WITHDRAWN

SMITHSONIAN INSTITUTION
INSTITUTE OF SOCIAL ANTHROPOLOGY
PUBLICATION NO. 3

MOCHE
A PERUVIAN COASTAL COMMUNITY

by

JOHN Philip GILLIN

GREENWOOD PRESS, PUBLISHERS
WESTPORT, CONNECTICUT

The Library of Congress has catalogued this publication as follows:

Library of Congress Cataloging in Publication Data

Gillin, John Philip, 1907-
   Moche, a Peruvian coastal community.

      Reprint of the 1947 ed., which was issued as Publica-
   tion no. 3 of the Smithsonian Institution, Institute of
   Social Anthropology.
      Bibliography: p.
      1. Moche, Peru. 2. Indians of South America--
   Peru--Social life and customs. I. Title. II. Series:
   Smithsonian Institution. Institute of Social Anthro-
   pology. Publication no. 3.
   F3611.M62G54 1973   309.1'85'1063   75-118758
   ISBN 0-8371-5075-2

LETTER OF TRANSMITTAL

SMITHSONIAN INSTITUTION,
INSTITUTE OF SOCIAL ANTHROPOLOGY,
Washington 25, D. C., June 15, 1945.

SIR: I have the honor to transmit herewith a manuscript entitled "Moche: A Peruvian Coastal Community," by John Gillin, and to recommend that it be published as Publication Number 3 of the Institute of Social Anthropology, which has been established by the Smithsonian Institution as an autonomous unit of the Bureau of American Ethnology to carry out cooperative work in social anthropology with the American Republics as part of the program of the Interdepartmental Committee on Scientific and Cultural Cooperation.

Very respectfully yours,

JULIAN H. STEWARD, *Director.*

DR. ALEXANDER WETMORE,
   Secretary of the Smithsonian Institution.

II

Originally published in 1947
by the United States Government Printing Office, Washington

First Greenwood Reprinting 1973

Library of Congress Catalogue Card Number 75-118758

ISBN 0-8371-5075-2

Printed in the United States of America

CONTENTS

IV

ILLUSTRATIONS

PLATES

(All plates at end of book)

FIGURES

MAP

FOREWORD

By Julian H. Steward

The purpose of the publications of the Institute of Social Anthropology is to further an understanding of the basic cultures of America through making generally available the results of cooperative studies. These studies at present are more concerned with the basic rural populations that are partly Indian and partly European than with the varied manifestations of western civilization. They are essentially acculturational, the various communities selected for investigations ranging in degree of assimilation from self-sufficient and self-contained preliterate Indian groups to strongly mestizoized, literate, Spanish-speaking villages, which are more or less integrated into national life.

The preceding monograph, "Cherán: A Sierra Tarascan Village," by Ralph L. Beals, Publication No. 2 of the Institute of Social Anthropology, describes a community which is increasingly feeling the impact of European civilization but is still thought of as "Indian." The present study of Moche, a coast village of northern Peru, reveals a community that is in the last stages of losing its identity as an Indian group and of being absorbed into Peruvian national life. Insofar as these communities are atypical of their nations, however, both are probably more 16th-century Spain than native Indian.

Surrounded by large, modernized haciendas, Moche is "Indian" only in that its population is largely Indian in a racial sense, that it has retained much of its own lands, that it exists in a certain social isolation from surrounding peoples, retaining a community life organized on a modified kinship basis, mainly of Spanish derivation, and that it preserves a considerable belief in witchcraft and a scattering of minor aboriginal culture elements. Its lands, however, are now owned individually, and they are being alienated through sale and litigation. It is on a cash rather than subsistence basis economically, and, though much of its produce is for home consumption, it relies increasingly on purchase of goods with money earned by sale of agricultural and dairy products. Many Mocheros even work outside the community for wages, and some are in professions. Moche clothing, household goods, utensils, implements, domesticated animals, many crops, art, music, and formal religion are all of Peruvian national types. The community is Spanish-speaking and another generation will find it largely literate. Formal aspects of native social organization have disappeared, and contacts with the outside world are increasing. Politically, Moche is completely under national and provincial administration.

Dr. Gillin's present excellent analysis of Moche is the first of a series of studies projected for Peru. It will help set in perspective the cultures and culture changes among the highland Quechua Indian communities, which the Institute of Social Anthropology, in cooperation with Peruvian authorities, is now studying. The field work at Moche, however, was done at a time when the plan for cooperation between these institutions had not yet been consummated, and, although Dr. Gillin had the greatest possible assistance and all courtesies from Peruvians, both officially and privately, it was not yet possible to arrange their participation in the work. Thanks to Dr. Gillin's part in developing the program, truly cooperative field work is now in progress.

Moche: A Peruvian Coastal Community

By John Gillin

INTRODUCTION

This monograph is an attempt to increase mutual understanding in the Americas by portraying in some detail the patterns of life of a Peruvian coastal community that I studied with ethnological methods during a period of service in Peru as representative of the Institute of Social Anthropology of the Smithsonian Institution.

Moche is a community of "little men" or "common people" in terms of their individual economic, social, and political influence in the country as a whole, and in that respect it is, of course, typical of the overwhelming majority of rural communities of Peru. The mode of life in Moche has many features in common with other coastal communities, but it is unusual in some respects, especially in the fact that the bulk of its land area is still in the hands of peasant owners.

It seems to me that some of the past difficulties encountered by foreign nations in dealing with the United States have been based on ignorance of the "common people" of our country. Our so-called former "isolationism" and "distrust of foreign intrigues," for example, cannot really be understood by anyone who does not have acquaintance with some of the thousands of small towns and rural neighborhoods scattered throughout our country. We should be well advised not to make the same mistake in our relations with other nations. Although a little less than half of our own population live in small towns and rural neighborhoods, a very large majority of Peruvians are members of rural communities of one type or another. Moche is not, of course, typical of all of them. A good many more reports on Peruvian communities would be necessary to complete the picture, and it is hoped that they will be forthcoming.

I undertook the collection of the data herein presented during the first year of the Institute of Social Anthropology's activities in Peru. I spent a total of some 22 months in Peru in 1943–44, although during the first year of this period I was attached to the Embassy in a nonethnological capacity. On a previous mission in 1934–35, I had spent about 5 months in the Peruvian-Ecuadorean Montaña. The period of field work in Moche totaled nearly 6 months in 1944.

In June of 1944, I accepted an invitation from the University of Trujillo to establish a course and deliver a series of lectures on cultural anthropology at that institution. While engaged in these activities, I initiated the study of the community of Moche, some 7 km. from the city of Trujillo. I rented a house in the town of Moche for interviewing and here spent some nights, but for want of furniture and kitchen equipment for the Moche house, I made my home and general headquarters in the Hotel Trujillo in Trujillo.

Because of the pressure of other commitments and the exigencies of the publishing schedule, the entire monograph in its present form was written and the illustrations were prepared for publication between December 15, 1944, and February 1, 1945, with the result that a certain amount of material gathered in the field has had to be held out for later publication because of sheer lack of time to prepare it.

An attempt has been made in the present work to present Moche culture as it exists at the present time, and for this reason those who may have been acquainted with Moche some years ago are asked to remember that the processes of cultural change have apparently been operating at a fairly rapid and steady pace. Some of my friends in Trujillo, for

example, were certain that the Mocheras still practiced weaving as a generalized activity, and for a
time I was disturbed by the fact that I could find
no looms or women devoted to this activity. It
turned out that as late as 15 years ago not a few
women were still operating their hand looms, but
that by 1944 they had all (with one possible exception) discarded them. Moche as a composite culture
and as a changing culture is the emphasis of the
present account.

From the technical point of view of an ethnologist
trying to do his work, Moche is not an easy problem.
One has to contend with a tendency to polite withdrawal which characterizes the Mocheros' dealings
with strangers and foreigners and which is to a
considerable extent based upon their fear of inroads
upon their land holdings. On the other hand,
although in my experience I have never encountered
a group whose confidence was so difficult to obtain,
I have never met people who, once their confidence
was gained, were so hospitable. The Mocheros like
to spend a good part of their not inconsiderable
leisure sitting about drinking, eating, and talking.
Once the ethnologist is admitted to such sessions,
he becomes privy to a great deal of gossip and general comment and is able to conduct a large number
of "indirect interviews." On the other hand, this
very pattern of relaxation makes it difficult to arrange long, serious, confidential interview sessions.
The typical Mochero does not like to sit down for
hours at a time and concentrate with an ethnologist
who painstakingly goes over apparently minor points
time after time and writes the answers down in a
notebook. I was fortunate, however, in securing the
services, partly voluntary and partly paid, of a group
of informants representing both the Mocheros and
forasteros (outside settlers in Moche) who were
willing to do this very thing as well as to write out
reports of their own on topics which were of interest
in the study. Since only a part of a year was spent
in the culture, a good many features of the yearly
round described herein, especially those concerned
with agriculture and fiestas which were not observed
personally, had to be obtained from informants
alone and are unsupported by personal observation or
participation. Any apparently significant differences
between informants have been indicated in the text.
In the field, notes were typed off onto 4- by 6-inch
sheets of paper, usually each night if possible, and
filed according to the 55 principal categories of the
Yale "Outline of Cultural Materials" (Murdock et

al., 1938) plus a few other categories of particular
interest to the present investigation.

A certain amount of material on Moche personalities and on the "typical" life cycle will, it is hoped,
be published at a later date.

Finally, two aspects of method should be mentioned which, because of the circumstances, could
not be fully carried out in the present case, but which,
it is believed, should be considered in future investigations of this sort. In the realization of both,
the full collaboration of official government agencies
of the country concerned would be invaluable. They
are as follows:

1. Practically all Latin American rural communities of actual or potential and cumulative significance
in present and future national and world affairs, are
cultural composites, or mixtures, and their cultural
systems are all in a condition of flux and change.[1]
This means that both the cultural patterns and the
behavior may show a considerable amount of variation and inconsistency. The only way to describe
the variability with a completely satisfying degree
of scientific accuracy is on a basis of systematic collection of quantitative material that is susceptible of
at least simple statistical treatment. This does not
mean discarding the technique of indirect interview
and other time-tested ethnological techniques in favor
of the exclusive use of questionnaires and similar
procedures, but it does mean applying techniques to
all the population or to large and controlled samples
and tabulating certain information obtained thereby
that has statistical or numerical significance. For
example, I am convinced by agreement among all of
my informants that quarreling over land is common
among the Mocheros, but I am unable to say with
accuracy how common it is, i. e., what percentage
of the adult Mocheros have been engaged in such
feuds, what percentage of the feuds involve members
of the same family, etc. It would be a great help
if the whole of the cultural variations in behavior
(amenable to such treatment) could be reduced to
percentages or other simple constants representing
the distribution of the various alternatives, because
such treatment would not only permit a more accurate description of the position of the various
cultural alternatives in the existing system, but would
also provide a more precise basis for measuring

[1] Isolated "primitive" cultures in Latin America are, of course,
important from the viewpoints of historical and general ethnology, but
by the time they have become significant to an understanding of national
or international developments, they have invariably become "acculturated."

changes in the culture in subsequent re-studies of the situation. The actual scientific techniques involved in such quantitative studies are relatively simple and easy to apply, provided rapport with the group has been established, but they require the services of a staff with some training if they are to be effectively applied to the whole range of the culture in a reasonable period of time. In the present case I have attempted to provide some statistical measures, especially with respect to diet and certain aspects of kinship and relationship between the sexes, but I could wish for more.

2. In studies of Latin American communities it is extremely desirable to have full field collaboration between Latin American and North American workers, i. e., trained investigators from both countries should work together in the field on the same investigation. One of the objectives of the program of the Institute of Social Anthropology is to assist in the development of a trained body of Latin American cultural anthropologists. In most cases the North American working in Latin America enjoys the advantage of technical training, wide experience, and a certain objectivity, but he suffers from a lack of native knowledge of Spanish, even though his workaday conversation and writing of the language be fluent, and he does not have the background of Latin American culture which is "second nature" with his Latin American colleague. The latter has a much more profound acquaintance-ship with the language and culture of his country, but for that very reason is inclined to overlook and to take for granted features in which an outsider sees significance.

It should be understood that the present tense as used in the following description and analysis refers to conditions as of 1944.

ACKNOWLEDGMENTS

The program of the Institute of Social Anthropology, under the able direction of Dr. Julian H. Steward, has already claimed the respect of both Latin American and North American social scientists, and it will, I am sure, serve as an inspiration for a new period of scientific collaboration between the Americas. I am happy to have had the opportunity to participate in this program, even for a relatively short period of active work and during its formative stages.

In connection with the present study, I wish to acknowledge my gratitude to the following Peruvian scientists and men of affairs: Dr. Luís Valcárcel, Director of the Museo Nacional de Arqueología; Señor Rafael Larco Herrera, Vice President of the Republic of Peru; Señor Rafael Larco Hoyle, Director of the Museo Arqueológico "Rafael Larco Herrera" of Chiclín; Señor Jorje Muelle, Chief of the Technical Section of the National Museum of Archeology and Professor of Anthropology in the University of Cuzco; Señor José Angel Miñano, formerly of the University of Trujillo; Dr. Hans Horkheimer, of the University of Trujillo; Dr. Alberto Arca Parro, Chief of the Dirección Nacional de Estadística; Señor Coronel Juan Dongo M., Prefect of the Department of La Libertad; and many other Peruvian friends and acquaintances who were interested in my work in Moche and who endeavored to make the sojourn of my family and myself in Trujillo and in Peru agreeable. Among my friends in the American Embassy in Lima, I am grateful to the following for special assistance in various matters concerned with my official duties during or before the period of this investigation: Jefferson Patterson, Counselor of Embassy; Dr. George C. Vaillant, formerly Cultural Attaché; Dr. Albert Giesecke, who performed the duties of Civil Attaché. Dr. Vaillant left Peru before the beginning of this study, but his earlier counsel was invaluable.

The list of my acquaintances in Moche is so long as to render practically impossible its publication here. A few names are mentioned in the text, but the rest shall remain anonymous. Even the initials used in the text to identify certain individuals and "cases" are not the true initials of the individuals involved, but refer to key letters in my notes. Nothing said in this report can properly be used to foment strife or trouble for any individual in Moche. But I should like the people of Moche to know that I enjoyed their hospitality, appreciated their help to me in my efforts to understand the local mode of life, and carry with me a persistent fondness for their corner of Peru and the people who inhabit it.

In connection with preparation of the material for publication, I should like to mention Miss Doris Chestnut who has worked with unusual persistence and intelligence on the typing of the manuscript. Miss Christina Changaris did the line drawings which appear herein. All photographs were taken by me.

Finally, I wish to acknowledge gratefully the constant helpfulness and courtesy of the Government of the Republic of Peru as manifested through its various officers with whom I came in contact, and I hope that the present report, whatever defects it may possess, will prove to be of some value to the Peruvian Nation, which occupies so prominent a position in hemispheric and global affairs.

BACKGROUND OF MOCHE

THE SETTING

Traveling over the asphalted Pan-American Highway from Trujillo to Lima, your car passes through the outskirts of the village of Moche, about 7 km. after leaving Trujillo, just before the highway enters the desert and starts up the long grade leading over the divide toward Virú, the next coastal valley southeastward. To the ordinary traveler, passing by it in this way, Moche offers nothing distinctive or particularly interesting. The adobe and white-plastered houses stand flush with the cobblestone and dirt streets, which are laid out in a rectangular grid, as in so many other Peruvian coastal villages. The *campiña,* or irrigated countryside, is scarcely noticeable from the road, since travelers are usually straining their eyes to see the imposing ruined pyramid of the Huaca del Sol standing in the background at the far edge of the area of green fields and willow tops. Your car gathers speed for the long rise ahead, the green fields end sharply at the edge of a desert of drifted sand and bare rocks, and Moche is left to its own devices.

This, in fact, has been Moche's fate and fortune since the Spanish Conquest over 400 years ago—to be left in large measure to its own devices. Yet the ruins of the Huaca del Sol, probably the largest single adobe structure in the world, and the nearby Huaca de la Luna testify that this region in times past was a center of human activity and organized effort on a large scale. It was here that the ancient culture, now known as Mochica, was first clearly differentiated from other antique remains by Max Uhle.[2] This archeological culture is known even to laymen by reason of the mold-made ceramics which, with unusual vivacity, realism, and freedom from artificial artistic conventions, convey perhaps a clearer idea of persons, physical type, and the material aspects of a bygone age than the pottery of any other ancient people of the Western Hemisphere. In Peru, it is customary to think of the present-day inhabitants of Moche as descendants or survivors of the people who created this coastal civilization. Although the Mocheros themselves do not seem to recognize such a connection, this belief is strengthened by the fact that the Mocheros of today are "different" from the ordinary run of folks living along the coast.[3] They are more "Indian" in physical type[4] than is the usual cholo, they are somewhat conservative in their customs, preserving certain modes of life of a former day, and they tend to keep to themselves rather than allow themselves to become absorbed in the general Peruvian population. The Mocheros have preserved a large measure of individual ownership of the small farms of their *campiña* in their own hands, and the district thus constitutes an enclave, as it were, in a region now mainly occupied by a highly mixed cholo population and largely owned by a few giant haciendas.

Thus, aside from the natural attractions of its setting and of its people, Moche offers interest in at least two senses of a more general nature. It may be regarded, on the one hand, as a remnant or survivor of a basic ancient population and culture of the north Peruvian coast. On the other hand, we may see in Moche a modern example of rural life in this region as it is and as it was before many of the coastal villages were absorbed into the enormous sugar, rice, and cotton haciendas which at present dominate the Pacific valleys and which have radically reorganized the manner of living and the habits of work of the rural citizen.

The entire coast of Peru, south of Tumbes, is one of the driest deserts in the world, with an average annual precipitation of 0.5 cm. (Romero, 1944, p. 20) which in normal years is provided exclusively

---

[2] It will be recalled that Uhle called this "Proto-Chimu." Although he published some of his material as early as 1900 in an article in the Trujillo newspaper "La Industria," his first comprehensive account of the excavations at the Moche ruins themselves was published in 1913 (Uhle, 1913; Kroeber, 1925, 1926).

[3] For example, "Diccionario de 'La Crónica,'" (1918, pp. 300–301) states: "The characteristic trait of the Moche district is the tendency of the inhabitants not to make a common life with the whites, for which reason they still retain many of their customs anterior to colonial times."

[4] It should be noted, however, that even during Mochica times, the population was not uniformly "Indian" in the sense of being invariably mongoloid in physical type. Although the mongoloid physical type seems to be numerically the most numerous in the portrait vases, faces are also portrayed which possess marked "white" features (e. g., high-bridged noses, beards and moustaches of "white" race type, external epicanthic folds, etc.) as well as others showing presumable negroid characteristics (Larco Hoyle, 1938–39, vol. 2, ch. 3).

by the "garúa" mist of the winter season. Human life and economic activity are therefore, in the main, confined to a limited number [5] of irrigated river valleys whose waters have been used to create oases of sharply restricted extension. These conditions have obtained since prehistoric times, and there is good reason to believe that under the Inca domination actually more coastal land was under irrigation than at present. Nevertheless, in modern times, with the introduction of capitalistic economic organization and expensive "scientific" methods of farming export crops, these peculiar conditions of the Peruvian coastal valleys have easily lent themselves to a tendency toward monopolization of the land and to centralized organization of the working population. It is natural that the large haciendas should grow larger, that they should absorb towns no longer conveniently located from the point of view of production of the cash crop, that they should concentrate the working population in their own housing units at chosen points, and that they should dominate, however paternalistically, the life of the common people. Especially in the production of sugar on a large and profitable scale, the natural tendency is toward the establishment of "factories in the fields." There is one hacienda in the Valley of Chicama that now stretches from the Pacific coast to the jungles of the Marañón River and its domain is said to give livelihood to 50,000 persons, including workers and their families. It is still increasing.

For better or worse, the Moche community is different and in many respects still preserves the advantages and disadvantages of free peasant life. The Mocheros are outstanding exponents of rugged individualism, and there is little or nothing "socialistic" about life in Moche.

At first glance, then, the Moche District seems to present several contradictions. Although it lies about halfway between the city of Trujillo and the ocean port of Salaverry, it is neither urban nor industrialized. The town is served by excellent asphalted highways and railroads, but the "tone" of life is that of comparative cultural isolation. More than 100 families of outsiders live in the community, but they have not as yet made over the culture in their own patterns, nor are they socially accepted in the community as a whole. Some of the most

imposing of the ancient Mochica ruins stand in the Mocha countryside, but the modern Mocheros recognize no ancestral link to the people who built them.

GENERAL COMPOSITION OF POPULATION

Among the inhabitants, there is a distinction made between Mocheros and "forasteros" (strangers). Although there are no official figures on the latter, a count made by myself indicates that there are 111 forastero families living in the community, of which 16 live in the campiña and 95 in town. If one estimates the total forastero population at about 500, it would represent about 13 percent of the total population of the District of Moche, which was 3,773, according to the 1940 census. There has been an attempt on the part of Trujillanos to make a sort of residential suburb of Moche, because houses are cheaper there and the climate is reputed to be healthier. The Mocheros have resented and resisted this tendency, and there are only 4 or 5 forastero men who have succeeded in establishing intimate social relations with the Mocheros in general. Only 15 of the forastero households belong to foreigners while the remaining 96 are Peruvian. Even so, they are "outsiders."

There is also a territorial subdivision of the population. Although the pueblo has no barrios (wards or similar subdivisions), Mocheros as a whole are classified as being from the pueblo, from the playa (seashore), or from the campiña, depending on where they have their principal or only dwellings. The playa group at present consists of only about 30 poor fishing families, although it was formerly said to be larger. None of the playeros, properly speaking, maintains an establishment in the other subdivisions. However, some persons who are identified as being "from the campiña" also maintain houses in the pueblo, and vice versa. As will be seen later, the campiña falls into three sections—north, south, and west.

In describing Moche, we shall deal mainly with the Mocheros, or "Mocheros netos" (real Mocheros), since, on the whole, forasteros "only live there."

ENVIRONMENT

The District of Moche lies within the last bend of the Río Moche before it debouches into the Pacific. The District is bounded on the north and northwest by the river, as shown on plate 2. To the east the irrigated land ends abruptly in a sandy desert

---

[5] Romero lists 50 rivers, of which 27 are of the first class with water all the year around, 14 are second class usually with water throughout the year, and 9 are third class with only seasonal flows in normal years. The Moche River is of the first class (Romero, 1944, pp. 20–21).

from which abruptly rises a small barren mountain range, the two most prominent features of which are the Cerro Blanco and the Cerro Comunero. The river makes a bend around the northern point of the Cerro Blanco, and here stands the great ruined pyramid platform of the Huaca del Sol, which dominates all views of the *campiña*. To the south and southeast, the rich level land of the District gives way to low sand dunes a kilometer or so from the sea and finally meets the broad beach of the Pacific, which during the winter months (from June to December) is almost constantly pounded by a heavy surf.

Moche is geographically in the Tropics. The District of Moche lies between the parallels 8°8″ and 8°12″ south latitude and 79°00″ and 79°03″ west longitude (pl. 1). But the Peruvian coast is not "the Tropics" as North Americans are accustomed to think of them. The most outstanding feature of the climate is that "it never rains," except at very long intervals. The last rain in Moche occurred in 1925 and was, naturally, a major disaster that destroyed numerous houses and considerable property, for the houses here are not built for rain. A roof, for example, normally is expected to fulfill only the functions of providing shade and privacy. Moche occupies an oasis, dependent upon irrigation, and all water comes either from the river or from underground seepage. This fact has decided consequences in such matters as personal hygiene and household cleanliness. The water supply occupies men's thoughts continuously. Land without water is worthless, regardless of the amount of work one may expend upon it.

In the summer (December to June) it is hot in Moche, with a dry desert heat, mitigated, however, by the sea breeze; but during the remainder of the year the temperature is moderate, with a tendency toward chilly nights and mornings. During part of the winter season (July to October, inclusive) the sky is overcast practically every morning until noon or after, and frequently the low-hanging clouds precipitate a thin, cold drizzle, the *garúa*. The nearest official weather station is at the Hacienda Casa Grande in the Valley of Chicama, about 60 km. north of Moche and some 25 km. farther inland. In 1942 this station registered a total precipitation of 7.5 mm. per square meter and an average atmospheric pressure of 1,010.8 milibars. The highest absolute temperature during the year was 30.9° C. and the lowest 10.0° C. The highest mean temperature per 24

hours was 24.2° C. and the lowest 16.6° C. Mean temperatures during warm days might average slightly lower in Moche, owing to proximity to the sea. Although it never actually freezes in Moche, cold nights, called *"heladas"* (freezers), occasionally occur during the winter, which are said to damage the alfalfa crops.

With the exception of the Moche District, most of the arable lands of the Río Moche drainage have been preempted by haciendas, and since Moche lies at the lower end of the valley, there is constant preoccupation and not a few accusations that water users higher up are robbing Moche of its needed moisture. The Río Moche rises in the Cordilleras Blanca and Negro and has a basin of about 800 sq. km. The river meter at Menocucho, 30 km. from the mouth and 200 m. above sea level, indicates that the flow varies from 170,000 cu. m. per second to 100 cu. m. per second, with an average annual discharge over 4 years of 268,187,500 cu. m. (Romero, 1944, pp. 26–27). By the time the river reaches Moche, this flow has been reduced by irrigation tapping to a mere trickle, especially in the dry season. (See pl. 3.)

THE "MOCHICA VILLAGES"

Moche is generally regarded as one of a number of "Mochica villages" scattered along the coast from the Valley of the Río Chao to and including the drainage of the Río de la Leche. According to my experience, the inhabitants of the Moche villages themselves do not dwell upon the possibility that they may be united by a common inheritance of ancient culture, nor, in fact, are the majority of individuals aware that this may be the case. However, a rather vague bond of likeness and kinship is recognized. True members of any one of these villages know that they have closer social ties with members of the other Mochica villages than with people in general, that it has been traditional for one marrying outside his own village to prefer persons from other Mochica communities, and that the customary movement back and forth to fiestas, and similar social intercourse, has tended to flow between the Mochica villages rather than in other channels. This may be a survival of the confederating influence of the Chimu "empire" rather than Mochica ethnocentrism, and at all events at present is an informal thing, not based on a conscious or apparent organization.

At the present time the following villages are regarded as forming parts of the "Mochica group": Moche, Eten (between Chiclayo and the sea), Monsefú (between Eten and Chiclayo), San José (fishing village on the coast north of Pimentel), Santa Rosa (fishing town on the coast southeast of Puerto Eten), Reque (inland from Eten), Morrupe, Motupe, Jayanca, Salas (all in the drainage of the Río de la Leche), Magdalena de Cao (near the coast a short distance north of the mouth of the Río Chicama), Santiago de Cao (near the coast, just southeast of the mouth of the Río Chicama), Huamán (a small *caserío* about 5 km. northwest of Moche on the other side of the Río Moche), Simbal (inland from Trujillo), Guañape (a small fishing village and port near the mouth of the Río Virú), Chao (at the mouth of the river of the same name), and Huanchaco (a fishing village some 17 km. northeast from the Moche *playa* along the coast).

In 1644, according to Fernando de la Carrera, priest of San Martín de Reque, the Mochica or "Yunga" language was spoken in the following places by a total of some 40,000 persons: Santiago, Magdalena de Cao, Chocope, Valle de Chicama, Paiján (in the Corregimiento de Trujillo), San Pedro de Lloc, Chepén, Jequetepeque, Guadalupe, Pueblo Nuevo, Eten, Chiclaiep, San Miguel, Santa Lucia de Moche, Parroquia de Saña, Lambayeque Reque, Omensefec, Firruñap, Túcume, Illimo, Pacora, Morrope, Jayanca (in the Corregimiento de Saña), Motupe, Salas (in the Corregimiento de Piura), Santa Cruz, San Miguel de Sierra, Ñopos, San Pablo, la doctrina de las Balsas del Marañón, una parcialidad de Cajamarca, Cachén, Gamboa, various other parts of the Sierra around Cajamarca, such as the Valley of Condebamba (in the Corregimiento de Cajamarca). The presence of Mochica speakers in the Sierra region of Cajamarca in 1644 is explained as due to previous deportation of the natives from the coast by the Inca conquerors.[6]

LANGUAGE

At the present time no one in Moche knows anything of the ancient language, and only Spanish is spoken. In fact, the only one of the Mochica villages where survivals of the language have been found in recent times seems to be Eten, where Larco Hoyle

(1938–39, vol. 2, pp. 77–82) and his agents collected 174 words during the 1930's.[7]

RECENT LITERARY MENTION OF MOCHE

Although there is an abundant literature on the ancient Mochica culture in general, as well as scientific reports of archeological excavations on the Moche ruins themselves, literary treatment of the living population of the District, during either colonial or modern times, is scarce and confined in the main to passing references or impressionistic accounts. Perhaps the two most ambitious modern treatments are those of Jimenez Borja (1937, pp. unnumbered) and Larco Hoyle (1938–39, vol. 2, pp. 28–38). Jimenez Borja's "Moche" is an impressionistic attempt to connect the ancient archeological culture with the present day in Moche and Huanchaco, and endeavors to suggest such a cultural continuity by a search for parallels between the decorative motifs of ancient Mochica art and present-day features of the natural environment, rather than by a close analysis of the customs and organization of modern Mocheros. From the ethnological point of view, the chapter entitled "La Campiña" is doubtless the best. Larco Hoyle is much more precise in the few pages that he gives to modern Moche ethnology; his collecting of material was, however, incidental to his main work as a means of enlivening and enlightening his very valuable archeological contributions. A few other writers have described the Moche *campiña* in terms of "local color" or have alluded to the alleged joys of drinking *chicha* in the shadow of the Huaca del Sol. Among these writers we may mention Alayza Paz Soldán [8] and Miro Quesada.[9]

DETAILED DISTRIBUTION OF POPULATION

According to the National Census of 1940, the total population of the District, amounted to 3,773, of which 1,857 were males and 1,916 were females. The population was classified by the census from

---

[7] Prof. Hans Horkheimer, of the Universidad Nacional de Trujillo, has compiled a definitive as yet unpublished vocabulary from all the published sources. With duplications ruled out, this amounts to a total of about 1,200 words. Sources are Bastian, 1878; Brüning, 1922; Calancha, 1638; Juan and Ulloa, 1751; Middendorf, 1892; Ore, 1607; Carrera, 1644; Villareal, 1921; Larco Hoyle, 1938–39; Zevallos Quiñones, 1941; Romero, 1909.

[8] 1939, pp. 359–361, a short popular account of Moche archeology and present scene in the manner of a newspaper feature article; 1940, pp. 403–405, an impressionistic account of a visit to the Huacas.

[9] 1938, pp. 27–30; impressionistic reference to an afternoon spent visiting the ruins and drinking *chicha* in the *campiña*.

---

[6] Carrera, 1644 (I have seen only the corrected and amplified version of Villareal, 1921). According to Camino Calderon (1942, p. 41) remnants of the Mochica deported to the Sierra by the Inca still exist in Santa Cruz, San Miguel, and Niepos (Napos).

the racial point of view as follows: White and Mestizo, 1,892 (914 males, 978 females); undeclared, 18 (10 males, 8 females); Indians, 1,849 (921 males, 928 females); Yellow, 14 (12 males, 2 females); Negro, none.[10] The racial classification as between Whites, Mestizos, and Indians, must be taken with reserve, as the census itself declares. Two things are worth remarking, however. First, there are no Negroes in Moche, a condition which contrasts strongly with most coastal communities. Second, 1,849 persons, or nearly half, apparently consider themselves pure Indians and do not hesitate to declare themselves as such. Of the "yellow race" there are 7 Chinese men in the town, 2 with Chinese wives, and 5 Japanese men.

The census counted families, as well as individuals. Although at the date of this writing these figures have not yet been published, they have been kindly placed at my disposal by Dr. Alberto Arca Parró, Director of the Census and of the National Bureau of Statistics (a dependency of the Ministerio de Hacienda y Comercio). Table 1 shows the number of families and the number of individuals in the various local subdivisions of the District in 1940.

TABLE 1.—*Families and individuals of Moche by census subdivision, 1940*

Locality	Families	Individuals
Pueblo of Moche	442	2,148
Sun	61	356
Chochoc	54	333
Huaca del Sol	62	437
Chorobal	16	67
Delicias, Las (the *playa*)	37	205
La Barranca	16	92
La Haciendita	23	95
Hacienda Moche	12	40
Total	723	3,773

As mentioned below, there are 111 *forastero* families in the community, 95 of them in the pueblo. The "Hacienda Moche" of the census is an error, being actually a part of the *campiña* near the pueblo, mostly worked by the Escuela de Agricultura. The 23 families, involving 95 persons belonging to the Haciendita, can also be eliminated from consideration in the pure Moche group, since they are practically all cholo workers from other parts. The average family, or household, in Moche consists of 4.8 persons. We therefore assign an arbitrary number of 500 to the *forasteros* in the District in addition to those on the hacienda property. If these groups are subtracted from the total 1940 population of the District, there are 589 true Mochero

[10] Extracto Estadístico, 1942, p. 21.

families and 3,178 persons. It should be noted, however, that the *forasteros* living in the community participate to some extent, even as outsiders, and have some influence, even though indirect, on Moche life, while this is not true of the hacienda dwellers.

I made a census of the *forasteros,* and the location of their houses is shown on map 1 in order to show the pattern of their residential relationships within the Moche community. Since I have more confidence in my count of *forastero* households than in my count of the absolute number of persons belonging to them (owing to obscurities regarding illegitimate children, former wives or companions, etc.), only the distribution of households is listed in table 2.

TABLE 2.—*Forastero households in the Moche community*

Locality of origin	Residence in Moche		Total
	Pueblo	Campiña	
Peruvian:			
Trujillo	38	4	42
Sierra of Dept. Libertad	15	8	23
San Pedro de Lloc	7	0	7
Paiján	1	2	3
Ascope	3	0	3
Piura	3	0	3
Chiclayo	1	1	2
Pacasmayo	2	0	2
Lima	2	0	2
Chocope	2	0	2
Magdalena de Cao	1	0	1
Chicama	1	0	1
Virú	0	1	1
Salaverry	2	0	2
Cajamarca	1	0	1
Total	79	16	95
Foreign:			
Chinese	7	0	7
Japanese	5	0	5
Spanish	1	0	1
Italian	1	0	1
Russian	1	0	1
German	1	0	1
Total	16	0	16
Grand total	95	16	111

The identification of *forastero* households was made with the consensus of opinion among my true Mochero informants and indicates again the feeling of vague solidarity among the "Mochica villages." Although several individuals and households in Moche have migrated here from other Mochica villages, they are not considered outsiders by the Mocheros, with the exception of one definitely cholo family which came from Magdalena de Cao. Except in this one instance, the Mochica villages are not included in table 2. It will be noticed that the great majority of *forasteros* live in the pueblo and do not engage in agriculture, which is the basis of Moche life. The majority of *forasteros* who are settled in the *campiña* are Indian agriculturists from the

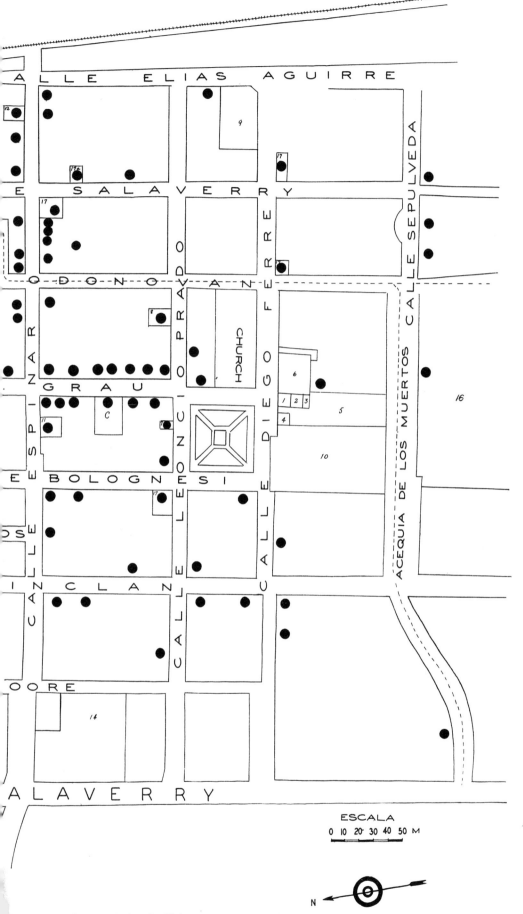

ngles locate buildings or institutions of public interest, as
lic market (*mercado*); 7, justice of the peace (*juzgado de*
ne office; 12, post office; 13, School of Agriculture; 14,
mercial poultry- and swine-raising establishment; belongs

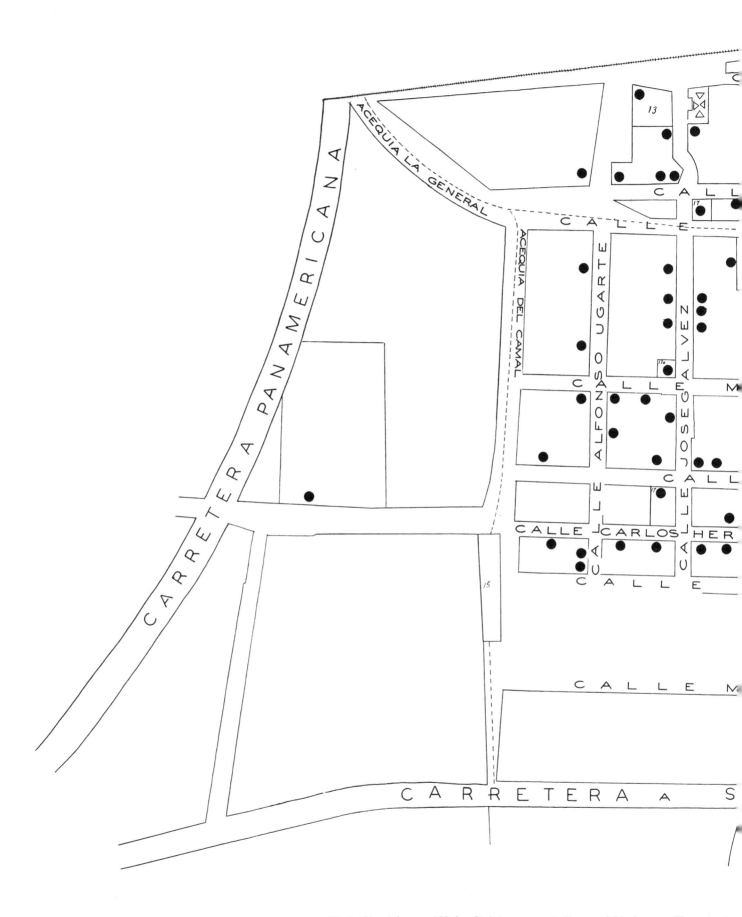

MAP 1.—Plan of the town of Moche. Black dots represent dwellings occupied by *forasteros*. The numbered
follows: *1*, Municipalidad; *2–3*, municipal storehouse; *4*, Gobernación; *5*, girls' school (*centro escolar*); *6*
paz); *8*, police station (*puesto de guardia civil*); *9*, boys' school; *10*, priest's dwelling (*parroquia*); *11*, t
residence used for summer season by Las Madres de Santa Rosa, in Trujillo; *15*, slaughterhouse; *16*, leadin-
to a *forastero*; *17*, shops belonging to Chinese; *17a*, shop belonging to a Peruvian; *C*, moving picture the

Sierra who originally came to the coast to work as peons on the haciendas and later settled in Moche through friendship or marriage.

VITAL STATISTICS

Crude vital statistics for 5 years, as compiled officially by the Municipalidad, are set forth in table 3.[11]

TABLE 3.—*Births, deaths, and marriages in Moche District, 1939–1944*

Year	Births	Deaths	Marriages
1939	160	80	42
1940	184	62	64
1941	147	60	60
1942	162	116	47
1943	175	60	59
1944 [1]	82	21	39

[1] First 6 months.

From these figures may be calculated yearly averages for the years 1939–43, inclusive, of 165.6 births, 75.6 deaths, and 54.4 marriages. This gives an average annual excess of births over deaths of 90, or a ratio of births to deaths of 2.19 over a 5-year period. No attempt has been made to test the accuracy of these figures by means of independent recordings,[12] which would clearly have been an impossibility for me. I believe, however, that the figures are reasonably accurate, because the District is small and relations are largely those of an in-group in which everyone's business is generally known, so that there is little opportunity for evading the legal requirements for the registration of births and deaths, even were there a desire to do so. During the 5 years under review, no stillbirths were recorded, which may be an indication of the general healthfulness of the population.

As will appear later, the registered figures on "marriages" have relatively little significance, since it is not customary in Moche to consider an official marriage a necessary preliminary for the establishment of a communal life or household by a man and a woman.

PHYSICAL TYPES AND CONSTITUTIONS

Since I was unable to secure a set of anthropometric instruments, either in Peru or in the United States, during the period of the investigation, I am unable to give precise data concerning the physical type and must be content with impressionistic remarks, based upon some observation of Indian populations and upon a fair intimacy with the various physical groups of Peru. The so-called cholos of the northern Peruvian coast appear to be a mixture of brunette Spanish, Indian, Asiatic (usually Chinese), and Negro. The mixture is probably not genetically stabilized, because it shows considerable variability, and my impression is that it does not breed true, except within broad limits. Generally speaking from an observational point of view, however, cholo men usually show more beard and body hair than do pure Indians, while both sexes generally exhibit wavy or curly hair. In contrast, the "true Mocheros" are more "Indian" in physical appearance, as plates 4 and 5 indicate. However, I do not believe that the true Mocheros are a pure Indian group, genetically considered. Phenotypically, they often show traits of mixture with a brunette white strain. Also, despite the Moche tradition of not breeding with outsiders, genealogical material indicates that it has occurred in the last few generations, and probably sporadically for centuries. The result of these assumed factors is a wide variability in physical type at present.

In general one may describe the true Mochero type as follows: Short to medium-short stature; copper-colored skin; nose bridge of medium height; nasal index probably medium; head brachy to meso-cephalic; black straight hair; fatty deposits about eyes, which, however, are seldom oblique; membraneous lips medium; integumental lips, thick; chin prominence, small; beard and body hair, sparse to medium; brownish rather than blackish hair, streaked with gray in aged persons. Even slight baldness is rare in "true Mocheros." Body build tends toward the "lateral" type.

I have no conclusive data on the physical constitution and longevity of the Mocheros, but personally know and have had social relations with 16 individuals who claim they are more than 80 years of age. Five of these claim to be more than 90 years old, and 3 between 99 and 101 years old. It is impossible to prove their ages, however, owing to the fact that the Libros de Bautismo of the local church were destroyed in the flood of 1925, and one can never be sure in talking with the old people that the historical events they claim to have witnessed are not the result of later information. Only one of these individuals is what might be called bedridden. This is an old woman,

[11] From the official books of the Municipalidad, copied off by the Secretario, Segundo Celestino, on the official letterhead, stamped with the official rubber stamp, and presented to me on June 30, 1944.

[12] The published figures for 1940 in Extracto Estadístico (1942, p. 78) show slight variations from those for the same year provided by the Municipalidad. The published table lists 182 births and 63 deaths for 1940.

supposedly 88 years of age, who, suffering from paralysis or weakness of the legs, spends most of her time on a mat on the floor of her house, but gets about by crawling on all fours. Eleven of these old people are women and 5 are men. With the exception noted, all are vigorous enough to take care of their houses, go about normal business (other than heavy field work), and drink heavily in company with younger friends and relatives.

Conclusive data are also lacking with respect to fertility. Perhaps the best available is obtained from the genealogical material, which shows an average of 6.73 children for each woman over 50 years of age. However, since in the case of several women whom I knew better than the average I discovered that it was not unusual for them to suppress or forget an illegitimate or deceased child or two when giving the genealogy, the average may well be higher. The most fecund woman is aged 48, a Mochera, and the mother of 21 children, including 2 pairs of twins. The mother of 1 of my informants, a *forastera*, had 18 children by single births and died at the age of 72.

LAND HOLDINGS

According to the records of the Administration of Irrigation in Trujillo, the irrigated land of the District of Moche amounts to 1,203.9569 hectares (2,974.98885 acres or 4.63 sq. miles), of which the Haciendita, an old Spanish land grant which obtrudes into the *campiña*, comprises 113.1380 hectares. This leaves approximately 976 hectares as lands of 803 small proprietors, who pay water rents. This gives an average holding of 1.3580 hectares. The smallest holding is 880 sq. m. and the largest 21.8781 hectares. The smallest and largest lots happen to be the sole landed property of their respective owners, but it is probable that the average holding per individual owner would be larger than that shown above, inasmuch as several men appear on the lists as holders of two or more lots. At the moment of this writing a new *catastro*, based for the first time on accurate surveys and examination of titles, is in the process of composition, and until this is complete the above figures and estimates must suffice. My own guess is that there are slightly over 700 farmers in the Moche District, and that the average amount of land managed by one man is about 1.6 hectares (3.9536 acres).

Whatever the exact figures may prove to be, it is clear that Moche is a community of small landholders and land workers.

HISTORICAL DATA

Historical data concerning Moche itself are very scarce, at least in the experience of the present writer. It is hoped that the present account of modern life in Moche may arouse sufficient interest on the part of Peruvian historians so that they will do the necessary research and make available an adequate historical account of this community, if such is possible. The records of the local church were either destroyed or removed to parts unknown in the flood of 1925. At least, neither the local priest, nor the Archbishop, nor the librarian of the Archdiocese of Trujillo was able to provide me with information concerning them, and no authority consulted has been able to give historical proof of the precise date of the founding of Moche during historical times. From all this ignorance seems to emerge, at least, the fact that Moche has been considered of little importance since the time of the Conquest; however, it would be interesting to have some picture of the condition of the people in the period of the first Spanish settlement.

If one accepts 1535 as the date of the founding of Trujillo,[13] it would be difficult to believe that Spanish control was not established in Moche almost immediately if a community of Indians in fact existed there at that time.

The earliest reference to Moche which it has been my fortune to encounter is that which figures in the list of *parroquias* visited in 1593 by Santo Toribio (Archbishop Toribio Alfonso de Mogrovejo): "Moche, que servía el P. Fray Alonzo Diaz de las Mercedes."[14] In 1613, in the *Auto* establishing the new diocese of Trujillo, "Mochi" figures as 1 of 22 *curas* of the "Corregimiento de Chiclaio"; one friar of the Order de la Merced is assigned to this church (Monografía de la Diócesis, 1930–31, vol. 1, p. 148). The church of Moche is mentioned specifically as having suffered serious damage in the earthquake of September 2, 1759, although nothing is said in the official church history regarding the fate of the parishioners in this disaster (ibid., vol. 2, p. 144).

The most extensive account of Moche published during colonial times seems to be that of Feijóo, which is herewith translated and quoted in full:

---

[13] See the wordy and sometimes acrimonious debate on the exact date as published in Apuntes y estudios históricos sobre la fecha de la Fundación de la ciudad de Trujillo (1935).

[14] Monografía de la Diócesis, 1930–31, vol. 1, p. 119. The original seems to be "Libro de Visitas de Santo Toribio," in the Archivo Capitular de Lima. During my hurried visit to this source, the librarian was unable to find this document or any others pertaining to Moche.

The pueblo of Santa Lucía de Moche, near the sea and separated from the city [of Trujillo] by two leagues to the southeast on the Royal Road to Lima, is composed of 118 male Indians and 157 female Indians; with their 125 small sons and 75 daughters they are dedicated to agricultural work [labranza] and generally to being fishermen. The church was damaged in the earthquake [of September 2, 1759] but is now being repaired by reason of the pious diligence of the Indians, stimulated by their priest. The Indians of the pueblos mentioned [Moche and Santiago de Guamanga] pay in royal tribute six pesos and four reales per year. [Moche] does not have its own cacique; and the collection of the royal tribute is entrusted to a collector named by the royal officials of this city [Trujillo] to whom belongs this incumbency. According to the book of distribution, the said Indians of the two pueblos [this includes Santiago de Guamanga] enjoy 206 fanegas of land, being a very small assignment for their subsistence and welfare. The priest of both pueblos is a religious of the royal and military order of Nuestra Señora de las Mercedes. The allowance for missionary activity [sínodo] is 154 pesos annually, and with obventions and other rights amounts to 2,000 pesos. [Feijóo, 1763 (reprint, undated, p. 36).]

Feijóo also published two maps,[15] "Descripción del Valle del Chimú planisférica de la ciudad de Trujillo del Perú" and "Carta topográfica de la provincia de Trujillo del Perú," both of which show the pueblo of Moche as of 1760, in approximately its present location.

One colonial reference that has come to my notice is perhaps of small importance; it is found in Medina and refers to the year 1650:

The thirtieth of January, 1650 (? en 30 dias del mes de enero de 1650 años), Lorenzo Huamán, aged Indian of the "aillo" of Amey, accused [delató] Francisca Beatriz, aged Indian woman of the "aillo" of "Mocha", affirming under oath that she is malificient, a witch, and practitioner of the indigenous rites (ritos gentílicios). [Medina, 1650 (edition, 1920, p. 98).]

This is the only indication I have that Moche was ever an ayllu, and I believe the word is used in a general sense by a reporter accustomed to think of all Indian villages in this terminology. This reference also provides proof, if any were needed, that brujería (witchcraft) was practiced as far back as 1650.

In 1818, the diocesan history provides another reference to Moche (Monografía de la Diócesis, 1930–31, vol. 3, pp. 256–258). The third volume of this compilation, "El Cabildo Eclesiástico a través de tres siglos," reveals that for nearly 200 years, since 1631[16] to be exact, this body had been periodically exercised

over the problem of securing a new clock and bell for the towers of the cathedral. By September 4, 1818, a clock had been secured, and the following year the bell was obtained (ibid., vol. 3, pp. 256–257). This is the only reference to Moche in the diocesan history.

Although in 1818–19 Moche enjoyed the services of a priest, the church historians have not published any information concerning the people under his care. Perhaps he made no reports; if he did, it is to be hoped that the church may publish them.

Juan and Ulloa (1751, p. 368) mention Moche in 1751 as being located at 8°24′59″ south latitude and consisting of 50 "baraque" houses with 70 families, composed of Spanish, Indians, and Mestizos.

Squier (1877, ch. 8) published an amusing account of his visit to Moche, in which he described certain drinking customs of the people there that do not sound so very different from present usages. He also provides us with the first serious measurements and descriptions of the ruins.

A short summary of the ancient cultural sequence in this area is given, relying mainly upon Kroeber's 1944 publication, the latest printed statement (Kroeber, 1944, pp. 42–80, especially pp. 78–80; also table on p. 112. See also Bennett, 1937, 1939; Kroeber, 1925, 1926; Squier, 1877; Uhle, 1913; Larco Hoyle, 1938–39, 1941; also Horkheimer, 1944, p. 11). According to this scheme, which aims to represent present knowledge, the succession of cultures in the north coast area may be arranged in the following column, with the oldest at the bottom:

Chimu, Inca period.
Chimu, pre-Inca.
Tiahuanacoid, later.
Tiahuanacoid, Earlier, Cajamarca associated.
Negative or Gallinazo.
Mochica.
Salinar.
Cupisnique.
Archaic (?) no remnants found in Moche area.

To date, no geological or other direct evidence for absolute dating has come to light, with the result that the chronology is based upon stratigraphy, typology, and the judgment of the investigators. Kroeber is inclined to estimate the beginning of Cupisnique period (Libertad equivalent of Tello's Chavin of the Coast) at about A. D. 500, the beginning of the Mochica period at about A. D. 700, the beginning of the Tiahuanaco period at about A. D. 1000 (Kroeber, 1944, pp. 114–115). This would give the true Mochica culture a period of about 300 years, beginning about 1,250 years ago. Others are inclined to

---

[15] I have seen only the reproductions published in Apuntes y estudios . . . 1935; the maps face pp. 80 and 88, respectively.

[16] Ibid., vol. 3, pp. 51–52, resumen of the Cabildo for the year 1631. Repeated references to this problem occur hereafter.

see the beginning of the Mochica period some 400 to 500 years earlier.[17] All archeologists, however, are agreed that the Mochica culture was followed and modified in prehistoric times by so-called Tiahuanacoid cultures from the Sierra out of which overlay and mixture developed the Chimu culture of the north coast area, which in turn was modified by mixture and overlay of Inca cultural influences, as a result of the Inca conquest of the Chimus, probably in the 15th century A. D.

Thus one cannot expect the Mocheros of today, even if regarded as lineal descendants of the Mochicas of antiquity, to exhibit Mochica culture in its pure form. The aboriginal cultural base in Moche is composed of elements of Mochica, Tiahuanaco, Chimu, and Inca cultures. And the aboriginal base itself has been mixed and modified by four centuries of contact with European cultural influences.

Our knowledge of Mochica culture is derived in the main from the realistic pottery, mentioned previously, of which the world's largest and best studied collection exists in the Museo Arqueológico "Rafael Larco Herrera," in the Hacienda Chiclín, some 56 km. from the village of Moche. This collection has been acquired and studied by Rafael Larco Hoyle, the well-known Peruvian archeologist, and it will be necessary to rely largely upon his findings in order to identify the still existing Mochica elements in Moche. The later prehistoric cultures of the region are known from archeology and also from accounts of Spanish chroniclers in the epoch of the Conquest. The most detailed description of the Chimu culture existing at the time of the Conquest is that of Calancha (1638). Rather than attempt to set forth a trait list of the several prehistoric cultures, so far as they are known, at the present point, a discussion of the prehistoric survivals will be postponed until a later section (p. 154 ff.).

As for the meaning of the word "Moche," opinions differ. According to Paz Soldán (1877, p. 590) "mocha" is a corruption of "mochi," Quechua for "to rinse the mouth" or "to chew corn to make *chicha*." This, in view of the modern habits of the Mocheros, would be a very appropriate definition. On the other hand, in Villagomes (1919, p. 210, footnote) is found the verb "mochar" defined as "to cut or lop off" and also as "to kiss or render religious homage." This source does not tell whether the word is Quechua or Mochica. My friend, Señor Manuel Briceño, who maintains a residence in Moche and who has enjoyed a long period of collaboration with Señor Rafael Larco Hoyle in the study of the ancient and modern Mochica culture and language, claims that the word is Mochica, meaning "to worship or adore religiously." I have been unable to locate the word in any published vocabulary of the Mochica language. My friend, Dr. J. M. B. Farfán, the well-known Quechua scholar, is inclined to derive the word from the Quechua word *"muchhi,"* meaning "pimple" or "acne."[18]

Finally, before leaving this review of the scanty historical material, it will be recalled that, according to Uhle's excavations, the town during Mochica times was located on the plain, or *llano,* lying between the Huaca del Sol and the Huaca de la Luna (Uhle, 1913, fig. 1 and p. 98), a site covered by the remains of small house mounds with numerous burials nearby. From the pottery, Uhle concluded that the site had been occupied by the Chimu and Inca following the Mochica period. At the present time this site lies in the extreme northern corner of the area which we are studying. There is no archeological evidence that an ancient Mochica town occupied the present site of the pueblo of Moche. Although at present this is mere speculation, I would not be surprised that the appropriate church and colonial documents, if and when they eventually come to light, would show that the present pueblo was established shortly after the Conquest following an early subdivision of other lands among the Spaniards. The lands and Indians northwest of the river and upstream from the Huacas were probably granted in *encomiendas,* leaving a group of Indians confined to the area corresponding to the present District of Moche, scattered about a small land grant, now known as the Haciendita.

A later section (p. 154) deals with possible survivals of earlier cultures in the present cultures of Moche.

SUSTENANCE AND BASIC ECONOMY

One of the distinctions enjoyed by Moche is that it is still a community of independent farmers, whereas most of the other Peruvian coastal communities have been absorbed into large haciendas. The basic economic activity at the present day is small-scale, irrigated farming, supplemented by a, diminishing amount of fishing, and there is good reason to believe

[17] E. g., Horkheimer, 1944, p. 10: "in the second or third century A. D."

[18] Farfán, personal communication.

that this has been true since Mochica times. However, at present, various accretions ("acculturations") have appeared in farming techniques, and, with the gradual increase in population, an increasingly larger proportion of the younger generation go out of the community to seek work as laborers on the roads, on haciendas, and in factories in Lima, with a few even entering the learned professions.

The farming and fishing of Moche are carried on both for subsistence and in order to produce income, either through money exchanges or barter. In fact, one of the changes of recent years has been an increasing emphasis upon cash "crops," such as alfalfa and milk, which are sold in Trujillo, while the fishing industry, although at present small, sells practically all of its production, other than that consumed by the fishing families themselves, to the Trujillo market, where the remaining Mocheros must go to purchase it. Although the Mocheros, or, more properly, their women, are actively engaged in trade in the sense of disposing of their production commercially, nevertheless trading, as an occupation in itself, seems to hold little interest for the people. All retail establishments in Moche pueblo itself are in the hands either of *forasteros* or of *extanjeros,* and I am not aware that any Mochero has left the community to set up or take part in a strictly trading or commercial enterprise elsewhere.

In this section no attempt is made to give a thoroughgoing description of agriculture in Moche from the point of view of an agronomist or other type of agricultural specialist. This is a task requiring the collaboration of a competent authority in this field. Our main interest in this report is to consider the place of agriculture and other economic activities in the cultural life of the community, with particular attention to the trends of cultural change. The orientation is cultural or ethnological rather than economic or agricultural in the full academic implications of those words. Certain omissions may occur, since I was working with the community only about 6 months and therefore was unable to observe the full yearly cycle.

SKETCH OF MOCHE AGRICULTURE OF THE CAMPIÑA

The most charming part of the Moche District is the *campiña,* or rural farming area, which surrounds the town on all sides, as can be seen from the aerial photographs (pls. 1 and 2). This is a region of sandy lanes shaded by willow trees overhanging the *acequia* (irrigation) ditches alongside, of small fields,

quaint houses with cool outdoor arbors, and a quiet peasant country life somehow out of the world. In the *campiña* the quaintest and most primitive aspects of the culture are best developed, and sophistication lies low. A single lane (pl. 18, *upper (left)*) is sufficiently passable to permit automobiles to drive through a part of the *campiña,* although in an exceedingly bone-shaking and axle-breaking manner. It branches off from the Pan-American Highway to the right about 800 m. from the pueblo, proceeds through the holdings of the Haciendita, passes through the small rural center of Sun, and on northward to the base of the Huaca del Sol. Leaving the Huaca, it fords the river and leaves the Moche District, proceeding northwestward through the Hacienda de Santa Rosa, to enter the city of Trujillo via the *barrio* of Chicago. This sole means of modern intrusion into the isolation of the *campiña* is traversed by only a very occasional automobile carrying intrepid tourists or visiting archeologists bent upon seeing the ruins, and, to date, has had no practical effect upon the quiet life of the Moche countryside, most of which is accessible only afoot or by donkey or horseback, traversing the willow-shaded sandy lanes.

On one or both sides of the lanes are irrigation ditches, tapped at frequent intervals by branches leading into the various land holdings. During the dry season the water is turned into any given ditch only once every 9 days, but the major ditches, when they contain water, are veritable small rivers or creeks, practically always shaded by overhanging trees. The fields, usually green at all times of the year, are bordered, as a rule, by solid-looking fences or walls of *tapia* (mold-laid mud; see p. 38), frequently partially hidden by bushes and small trees growing in the field borders against the inside surfaces. A *tapia* wall or fence is practically invariably found on the side of a holding which borders a lane. The houses are located at frequent intervals and are usually well shaded by large shade and fruit trees in their *huertas* (surrounding garden orchards). As a rule they are situated in the corners of the land holdings, sometimes so well surrounded by vegetation as to be almost invisible from the lane.

As one passes along, one sees quiet groups of cattle tethered by neck ropes or horn ropes, grazing in small alfalfa pastures inside the *tapia* walls, and often guarded by small boys and girls. In the mornings, if it is not planting or harvesting season, men working with shovels either singly or in pairs are seen in the cultivations, and from about 10 a. m. onward throughout the day, one will be frequently passed by Moche women returning from the Trujillo market atop small gray donkeys. The load of one of these beasts generally includes a woman, a child in arms, and various empty milk cans, baskets of food, and other materials acquired in the city. During the planting or harvesting seasons one will see groups of men working in the fields together, attended by a coterie of women in the shady field corner preparing and purveying food and drink.

This peaceful landscape, which is sunlighted practically every afternoon of the year and all day long from November until July, is dominated by the great pyramidal Huaca del Sol standing at the northernmost extremity. The *campiña* itself is flat, without hills or undulations, so that from one end to the other, one has only to look to the north to see the famous ruin, frequently framed in the branches of trees. The Moche Mountains, of which the Cerro Blanco is outstanding, dominate the northeastern border of the *campiña*. They are utterly devoid of visible vegetation and are of a basic gray-white color, which, however, changes hue with the varying angles and brilliancies of the sunlight. To the east, the *campiña* ends abruptly at the limit of irrigation. In many places this border with the desert is a startlingly precise line, and one can stand with one foot on a green, cultivated patch of ground and the other foot in the sandy dust of the desert. Along this border the trees are fewer and scrubbier than in the better watered parts of the area. The remains of old irrigation ditches in the desert to the east indicate that the present irrigated area is less extensive than in ancient times.

Strange as it may seem in an area so small in North American eyes, the farming area of Moche is divided into three sections—northern, southern, and western.

The foregoing description is characteristic of the *campiña* in general, but is found best developed in the section north of town. This seems to be the best-watered area, is most intensively cultivated, possesses the most desirable soil, and has the best-made houses. It also lies nearest the ruins, so that there may be historical as well as geographical reasons for its apparently richer cultural development.

The southern section of the *campiña* is drier than those portions north and west of the town. As the land approaches the sea, the soil becomes sandier, and the landscape to the south is dominated by a series of dunes 20 to 35 feet high, partially covered by scrubby grass. Thus the *campiña* is definitely separated from

the *playa*. In this part of the farming area one can hear the roar of the surf mingled with a faint but constant singing of the sea wind through the scrub grass, but in the fields one does not see the sea itself because of the dunes.

The third section of the *campiña* lies across the road to the west. It is often called Barranca, although this properly refers only to the northern part. Barranca is actually the name of a large irrigation ditch. This western section is dominated by the river. Here the brush and trees are wilder and more abundant. Along the left bank of the river itself is an area almost entirely given over to wild brush growth, whose owners derive an income from the sale of wooden building beams, firewood, and *caña brava* (cane) harvested in this miniature jungle. In this section there is also considerably more natural pasture than in other portions of the *campiña*. Although in the dry season the visible water of the river is reduced to the trickle of a medium-sized brook, nevertheless the subterranean seepage water seems to be considerable.

Thus it is that the *campiña* is like a small country in itself, the three regions—north, south, and west— each having somewhat different conditions and landscape. Although visiting takes place back and forth, there is a tendency, owing to factors of transportation, toward ethnocentrism in each of these areas. The normal communication lines run from each area to the town or from each area to the city of Trujillo, rather than from area to area. Therefore, contacts between the three sections are most regularly renewed on feast days in the pueblo. It is not uncommon to hear two men from different sections of the *campiña* inquiring at a fiesta about events and personages of each other's neighborhood as if they actually lived in different parts of Peru. However, this tendency toward separatism or regionalism has not reached a stage where it is the basis for formal differentiation in the social or political organization. The three sections of the *campiña* do not even have names that are in common use by the whole Moche community. In Moche, one does not say that he lives in "the northern section." He says that he lives *"por la Huaca"* (toward the Huaca), *"por este lado de Sun"* (this side of Sun), or near some other landmark or person known to be in the northern section. If one lives in the southern section, one is identified as being *"por la playa"* (toward the beach), or *"cerca de Chorobal"* (the water wells), etc. In the western section, one may be *"del otro lado de la carreterra"* (from the other side of the highway), *"de Barranca"* or *"de la boca del rio"* (from around the mouth of the river), etc.

Straddling the road and occupying central portions of both the northern and western sections are the lands of the Haciendita, apparent as comparatively large unsubdivided fields in the aerial photographs (pls. 1 and 2). This land, totaling about 113 hectares, is not a part of the Moche *campiña* in any sense other than the geographical. A few Mocheros work as peons on the Haciendita, but otherwise the crops, methods, organization, and personnel are outside the Moche picture. Another, smaller area of *forastero* intrusion is visible (pls. 1 and 2) as comparatively extensive, unbroken fields, about 30 acres in extent, off the northeast corner of the pueblo. Most of this is at present leased to the Government-supported agricultural school, which, as will be pointed out below, also plays no part in the agricultural configuration of the community.

CULTIVATED LANDS AND THEIR MANAGEMENT

Planting and care of domesticated plants occur in Moche in three types of locations: (1) Fields, (2) garden orchards (*huertas*), and (3) field borders.

Many a Moche "field" would perhaps appear to a North American farmer to be too small to be worth cultivating. The average land holding seems to be about 1.6 hectares, or 3.9 acres, with a wide range about the average. The individual field, however, would average much smaller. When the official *catastro* is completed we shall have, it is to be hoped, accurate figures on this matter, but it is doubtful that the average cultivated field or planted plot exceeds 1,000 sq. m. I know of several fields in cultivation which do not exceed 100 sq. m., and the largest single field of which I know is probably not over 4 hectares (40,000 sq. m.).[19]

Although land holdings are usually divided by *tapia* fences, this is not necessarily true of fields, and a single fenced piece of ground may contain two or more fields or cultivated plots, each given over to a different crop or to different plantings of the same crop.

Among the Mocheros a farm, or land holding, is usually called a *chacra;*[20] a person also refers to "mis terrenos" (my lands) and "mi propiedad" (my property). The word *granja* is used in Moche to refer only to a poultry farm or a small stock farm raising swine. There are three commercial *granjas* in Moche, all operated by *forasteros* for the Trujillo market. "Fields," in the sense of individual cultivated plots, are usually called *campos* or *sembrados;* occasionally one uses the word *cosecha* (harvest or crop) when referring to a given plot, identifying the piece of land with the crop growing upon it. "Crop" is also known as *"siembra."* Mocheros use the word *fanegada* when speaking of land areas more often than the word *hectarea;* there seems to be general agreement that a *fanegada* is equal to about 3 *hectareas,* but informants are never precise or sure. The *fanegada* is a Spanish land measure introduced during colonial times, and it is apparent that most Mocheros still think in terms of it and have not yet become accustomed to translating *fanegadas* readily into *hectareas.*

There are no clearly defined planting times in Moche to which all farmers adhere. The general rule is that there be sufficient water to get the new crop started properly. Except alfalfa and yuca (sweet manioc), which are planted only once a year or less often, a farmer may expect to plant and harvest two crops per year of such crops as corn, lentils, beans, and sweetpotatoes. In most years and on most lands, December is regarded as the time for putting in the wet-season crop (*tiempo de abundancia*), which is harvested in May, and June is the time for putting in the dry-season crop (*tiempo de escasez*), with the harvest beginning in October. Individual conditions may vary somewhat. The fiesta of San Isidro in May serves as a sort of harvest festival for the first crop, and the October fiesta serves as the harbinger of the second harvest.

No fertilizer other than the droppings of livestock made directly on the fields is used in Moche farming. The constant planting of leguminous crops like alfalfa, beans, and lentils doubtless restores the nitrogen to the soil satisfactorily.

A nonrigid or informal crop rotation is practiced, of which the following example may give an idea. The field described was planted to corn and lentils in the first crop of 1938. During the second crop it stood idle, i.e., cattle were allowed to forage on the cornstalks. Corn and lentils were again put in for the first crop of 1939, and the second crop was beans. Early in 1940 it was planted to alfalfa and sorghum.

---

[19] Compare the aerial photographs (pls. 1 and 2). It must be remembered that the Haciendita, comprising some 113 hectares, lies geographically within the *campiña*, but is not considered a part of it, either from the community or cultural point of view. The broad open fields visible in the center of the farming area to the north of the town belong to the Haciendita, whereas the small subdivisions seen covering most of the remainder of the area are the holdings of Mocheros.

[20] From the Quechua, according to De Arona (1938, p. 157).

Six crops of alfalfa were taken from it during the year. It was allowed to stand untouched for about 3 months after the last cutting, and was then turned into pasture. Cattle occupied the field during most of 1941 and up to June 1942, when the alfalfa began to thin out. It was plowed and a crop of corn and lentils put in, which did not do well because of lack of water. In January 1943, it was planted to yuca and corn. In 1944 it was once more in alfalfa.

IRRIGATION

The irrigation system is now under control of an official dependency of the Ministerio de Fomento, which maintains a subadministrator in Moche (under the immediate supervision of the Administración de Aguas del Rio Moche, which has offices in Trujillo). This authority lays down the regulations concerning the time of water flow and the care of the ditches. The *"república,"* or democratic organization of water users which is said formerly to have handled all matters of irrigation, has thus been superseded. Perhaps as a substitute the Government has permitted the organization of a group known as the Association of Irrigators of Moche (Asociación de Regantes de Moche) which is supposed to serve in an advisory capacity to the subadministrator and as a vehicle for making complaints to the higher authorities. The president of this group at present is the proprietor of the Haciendita, which is the largest single water user in the District. Although the Mocheros complain mightily that the Haciendita is favored over the smaller land holdings in the distribution of the water and also that the haciendas farther up the valley are obtaining more than their share of the river flow, nevertheless the natives have been unable to unite on a candidate of their own whereby they might obtain more effective control of the organization. An organization of younger progressive natives, called Moche en Marcha (Moche in Movement), is at present strenuously attempting to unite the Mocheros for this and other purposes involving the common welfare.

The irrigation administration is primarily concerned with the distribution of the water, which is most abundant in March and scarcest in October. During the dry season the river water is turned into each trunk ditch only once every 9 days. The principle of distribution of water to individual land holdings or fields is time. Each holding, or, more properly, each side ditch running into a holding is assigned so many minutes of water during the time that water is running in the main ditch. This time may

be changed in theory by appeal to the authorities, but as of any given moment is recorded in the official *catastro* (property list) and is one of the rights which go with the parcel of land if and when it changes hands. An annual tax is levied upon each parcel of land to support the irrigation service, and this is based upon the amount of water time assigned to the parcel, which in turn is theoretically based upon the area of the parcel of land and a consideration of its needs (e.g., land near the river with considerable underground seepage water is not considered to need so much irrigation per unit of area). It is because the areas of the land holdings were previously only imperfectly known that the Government undertook the precise survey in 1944 which should result in a new *catastro,* mentioned previously. The time limit on water applies, of course, during the season of scarce water; in the season of abundance each farmer has as much water as he desires. According to the 1944 *catastro,* the lowest annual water rent paid by a Mochero was 26 centavos, and the highest 16.42 soles. (One sole equaled approximately 15.3 cents and 1 centavo approximately 1/7 of a cent in terms of United States currency at the time the study was made.) The water rent goes toward the maintenance of the system of administration.

In order to operate this system the subadministrator depends upon the services of the farmers themselves, who are assigned to water watching according to a rotating list. The night duty is the most onerous and involves regulating the main gates at the proper intervals and patrolling the side-ditch outlets. Night duty rotates to most farmers about once every 2 or 2½ months and is called *mala noche* ("bad night," a term which also refers to any night spent without sleep, whatever the reason). It is, of course, the responsibility of the individual farmers to care for their private ditches. Irrigation ditches of all kinds are called *acequias.* It is said that rich or powerful water users are able to obtain more than their proper share by (1) bribing or otherwise influencing the subadministrator to increase their time on the list and (2) by influencing the watchers to allow certain ditches to run longer than the official time. I have no evidence that this is true.

The principal irrigation ditches are named. For example, there are the ditches named Sun—one of the main trunks which taps the river above the Huaca del Sol and probably dates from prehistoric times—Chocchoc, Güerequeque, Barranca, Esperanza, los Muertos, el Muelle, etc.

Although each landholder cleans and keeps in repair his own ditches, the upkeep of the main communal ditches of the system of distribution is done on a communal unpaid basis. Periodically the call goes out for the *destajos* (task work), and gangs of men assemble with spades. Each man is obliged to work a length of time proportional to his amount of irrigated land. Often he is merely assigned to certain proportional length of the communal ditch to clean. The work consists in digging out the vegetation, mud, stones, and other accumulations in the channel. Formerly, it is said that this task was performed in festive mood to the accompaniment of food and drink after the manner of a *minga* (reciprocal work parties), but at the present time one sees none of this. It is a job to be done, and that is all.

The principal heads of the main communal ditches are provided with cement sluices and steel gates, but water is diverted into small side ditches by earth dams bolstered by a couple of horizontal sticks or boards held in place with wooden stakes, as illustrated in plate 5, *lower* (*left*). Men may water small house plots by ladling water out of the communal ditch with buckets. This is not considered stealing the water if it is done on a small scale.

The distribution of the water on the field itself follows several patterns, depending upon the crop and its stage of growth. Although I know of the following three types, there may be more. (1) A thin sheet of water is spread over the ground before plowing if it is very hard and dry; young plots of alfalfa and newly planted gardens are frequently given a similar treatment. Fields are divided into rectangular plots, *melgares;* the system is called *de pozas*. This is accomplished usually by simply opening the ditch in one or more places alongside the field and allowing the water to spread out over the ground. (2) In the second method a series of small parallel straight ditches (*regaderas* or *reventeros*) run off the feeder ditch (*regadero*) from one side of the field to the other. Corn and beans are usually irrigated this way, as well as yuca. (3) Winding irrigation channels (*de caracol*) are sometimes used to irrigate yuca; the channel runs down one side of the row, turns back to run down the other side of the row, and so on, irrigating the entire field from a single outlet of the feeder ditch.

IMPLEMENTS

Fields are prepared for planting by plowing. A yoke of oxen is used for traction, but the implement itself is a single-handled one-way walking plow, all of iron, and manufactured in the United States. No wooden plows are to be found in the Moche countryside at present. The technique of handling the plow is, however, apparently much as it was when the Spanish wooden plow with iron point was used (pl. 6, *lower* (*left*)). This type of plow, although it has a curved moldboard of iron, cuts a furrow only about 4 inches deep and often less. The depth of the furrow depends upon the skill of the driver. The driver is accompanied by an assistant who breaks the clods, either with his feet or, more often, with a wooden stick or iron crowbar which he carries for the purpose. No harrow is used. The driver guides the oxen by voice and with a whip which has a wooden handle about 2 feet long and a leather thong 5 to 6 feet long. Oxen have individual names to which they respond and they also are taught to obey commands of a limited range. Oxen are usually castrated between the ages of 1 and 2 years. However, bulls are frequently used under the yoke. Both are called *"bueyes."* When a distinction is made, the gelded animal is simply called *un buey castrado*. A team of oxen is called a *yunta* (yoke). The actual yokes are made of wood obtained in the *campiña* and fastened to the horns with rawhide straps or thongs. Willow wood is said to be most commonly used, although oak (*roble*), if it can be obtained, is preferred. Almost any farmer can make a yoke himself, although certain ones are considered specialists and are employed to make yokes for others. The yoke is attached to the plow by an iron chain, not by a shaft.

Many farmers do not possess ox teams or plows and are required to hire their plowing done on a custom basis. In 1944 the standard rate was 8 soles per day for team, plow, driver, and his assistant. The hours are carefully watched, and work is supposed to continue without interruption from 8 to 11 a. m. and from 1 to 5 p. m. The acreage which can be plowed in a day depends upon a great many factors—driver, oxen, condition of the soil—but *yuntas* are usually hired by the day only. If the work is finished before the end of the day, no rebate is made. To be sure, as in all Moche deals, payment may be made in produce rather than in cash money, but there is little sharing of work which involves oxen. Even brothers enter plowing deals with each other which involve payment in terms of money.

The plow is used for preparing the ground, as just described. It is also used, after the ground has been plowed once, to produce furrows in which various crops are planted. The plow produces a shallow fur-row and also throws out a ridge of earth on one side. There seem to be three types of furrows: (1) The simple furrow with a ridge of earth alongside; (2) the double furrow, with ridge of earth on each side, produced by plowing a second furrow alongside the first one in the opposite direction, called *surco hembra* (female furrow); the central furrow usually serves as an irrigation channel; (3) the double furrow with a double ridge of earth in the center and furrows on each side of it, called *surco macho* (male furrow). In planting certain crops, such as sorghum, maize, and beans, it is said that the seeds are placed in the furrow, although actually they are placed in the base of the ridge of earth with the effect that the plants usually are seen growing out of a low ridge of earth rather than from the depression of the furrow. This method of planting must obviously be a comparatively recent innovation, since it seems to depend upon the presence of a plowshare and moldboard of modern type capable of producing a clear furrow and turning over a ridge of earth, features impossible with the old-fashioned wooden plow of colonial times.

Oxen are not used to pull wheeled vehicles of any kind. Neither are horses and donkeys used to pull wheeled vehicles in Moche, with the exception of a two-wheeled garbage cart drawn by a single horse and maintained by the Municipalidad. Otherwise, the only wheeled vehicles seen in the Moche District are automobiles and railroad vehicles. Neither of these types is owned by Mocheros, nor can they be consid-ered a part of the material equipment of the com-munity.

The plow is the only power implement used in Moche agriculture (ox power). The hand imple-ments are as follows (pls. 5, *lower* (*right*); 6, *cen-ter*): (1) The short-handled shovel or spade (*palana*); (2) the *machete*, a one-handed heavy knife of the type familiar under this name to North Ameri-can readers, used for clearing brush and weeds and for splitting firewood; (3) the *calabozo*, a heavy "bush" knife with a hooklike projection at the end of the blade, fitted to a long wooden handle and used for clearing brush and weeds from the land; (4) the *barro*, a wooden clublike stick, used for breaking earth clods after plowing and for making holes for plant-ing; (5) the iron or steel crowbar (*barro de hierro*), used for breaking clods and for other purposes, such as moving stones, logs, and other weights; (6) the pickax (*pico*), for breaking hard ground, especially in irrigation ditches; (7) the ax (*hacha*), a single-bladed implement of European type, used for felling and splitting wood and for clearing brush from the land; (8) the *horca*, a tined fork, made from a single, branched tree limb; and (9) a modern, wooden-handled, iron rake or *rastro*, used by some men.

It is curious that the hoe is not present in modern Moche, but, on the other hand, there is no clear evi-dence that it was ever used in prehistoric times. The implements recovered from Mochica and Chimu cul-tures are of the spade type, i.e., the blade of the imple-ment lies in the same axis as that of the handle. Present-day spades are of modern European or North American design (most are imported from these two sources, although lately at least two Peruvian con-cerns have begun manufacturing these implements), but are used for "hilling up" corn and other crops, for making holes for planting etc., and for cultivating around standing plants, as well as for cleaning irriga-tion ditches and for all tasks involving the movement of earth by hand. In many of these efforts it would seem that the hoe would be a more useful implement. Moreover, it is available in Trujillo hardware stores. Such is the power of tradition, or the resistance to acculturation. Plate 6, *upper* (*right*), shows a man working with a spade.

The *calabozo* is likewise, apparently, a prehistoric implement. In the Museo Arqueológico "Rafael Larco Herrera" in Chiclín, blades of the same type as those in use at present occur in great numbers, but it is not clear whether they are of Mochica or Chimu provenience.

Likewise it is quite possible that the *barro*, the clod-breaking wooden bar, is prehistoric in origin. There is some reason to believe that the Mochicas and Chimus used a digging stick with which they punched holes in the earth for planting. The ancient idea behind this implement (symbolic pattern) seems to have disappeared in its original form in modern Moche, possibly owing to displacement by the plow in the planting complex, although the *barro* is used for poking seed holes in furrows prepared by the plow.

TECHNIQUES WITH FIELD CROPS

The actual planting of field crops is usually done on a shared work basis, in the pattern of a *minga*. The owner of the land invites certain friends or rela-tives to assist him with the planting. The women of his household provide food and *chicha*. It is also un-derstood that today's host will lend his services to his fellows during the following days. I have not had the opportunity to observe a large number of these work parties over a long period of time, but informants state that, contrary to expectations, they are not permanent or organized, i.e., members of the same groups do not exchange work with one another invariably year after year, with an organization of leadership, etc. However, there does seem to be a natural tendency toward a relative permanency among neighbors. Although relatives are frequently included in the planting parties, there seems to be no rule to this effect.

Techniques involved with a few of the more common field crops can be briefly described as follows.

Alfalfa, which occupies perhaps three-fifths of the cultivated land of Moche at present, is always planted in the same field with sorghum (*sorgo*),[21] as illustrated (pl. 3, *upper* and *lower* (*left*)). Patches of alfalfa 2 to 3 m. wide[22] alternate with rows of sorghum in parallel series across the field. Alfalfa seed is purchased in the *tiendas* in the pueblo, or threshed by the farmer himself. It is sown broadcast from a cloth bag.

The earth where the rows of sorghum are to be planted is usually heaped up by the plow in a ridge about 3 inches above the surface of the alfalfa bed before planting. The sorghum is then planted in shallow holes about 1 m. apart or less near the base of the ridge of earth. Six seeds are placed in each hole. Another method is to plant the sorghum in two parallel ridges made by plowing two furrows, side by side, one in each direction to produce a shallow irrigation channel between them—a "female furrow." The sorghum shoots up faster than the alfalfa and appears as a line of tufts of light green above the darker green of the surrounding young alfalfa. By this combination of the two plants, one is able to obtain forage for cattle within 10 to 14 days after planting, without waiting for the alfalfa to produce a crop. Many such fields are used simply as pasture, with the cattle being turned in as soon as the sorghum has reached a height of 9 inches or a foot. Some sorghum and alfalfa is cut with a sickle and carried to other

places on the farm as cattle feed, while a not inconsiderable quantity of both crops is carried on donkeyback to Trujillo for sale fresh, mostly to the army as feed for its horses. One of my friends reported that during one morning he counted 23 donkey loads pass the *chacra* where he was working, en route to Trujillo. Finally, a farmer may sell part of his crop to other farmers in temporary need of cattle feed. Sorghum and alfalfa are always cut and used fresh, if cut at all. No dried haystacks are to be found in the Moche area. In the pueblo there is a cement silo, erected some years ago by a progressive *forastero*, which apparently has been a failure. Sorghum and cornstalks put into it as ensilage are said to spoil and become useless as cattle feed. Whether this is due to climate or faulty technique, I do not know. Four to six crops of alfalfa per year are expected, if the crop is cut. For seed, alfalfa is cut ripe and piled up to dry. It is then either carried to the house or threshed in the field. At all events a mat (*petate*) is placed under the pile, which is then pounded with a heavy stick. (This is not hinged like the old-fashioned American flails.) This treatment is to *sacar la gavilla* (break up the stalks and bunches). Afterward the alfalfa is picked up in small bunches and these are whipped over a basket with a small stick or switch to knock off the seeds. Occasionally the highland method of threshing wheat is used. The alfalfa is spread out on a hard dirt floor with a heavy stake or post set up in the middle. A pair or more of horses are driven round and round the stake, and after this the residue is tossed into the air and winnowed in the wind.

Corn (maize) is planted in rows about 18 inches apart, hilled up with the spade or plow before planting into low ridges produced by plowing a furrow. Corn is frequently planted with lentils (*lentejas*) in the same hole. The holes are about 3 feet (1 pace) apart. The method is to place two kernels of corn and three seeds of lentil in the first hole, three kernels of corn and two seeds of lentil in the second hole, and so on successively. The planter is usually followed by another person who covers the hole and tamps it down with his feet. Lentils are often harvested before the corn has eared, but hard, dry lentils may also be harvested even after the corn has been husked. Lentils are harvested, as a rule, by pulling them up by the roots and carrying the whole plant to a convenient spot where the seeds are taken out of the pods or (in the case of green lentils) the pods are removed from the plant. Corn

---

[21] A list of scientific names of certain plants with remarks concerning their origin, follows this section. This list is given only as an aid to the reader interested in the matter. The scientific names have been culled from the literature and the records of the Museo Arqueológico "Rafael Larco Herrera" in Chiclín.

[22] I may be making too much of this, but informants repeatedly insisted that the alfalfa patches (*melgares*) were 5 to 6 m. wide, whereas on inspection I was unable to find one more than 3 m. wide. This tendency to exaggerate numerical values occurs fairly frequently. Whether it represents an incomplete association of the numerical symbol with its referent or a form of ego inflation through the telling of a good story, I am unable to say with certainty at present.

is harvested green to be eaten boiled on the cob (*choclo*). It is also harvested ripe, about 6 months after planting. In both cases it is husked on the stalk in the field. For this purpose a bone or wooden pick, 5 to 6 inches long, perforated at the butt end and attached to the wrist by a thong passing through the perforation, is used as an aid in opening the husks. Rarer are picks made from iron spikes. As a general rule, the stalks are allowed to stand in the field after harvest and cattle are turned in to eat them and trample them down, after which they are burned. Harvesting may be done by individuals working alone, in pairs or small groups, and also in the *minga* arrangement. When planted in the same plot with yuca, the corn seeds are deposited in individual holes made with the spade.

Various types of beans are planted in rows or ridges as is corn, three seeds to a hole usually. Beans are harvested by pulling the whole plant up by the roots. They are threshed by hand as is alfalfa, by beating (although horses are never used, because they crush the seeds). Beans are not cut with a sickle. Seed beans are still stored by some people in a box full of sand, a procedure which seems to date from Mochica times. This keeps them dry and also is said to protect them from the attacks of insects that eat out the inside of the bean and destroy its germinating power. The more modern method, however, is to store the beans in stoppered bottles or in tin cans sealed with sticking plaster.

Yuca (also known in English as manioc and cassava) is planted from cuttings about 5 inches long taken from the stalks. The cutting must be in the state in which milky juice issues from the wound. The surface of the cutting is covered at intervals by buds, which on the growing stalk point upward. In Moche a bud is called *"nuez del palo"* (nut of the stick). In planting, the cuttings must be so laid that the buds point into the ridge of earth alongside the furrow. Cuttings are planted about a meter apart. Three methods of planting are in use. (1) In the *pisada* method, the cuttings are laid crosswise in a simple furrow, pointing toward the ridge of earth, and are tamped down with the feet. A small portion must protrude above the surface of the hill. (2) To *sembrar a estaca,* the cuttings are thrust into the moist soil of a hill ridge made by a "male furrow," leaving an inch or so to protrude. (3) In the *de acequia* method a "female furrow" is made first. Then the cuttings are laid crosswise, but so placed that the buds of alternate cuttings point in

opposite directions. Again it is necessary that a small portion of the cutting protrude through the hill. Then water is turned into the female furrow. Yuca is usually ready to harvest in 9 months and produces large bunches of heavy roots, often as large as a man's lower leg. Yuca is harvested simply by grasping the stalks above ground and pulling up the roots, which may be left in piles on the field for a few hours to dry.

Although alfalfa, sorghum, maize, lentils, beans, and yuca are the principal or largest field crops, many others included in the list below are also planted and grown in fields, as well as in garden orchards and field borders.

Weeding is done by hand, and with spade, machete, and *calabozo*.

Every house in the *campiña* is surrounded by a *huerta* and most houses in the pueblo have an attempt at one in the back yard. These are usually relatively small areas containing a great variety of fruit trees, bushes, and small plots of decorative flowers and kitchen vegetables. In the vegetable plots it is not unusual to see onions, cabbage, lettuce, azafrán, and radishes, for example, all growing in one plot, either in alternate rows or mixed up together more or less indiscriminately. Usually the small vegetable plots are surrounded by a fence of cane to keep out poultry and dogs. The fruit trees and bushes provide shade and protection from the wind as well as edible products.

The field borders are usually 3 to 6 feet wide, up next to the enclosing *tapia* fence of the property. Fruit trees, shade trees, and a variety of bushes and even planted products are to be found here.

The field crops mentioned above are seldom grown in any quantity in *huertas* and field borders, but practically all other types of domesticated or useful plants are to be found in both *huertas* and borders and often in fields themselves.

OTHER CROPS AND USEFUL PLANTS

Following are lists of domestic and useful plants one will find in the Moche *campiña*. The lists are not necessarily exhaustive.

First are listed the domesticated plants, planted in fields, gardens, or both:

Ají (chili peppers). Several varieties, large, small, green, yellow, and red; usually planted in *huerta.*

Alvaja de comida (albahaca? sweet basil). Plant grown in fenced enclosures in *huertas* and used for making soup and for flavoring other dishes.

Alverjas (vetches). Planted either in fields or gardens; plants look like those of common sweetpea; produces small, podded, pealike fruit; several varieties.

Azafrán. Usually planted in field borders and garden orchards; produces a dark orange-red flower, which is dried and toasted over the fire, then rubbed to a powder between the hands. The powder is used to color foods, and is an essential ingredient of *sopa teóloga*.

Caigua of various varieties. A low, creeping plant producing a soft squashlike fruit, which is eaten as a vegetable and also stuffed with meat to make *albóndigas*. Usually planted in field borders near irrigation ditches.

Camotes (sweetpotatoes). Planted systematically in fields. Several varieties. The following types of *camotes* are grown: *sangriento* (bloody), *colorado* (red), *boca de chizco, espelina, pierna de la viuda* ("widow's leg," large, long, white, and big in diameter), *niño* ("child," but, curiously, also large and white), and *morado* (purple).

Capulí. Planted in fields and elsewhere; low plant; fruit looks like North American "groundcherry."

Carrizo. A stiff reed used for making baskets; sometimes planted in fields, it also grows in field borders and alongside irrigation ditches. Although this plant seems to have a tougher, harder surfaced stem than *caña brava*, I am not sure that botanically it is a distinct plant.

Cebolla (onion). Planted in gardens and fields; some raised for the market.

Culantro. Planted; used as food seasoning.

Garbanzo (chickpea). Planted, usually in field borders.

Lechuga (lettuce). Planted in gardens only.

Maní (peanuts). Planted in fields, but on a small scale by the Mocheros. One of the local landholding *forasteros* grows peanuts commercially.

Papas (white potatoes). Very rarely planted in Moche because they do not do well.

Plátano (banana). The following types are recognized: *Rabanete* (literally "radishlike"); *de la isla* (island banana), especially favored in fried form; *mansano* ("apple banana"), sweet and eaten raw; *naranjo* ("orange"), orange colored and with a slightly tart taste; *de seda* ("silky"); *guineo* ("Guinea banana"), large yellow.

Rábano (radish). Planted in gardens only.

Repollo (cabbage). Planted in fields and gardens.

Sandía (watermelon). Several varieties planted, all striped.

Tomate. Garden tomatoes; there is also said to be a wild tomato which grows in the field borders, producing a small, tasty fruit. (I have not seen it.)

Tumbo. A climbing vine, producing an edible fruit about the size of a muskmelon; planted around houses as cover for outdoor arbors. It is said that each plant has a guardian serpent, which attacks strangers attempting to steal the fruit or harm the plant.

Zanahoria (carrot). Planted in gardens.

Sugarcane (*caña de azucar*), which constitutes the principal field crop of the haciendas of the entire Trujillo region, including the Haciendita of the Moche District, is not grown by the Mocheros, except for an occasional plant. Its only use as a plant among the Mocheros is to chew the stalk as a confection, sucking out the sweet juice.

Fruit trees and bushes planted either in *huertas* or in field borders include the following:

Algodón pardo (brown cotton). A few persons have planted bushes in their *huertas,* while other plants are to be found growing untended by roadsides (pl. 5, *middle*). The bushes assume a large, spreading form, as much as 9 feet high and 12 feet in diameter, and are not trimmed. They are rare in Moche, but the product is much prized for its use in certain types of curing.

Blanquillo. Brush with edible fruit.

Calabazo (gourd tree). There are apparently several varieties of these bushes; although the best-decorated gourd containers in use in Moche are obtained in trade (usually from the region of Chiclayo), gourds are grown in Moche for ordinary use. The product varies in size and shape from a wide, shallow, platelike container up to 15 inches in diameter, to small cups 3 inches in diameter, and long-necked *chicha* bottles with globular bodies. The branches of the producing bushes are supported by sticks and the fruits themselves are bound with bandages intended to control their shapes. The plants, which are all of an "over-sized" bush type, are usually planted and tended in *huertas.*

Cerezo (cherry).

Chirimoyo. Fruit tree in *huertas.*

Ciruela. Plum; planted both in *huertas* and field borders.

Higo (fig). Tree valued for the fruit and also for the large five-pointed leaves which are used to flavor the dish known as *sancochado.*

Limon ágrio (common lemon).

Limon real. Large, sweetish lemon; some are almost orange in color.

Limon sutil (lime).

Lúcumo. Fruits are picked, placed in the sun for a day or two, and wrapped in rags or straw to ripen.

Mamey. Fruit tree in *huertas.*

Mango. Fruit tree in *huertas.*

Membrillo. A woody bush bearing a small fruit.

Naranjo ágrio. Bitter orange, usually green when "ripe." Sucked to relieve thirst, but mainly used in *seviches* and *escaviches.*

Narango dulce. Sweet orange.

Pacay (guava).

Palto (alligator pear). Usually found near the house.

Papayo (papaya). Has male and female forms. Male trees have yellow flowers, and their fruit, when it occurs, is small. Female trees have white flowers and smaller leaves. Mocheros believe that only a man can prune the female trees, and only a woman can prune the male trees. If this rule is not followed, fruit shrivels or does not appear.

Other plants encountered in the *campiña* are the following. Most are half-domesticated, as very little grows wild in an irrigated countryside without at least the tolerance of the human occupants. Some are planted more or less regularly, some not; but none are systematically tended as are the domesticated "crops."

Alelí. Small, narrow-leaved tree; flowers are used for decoration and sold in the market.

Algarroba. Wood of the tree used for supports and beams in houses; sweetish, large beanlike fruit eaten or sucked.

Cactus. Various types are found rarely in the Moche countryside, and mostly near the borders of irrigation. Cultivation is intense enough to keep most of the plants rooted out of the farming area. The most useful is *penca* (name of the plant), which is a fleshy, low cactus, producing a fruit called *tuna*, which is gathered and eaten. Cactus plants are not regularly planted as fences or on top of *tapia* fences as in certain other Latin American countries, e. g., parts of Mexico.

Caña brava (cane). Grows wild along the edge of certain irrigation ditches and also in large quantities near the river. Used in making house roofs and *quincha* walls, etc.

Choloque. Tree which has a fruit encased in a green-yellow shell; the shell, removed from the fruit produces "suds" when rubbed in water and is considered the best "soap" for washing woolen goods; inside the shell, which is soft and sticky, is the fruit, a hard, dark purple, practically round ball about three-eighths of an inch in diameter, which is used in the marbles games of small boys.

Cinamon. Tree used for wood in construction.

Higarón. A large tree, with large rubbery leaves; when twigs are broken, a white, milky, sticky sap oozes out, which is much prized for curing *quebradura* (umbilical hernia in children). The tree usually grows in *huertas,* although it is also found in field borders.

Ingrio blanco (also a variety called *colorado*). Plant looks somewhat like castor-bean; produces seeds covered with a burr, which contain oil; sometimes planted, but mainly regarded either as a weed or as decoration about the house.

Norbo. A climbing vine, somewhat like a morning-glory, which produces a daisylike flower; usually grows wild in field borders, sometimes planted as cover for outdoor arbors.

Pajarito. A small bush, producing a blue flower with a white center; usually wild, but sometimes transplanted to a *huerta* for decoration.

Pegopego. A weed, somewhat like a nettle, which grows along the sides of the irrigation ditches and in field borders. It is said that the wild doves (*palomas*) become entangled in it and are easily caught.

Uña de gato (literally cat's claws). Grows alongside of *tapias* and irrigation ditches and is frequently planted to serve as a fence and to keep livestock from wandering. It is covered with spines.

Yerba luiza. A grass, the leaf of which looks much like that of sorghum, but which, when rubbed, is aromatic. It is much used in an infusion to make a beverage, taken either hot or cold. When one speaks of "tea" (*té*) in Moche, the reference is practically always to this beverage of *yerba luiza,* rather than to India or China tea.

Yuyu. A low plant which looks something like ragweed; not usually planted, but leaves are cooked and eaten as greens.

A partial list of wild plants gathered for their medicinal properties follows, in order to give some idea of the knowledge of nature which a Mochero possesses. A man or woman walking through the countryside is frequently engaged in casually picking certain herbs as he goes along, to be taken back to the house for future use. A more complete list of medicinal plants will be found in the section dealing with medicine and curing. Certain families transplant some of these plants to their garden orchards in order to have them ready to hand in case of need.

Altamís. When one has bone ache, or cold bones (*huesos fríos*), the leaves of this plant are heated and bound on to the leg or arm in order "to get rid of the cold" (*quitar el frío*).

Brocamelia. Flowers are made into an infusion as remedy for cough.

Campana (floribundo). A small tree with lilylike leaves; the flowers are rubbed together in the hands and used as a poultice to relieve inflammation.

Chamico. A weed, the dried leaves of which are smoked in cigarettes for the cure of asthma.

Chilco macho. A tree, the leaves of which are heated and bound as a poultice over a broken bone in order "to keep out the cold."

Flor muerta. A yellow flower; this is cooked into a paste and stuffed into an aching tooth.

Malva real. A roadside green plant (not to be confused with *malva de olor*); stems and leaves used for enemas.

Rabo flaire. A plant with an appearance like that of burdock; root is mashed up and used in an infusion with *chicoria, verbena,* etc., for enemas.

San Juan. A creeping vine with a yellow flower; the body of an *asustado* (literally, "frightened"; a type of illness prevalent in Moche) is rubbed with the whole plant.

Sombrerita. A lilylike, low, ground plant; an infusion like tea is made from the leaves to cure kidney trouble (*dolor de los riñones*); this infusion is usually made together with the leaves of *amor seco* and *grama dulce.*

Tamarindo. Tree, the fruit of which is used as a purgative.

Verbena. Root only is used in an infusion for the cure of malaria and other fevers.

Yerba mora. Small vine with long white flowers, used for enemas.

Yerba santa. Grows wild; leaves are boiled and bound onto boils as a poultice.

From the point of view of acculturation, it is worth noting that many cultivated plants in Moche bear names, now in common use among the natives, which are native neither to this region nor to Peru. As Herrera and others have pointed out,[23] the words *ají, caygua* (*caigua*), *guayaba, maíz, maní, papaya, tomate, tuna, yuca* are Haitian in origin; *camote* and

---

[23] Herrera, 1942; also Arona, 1938 (see various words in his dictionary); Valdizán and Maldonado, 1922, vol. 2, p. 57 and passim.

chirimoyo are Mexican (Aztec); and *palta* is said to be Ecuadorean (non-Quechuan) in origin.

According to Valdizán and Maldonado[24] the following plants now growing in Moche are foreign to Peru, but were introduced from other parts of the Western Hemisphere:

Capulí (*Prunus capuli*), probably from Mexico; there is no Quechua or Aymara word for it.
Chirimoyo (*Annona cherimola*), probably indigenous to Central America.

The same authors identify the following plants as native to Peru:

Maní, peanuts (*Arachis hypogaea*), cultivated prehistorically in the warm parts of Peru.
Carrizo (*Arundo donax*), probably native to Peru.
Algarrobo (*Prosopis limensis; P. juliflora*).
Molle (*Schinus molle*).
Mamey (*Mammea americana*).
Granadilla (*Passiflora ligularis*).
Tumbo (*Passiflora quadrangularis*).
Culantro (*Coriandrum sativum*).
Lúcumo (*Lucuma obovata*).
Ají (*Capsicum annuum; C. frutescens; C. pubescens*).
Caigua (*Cyclanthera pedata* var. *edulis*).
Zapallo (*Cucurbita maxima*).
Poto, *mate* (*Lagenaria siceraria*).

They identify the following as having been introduced from Europe by Spaniards or other Europeans:

Garbanzo (*Cicer arietinum*).
Haba (*Vicia faba*).
Alverja, arveja (*Pisum sativum*).
Alfalfa (*Medicago sativa*). It is said that alfalfa seed was brought from Valencia at the beginning of the Conquest by a Portuguese, Cristóbal Gazo, and was first sown in Lima.
Caña de azucar (*Saccharum officinarum*). Brought to America on the second voyage of Columbus. The first Peruvian plantings were made in 1570.
Ajo, garlic (*Allium sativum*).
Cebolla, onion (*Allium cepa*).
Rábano, radish (*Raphanus sativus*).
Melon (*Cucumis melo*).

The Museo Arqueológico "Rafael Larco Herrera" in Chiclín has identified the following list of plants now growing in Moche as having been known to the Mochicas from the evidence of actual preserved finds or their portrayal in sculptured or painted vases.

Maize (*Zea mays*).
Chirimoyo (*Annona cherimola*). Both Herrera and Valdizán and Maldonado, cited above, regard this plant as of Central American origin. If this view is true and also if

it can be sustained that the *chirimoyo* was known on the Peruvian coast as early as Mochica times, we have an interesting evidence of prehistoric contact between this region and Central America. Zevallos Quiñones (1944) points out many supposed parallels in place names between the northern Peruvian coast and Central America. The legend of Naymlap, the allegedly Central American prehistoric conqueror of the Lambayeque region, is well known. (See Calancha, 1638.)

Guanábana (*Annona muricata*).
Palta (*Persea americana*).
Beans (*Phaseolus vulgaris*).
Pallares, *lima bean* (*Phaseolus lunatus*).
Maní, peanut (*Arachis hypogaea*).
Pacay, guava (*Inga feuillei*).
Yuca, manioc (*Manihot utilissima*).
Algodón pardo (not specifically identified).
Papaya (*Carica papaya*).
Guayaba (*Psidium guayava*).
Camote, sweetpotato (*Ipomoea batatas*).
Ají, pepper (*Capsicum*).
Tomate, small wild tomato (*Solanum lycopersicum*).
Potato (*Solanum tuberosum*).
Caigua (*Cyclanthera pedata*).
Pepino (*Solanum muricatum*).
Zapallo (*Cucurbita maxima*).

Several crops mentioned as formerly important in Moche are no longer cultivated to my knowledge. Stiglich says, "Since 1891 the prosperity of this valley, where only coca and fruit were cultivated, has begun . . . The coca is always carried to Trujillo by arrieros . . ."[25] I have not obtained clear evidence from informants that coca was ever cultivated on a large scale in the present District of Moche, so am inclined to regard Stiglich's remarks as referring to the upper Moche valley. However, a number of informants claim that small-scale cultivation of coca plants in *huertas* for personal use was practiced until 30 to 40 years ago in the Moche community. At present, so far as I know, there is no growing coca plant in the District. Coca is used occasionally by Mocheros, mainly as a means of keeping awake during sessions of all-night work on the irrigation ditches or at certain ceremonies, but it is obtained in dried form from the local *tiendas*. The use of coca is not habitual among Mocheros at present.

Squier (1877) mentions that the nopal was formerly extensively cultivated in Moche, together with cochineal bugs, but that this industry had largely disappeared by the time of his visit in the 1870's. One informant, an old man claiming to be 99 years old, stated, without suggestion from me, that the growing of cochineal was common in his youth. All

---

[24] 1922, vol. 2, passim. The lists herewith given are not exhaustive. They contain only items identified by the source under the common names used in Moche.

[25] Stiglich (1922, p. 688).

of this has disappeared at the present time. Squier also mentions fields of cotton and rice in the Moche countryside, which are now entirely absent, not only from Moche, but also from the region of Trujillo.

A Government-supported agricultural school is established in the town (map 1, No. 13) and farms several tracts of land belonging to a *forastero* family north and east of town. The school normally has from 4 to 6 instructors or staff members and about 20 students. The latter are boys in their teens from various localities of the region, who are being trained to act as foremen and field bosses on the haciendas. The school at present has very little, if any, influence on agricultural methods in the Moche *campiña* itself. No demonstrations or "extension" programs are carried out for the benefit of the Mocheros.

DOMESTIC ANIMALS AND STOCK RAISING

An estimated three-fifths of the farming land of Moche is devoted to alfalfa, used to pasture and feed milk cows. The present emphasis on dairying seems to be a recent development of the past 10 years. Previous to this phase, Moche agriculture was devoted primarily to the raising of garden crops for the Trujillo market, and previous to the garden-crop phases there were probably other periods of emphasis, such as that centering about the production of cochineal. This is to be expected, since the marketing of Moche products is largely dependent upon the changing conditions of the Trujillo demand and supply situation. Garden crops for the Trujillo market are still produced in Moche on a small scale, but with the advent of Japanese truck gardeners about the city and the rise in the price of milk, there has been a shift in favor of dairy cattle.

The bulk of the milk is taken to Trujillo, either by the wives of the producers themselves or by certain women who act as commission saleswomen, known as *revendadoras*, who collect the milk from the producers in Moche at a discount price. Some of the Moche milk is sold in the port town of Salaverry. In 1944 the average price per liter obtained in Trujillo was about 30 centavos (a little over 4½ cents in United States money; a liter is slightly more than a United States quart). I have no thorough statistical data on milk production. One of the apparently more prosperous producers said that he obtains from his 10 cows about 130 l. per day for an average of between 5 and 6 months of the year; the other 6 months average only between 30 and 40 l. per day. During the season of heavy produc-

tion his income from milk is about 40 soles ($6.12) per day. There may be 20 producers in the Moche community who do this well. Many, however, during my stay in the community were selling only 3 or 4 l. per day. The general practice seems to be to milk the cows only once a day, in the early morning, allowing the calves access to the cows during the day. The men milk the cows, which are usually kept tied in the fields during the night, very early in the morning, usually between 3 and 4 o'clock, so that the women may leave for Trujillo on the first bus at 5 a. m. Milking takes place in the field, an earthen pot being used, as a rule (some use metal buckets); a milking stool is rarely used.

Service of a good Holstein bull costs 75 soles, although service from nonblooded bulls may be had for as little as 20 soles. Some farmers maintain bulls, but the majority sell their bull calves for beef or geld them to use as oxen. I do not know the number of breeding bulls in the community. A yearling calf brings between 150 and 200 soles for beef, but a yearling heifer will bring 200 soles at the least.

Milk cows in Moche are not fed small grain, although they are occasionally given maize on the cob and sweetpotatoes. In addition to feeding on alfalfa, sorghum, and such wild grass as may be available in field borders, the cows are also allowed to forage in fields of standing cornstalks after the ears have been removed, as previously mentioned. In the mountains to the southeast there is temporary pasture some years during the month of August. This pasture is watered by the *garúa* (mist) and consists mainly of clover and *capuli;* cattle are driven to these areas for short periods if the springs and normally dry stream beds contain sufficient water for them to drink.

Milk is transported to Trujillo or Salaverry in metal cans with narrow-collared necks and tight-fitting lids; the cans are of various sizes, the standard being 10 l. Most of the milk is carried by women riding the bus, although not a few still go to Trujillo, carrying their milk cans on burros. A donkey with a pack saddle carries normally four 10-l. cans, two on each side. The buses have railed baggage space on the roofs where milk cans, baskets jars, and other luggage are carried. The whole milk is sold and, so far as known, there is no systematic skimming in the Moche households, nor any regular industry of cheese or butter making.

Among the Mocheros (as distinguished from th

Haciendita and other *forastero* developments) it is not the general practice to provide sheds or stables for cattle. The animals are kept tethered by horn ropes or neck ropes to stakes set in the fields or pasture grounds and are driven out twice a day to the nearest running ditch for watering, when there is no water on the land. The stakes and the area of grazing of each animal are constantly moved with a view to prevent overgrazing of the pasture. Some owners permit their cattle to run loose, if the field is well closed by *tapia* fences, but even then children are frequently assigned to watch them. A few owners having houses in town maintain corrals for livestock in the back yard of the house, but this is not a general custom. Informants agree on a rough estimate of 3,000 cattle maintained by the Mocheros.

Milk is very little used by adult Mocheros, although in the food survey (pp. 54-60) it figures as a breakfast drink for about 35 percent of Mochero school children of both sexes. (In the breakfasts of *forastero* girls it appears 60 percent of the time, and of boys 64 percent.) The emphasis upon dairying, in other words, is primarily due to the fact that it is a cash-money product.

In addition to cattle, which, as we have seen, are of importance for milk, meat, and traction for plows, the other most important domestic animals in Moche are donkeys, or burros. These small and patient beasts are by all odds the principal means of transportation of cargo, and only recently have been relegated to second place by the development of bus transportation for the transport of persons to Trujillo and other outside centers. Riding saddles are not used on burros; the rider is cushioned by one or two gunny sacks thrown over the animal's rear quarters. Pack saddles are of the usual type. Loads are also frequently attached simply to a padding and girth combination. A few peculiar customs involving donkeys may, however, be mentioned. The word "burro" is used in personal insults and, therefore, is not permissible in polite conversation in Moche. The polite word for burro is *pieajeno* or *pieajenito*. Even this reference is usually accompanied by an apology. Thus one will say, *"Monté mi pieajenito—perdón, compadre—hasta Trujillo."* ("I rode my donkey—pardon, *compadre*—as far as Trujillo.") The sense of *pieajeno* is "my other foot," or "substitute for feet." When speaking to the animal itself, the word "burro" or a derivative is used, as when a woman, belaboring her donkey, will scream, *"Ya, véte, pues, burro."* On the other hand, to call a person a "burro" carries a heavier emotional charge than to call one a "donkey" among North Americans. A donkey is often ridden at the same time it is carrying a load in a pack saddle. The rider seats himself astride the rear quarters of the beast; women frequently curl the left leg up over the back, although sitting or kneeling fully astride is not considered immodest. The animal is usually mounted by hooking the great toe over the pack saddle strap which goes around the donkey's rump (this is the explanation given for the fact that many Mocheros of both sexes possess great toes widely divergent from the other toes and the main axis of the foot). The *alforja,* a double "saddle bag" (also used as a shoulder bag) is constantly present, thrown over the donkey's back. Donkeys, when not working, are kept in the fields, although there are several *arrieros* (professional donkey drivers) in the town, who maintain corrals and buy feed. Informants estimate that there are 900 to 1,000 donkeys.

Only a few of the wealthier Mocheros own horses. Most of these animals in the community belong to *forasteros*. They are ridden with saddles, with gunny sack cushions, and bareback. A few riding mules are kept in the community.

It is common for two persons to ride one burro when it is carrying no other load. The heavier of the two is mounted over the hind quarters of the animal. Wooden saddles, lightly covered with leather and many nails, are used for horseback riding, although horses are also ridden simply with pad and girth, or bareback. Except for the most calloused buttocks, a blanket must be thrown over the saddle as protection from the rough corners and nailheads. Donkeys are managed only with a halter and a single tie rope, and they are prodded along with a stick, which is periodically rammed into the hind quarters. Horses are handled with rawhide or woven-leather halters. Bits are very rarely used. The reins are attached to a muzzle consisting of a single strap or line of woven leather, which goes around the horse's nostrils and under its lower jaw. A hard pull compresses the horse's nostrils as well as lifts the head. Usually the traveling gait is a soft trot. The horses belong to the so-called Peruvian breed (not a pedigreed stock as yet), which is characterized by an unusually long pastern, making for an easy trot.

A donkey is worth from 30 soles up, a horse from 200 soles up, and a riding saddle from 200 soles up.

Practically every household, whether in town or in

the country, keeps poultry—chickens, ducks, and/or turkeys. Eggs are a common article of diet among the Mocheros, and poultry flesh also is consumed, although not so frequently. Both products are also sold. Poultry is frequently kept in small houses in the yard, made either of *totora* matting (*esteras*) or of *caña brava*. Sometimes houses of the latter are built on small platforms 4 to 5 feet off the ground as a protection from weasels and dogs. The birds roost in these shelters at night, but usually have their laying nests either in corners of the human dwelling or about the *huerta*. Ordinary chickens are called *"jira chuzca raza."* A mottled gray-and-white type is called *carioca chuzca*. Fighting cocks are not bred here as a general rule. There is no cock-fighting arena in the community and little interest is shown in the sport; except in the event of an occasionally arranged local affair, the followers of the sport must go to Trujillo to follow their interest.

Swine are kept by some Mocheros, although comparatively rarely. Most of the swine in the community are the property of *forasteros*. Sheep are also kept on a comparatively small scale mainly by those who own or have access to the natural pasture land near the river.

Dogs are the only other regularly kept domestic animals. These are numerous, and each household is guarded by two or three at least. They seem to be mongrels, with houndlike smooth-haired varieties in the majority, although large hairy brutes, derived from something like an English shepherd dog are not uncommon. Not a few households have "Chinese dogs" (*perros de los chinos*), a practically hairless breed of dog about the size of a terrier, with black skin, ratlike tail, and thin, spindly legs. Although the Mocheros stoutly maintain that only the Chinese eat these dogs, I am not above the suspicion that certain natives have consumed them. The larger dogs, aside from serving as noisy announcers of the approach of strangers, also aid in herding cattle when they are being driven along a road or lane.

Some households keep cats, but these animals are by no means as universal as dogs.

It is said that guinea pigs (*cuyes*) were formerly kept in Moche as house animals. So far as I could discover there are none now, and even curing *brujos*, who use the animals in divining, say that they are forced to obtain the guinea pigs from outside the community.

Goats, so far as could be determined, are raised even less frequently than sheep, and they also are maintained on the natural grazing grounds near the river. Both of these animals are raised mainly for meat, rather than for wool or hair. Although kid, and to a lesser extent, mutton, is a favorite food of the Mocheros, the major part of the meat is bought in the Trujillo markets. The lack of emphasis upon sheep and goat raising is explained by the fact that pasture suitable for these animals is scarce and that maintaining them on the alfalfa pastures would be uneconomical.

HUNTING AND TRAPPING

Hunting has practically disappeared except as a sport. Occasional forays are made into the mountains, but very few Mocheros have guns, which have to be licensed by the police. Opossums, weasels, and rodents are trapped in box traps with figure-4 triggers of wood and a drop entrance door, a European or North American pattern. The only animals extensively trapped for food are, I believe, the small lizards (*cañanes*). These are hunted by small boys, who kill them on the run with sticks. It is also said that they are trapped according to the Mochica method. This consists of standing up a long roll of matting in the form of a fence across a field and with an inward curl of the matting at each end. The lizards are stopped by the barrier and are too stupid to go backward or around the curled ends to escape. The *cañan* lives near algorroba trees because he eats the seeds (*faiques*). The *cañanes* are not to be confused with other small lizards called *largartijas*.

During the moist winter season occasional expeditions are made to the nearby mountains to the east to gather large ground snails, which appear there at that season. They are steamed and eaten.

RELIGIOUS ASPECTS

A certain amount of superstition and religious beliefs is involved in agricultural and horticultural activities, of which the following are given:

It is believed that every *huerta* has a serpent guardian. This serpent is called a "culambra" (this word does not occur in Spanish dictionaries, including that of the Royal Academy). If a stranger enters the *huerta*, the culambra wraps itself around him until the master of the *huerta* arrives. When the master arrives, he must beat or otherwise punish the snake. If he does not do so, the snake will wrap itself around him also. These snakes are not poisonous, but are said to reach a length of a meter or more and to be as big around as a boy's arm.

The belief has been previously mentioned that each *tumbo* vine also has a serpent guardian. I personally have never succeeded in seeing a snake of any kind in a *huerta* and therefore am unable to say from direct experience whether this belief is based on materialistic experience, or not.

Witchcraft (*brujería*) can be used to damage crops as it can be used to do harm to almost anything else. Certain individuals are believed to possess the power of casting blights upon crops. By way of illustration, the following two experiences are presented, recorded directly from informants and checked and approved by others:

M. R., an old woman, was known as a witch in the pueblo. But, although it is said that witches cannot enter the church without being struck dead, nevertheless, M. R. regularly attended church and spoke to all the people. This is regarded as proof of her extraordinary power. One day the old woman fell sick. Her son, with whom she lived in the pueblo, went out in the evening to visit friends, leaving the invalid in the house. Upon returning he found that his mother was gone. He and his family went out searching for her all over town. No one had seen her. After 2 days they received a report from a farmer living near the Huaquita, saying that the old woman had been seen near his *chacra*—in the form of a cow. How did he know it was she? Because he had hit the cow to force it out of a field, and it had yelled out in human words, "Don't hit me. I am M. R." Also, this farmer had noticed that several days previously his alfalfa crop had started to wither and go bad. He suddenly realized that it had been bewitched and that this apparition of the *bruja* in the form of a cow explained everything. The farmer and his sons beat the cow violently with sticks to drive it away, despite its human screams. Two days later the old woman appeared in the town at the house of her son. The story of the farmer about the cow was obviously true, because the old woman bore marks on her back showing that she had been beaten with a stick. A few days later she died, as must happen to all transfigured witches discovered in their disguise.

Everyone consulted obviously believes this story, even one of my principal informants, an enlightened "accepted *forastero*."

Another story has to do with old J. B. It is said that one day he came to the house of a neighbor, one of my informants. J. B. had a general reputation as a malevolent *brujo*, or witch, although he does no harm to persons, as a general rule. He asked the wife of my informant if she had any *chicha* (corn beer). The woman said, "No," rather brusquely. "All right," said J. B., and went away without further comment. It was not more than an hour after his departure before the *chicha* in the house turned to vinegar, and the next day a blight appeared upon the field crops. A week or so later J. B. again appeared at the house and asked

if there were *chicha*. The lady of the house had drawn her own conclusions and said "Yes, indeed," with alacrity, forcing J. B. to drink as much as he could hold. Then she brought up the matter of the blight which had fallen on the crops and the *chicha*, and asked J. B. tactfully if he could not do something about it. He replied hesitatingly that he would see. She gave him several bottles of *chicha* to take with him when he left. The next day the blights on *chicha* and field crops disappeared. This is only one of a number of similar incidents which are supposed, according to one of my informants, to prove that J. B. is a witch.

In summary, it is believed that witches may cast spells on crops and that they may be hired by rivals to do so. Likewise, the victim may seek out another *brujo* (witch) who may succeed in counteracting the spell, or, on the other hand, the victim may placate the witch and induce him to remove the spell.

San Isidro the Laborer,[26] whose feast day is May 15, is celebrated as the patron of agriculturists. The image of the saint is taken out of the church under the care of a group of devotees (*mayordomía*) to make a pilgrimage about the countryside, stopping in the houses of those who have raised altars in his honor. People say that the purpose of this journey is *"Pa que haga la bendición en las siembras"* ("In order that he bless the crops"). Formerly, it is said, special crops were planted in the plaza for San Isidro, but this custom went out of practice 40 years or more ago. My period of contact did not include the day of San Isidro, so the translation of the written description of one of my informants is quoted:

The 5th of May, the Saint goes forth from the parochial church en route to the *campiña* where he spends the night at various altars erected by individual families and where also religious ceremonies take place. These frequently turn into carousals (*se tornan en jaranas*) and gorgings (*comilonas*) where the *chicha*, the liquor of the Incas, flows from gourd to gourd (*de poto en poto*) and from mouth to mouth. Great quantities are consumed until the Saint arrives at an altar near the Huaca del Sol. From that point commences what is known as the "descent of the Saint" (*la bajada del Santo*) and exactly in the evening of the 14th the Patron of the Crops enters the pueblo accompanied by a great crowd which has dressed in its best clothes (*de gala*) for the occasion. A curious note in the celebration is the dance of the Devils (Diablos) who do not cease to dance from the moment of the Saint's entrance until the evening of the 16th, enlivened by drinks (*avivados por las copas*) and the joy of serving the Saint. A band of musicians welcomes the Saint upon his entrance into the pueblo and he leads the procession to his altar erected beside the church. Covered with flowers, the progress of the Saint is the center of attention for natives and strangers. Afterward come the vespers, which have two stages, one inside the church and the other outside. The fol-

---

[26] Not to be confused with St. Isidore of Seville, whose feast day is April 4 (Cabrol, 1934, pp. liv and 841).

lowing day the Mass is celebrated and afterward a procession through the pueblo. At 3 p. m. the distribution of fruits of the harvest takes place. An arch erected over the Saint and his scepter (*bastón*) are loaded with offerings for the Señor priest (*Sr. cura*), and the remaining offerings are distributed to the poor. The following day (the 16th of May), the will (*testimonio*) of San Isidro is read, which assigns tasks to those who have not fulfilled their obligations to the Saint.

FISHING

The third and, from the point of view of the number of inhabitants, smallest of the three major divisions of the Moche community is the *playa,* or beach. Physically the beach is squarely divided by a recently built summer resort called Las Delicias, given over during the hot season to the pleasure of Trujillo residents who can afford to own or rent cottages there. A number of shops, a cement-sidewalked plaza with electric lights, a seaside promenade, and a casino made of planks constitute this vacation settlement, in addition to some 30 cottages (pl. 8, *middle, left*). However, Las Delicias normally is inhabited only during the latter part of December and the months of January and February. It is an outside intrusion which plays no functional part in the community life of Moche, other than as a temporary source of sales and employment for a few Mocheros during the "season." During the remainder of the year it is totally deserted. The professional fishing families of Moche are distributed along the dunes overlooking the beach for about a half mile on each side of Las Delicias. There are seven houses to the northwest and seven to the southeast. Counting a few *chozas* about the mouth of the river to the northeast and a few more fisher families who maintain their dwellings back from the beach (*mas adentro*), the total fishing community consists of perhaps 30 families. It is said that this is considerably less than in former times, and that as recently as 10 years ago there were as many as 50 fishermen's houses on the beach.

When speaking of the fishing element in the community, I refer to those families whose principal activity is devoted to fishing, which is their main source of livelihood. Almost everyone in the Moche community goes to the beach occasionally to try his luck, and also fishes in the ditches and the river, but only the fishers (*pescadores*), properly speaking, try to make a living out of it.

Except for occasional short trips with the Huanchaco fishermen, who sometimes visit these waters during the summer season, the Moche fishermen use no water craft in their profession and all fishing is done either from the shore of the sea or in the river or the irrigation ditches. The following fishing apparatus is used: (1) The *cahuán,* a dip net for catching shrimp, crabs, etc. (pl. 8, *lower (right)*); (2) the *chinchorro* (pl. 8, *upper (right)*), a large two-man net of the general shape of a tennis net, but wider and longer, used for fishing off the beach by wading into the surf; (3) the *atarraya,* a casting net; (4) the *red,* a set net staked out at night; (5) the *naza,* a conical trap of cane set out in the river or irrigation ditch; and (6) the *espinel,* a setline with hooks (fig. 1).

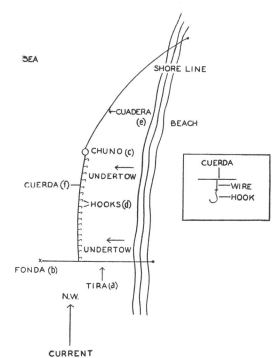

FIGURE 1.—Explanatory diagram of setline used for fishing (*espinel*). (For explanation, see p. 29.)

All of these appliances are made by the fishermen themselves. The *cahuán* is made of cotton thread. As can be seen from the photograph (pl. 8, *lower (right)*), the net is a purse-shaped affair supported on two sticks held in the hands. Across the front edge runs a thin rope to which are attached several small lead weights, totaling about one-half pound, which keeps this edge deep in the water when fishing for shrimp, crabs, and small fish. The mesh is fine, about one-quarter of an inch. The net is used both in the sea and in fresh water. Two kinds of shrimp are caught, *muy-muy* (sea shrimp), also called *camarones del mar,* and *camarones del rio* (fresh-water shrimp). The *muy-muy* are about the size of half of an English walnut shell and do not have the long, meaty "tail" of the fresh water shrimp. The usual method of eating them is to take the whole animal in the mouth, audibly sucking out the meat inside the shell, and finally spitting the remains onto the floor.

The *chinchorro* varies in length, one being as long as 100 feet; 40 to 50 feet is the more usual length. The net is about 5 feet wide and the mesh is about an inch. The bottom edge is weighted with small lumps of lead and the top edge is supported by floats made of globular gourds (*chunos*). At each end the net is attached by small ropes to a wooden stick about 5 feet 4 inches long. One man grasps each stick and the team walks into the sea, dragging the net between them. Plate 8, *upper (right),* shows one of these nets drying over a wooden framework on the beach; the small boy is holding one of the end sticks. Although there is no direct evidence that the ancient Mochicas used this type of net for fishing, a similar net was used by them for hunting on land.

The *atarraya* net is roughly circular in shape. A thin rope is threaded through the edge around the circumference and is weighted with small lumps of lead. A slit or opening leads from the circumference of the circle to the center and hand ropes or cords are attached to each side of this opening on the circumference. In use, the fisherman holds one of these in his mouth or in his hand, makes the rest of the net into a bundle, and flings it over the water so that it lands spread out on the surface and the weighted edges quickly sink to the bottom. With the hand ropes the net is drawn together and pulled to shore, with the fish imprisoned within.

The *red* (net) is usually a comparatively short, rectangular net somewhat like the *chinchorro* in shape but provided with larger meshes. It is staked out overnight in a stream, rarely in the sea. It is a gill net in which the fish are caught by poking their heads into the meshes.

The *naza* is a conical basket trap made of *caña brava* or bamboo (Guayaquil cane). It may vary in measurements, but a useful size is about 5 feet long by 18 inches in diameter at the mouth, from which it tapers to a point at the rear end. The pattern seems to have first appeared in the Chimu culture. The trap is staked down in a small channel of the river or an irrigation ditch overnight, with the open mouth upward.

The *espinel* or setline is perhaps used more on the Moche *playa* than any of the other types of equipment. In the sketch in figure 1, *a–f,* the various parts of this apparatus are shown. The *tira* (*a*) is a light three-ply rope which runs out to the sea perpendicularly from the shore line to the *fondo* (*b*), an anchor of stone or old iron. The other end of the *tira* is fastened to the shore above high water mark. About 30 feet out from shore the *cuerda* (*f*), a cotton three-ply line, carrying the hooks, is attached. Hooks are attached to the *cuerda* about every 7 feet, and a good *espinel* will carry about 100 hooks. The hooks (*d*) are pointed but without barbs (this seems to be a Mochica survival) and are attached to the *cuerda,* as shown in the inset of the sketch, by wire 5 to 6 inches long. (This is the "best type" of *espinel;* some do not have wire attachments, and consequently lose many hooks.) The hooks vary in size according to the type of fish sought, but the most generally used size is about 3 inches long (about $4\frac{1}{4}$ inches long, if straightened out). The hooks are baited with two *muy-muy* each. At the farther end of the *cuerda* is attached the gourd float or *chuno* (*c*) which in shape and method of binding also seems to be a Mochica survival. From the *chuno* a light rope, called the *cuadera* (*e*), continues onward some distance parallel to the shore line and is eventually carried ashore and fastened on the beach. Total length of *cuerda* and *cuadera* may reach 1,500 feet. The purpose of the *tira* and anchor is to hold the *cuerda* with its hooks out from the shore at a controlled distance and at a controlled depth. The prevailing current up the coast from the southeast keeps the *cuerda* with its hooks stretched out along the shore to the northwest, while the undertow from the surf tends to keep it offshore. The *chuno* float keeps the line from dragging on the bottom. The large types of fish are caught with this equipment— the bonito, bacalao, corvina, etc.

Two main types of instruments are used in making nets, needles (*agujas*) and blocks (*malleros*). These are used in various sizes for the different types of nets. The needle is made of bamboo, and has a point and a cut-out tongue. I have not made a study of the knots used, but have been told that two types are current, *de chinchorro* and *de red.* Fishermen are usually at work on their nets, when not otherwise employed. It is said to require about 3 months of part-time work of this sort for one man to make a *chinchorro,* and the material which goes into it costs about 50 soles ($7.65). The material in a *cahuán* costs about 8 soles, but a ready-made article sells for 20 soles. The *playa* dwellers obtain a certain income from making dip nets and casting nets, which they sell to Mocheros of the *campiña* for fishing in the river and in the irrigation ditches for shrimp and small fish about the size of sardines.

The fishermen rise between 3 and 4 o'clock in the morning. The night's catch and that of the day before are placed in baskets and their women carry them by bus to the markets in Trujillo and Salaverry.

The fishing community is apart from the rest of Moche physically and to some extent socially. As a rule the people are poorer than the pueblo and *campiña* Mocheros and are looked down upon slightly. Also, they have a reputation of being very irritable and hard to get along with (*coléricos*). They do not seem to be united even among themselves and, in keeping with the general Moche pattern of individualism, are engaged in feuds and quarrels. Several families living side by side on the beach do not speak to one another, and refuse to visit one another's houses. The seven houses to the northwest of Las Delicias all belong to families named G., who are relatives. Five of the houses to the southeast are occupied by families of the name of S. The fishing occupation seems to be traditional and is passed on from father to son. Most of the fishing families have a *chacra* somewhere in the *campiña* and supplement their subsistence from it. In a number of cases, however, a single *chacra* has been inherited by the heads of a number of immediate families in common, a fact which seems to account for some of the quarreling.

Fishing has become a distinctly secondary activity in the economic life of Moche itself. In order to round out a picture of fishing along this immediate coast, some notes on the village of Huanchaco, where fishing is the primary activity of the community, are presented below.

NOTES ON THE FISHING VILLAGE OF HUANCHACO [27]

Following the coast line about 17 km. northwest from Las Delicias (the resort settlement on the Moche *playa*) one comes to the fishing village of Huanchaco (pl. 1). By highway, passing through Trujillo, the distance is about 21 km. In the region of Huanchaco it is considered that it is a "Moche village," that it (together with Huamán and Moche) is one of the remnants of the prehistoric population, and that certain aspects of its modern life are "survivals" of ancient times. Since the natives of Huanchaco are on the whole dedicated to professional fishing, both deep-sea and inshore, a brief description of their methods and organization is of interest from a comparative point of view.

At present Huanchaco is a village of about 700 inhabitants situated in a shallow and arid indentation or bay of the coast. The beach slopes upward gently for a distance of about half a mile from the sea to the foot of an escarpment 150 to 300 feet above sea level which rises to the general level of the coastal plain stretching inland to the foothills of the Andes. A large church, rebuilt in modern times, sits on the lip of the escarpment and dominates all views of the town below, which is laid out back from the beach. During the early years of this century the town was developed into a port for the shipment of sugar and as a summer resort for residents of Trujillo. A railroad connected the port with the Hacienda Roma and also, according to my understanding, with Trujillo. The motivator of this development was the late Señor Victor Larco Herrera, the well-known Peruvian millionaire and philanthropist. He is still spoken of as the *"patrón"* of the pueblo. About 1925, however, Señor Larco disposed of his plantation holdings. The railroad tracks were removed and the summer visitors abandoned their villas in Huanchaco. The town was left once more to its native inhabitants and the summer villas stand now, mostly in a semiruined state, along the street nearest the seashore. Señor Larco's house on the beach has been turned into a Government-supported rest school for the underprivileged and tuberculous children.[28] A good pier with steel supports and wooden flooring, also owned and maintained by the Government, provides tie-up facilities for sailing boats and launches and is the central feature of the beach. The sea bottom close inshore is covered with cobblestones to which cling several varieties of seaweed and shellfish, which are gathered by the women of the community; back of the high water mark the shore is covered for the most part with smooth sand, over which *caballitos del mar* (small rafts made of *totora*, a species of reed; see fig. 2; pls. 8, *lower (left)*, 9, *lower and middle (left)*) as well as wooden fishing boats of larger dimensions can be hauled without damage. The

[27] My friend Señor José Angel Miñano of Trujillo has allowed me to check his notes against my own, has discussed the material with me, and, on one occasion, accompanied me to Huanchaco and put me in touch with many persons I would not otherwise have known.

[28] I wish to acknowledge the helpfulness and hospitality of Señor Daniel F. Ugarriza, Director of the Colonia Victor Larco Herrera in Huanchaco, who entertained me royally in the village.

wooden-hulled sailing boats used for deep-sea fishing are also made and repaired on crude scaffoldings erected on the beach.

The people of Huanchaco are Indians and *cholos*. Although one gains the impression that the proportion of white blood is slightly greater than in the population of Moche, the Huanchaqueros are on the whole definitely more Indian in physical features than the general population of Trujillo. However, consciousness of an ethnic bond uniting Moche and Huanchaco, if it ever existed, seems to have dimmed with the years in both communities. Family relationships uniting the two communities seem to be very few, or, at least, very poorly remembered. A few Mocheros have friends in Huanchaco, and the converse is also true, but the number of friendship bonds between Moche and Huanchaco at present seems to be less than those involving Moche and Paiján, Ascope, and other villages. Most of the Huanchaquero contacts with Mocheros are with the inhabitants of the Moche *playa*, because at certain times of the year the Huanchaco boats come down the coast and pick up Mochero fishermen for several days of joint activity. Following is a list of the principal family names in Huanchaco. These are all family names of "true Huanchaqueros," as distinguished from *forasteros*.

Aguilar	Huamanchumo
Aguirre	Leytón (from "Leighton"?)
Arroyo	Ordío
Asencio	Pimichumo
Azola	Sánchez
Beltrán	Segura
Berna	Ucañan
Carranza	Urcía
Chilmaza	Vanegas
Cumplida	Villacorta
Díaz	Villaneuva

It is to be noted that only two of these—Huamanchumo and Sánchez—are to be found in our list of Moche patronyms on page 103. Of the Huanchaco list, only the following appear to be possibly aboriginal: Chilmaza, Huamanchumo, Pimichumo, and Ucañan. It is doubtful that any of these four is Mochica or Chimu in derivation.

Inland, back of the church, are cultivated lands belonging to the community. But they have water only during the *tiempo de abundancia* (January–March) and, therefore, produce only one crop per year. These lands are rented to individuals by the *municipalidad* (local government), and most families have one of these plots on which they raise small crops of maize, rice, beans, etc., for family use. However, these agricultural activities are insufficient to maintain the people and are distinctly secondary to fishing.

Four general methods of obtaining sea products are practiced by the Huanchaqueros: (1) Fishing from sailboats or motorboats of wood; (2) fishing from *caballitos del mar* (literally "little horses of the sea"); (3) gathering of shellfish and sea plants by wading; (4) fishing with hooks and lines from the shore.

FISHING FROM BOATS

The boats are made of planks, with wooden keel, ribs, and gunwales, in the European fashion. They have square sterns, are open (without decking except for a short weather cowling aft of the bow), and contain wooden crosswise benches. They are from 18 to 21 feet in over-all length, from 4½ to 5½ feet in beam at the gunwale, and draw about 4 feet of water when loaded. Each sailboat has a single mast stepped into the keel about one-third of the distance aft of the bow. The mast is steadied by four guy-ropes attached two to each gunwale, while a fifth guy-rope runs from the masthead to the bow. The sails are triangular, but of the latan type. The longest side of the triangular sail is attached to a single boom, one end of which is attached to the bow of the boat, while the boom as a whole is suspended from the top of the mast by a pulley rope attached to the boom about one-fourth of the distance from its upper end, as illustrated in plate 8, *upper* (*left*). It is possible to tack against the wind with this type of sail, but when the tack is changed the sail must be lowered and then raised again for best results.

These sailboats are made in Huanchaco and also in Salaverry. In 1944 there were two specialist boat-wrights in Huanchaco. A boat costs between 5,000 and 6,000 soles ($765 to $918), and this price does not include the sail, fishing nets, and other equipment. Although this is a large investment according to local standards, a boat, if properly handled, will serve, with luck, for as long as 30 years. After building, the boat is launched by a *minga*, in which a group of 20 to 25 friends join to provide their strength in return for festive food and drink provided by the owner and his wife.

There are 20 sailboats in the Huanchaco fleet. In addition, there are 6 *lanchas* (motorboats), powered with Diesel engines (pl. 9, *lower* (*right*)). The *lanchas* are decked fore and aft and have a cockpit in the middle. None are being built along this coast at present owing to inability to obtain motors, but before World War II, it is said, a motor-boat cost about 50 percent more than a sailboat. Its advantage lies, of course, in greater speed, independence of wind conditions, and ability to operate with smaller crew.

All boats of the Huanchaco fleet are painted yellow, to distinguish them from boats based on Salaverry (blue) and Puerto Chicama (white). Each boat has a name, often, though not invariably, painted on the stern. Following are some of the names. Sailboats: Santa Cecelia, San Gabriel, Intendente de la Torre, Huascar, Defensor Cahuide, Santa Cruz, San José, San Lorenzo, San Andrés, San Francisco, Santa Fe, San Miguel, Miguel Grau, Compañero del Mar, Santa Lucía, Santa Barbara, San Antonio, and Jesús del Gran Poder. Motor-boats: Nuestra Señora de Socorro, Santa Rita, Santa María, Santa Luiza, and Santa Isabel. Every boat carries a saint's image or picture, even those which do not bear saints' names, usually placed under the weather cowling at the bow. The saints involved serve as protectors of the boat, and when a boat carries a saint's name it also carries the saint's image and protection.

As a rule each boat has a single owner, although two of the motorboats are owned by a partnership of three men. The owner of the boat sometimes owns one or more nets, but not necessarily so. The proper crew for a sailboat is four men, one of whom is usually the owner of the boat. One of the men (not necessarily the boat owner) is the commander or *patrón*. He is an expert in managing the boat and the other three crew members take their orders from him. He has no other privileges except his power to give orders and to exact obedience. Failure of a crew member to obey the *patrón* results in his exclusion from the crew and inability to sail under this *patrón* in the future. Other *patrones* will also be chary of taking him into their crews. The individuals forming a crew are sometimes relatives, but just as often not. Election or recognition as a *patrón* is said to depend upon an innate ability or knack; frequently the *patrón* is the youngest man in the boat. Take the boat, *Santa Fe,* for example. Mercedes Arroyo is *patrón;* he is about 21 years old, and all the other members of the crew are older men. Pedro Pimichumo is owner, but when at sea, takes orders from Mercedes. The other members of the crew are Manuel Arroyo and Antonio Gordillo. Manuel is

the oldest of the crew and is uncle of Mercedes and Antonio. Pedro, the boat's owner, does not sail every day and when on the beach substitutes his son in the crew. *Santa Fe* operates four nets.

The division and counting of the catch also follow a peculiar system. Nets belong to individuals, not to boats (although the owner of a boat may also be the owner of one or more nets). There is no definite number of nets which a boat should operate, although 4 for each is regarded as a proper minimum while some boats carry as many as 20. The catch from each net is divided into two parts: one-half of the catch "belongs to the net" (i. e., the owner of the net), while the other half is divided share and share alike among the members of the crew *and the boat.* Thus, if there are four crew members, the second half of the catch is divided into five parts. The boat receives a share equal to that of one crew member. The *patrón,* or commander of the boat, receives the same share as the other crew members. As each net is drawn up, the fish from it are marked with a knife cut which identifies them as having come from that net. For example, a chip from the left side near the head marks the fish from one net, from the right side near the tail, another net, and so on. When the boat returns to shore, the fish are unloaded from the boat by stringing them through the gills onto large poles of "Guayaquil cane," about 2 inches in diameter and 8 to 9 feet long, which, with their loads, are carried between the shoulders of two men. On the beach the fish are first sorted into separate piles belonging to their respective nets. Each pile is then sorted into separate piles by species of fish (which approximates sorting by size). Division by halves then takes place with the "net's half" being set aside, and the crew's and boat's shares being placed in common piles (according to species or size). After all the net shares have been separated, the crew and boat shares are counted off into piles, beginning with the large fish and working into the smaller ones.

The whole fleet and the profession are organized informally. Felipe Carranza, the best *patrón,* is recognized as "chief pilot" of the fleet, and Lino Segura is called "chief of the port" and also *primer sargento de los pescadores* (first sergeant of the fishermen). These titles are recognized by the departmental government in some vague way, which is not entirely clear to me, but the real authority of the offices depends upon respect accorded to them by the other fishermen. Thus, all boats are bound by the opinion of the chief pilot regarding the weather. If, in his judgment, a storm is brewing and he advises against sallying forth, no boats leave port. The chief of the port assigns anchorages and tie posts to the various craft and settles disputes, which, however, are said to be very rare. He also acts as a spokesman for the fishermen, who are not yet organized as an official "syndicate" (legal union or workers' group) under the provisions of the Peruvian labor laws.

Sails are made in Huanchaco and in Salaverry of regular sailcloth, which has been scarce during the war. Specialists do the best work, although a number of boat owners make their own sails. A good sail is said to cost about 200 soles ($30.60) or more. Sail ropes must be of manila fiber.

On the other hand, everyone, even women, knows how to make nets. They are of the same general shape as a tennis net, although both longer and wider, about 4½ feet wide by about 100 feet long. About every 3 feet along the upper edge is fastened a slab of cork, so that an ordinary net has from 30 to 35 of these floats to support it in the water. Along the lower edge are affixed an equal number of lead weights. At each end of the upper edge is a lateral projection or extension called a *cabecera* (head) or an *oreja* (ear). To each of these ears is attached a *chuno,* a float made from a large spherical gourd about 12 to 15 inches in diameter held by a binding of light rope. One is larger than the other and serves as a marker buoy in case the net is detached from the boat. Also extending from each ear of the net is a hand rope, made of manila fiber, about one-half inch in diameter and varying in length from a few feet up to more than 100 feet. Although occasionally these nets are trawled between two boats, the usual pattern is to cast them out from a single boat, with both ends of the net secured to the boat by the hand ropes. Motion of the boat and the current carry the fish against the net. The interstices of the net are about 1½ to 2 inches on a side. They are holding nets, which catch the fish behind the gills.

Nets are made from three-ply cotton twine purchased in the stores at a price now varying between 10 and 12 soles ($1.53 to $1.84) per pound. At this rate a net costs up to 150 soles ($22.95) for materials alone. The fishermen complain loudly of being exploited by speculators. Nets are made in the same manner as at Moche, using the bare foot and toes to hold the line, and a netting needle of cane with cut-out and small tongue. Two types of knots are used, *el derecho,* a slip knot, and *el cruzado,* a tight knot.

Ropes for nets are made of *cabo* fiber, which is made in factories and bought by the fisherman in stores, but which they themselves twine into ropes in Huanchaco. Net ropes are called *tayas.*

When a new net has been completed and before it is used for the first time, it is subjected to ceremonial treatment. The owner finds a *brujo curandero* (curing witch), who "cures" the net. Although I have not seen this treatment, it is said to involve filling the *chunos* with juice of herbs, pouring it out, and officially sealing them, together with sprinkling of the net itself with herbs and powders used in ordinary *brujería* (witchcraft). Also, each net before it is wetted (*antes de mojarla*) undergoes a *padrinazgo* ceremony. The owner chooses a *padrino* (godfather) and *madrina* (godmother) for the net. Their relationship to the owner is expressed as *compañeros de la red* (companions or partners of the net). They have only the obligation of arranging (and paying for) the *fiesta* on this occasion. The principal ceremonial activity of the *fiesta* consists of laying out the net in the form of a cross and sprinkling it with holy water.

Occasionally a net falls into a period in which it seems to be unable to catch anything. The owner will soon come to the conclusion that someone *ha hecho daño a la red* (has done harm to the net), in other words, some enemy has hired a *malero* (evil witch) to cast a spell upon it. In this case, the owner again seeks out a *brujo curandero* to "cure" the net once more.

The daily fishing cycle begins about noon, when, if the weather is favorable, the fleet leaves port for the high seas (pl. 8, *middle* (*right*)). Each boat is loaded by its crew with their personal belongings, the nets (which have now been dried, repaired, and folded into bundles on the beach), food, and ballast (gunny sacks full of sand, which may be dumped overboard as the catch loads down the boat). Oars may be used to move the boat out of the lee of the dock. Since there is always a heavy swell, at least, running in from the Pacific, the boats are tossed excitingly as they climb the swells and disappear into the troughs until they are well out at sea. The daily sailing of the fleet is a decidedly picturesque spectacle, with the women, children, and old men lining the dock and the beach and waving farewell to the sailors. Several men and boats are lost each year, so that each sailing has an element of some uncertainty.

The boats stay at sea, often well out of sight of land, until dawn of the following morning. The crews carry food and *chicha* for the voyage and normally sleep several hours, in shifts, during the night. The night is spent in darkness, as a light in a boat attracts sharks and sea-lion which damage the nets. Time is kept by the stars. For example, according to Felipe Carranza, the *Lucero de la Mañana* appears in November at about 4 a. m.; *Las Cabrillas* (Pleiades) about 3 a. m.; and *El Arado* sets between 3 and 4 a. m., at about the same time that the *Cruz de Mayo* appears. When these astronomical signs show that the hour is between 3 and 4 o'clock in the morning, the boats begin to return to port. Usually the boats are out about 16 to 20 miles and require between 2 and 3 hours to reach Huanchaco in the first gray dawn. Arrived at port, the boats tie up to the lee side of the dock and the fish are carried to the beach on poles as already described, or, in the case of large fish, one man may carry a fish in each hand by the gills. The women, children, and old men are waiting. After the catch has been properly divided, as described above, the women of those who have participated in the division proceed immediately to clean the fish on the beach, using the sea water in the process. Livers are collected by three men, who ship them to Lima, but the other viscera are usually thrown into the sea. Although this practice serves to attract some fish and crustaceans to the Huanchaco beach, larger numbers could probably be attracted by collecting the fish viscera and throwing them into the sea at a point of the coast a kilometer or so southeast of the town, since the prevailing current along the shore sets from the southeast.

In the division of the catch, a few odd-sized fish are usually given to one or the other of a half-dozen town indigents who gather at the beach for this purpose. They are four superannuated fishermen and two wives of fishermen lost at sea.

By 6 a. m. the women have usually completed their work and have packed their fish in baskets, ready to take to the market at Trujillo. They usually leave on the truck at 6 o'clock. Transportation is a sore spot with the Huanchaqueros at present, because of what they consider the high fares. Round-trip fare for a person is 1 sol ($0.153); the charge for each basket of fish is 80 centavos; and for a single large fish, 20 centavos. Many of the women have no *plaza* (stall) in the Trujillo market and have to sell their fish at a discount to other women (*revendadoras*) more fortunate. However, all commercial transactions involved in marketing the fish are in the hands of the women, just as marketing produce is women's prerogative in Moche.

The men, having cleaned up their boats, carry the nets ashore, using the same pole of Guayaquil cane between two men as was used in unloading the fish. The nets are laid out on the beach to dry. Then the men go to their houses for breakfast and an hour or two of sleep. Between 9 and 10 o'clock they again appear on the beach and set to work mending the nets. By about 11:30 a. m. the nets are mended and dried. They are then folded into neat bundles and, by the more careful owners, put into gunny sacks. Suspended on two-man poles they are carried aboard the boats about noon. By this time the women have returned from the market, and the daily cycle begins again.

Summer (December to June) is regarded as the best fishing season. During this period the fish run closer to the surface of the sea. In the winter when the fish are deep the nets are frequently submerged with anchors of rock. The winter season is bad off Huanchaco, and the boats usually fish off Guañape, Chao, and as far south as the mouth of the Rio Santa. However, in any season *"la buena pesca depende de la buena comedura"* (good fishing depends on good fish food). The *comedura* consists of schools of anchovy upon which the larger fish feed. Also, it is said, *"el bufeo trae la lisa y la lisa la larna, y la larna la cachema,"* meaning that one type of fish is followed into a given fishing ground by a series of others in succession. *"La pescadilla anuncia la buena pesca."* (Small fish announce good fishing.)

Certain persons are "unlucky" fishermen, as is stated by the common saying, *"Fulano no puede tocar mi red porque tiene mala mano."* (So-and-so can't touch my net because he has a bad hand.) Another common saying is, *"La luna nueve siempre trae buen aire, alborota el percado, y lo hace amainar."* (The new moon always brings good wind, wakes up the fish, and makes them tame.) *"Circulo del sol es mal augurio."* (A circle around the sun is a bad sign.) More faith is placed in the stars, however, than in the sun. For example, *"Rio Jordan claro, buena pesca."* (When the Milky Way is clear, there is good fishing.)

CABALLITOS DEL MAR

The use of the "little horses of the sea" is perhaps at once the most romantic and most "primitive" aspect of Huanchaco fishing. These craft are made of a species of reed (*totora*) bound in bundles into the shape shown in figure 2 and plate 9, *upper* (*left*), *lower* (*left*), and *middle* (*left*). In essence, the *cabillito* is a one-man raft with a pointed bow and a square stern, made of four tapering cylindrical bundles of reeds. The entire population, including children of 10 years and older, know how to make these craft, which are used by children for sport and by children and adults alike for line fishing and the catching of crabs. The *caballitos* vary from 9 feet 8 inches to 11 feet 4 inches in length (3 to 3.5 m.) and vary from 20 to 28 inches in width at the widest part. They are propelled by a paddle about 8 feet 1½ inches (2.5 m.) long and 3 to 4 inches wide. It is simply a flattened piece of split "Guayaquil cane," which is held by both hands in the middle and used as a double-ended paddle, but without having a special treatment at the ends in the form of paddle blades.

As shown in the sketch in figure 2, *a–e*, the typical

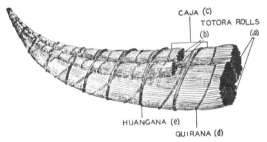

CAJA (c)
TOTORA ROLLS
(b)   (a)

HUANGANA (e)
QUIRANA (d)

FIGURE 2.—Explanatory diagram of a *caballito del mar,* as used in Huanchaco.

caballito consists of the following parts: Four bundles (*bastones*) of *totora* reed, two of which (*a*) are large, basal bundles tied side by side to form the body of the raft, and two smaller and shorter bundles (*b*), tied side by side and on top of the (*a*) bundles. Some *caballitos* consist of only the two (*a*) basal bundles (as in pl. 9, *middle* (*left*)). The (*b*) bundles end 18 to 24 inches forward of the stern of the craft, leaving a small flat cockpit (*c*), known as the *caja* of the *caballito*, where the operator sits or kneels and where he carries his fishing gear. The forward end of the *caja* is protected slightly from the waves by the wall formed by the ends of the (*b*) rolls of *totora*. The binding of the individual rolls of *totora* is called *quirana* (*d*) and is a light rope or heavy cord made of *hilo de pavilo*, which is wound around the *totoras* of the roll in spiral fashion. The heavier binding which, in turn, encircles the

four rolls and holds the entire craft in shape is called the *huangana* (*e*) and is made of *cabo de manila*. The *totora* itself is obtained from Huanchaquita, a small settlement situated a few kilometers down the coast, near the ruins of Chan Chan. Two soles will buy enough for a large *caballito*. If in constant use, one of these craft either becomes waterlogged or starts to disintegrate after 12 to 14 days of use. They are always dragged out of the water and stood up on the beach on the stern end when not being used.

In operation, the fisherman sits or kneels in the *caja*. Some prefer to dangle their legs in the water on each side, as in riding horseback (hence the name of the craft, perhaps), although this is chilly in winter. Otherwise, the legs are doubled up under the operator, who is kneeling in the *caja,* or in other cases straddle the part of the craft forward of the *caja*. Occasionally *caballitos* venture out of sight of land, but usually are used for fishing within a mile or two of shore, beyond the zone of breakers and heavy swells. Considerable practice is required to prevent a *caballito* from turning over in the sea, but an experienced operator has no difficulty in crossing heavy swells and breaking waves of considerable height. A favorite sport of young boys is to "ride the waves" with the craft in to shore in the manner of surfboard riders. Whatever the manner of operation, even the most experienced operator must be prepared to have at least the lower part of his body thoroughly wet. So far as I know, adult women among the Huanchaco population never venture out in these craft.

Deep-sea boat fishermen resort to *caballito* fishing during periods when the fish at sea are not running well. The craft is used for three types of fishing: crabbing, line fishing, and net fishing. Every craft carries a net, called a *calcal,* which is a bag net about 2 feet deep with a purse-string mouth, which can be opened up for casting when fishing, and can be drawn shut when the net is used as a container for crabs and other booty. The interstices of these nets are about 1 inch on a side.

The crab trap or *saca* is shown in plate 8, *lower* (*left*). As shown also in the sketch in figure 3, *a–g,* it consists of a square frame (*a*) of four pieces of cane (bamboo) tied together at the corners. Over these is stretched a net (*b*) which hangs down below the level of the frame to a depth of 6 to 8 inches in which the bait is tied in place. The four corners of the frame are weighted with cobblestones (*c*) tied in place for the purpose of carrying the apparatus beneath the surface of the water. To each corner are attached four suspension cords (d) of equal length which are in turn united to a cable, called a *rabiza* (e). This is about 23 feet long (7.0 m.) and attached to it at intervals are small bundles on

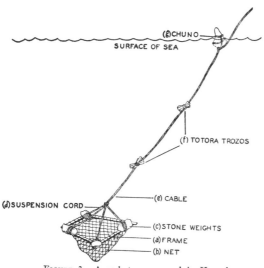

FIGURE 3.—A crab trap, as used in Huanchaco.

trozos of *totora* (f) which serve to give the line a certain underwater buoyancy and thus prevent its fouling on rocks along the bottom. Near the upper end of the line is a *chuno* (gourd float) (g), somewhat smaller than those used on deep-sea nets. Finally, the upper end of the line is either held in the hand or attached to the *caballito*. The bait, consisting of entrails of the bonito and other large fish, or of cow liver, etc., is tied to the net. The crab locks his pincers on the bait, gets them tangled in the net, and is thus held fast until drawn to the surface.

Lines may have one or more hooks and are also provided with a lead sinker and a *chuno* float. They are not used with poles. In fishing with line from the *caballito,* one drops the line overboard in still water, or attaches the line to the craft and trawls.

COLLECTING

Women and children collect a variety of small clams, snails, shrimp, crawfish and crabs, as well as several varieties of seaweed from the cobblestone bottom off the beach during low tide. There are three types of seaweed of which I am aware: *yuyu, mococho,* and *cochayuyu* (Quechua, "water plant"?). There are three types of crabs: (1) *cangrejos* and (2) *biquín,* both of which are found in the sea, and (3) *carreteros,* soft-shelled crabs of the beach. They

are used in the homes, and also considerable quantities are taken to the Trujillo market for sale. Much of such seaweed as is consumed in Moche comes from Huanchaco.

SHORE FISHING

Shore fishing with hook and line follows the same methods as those employed on the Moche *playa.* Relatively little attention is paid to this activity in Huanchaco, which regards it as a Moche speciality. It is recognized in Huanchaco that the use of *caballitos* is unsatisfactory on the Moche beach by reason of the high surf there almost the year around. During the summer months, the Huanchaco boats frequently stop off the Moche beach to pick up the Moche fishermen and their nets (and their advice). During this time of year the fish are near the surface and run close inshore to the Moche *playa.* While this attention to the Mocheros is a form of courtesy, it is also mutually advantageous to both sides. The usual rules of division of the catch prevail on such occasions.

It is estimated that an ordinary fisherman, with one net, but without a boat, is able to make from 600 to 1,200 soles ($91.80 to $183.60) per year in cash money. Many remain in this condition, however, because they spend their funds on liquor and fiestas instead of putting it into boats and nets. Three men, at least, are said to have incomes of over 10,000 soles ($1,530) per year.

RELIGIOUS ASPECTS

The patron saint of fishermen is San Pedro, whose feast day, June 29, is celebrated in the community. Ironically, at this season of the year there is relatively poor fishing. *La Virgen de Socorro* (The Virgin of Succor) is believed to take a special interest in Huanchaco and once every 5 years the image of the Virgin is brought on a pilgrimage from Trujillo, under the supervision of the *Hermandad de Socorro.* Leaving Trujillo the 30th of November the pilgrimage makes the journey by easy stages, one of which is a 3-day stop at the chapel built for this purpose about midway along the road by Don Victor Larco Herrera, and arrives in Huanchaco the 24th of December to pass Christmas. The principal dances at this fiesta are those of the *Pastores* (shepherds) and of the *Negritos de Cañete* (Negroes of Cañete).

Huanchaco has its Cross cult, as has Moche. Some seven crosses are to be seen on various heights back of town, each in charge of a *mayordomia* of four to six men, who have the obligation to take down their cross on the 3d of May, paint it, offer fruit and other products to it, and put it back up at the end of the month. In Huanchaco, in contrast to Moche, the crosses have no *padrinos*. The taking down and putting up, however, are occasions for a fiesta in charge of the members of the group.

The following two Huanchaco items are not found in Moche. When a child dies, the church bells toll *la seguidilla,* i. e., lightly and in rapid succession, which is said to sound like *"es angelito, es angelito"* (it's a little angel). When an adult dies the *doble* is sounded as in Moche. The dead in Huanchaco are buried with all of their personal belongings, even old items—all clothing, ornaments, pocket pieces, and the like.

In summary, we may see in Huanchaco a specialized fishing community which possibly has developed from the same prehistoric cultural matrix as Moche. At all events, the orientation in Moche has developed toward agriculture; in Huanchaco, toward fishing. And in both communities colonial and modern culture have overlaid the earlier elements very thickly.

HABITATIONS

TYPES OF STRUCTURES

As can be seen from plates 11 and 12, the house types and architecture of Moche show considerable variation. Generally speaking, the style of domestic architecture may be regarded as a simple colonial form in which, in many structures, has been incorporated certain elements reminiscent of prehistoric cultures. In the pueblo, especially, the houses do not look notably different from those seen in many a Peruvian coastal village or town. They stand in solid blocks with their white plastered fronts flush with the sidewalk (pl. 10, *lower (right)*). It is mainly in the *campiña* that one finds the "typical" Moche dwelling, which exhibits a variety of distinguishing characteristics.

When all minor variations are left out of account, Moche dwellings and shelters may be classified into the following types, in order of frequency: (1) Adobe houses, (2) *quincha* houses, (3) *totora* shelters, (4) *tapia* houses. In keeping with the very mixed character of all Moche culture, it is not infrequent to see a house embodying features of several of these types (pl. 11, *upper (right), middle (left)*).

Adobes are made by specialists. There are also some ordinary citizens possessing skill and facilities who make their own adobes when building their houses. In the pueblo the specialists are relied upon more than in the *campiña*, and in 1944 adobes sold for 60 soles ($9.18) per 1,000. Five years earlier they were obtainable for as little as 20 soles per 1,000, the rise in price being blamed on "the war." The adobes are of the common type used at present, so far as I know, throughout the coastal region.

They are rectangular, with right-angled edges, and, according to my measurements, vary from 18 to 24 inches in length, 12 to 14 inches in width, and 3 to 4 inches in thickness; the lower figure in all cases is "standard." The adobe is made of clayey dirt which is dug loose in the ground itself and puddled by pouring water over it. It is mixed with grass which has been chopped with a machete into lengths between 1 and 2 inches. A spade is used for mixing. It is usually carried from the mixing spot in gunny sacks (*camales*) to a nearby flat piece of ground where it is pressed into a wooden frame of proper size on a flat board platform. After it has been properly smoothed on top with the spade, the frame is removed and the adobe is slid off the board platform onto a clean flat piece of ground (sometimes covered by a *petate*), and left to dry in the sun. A week of drying before use is considered desirable.

Adobe walls are, by preference, laid up by professional masons (*albañiles*) of whom there are 15 in the community. In the *campiña*, however, many a house has been built by the householder with the help of a group of friends and relatives in a modified *minga*. In such a case it is considered desirable to hire a mason to supervise the job. Lines are stretched to keep the wall straight and a plumb line is occasionally hung from the top to maintain verticality. Occasionally scaffoldings or boards are used to support the workers, but more often than not a heap of dirt on the inside of the wall serves the purpose. It is built up as the wall increases in height and shoveled away when the job is finished.

Adobe walls may stand in their original state (pl. 10, *upper (right)*), or may be plastered (pl. 10, *lower* (*right*); 11, *middle* (*right*)). The latter is the ideal of all house owners, but many for want of time, money, or energy never get around to it. Plastering may take one of two forms; a white lime plaster made of purchased materials (as there is no lime kiln in the community itself) or a simple mud plaster simply spread over the adobes by hand and smoothed down with the edge of a board. The mud plaster is sometimes whitewashed, in which case it has an appearance resembling that of the lime-plastered walls.

Although no complete new houses were built during my time in Moche, I was told that a mason, when employed, helps to lay out the plan of a new house. The mason may stake out the position of the walls and partitions on the ground, connecting the stakes with cord lines. Often the house owner or the family lays out the plan "free hand," simply marking the position of the walls with lines drawn on the ground. Only the adobe and *tapia* houses are laid out with any care.

In the house with walls of *tapia* the walls are made in the same manner as that employed in constructing the *tapia* fences. The ancient Mochicas knew the *tapia* process, but seem not to have used it in house construction.[29] Plate 11, *upper* (*left*), shows a house constructed of *tapia*. Although this process is cheaper than adobe, it is not preferred because it produces a very thick wall which, with the technique in use, is hardly ever perfectly plumb. *Tapia* construction is often used to patch adobe walls and to make additions to adobe houses.

The procedure and artifacts in making *tapia*, whether in house walls or in fences, are as follow. The two principal artifacts, in addition to the spade, are the *cajón* (mold made of boards) and the *sogas* (ropes) for tying the *cajón* together. When a *tapia* is in two or more levels, the lower one is called *arrastrada* (creeping along the ground). For making this, four stakes are driven into the ground, one for each corner of the *cajón*, which actually consists of four parts, the four sides of the mold. Then the four elements of the *cajón* are tied to the stakes, tied together, and adjusted to give the proper shape and also to make certain that the *cajón* does not come apart. The earth of the ground alongside is wetted and left to stand for 4 days. Then it is mixed and puddled with the spade, and shoveled into the *cajón*. If the puddling place is distant from the site of the *tapia*, the wet earth is carried to the *cajón* in gunny sacks or baskets. Once in the mold it is stamped down by a man working barefooted therein. Then the sides of the mold are removed and the sides of the *tapia* while still moist are slapped with the flat of the spade in order to smooth and consolidate them. The upper block of a *tapia* is called *ensimada* (on top). Two bars of iron are laid across the lower block, one at each end, and to these are tied the *cajón*, so that it does not fall down. The tying is done with a double rope, and sticks are twisted into these ropes to tighten them. The sticks are called *toltol* and the capstanlike arrangement is called *cabresta*. (The Spanish Academy, I believe, favors "*cabrestantes*.")

A second type of wall, much used for patching *tapia* fences, is called *sanja tapia*.[30] This is made entirely with the spade and without a mold form. Moist earth is simply shaped by the spade. The top of a *tapia* fence is usually horizontal and is often used as a pathway, because it offers a better surface than the sandy lane. Some tops, however, are made in the form of a pitched roof, in order to prevent their use as sidewalks, which tends to wear down and to break down the fence. In Moche, practically all *tapia* making, whether for house or fence, is done by *minga* (cooperative work), but in other nearby communities it is done by specialists, who in 1944 charged 1.50 soles per *cajón* for their labor. Five years before that the price was 80 centavos.

The *quincha* type of wall is found throughout the Peruvian coastal communities. Two general types, a primitive and a sophisticated, occur. In both types upright canes (*caña brava*) are inserted side by side in line in the ground. They are usually stuck into the ground from 3 to 6 inches, and if the surface is dry, a crowbar may be used to make the hole. On occasion, however, the canes are not inserted at all but have a footing of mud built up around their butts to a height of 3 to 4 inches. The upright canes are then interlaced with two or more series of horizontal canes, called *tientos*. This is to say that every odd cane passes outside the horizontals and every even upright passes inside, as in checkerboard weaving. Usually there are only two series of horizontals, one about middle height of the wall and the other near the top. Sometimes there are three sets of horizontals. These horizontals are usually arranged in a series close together; the series varies from two to three.

---

[29] Personal communication of Rafael Larco Hoyle and Manuel Briceño.

[30] I have not secured a clear meaning for "*sanja*." Can it be Quechua, "sankhu," dense? See Farfán (1941, p. 22).

Most frequently there are three horizontals in the middle series, and two in the upper series. In the "primitive" type of *quincha*, stability is given to the construction by tying some or all of the upright members to the horizontal members with rawhide strips of cattle hide. In the "sophisticated" type, stability is provided by upright posts of sawed lumber, rectangular in cross section and about the size of a "2 by 4." These upright posts have holes bored in them into which the horizontal canes are inserted, thus providing stability and support. In this type of *quincha* the uprights and horizontals are seldom tied together. In a well-made *quincha* the projecting upper ends of the canes are cut off on a horizontal level to produce a clean-cut top, but this is not universally practiced. After the construction of the cane wall, as described, the inside and outside are plastered with mud in a very moist state, just short of liquid (much more maleable than is necessary in making adobes or *tapias*). A well-made job will have several layers of mud which completely eliminate any trace of the cane and which are smoothed down on the surface with the edge of a board and often plastered or whitewashed. In this case the wall is distinguishable from plastered adobe only by careful inspection. However, many *quincha* walls are only half-finished, even when incorporated in dwellings. Also, the *quincha* construction is used in conjunction with almost all dwellings as a form of windbreak for the outdoor arbor, in which case the canes are often only partially covered with mud and their tops are allowed to protrude in an irregular line toward the sky.

Shelters made of *totora* have no particular plan or shape. Only occasionally are complete dwellings made of this material (pl. 11, *lower (left)*) and usually only by families who are waiting to construct a more permanent house. Occasionally shelters of *totora* are erected for guests, and lean-to sheds, made of *totora* mats leaned against a house wall, are not uncommon. *Totora* mats are also used for partitions, as windbreaks for kitchens, very occasionally as shades for outdoor arbors, and in other ways as adjuncts to architecture.

Wooden rafters and uprights occur in all houses, except those of the *totora* type, in which a framework of saplings is used. In the more elegant houses in the pueblo, the rafters are made of sawn lumber, obtained in Trujillo, about the size and shape of "2 by 6's," and the roof framework is fastened to them with nails. In the *campiña* it is more common to construct the rafters of small logs of wood, usually willow, which grows along the banks of the *acequias* (irrigation ditches). These are cut and trimmed with steel axes of the usual European model. Not a few houses in the pueblo use this type of rafters as well.

In the pueblo all houses have doors of wood. Sawn lumber roof frames, doors, and door frames are usually fitted and made by professional carpenters, of which there are 19 in the community. A door may cost from 20 to 60 soles ($3.06 to $9.18), or even more, with hinges and lock, depending upon its elaboration. Doors frequently have barred, glassless openings in the upper panel. Except in houses built by *forasteros* in the "Peruvian coastal" style, windows are practically unknown in Moche houses. Light for the inner rooms is provided by a square or rectangular hole in the roof, which may be completely open, or may be covered by a hinged trap door which opens upward. In the most elaborate constructions a small square lantern or cupola with or without glass windows on all four sides covers the hole in the roof.

No roofs in Moche are watertight, and cracks of light are usually visible from within, even in the more permanent types. Since it "never rains" except at intervals of a generation, the roof serves mainly as protection against the sun and the wind. Whichever type of rafters is used, they are laid in parallel fashion, horizontally set into the adobe or *tapia* walls usually within 3 to 6 inches of the top of the walls, in some cases in mere notches in the top of the wall. In the house with *quincha* walls the rafters are supported on stringers which are in turn supported by upright forked logs, set in the ground, and irregularly placed, although tending toward two in each of the four corners. The framework is tied together with split reed used in basket making. The few houses having nothing but *quincha* walls, however, are, with one or two exceptions, all roofed with *petates* (reed mats), so that the supporting rafters and uprights do not have to be large. The *petates* are simply laid on and tied to a light framework of saplings, canes, or very thin logs.

In the "permanent" type of roof the rafters are crossed by a series of canes, laid side by side at right angles, and over this series lies another series of canes at an acute angle to the direction of the rafters (pl. 12, *lower (center)*). Over this second layer of canes is placed a layer of *petates*. The two layers are nailed to the rafters when the latter are sawed, and usually tied at intervals with split reed (*carrizo*) when the framework is of unsawed wood. Finally, a layer of mud, mixed with chopped grass, is laid over the whole for a thickness of 1 to 2 inches, and smoothed down. From an old roof there is a constant settling of fine dust, so that the furniture in the house will be covered with a film even in so short an interval as overnight.

So far as I know, tiles are not used for roofing on any house in Moche, the *campiña* or the *playa*. A few houses, however, have a layer of light cement over the mud covering of the roof, as a protection against the next heavy rain.

Although from street level one has the impression that most houses are flat-roofed, this is actually true in only about one-third of the cases. Practically all roofs have a low-grade slope. In the pueblo, this is most often a single slope from the front of the house to the back (pl. 12, *middle (left)*). Low pitched roofs occur in both pueblo and *campiña*, supported by ridge poles laid on the points of low gables (pl. 12, *upper (left)*). Single-slope roofs also occur with open-ended structures in the case of single rooms, arbors, and sheds. The pitched and the sloped roofs were characteristic of ancient Mochica domestic architecture. There seems to be no functional reason for their survival at the present time other than that these types of roof frame require fewer long heavy beams than the flat type.

In the pueblo houses the roof is often hidden from the beholder on the street by a low parapet.

In addition to the features outlined above, many other variant details and treatments occur, especially in the pueblo. Not uncommon is a series of metal spouts projecting through the parapet on the street wall. Although these are supposedly for the discharge of rain water, they are actually only decorative—if that—for those examined were stuffed with dirt from the rooftops. Since rain is practically nonexistent, their functional use is very infrequent at all events.

Windows of the Peruvian colonial type, with support, cap, and metal grill protruding outward from the wall, occur, but are rare. Occasionally a simple small window will be seen in a newer *campiña* house. Also, it should be mentioned that recently *forasteros* have constructed in the pueblo a half dozen cement walled houses with "modified colonial" architectural treatment.

The arrangement of the house is quite variable. In town, owing to the fact that all houses are flush

with the sidewalk, a certain uniformity is presented. In figure 4 is shown a typical house plan for a pueblo-

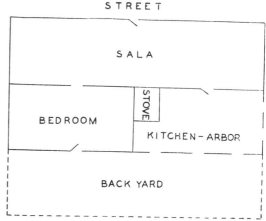

FIGURE 4.—Common plan of house in Moche pueblo.

dwelling Mochero's house. The patio is not a feature of the plan in Moche, but each house has an open space in the rear of its lot. In some cases this is nothing more than a dusty yard in which domestic animals and fowl are confined, but, if water is available, an attempt is usually made to cultivate flowers and fruit trees. Emerging from the back room of the house, one usually finds himself in an open-air, shaded arbor composed of a wooden trellis or framework. The shade may be provided by *petates* or vines. Among the latter, grape and *tumbo*[31] are favorites. There is a wooden plank table with benches (pl. 13, *upper (left)*) and perhaps a chair or two. This is the living and dining room of the family and the place where they usually meet their friends.

The Mocheros live in the open air. The closed rooms of the houses are only for sleeping and storage. In the *campiña* the house plans take numerous forms, often owing to the fact that new portions have been added at various times. One feature which is almost constant, however, is the partly open wall surrounding a sort of porchlike room (pl. 11, *middle (right)*; 12, *lower (left)*). At least one of the "porches" is found in houses of all types, usually located on the lee side of the house. (The prevailing wind is from the sea.) In these structures is often seen the use of square pillars (pl. 11, *middle (right)*) to hold up the roof. Although at present the "cutout" openwork walls of Mochica times do not exist, nevertheless, the partly open wall and the square

[31] *Passiflora quadrangularis* L.; this vine produces a large, melonlike fruit which is much prized for food; it is indigenous to the Peruvian coast.

pillar (which was a definite Mochica feature) are both reminiscent of Mochica architecture. The "porch" of the *playa* houses is always made of *quincha*, roofed with *petates*, and is located on the landward side. In addition to these open-air rooms, *campiña* houses usually possess an arbor and a garden (*huerta*) facing it, whereas arbors and gardens are at best only rudimentary on the *playa* owing to lack of irrigation water.

The great majority of floors are of hard-packed earth, which is preferred by the true Mochero, because he sleeps on an *estera* of *totora* laid on the floor, and he claims that cement and tile floors are too cold for comfort. In the pueblo some sophisticated and rich Mocheros live in houses with wooden plank floors, and one or two have cement and tile floors. The *forastero* houses usually have tile.

WATER SUPPLY

Water supply in most houses is a matter of fetch and carry. In the town there are six *pitas* or public spigots from underground pipes. When water is running in the *acequias* (irrigation ditches) in town, people also obtain water therefrom. Outside of town, water is obtained only from the *acequias*. During the dry season when a given ditch has water only every 9 or 10 days, considerable labor is sometimes required; for example, when the nearest running ditch is 2 km. away, on the other side of the *campiña*. In such cases donkeys with pack saddle and two metal cans are sometimes used. Otherwise, water is usually carried to the house from the source by women using pails or clay pots.

A number of houses in town—relatively few outside—have wells (*pozos*) in the back yard. I am unable to understand why all houses do not possess this convenience. In town the water level is between 2 and 3 m. below the surface, depending upon the season, so elaborate work is not required for the sinking of a well.[32] These wells are lined either with the shells of oil drums or with brick, and the water is drawn up by means of a metal bucket on the end of a rope.

SANITARY FACILITIES

Sanitary facilities consist of the nearest adobe wall or fence off the immediate premises. So far as I

know, there is no water closet, indoors or outdoors, available to any Mochero. One of my informants, visiting me at the hotel in Trujillo, found himself completely confused when I showed him into the bathroom. Small children relieve themselves on the street, the sidewalk, and almost any other public place, and I have never seen one reprimanded or punished for this behavior. Although women are modest, the sight of a man urinating or buttoning up his trousers in plain view of the general public is very common. Enamelware chamber pots are possessed by about a third of the Mochero families, according to my count, but the regularity with which they are used is questionable. During one night spent in a Mochero's house in the *campiña* in a curing session, I noticed that several members of the family sleeping in the adjoining room apparently openly urinated on the floor during the night.

Garbage and other refuse is commonly thrown into the middle of the street. There is a garbage man (*baja policía*), with a horse-drawn cart, who comes around at infrequent intervals to carry the refuse away.

In the pueblo the houses, as shown on map 1, are arranged along the streets, which are laid out in a rectangular, although slightly irregular, grid plan. In the *campiña*, they are located at irregular intervals, usually shaded by trees. A *campiña* house is usually located in the corner of the owner's land, not in the middle of the plot. On the beach, the fishermen's houses are strung out at irregular intervals for about 11 km. on each side of the small seaside resort of Las Delicias.

A good many *chacreros* have two houses, one in the pueblo and the other in the *campiña*, "on the *chacra*."

HOUSE FURNISHINGS AMONG TRUE MOCHEROS

A North American even of lower economic status might consider even the better furnished Moche houses somewhat bare and old-fashioned. Also, the constant sifting of fine dust from the ceiling prevents the rooms from ever looking spic-and-span in the sense employed by a good housekeeper. It is somewhat difficult to describe the furnishings of the "typical" Moche house at present, owing to the varying influences of acculturation and differentiations in wealth. As has been the case with many indigenous groups in various parts of the hemisphere, it would seem that Moche had achieved a form of "stabilized native-colonial" culture compounded of aboriginal

[32] In 1934, the water level of nine wells in the town ranged from 0.5 to 3 m. below the surface and averaged 2.28 m. Data from blueprint No. IT–APM–50, Consejo Provincial de Trujillo, Inspección Técnica de las Obras de Agua Potable, Agua Potable de Moche, Proyecto de la Red de Distribución, Diciembre, 1934.

and Spanish colonial elements. This rather stable culture seems to have persisted without great change from shortly after the Conquest—let us say, from the end of the 16th century until the beginning of the 20th century or perhaps a little later. Precise dates cannot be given in the absence of documentary records. Much of this native-colonial culture remains in the community at the present time, although constantly subject to intrusions of newer elements, overlays, and reorientations. As might be expected, the newer elements are found most frequently in the houses of the pueblo and among the more well-to-do families (*familias acomadadas*).

Until about 40 years ago at the most (as a conservative estimate), it would seem that the great majority of Moche households got along with the following basic furnishings (later introductions are suggested in parentheses) : Dirt floors (instead of floors of boards, tiles, or cement) ; *mates,* large plate-shaped shallow gourds for eating (instead of tinware and enamelware plates) ; wooden spoons, hand-carved, and frequently none at all, no forks (instead of metal factory-made spoons and forks) ; *potos,* globular cuplike gourds for drinking (instead of glass tumblers) ; earthenware cups for hot liquids (instead of glazed chinaware coffee cups) ; *esteras* of *totora* used for mattresses and partially for covering, for sleeping directly on the dirt floor (instead of cotton mattresses and wooden or metal bedsteads) ; woolen hand-made blankets obtained from the Sierra in trade (instead of cotton and woolen factory-made blankets) ; hand-made earthenware and shallow one-piece carved wooden vessels (*bateas*) as containers for liquids, for clothes washing, etc. (instead of metal, enamelware, and wooden board buckets, washtubs, water storage jars, etc.) ; earthenware cooking pots (instead of iron pots and pans) ; use of mats for sitting and eating (instead of tables and benches or chairs) ; woolen bags for storing clothes etc. (instead of wooden and metal trunks) ; for lighting, candles and earthenware tallow lamps with rag wick (instead of kerosene lamps of various degrees of elaboration) ; and long-necked gourd bottles (*porongos*) for *chicha* (instead of beer bottles of glass).

The following "native-colonial" items are present in practically all Moche houses today, rich or poor, although they may exist alongside newer items and may not be used in the old way. (1) Mats of reeds (*esteras de totora*) are found. (2) Fireplaces on the ground consisting of three or four stones to support a cooking pot are present (pl. 14, *lower (left)*). (3) "*Botijas*" for storing *chicha* are in use. These are elongated, cigar-shaped containers of baked earthenware understood to hold 100 beer bottles of *chicha*. The pattern seems to be Spanish, but those in Moche are said to have been imported from Pisco in times past, filled with the well-known brandy of the same name (pl. 13, *upper (right)*). Steel oil drums have supplemented these containers in certain *chicherías* requiring a comparatively large storage capacity, but practically every house has at least one. (4) Gourd drinking cups (*potos*) are present, even when the household possesses glasses and china cups. The Mochero prefers to drink his *chicha* from a *poto,* claiming that the true flavor can only be appreciated in this way.

Although kerosene is quite extensively used for lighting, there is, to my knowledge, no kerosene stove or metal stove of any type in the community. In the more elegant houses (usually in the pueblo) hanging kerosene chandeliers are present. There is no electric light, even for the streets, in the community. Factory-made furniture, such as carved dining-room tables, sideboards, dish cupboards, sofas, etc., occur in a few of the richer houses, as well as framed oil paintings by local artists, oleo portraits, and colored lithographs. In the poorer houses pictures from magazines and newspapers, colored advertisements, and religious calendars usually constitute the wall decorations, although several houses have had the inside walls decorated with frescoes by the owners or members of the family. Although door curtains of the portiere type are affected in one or two rich houses, rugs for the floor are totally unknown in Moche.

I was unable to make a systematic statistical survey of the houses for want of staff and for reasons of delicacy. The people suspect officious questionnaire filling as a scheme of the Government to collect taxes, and it was desirable that no such suspicions upset my relations with them at this stage of the work. However, three of the informants were each asked to visit what they would consider a poor house, a middle-type house, and a rich house, to memorize the furnishings of each, and to write them down. The lists given below are a collation of these data, together with observations made by myself in numerous visits to all types of houses, and are presented as the next best thing to a statistical survey.

There are no social classes formally defined and recognized in Moche, but there are differences in wealth or expenditure, which are readily recognizable, at least in house furnishings. A rough estimate, on which the informants are in substantial agreement, would indicate that about 70 percent of the families of the community use "poor-type" furnishings; about 25 percent live in "middle-type" surroundings; and probably not more than 5 percent live in houses furnished according to the "rich type." It is, however, improper to speak of "upper, middle, and lower classes" in Moche at the present time, at least when considering the true Mocheros alone. Many of the more respected older residents live in houses furnished in the poorest style. The three types of house furnishings among the true Mocheros are as follows:

List of House Furnishings

Poor-type house:

Two small tables, three benches.
Five enamelware plates.
Four *mates* (large flat gourds) for eating.
Five earthenware pots.
Five tablespoons of brass; seven hand-carved spoons of wood.
Seven or eight *potitos* (small gourds) for drinking.
Five *esteras* (mats) used on ground as beds.
One enamelware chamber pot.
Three blankets, and some rags of discarded clothing used as bed covering.
Fireplace on the ground, consisting of lumps of adobe and a few stones; burns manure.
Dirt floor.
Hand broom of brush.

Middle-type house:

Six modern chairs, one dining table.
One old, hand-propelled sewing machine.
One trunk.
Two kitchen tables with one bench of wood.
Two wooden beds with bedclothes, including sheets and pillows.
Two enamelware chamber pots.
Eight plates, mixed, part of enamelware, part of graniteware.
Seven tablespoons of brass (*latón*), and three kitchen knives of same.
Six earthenware kitchen pots of different sizes.
One iron frying pan.
Two *botijas* for *chicha*.
Tablecloth.
Adobe stove burning wood.
One large dishpan of enamelware.
Five glasses.
Eight small spoons of *latón*.
Dirt floor.
Hand broom and full-sized broom.

Rich-type house:

One sideboard (*aparador*) with sets of glasses, cups, *copita azapate,* large and small napkins, *garrafa* of crystal, one of earthenware (*barro*), tablecloth.
One dozen chairs (*sillas americanas*) and others.
One dining table.
Four trunks.
One clothes rack.
One Singer sewing machine.
Three bedsteads with bedclothes, sheets and pillows; one bedstead of brass.
Five enamelware chamber pots, two of children's size.
Two iron pots.
Ten earthenware *nacional* pots.
One frying pan (*sartén*), plates, cups, graniteware pots (about five visible), five iron plates, enamelware; a collection of tablespoons, forks, knives of imitation "alpaca" silverware with wooden case.
Two large kitchen tables of wood for service.
Four benches, six mats, one skimming ladle with holes.
Two *botijas* of *barro* for *chicha*.
One stove of adobe and stone adapted for wood.
Two *bateas* for washing clothes.
Wooden or tile floor.
Some curtains and textile hangings in the *sala* (parlor).
Two hand brooms and two full-sized brooms.

The foregoing lists include the essential furnishings of houses of the three classes considered. The Mocheros are not self-sufficient in furnishing their houses and must buy the majority of the articles in the markets or stores of Trujillo or other towns. All items of cloth, metal, glass, and pottery are either bought ready-made or are made of materials obtained from outside the community. The local carpenters make tables, benches, and chairs of the types used in lower- and middle-type houses. Finer finished wooden furniture is obtained elsewhere. A table capable of seating eight persons costs at present about 30 soles ($4.62). A small bench costs about 6 soles ($0.92). Adobe fireplaces are made in Moche as well as wooden spoons and containers, although the last two items are also purchased in outside markets.

THE TOWN

This section on habitations may be concluded by quoting, for comparison, Squier's description of Moche, published in 1877.

... A ride of another league, over a flat country and a dusty road, brought us to the Indian pueblo, a considerable town, regularly laid out, of low cane huts, their roofs of reed-matting supported by crooked algaroba posts, and covered with a thin layer of mud to keep them from blowing away. There were a few houses of crude adobes, roofed in like manner, the whole presenting an aspect of squalid monotony. We rode directly to the house of the *gobernador*, a full-blooded Indian. His dwelling was merely an immense shed, with some compartments fenced off with adobes or canes, for such of the occupants as affected privacy. The bare earthen floor was strewed with the *aparejo* of mules and rude implements of husbandry, for the *gobernador* was both muleteer and husbandman . . . We rode through the silent streets, fetlock-deep in dust, to the plaza, one side of which was occupied by the church, a quaint, old, tumble-down edifice, its bell-tower reached by a flight of stone steps outside the building. [Squier, 1877, pp. 126–127.]

The town of Moche seems to have been somewhat modernized since Squier's time, although many of the town dwellers still complain loudly of the "lack of attention on the part of the authorities." As can be seen in plate 10, *upper (left)*, the plaza is now paved with cobblestones and cement, and an ugly modern, imitation brick facade, erected after the flood of 1925, hides the old church referred to by Squier. Presumably, however, the original edifice remains behind this attempt at face-lifting, for the outside stone steps leading to the bell tower are still exposed to the sky, although hidden behind the new facade. About a third of the street mileage in the pueblo is now paved with cobblestones, and several streets near the plaza are bordered by cement sidewalks (pl. 10, *lower (right)*. The great majority of houses in the pueblo are now of adobe, or at least present a plastered adobe front to the street. And a considerable sprinkling of more elaborate *forastero* houses for outsiders who live here, using Moche as a suburb of Trujillo, or who

come here during the summer season, gives the town a "mixed" appearance, doubtless considerably different from the squalid Indian village of Squier's observations.

Among the "civilized" structures of Moche to be seen at present are (map 1, Nos. 1–17 and C): The two-story Escuela de Agricultura (School of Agriculture) near the railroad tracks (No. 13); the railroad tracks themselves, which skirt the east edge of town, although the former station has now been removed; the silo of Señor G.; the partially dilapidated, but formerly elegant, house of the O. family with elevated wooden lookout platform; the facade of the Government buildings (pl. 11, *upper (center)*; map 1, Nos. 1–5); the slaughter house (No. 15); the new school for boys (No. 9); the movie theater, rarely used and not impressive from the outside (C); two houses with second stories near the plaza.

This sprinkling of attempts at sophisticated architecture and hard-surfaced streets is mixed with the dominant atmosphere of adobe houses, *quincha* fences and windbreaks in the backyards, low sloping roofs, and dusty streets frequently littered with garbage and refuse. Moche is no longer "pure," and for that very reason is the more interesting to a student of cultural change. The over-all impression a stranger receives of the pueblo is one of ragged rusticity. In the *campiña* the rusticity is complete.

FOOD AND DRINK

THE CONTENT AND THE ETIQUETTE OF BOARD AND BOWL

The Mocheros are not an easy people to become acquainted with, but once one has established rapport with them, their hospitality is extensive and continuous. They are the envy of persons from all parts of the coast because of the time and the resources they lavish on the consumption of food and liquor. In fact, eating and drinking are their principal relaxation and recreation. Generally speaking, they are not gamblers, they care little for bullfighting and cockfighting, they have developed only a vapid interest in the movies, but they love their *causas* and their *chicha*.

Eating and drinking, in addition to being activities essential for the maintenance of life and health, are great socializers and producers of interaction, generally with a pleasant emotional overtone. The dishes served on Moche tables and their ingredients

are not exclusive to this community, but it is widely claimed that they have a flavor not found elsewhere. Although the use of peppers and other "hot" seasonings is common to most of Peru, the food of Moche makes an unusually sharp assault upon the taste buds of the novice and even brings tears to the eyes of the initiated. The Mocheros consider the flavoring of the cooking in other areas insipid. One of my friends spent 10 days in Lima and returned to Moche much disappointed. He told me that he could not get enough to eat, that the yucas were measly small things, the fish stale, and so on—but worst of all, the food had no flavor. He was under the suspicion that the Lima cooks substituted *achote* (a reddish coloring powder) for the strong, tear-jerking peppers of his native *campiña*.

To a North American the three most outstanding features of Moche repasts, aside from details of various recipes, would probably be the *picante*, the dishes made in various ways from raw fish, and the *chicha*, or maize beer. The first and second of these items in one form or another are characteristic of the whole of Peru, and dishes prepared from raw fish are found throughout the coast. Therefore, Moche is to some extent representative of Peru as a whole in a general way and unique primarily in details.

Picante is a general term referring to what North Americans might call "hot seasoning." It appears in various forms, but its principal ingredients are red and yellow peppers (the red are the hottest), salt (bought in the stores in the form of rock salt), black pepper (the berries are bought in the shops and ground at home), onions, garlic, parsely, *azafrán,* and citrus fruit juices, especially lime juice. Of all these, the red and yellow peppers (*ají colorado* and a*jí amarillo*) are the most important, since they appear in practically all food preparations. All cooked foods usually are blended with *picante* during the process of preparation, and raw fish (*seviche*) is "cooked" in citrus fruit juice and eaten with pepper. A small side dish or gourd of *picante* sauce usually stands on the table, in case one is not satisfied with the flavoring of the dishes set before him. And, just to make sure that one's gastric juices are sufficiently stimulated, one often holds a small green pepper (unripe red pepper) in one hand to nibble between mouthfuls, after dipping it generously into a dish of salt and black pepper. This faithful devotion to *picante* among the Mocheros has a certain appearance of masochism. Many a time I have dined with persons whose eyes were streaming with tears and whose mouths were admittedly burning, but who were apparently deriving huge pleasure from this self-inflicted pain. *"Ay, ay, caramba. Pica fuerte, no? Que bueno. Que rico."* (Ouch, my goodness. It stings sharply, doesn't it? -How good. How appetizing.)

Raw fish is served in the form of *seviches;* in this the fish is first "cooked" in lime juice, then covered with cold *picante* sauce, and served with corn on the cob, yuca, sweetpotato and often other vegetables, the whole garnished with leaves of lettuce. Crabs and shrimps are also eaten raw after similar treatment, as well as being steamed or boiled. A particularly charming custom is the *"bocadita";* a lady at the table, often the hostess, will pick up a *muy-muy* (sea shrimp) and after sucking it delicately will remove it from her mouth and insert it between the lips of a gentleman, accompanying the gesture with a kissing sound. This procedure may be employed with any other tidbits, and after the

chicha bowl has made the rounds a few times, the morsel may be transferred directly from the mouth of the lady to that of the gentleman. Only the more sophisticated persons think it necessary to use table forks or other implements for eating, and spoons are used only for soup. Frequently a single *mate* (calabash plate) is set in the middle of the table. Each guest takes a piece of lettuce which he places on the table before him, proceeding to lift the food with his fingers from the central dish either directly to his mouth or to the lettuce leaf at his place.

Water, as water, is considered to be essential for the irrigation of land, as useful in cooking vegetables and meats (although some cooks use only *chicha*), and as pleasant for an occasional bath, if convenient. But it is regarded as little short of poisonous if used as a drink by man. No doubt this is an eminently hygienic attitude, considering the fact that many available supplies of the liquid are possibly contaminated. Tea made of *yerba luiza* and also coffee are consumed by both children and adults, usually for breakfast only (also milk, cocoa, and soda water in comparatively small quantities by children). Nevertheless, the principal drink for all persons above the age of puberty is *chicha,* a maize beer.

Three main meals are consumed by the Mocheros, breakfast, lunch, and dinner or supper, but they are interspersed with lunches, called *causas* (verb, *causear*). Even when guests do not drop in or the family does not go out, it is normal to enjoy at least one *causa* during the morning and at least one during the afternoon. A lunch of this sort may consist of anything from a small bit of fish and a morsel of yuca to a meal consisting of several dishes, and it is always washed down with mature *chicha,* if it can be obtained. A friend visiting a house is always invited to sit down at the table in the arbor or in the back yard. Within a few minutes the lady of the house sets out a *causa,* which may consist of no more than a couple of boiled eggs, and the guest eats and then is offered *chicha*. The ethnologist visiting a number of houses during a day finds this hospitality agreeable, but also a burden upon his capacity. If one comes uninvited, it is customary to offer money to the hostess to pay for the *chicha* and food, although this will be refused if one is a *compadre* of the household or has elsewhere kept up his end of the entertaining. In addition to household hospitality of this sort, food and drink are obtainable upon payment in many houses operated on a small-scale commercial basis. Many a housewife augments the family income by making *chicha* and *causas* to sell. The *chicha* sells, according to quality, for 10 and 15 centavos a liter, and an ordinary *causa* is worth 10 centavos. Owing to the rigid etiquette of drinking which requires even a commercial hostess to drink with her guests, many of these women who sell *chicha* all day become more or less thoroughly intoxicated by evening. Such places of refreshment are called *chicherías*, although the word is less used than in certain other parts of Peru.

Some of the more conservative families still eat on *totora* mats placed on the dirt floor, but the great majority now have rough rectangular tables, somewhat like those for kitchen use in United States farmhouses, around which they sit to eat and drink on benches made of sawed boards.

There is no rule against men and women eating together and for ordinary meals and small gatherings this usually takes place. At festive meals the women of the household are usually in the kitchen during the meal, occupied with the preparation and serving of the food, and at any meal the women are usually up and down, serving the meals, moving back and forth between table and kitchen.

All responsibility of preparing, cooking, and serving the food and *chicha* is customarily in the hands of the women. Although the women do the work they also have the authority, and a man is supposed to secure the agreement of his wife before issuing invitations. If a visitor drops in, the man will ask his wife if she has something in the way of a *causa* and some *chicha*. If he wishes to buy *chicha*, he usually asks his wife for the money. To be sure, certain men dominate their wives or companions sufficiently to make these requests more in the nature of a command than a pleading, but in the pattern and phrasing of the eating and drinking situation the woman is supposed to have the controlling role.

Proper relaxation is required for the healthful digestion of food after eating, according to local belief. Reading, riding horseback, and sexual intercourse within an hour or two after a meal are regarded as extremely dangerous. This is summed up in a frequently quoted proverb, which I believe has a general Peruvian distribution:

> *Después de comer,*
> *ni un papelito para leer,*
> *ni caballo, ni mujer.*
>
> (After eating,
> neither a paper to read,
> nor a horse, nor a woman.)

During my time in Moche one of the local *forasteros* was suddenly taken ill and, 2 days after being removed to the Trujillo hospital, died of a ruptured duodenal ulcer, according to hospital attachés He was a strong, healthy man in his thirties, and the Mocheros were agreed that he met his end by reason of his habit of immediately mounting his horse and riding off to his work after eating.

CHICHA

This drink and the customs concerned with it deserve a fairly long section, not because of its inherent interest for tipplers unacquainted with the beverage, but because, for better or for worse, it plays so large a part in Moche life.

Maize grown in the countryside is used principally for roasting ears (*choclos*) and for making *chicha*. Certainly the latter use absorbs by far the major part of the maize consumed in the community. The consumption of *chicha*, according to my data, seems to average about 2 l. per day per adult (over 18 years of age) for its "normal" or thirst-quenching properties, as an accompaniment of meals etc., with an additional liter per day per adult as a conservative estimate for *chicha* consumed because of its festive properties. These are only estimates, based on relatively small samples of families, but seem to be on the conservative side, if anything; for when the Mocheros become festive, the amount of *chicha* consumed is prodigious. The fact that they are, for the most part, independent proprietors of their lands allows them the leisure and the opportunity for such relaxations.

The word "*chicha*" is in general use for rustic drinks in all parts of Spanish America, and it does not seem to be a term native to Peru.[33] The Quechua terms are "acca, aka, asuha, khusa, aqha." [34] The material preserved in the Museo Arqueológico "Rafael Larco Herrera" in Chiclín seems to show clearly that *chicha*, or a similar beverage, was in common use during Mochica times. Many informants have insisted that large sealed pots containing *chicha* in a "good state of preservation," i. e., potable, have been recovered from the Moche ruins

---

[33] Arona sees the word as an old Spanish term meaning "sustenance" or "nourishment," the same root involved in *salchicha* (sausage) (Arona, 1938, pp. 165–166), although in another place he raises the question whether it may not be an Antillean term (ibid., p. 177). It is impossible to translate the word as "beer," as will appear later, when beer itself is discussed. In Moche the word *jora* (actually the mash from which *chicha* is brewed) is used frequently to refer to the beverage.

[34] Valdizán and Maldonado, 1922, vol. 2, p. 69 ff.; *aqha* is Farfar's rendering (Farfan, 1941, p. 34).

themselves, although I have found no one who has personally seen or tasted this allegedly well-aged brew.

It is said that in Inca times all fiestas, as well as deaths, etc., were celebrated with *chicha*. According to Cieza de León, nobles and plebians alike drank to the point of being unable to hold their drinking utensils in their hands (Valdizán and Maldonado, loc. cit.). According to Garcilaso de la Vega, *chicha* was offered as a sacrifice to the sun, earth, and the *huacas*. It was customary first to dip a finger halfway into the *chicha*, gaze respectfully at the sun, and flip a drop of the liquid off the finger. After this they drank to their heart's content. During the Fiesta of the Sun,[35] called by Garcilaso *Intip Raymi*, the Inca drank from a gold vase and gave it to kneeling relatives to drink from. This *chicha* was made by the so-called Virgins of the Sun. The *curacas*, not being of royal blood, met in another plaza, *Cusipata*, and were given the unsanctified *chicha* which the Inca women drank. According to Juan de Betanzos (1880),[36] the cult of the Orejones owes its origin to *chicha*. The cult was founded, according to this source, by the Inca Yupanqui who required the Incas to begin a 30-day period of fasting. Before starting they were ordered to make four large jars of *chicha*. During the 30 days they had nothing but *chicha* made by a virgin. At the end of the month they were required to drink all of the four large jars of the liquor at once, whereupon they fell into an unconscious state and had their ears bored before they regained consciousness.

Although drunkenness was prohibited by Inca law and repeaters were supposed to be executed, it seems to have been fairly widespread, according to Guamán Poma de Ayala (1936). Lastres says—

A people essentially idolatrous and superstitious, they had to find release from their anxieties in the immoderate use of stupefacients. And *chicha* was the imperial drink of both nobles and commoners. From its immoderate use came psychic and organic upsets ranging from simple drunkenness to the *Hatunmachay*, or loss of judgment. [Lastres, 1941, p. 122.]

Thus, whatever else may be said about the *"chicha* complex" in modern Moche, it seems to be directly in line with the cultural usages of early (Mochica) as well as late (Inca) prehistoric times.

In Moche there is a sort of cycle involving eating

and *chicha* drinking. It is thought necessary for adults to "settle" (*sentar*) all meals except breakfast with *chicha* (although some individuals do not hesitate to "settle" breakfast as well). At least one bowl of *chicha* is essential for this process. *"Ya vamos a sentar el almuerzo"* simply means, "Now that we have had lunch, let's have a drink." Conversely, it is regarded as unseemly and unhealthy to consume any considerable amount of *chicha* on an empty stomach. Since one bowl of the liquor after lunch frequently induces the desire to have another, and so on, drinking and eating frequently progress hand in hand from midday until bedtime.[37]

Fresh *chicha* (*fresca*) with little or no alcoholic content is used, if available, as a thirst quencher at breakfast and to be carried in bottles to the fields, etc. This fresh drink is, of course, merely the regular product before it has fermented (when it is called *chicha madura*).

Judging by its effects (and not on myself alone), well-matured *chicha* must have an alcoholic content close to that of a heavy ale, perhaps 12 to 14 percent by volume. The strength of the brew is increased up to a certain point proportionately to the amount of *chancaca* (brown cake-sugar) or sirup mixed with the *jora* (mash made from sprouted grains of corn).

Except for the probably excessive consumption of alcohol which it induces, *chicha* in itself would seem to be a comparatively healthful beverage. As will be seen from the standard recipe in a later section (p. 53), it is made from sprouted corn or other grains. This is not chewed up and spit out as is done in the manufacture of certain beers in the jungle portions of South America. The mash, or *jora*, thus made is then boiled with water for from 24 to 48 hours, which is, of course, sufficient to kill contaminating germs. The fermentation process serves the same end.[38] It is, however, in the etiquette of drinking that all attention to modern rules of cleanliness disappears.

[35] Cited by Valdizán and Maldonado (1922, vol. 2, p. 75); see Garcilaso de la Vega (1919, vol. 2, pp. 188–193).

[36] Cited by Valdizán and Maldonado, loc. cit.

[37] In a footnote in Prado (1894), 1941, p. 181, the late Dr. Pablo Patrón sustains the thesis that *ají* and coca counteract the effects of alcohol and he gives references which I have been unable to locate that "English therapeutics" uses coca and *ají* to break the drink habit. If there is any truth in this, so far as *ají* is concerned, might there be something in the theory of *ají* as a counter irritant? Or would it be beneficial to alcoholics because of its allegedly high vitamin content?

[38] According to the anonymous author of "Relación de las costumbres antiguas de los naturales del Peru, Tres Relaciones . . ." 1879, the Inca physicians invented *chicha* as a means of preventing contamination from infected water, and at least one modern physician has recommended its use for this purpose, in order to prevent infection by drinking water in the *campiña* of Arequipa. See Escomel (1913), cited by Valdizán and Maldonado, vol. 2, pp. 69 ff., 1922.

The brew is stored in *botijas* [39] (large jars from Pisco) and ladled out with a small gourd called a *cojodito* ("little lame one") into a large gourd called a *poto*. Then the single *cojodito* serves as the drinking vessel for all who may be present. The affectation of certain more "modernized" Mocheros of serving the drink in a glass tumbler serves only to render visible the slime left by many mouths on the rim.

The etiquette is as follows. The host or hostess dips out a *cojodito* full of the drink, saying, usually, "*A ver, que usted tome conmigo*" (Look, drink with me). Frequently, this is shortened to merely, "*A ver.*" Sometimes it takes the form of "*A ver, salud, pues,*" or "*Que dice? A ver.*" The phrase of invitation is accompanied by a bow toward the guest and a raising of the cup to the mouth, followed by draining the contents at once. It is a gross insult to refuse an invitation of this sort and implies, as a refusal to shake hands among ourselves, that the guest wishes to have no social relations with the offerer of the drink. After swallowing the liquor, the host or proposer again fills the cup and passes it to the invitee or guest. The latter then makes a similar proposal to someone else present; the latter person, after draining the cup, then proposes to another, and the process is repeated. If one is a guest at a home or a fiesta, one must "drink with" every other person present in this manner; and minor quarrels sometimes occur because one person has overlooked this salutation to someone else present. The customary reticence of the Mocheros disappears as the bowl makes the rounds, and singing and dancing begin, together with the constant eating and drinking. Food is spread on the table and, after everyone has sat down to eat, there is usually a good deal of toasting. The general effect is often heightened by a few small glasses (*copitas*) of *pisco* brandy, or, more commonly, *cañaso* (drinking alcohol distilled from sugarcane juice). Among the more common toasts are the following:

> *A proporción del burro son los capachos.*
> (The *capachos*—rawhide containers fastened on pack saddles—are selected in proportion to the size of the donkey, i. e., some people can drink more than others.)

---

[39] The *botija* "has a yard and a half of height and a half-yard widest diameter; it has the form of an inverted cone; it contains 23½ regular flasks (*frascos*), and in them (the *botijas*) are sent to the kingdoms of Tierra Firme, Guatemala and New Spain, the wine, aguardiente, olives and other things." Quoted by Valdizán (1938, vol. 2, p. 187) from Alcedo, Diccionario de Peruanismos. Guamán Poma de Ayala (1936) also uses the word.

> *Paz para el alma, salud para el cuerpo.*
> (Peace for the spirit and health for the body.)

> *Jesús, te invoco que esto para mi es poco.*
> (This is not too much for me.)

> *Salú' compá'. Mi amor se va con usted.*
> (Health, *compadre*, my love goes with you.) Reply: *Esta y otra, lo que siento es la demora.* (This one and another, what I don't like is the delay.)

> *Tres cantos tiene la encula.*
> (The dove has three songs, i. e., the woman serving the drink has three drinks for me.)

> *Tomar y tomemos*
> *con gran placer y contento,*
> *y si no fuere así,*
> *se le fusile al momento.*
> (To drink, let us drink with great pleasure and happiness, and, if it were not so, one would be shot immediately.)

> *Esta copita de chimoy*
> *tome ahora porque contigo me voy.*
> (Chimoy is said to be the old name for Trujillo; translation: take this cup of Trujillo liquor, because I am going away with you now.)

> *No hay primara sin segunda.*
> (One is no good without a second.)

A man arriving at a house and wanting a drink will often use the phrase, "*Seco, laváo, y volteáo,*" (I am dry, washed, and upset).

The present writer is not sufficiently acquainted with rural drinking customs in other parts of Peru to know, but he believes that these toasts, except for the pronunciation, are not unique to Moche, but are fairly common throughout the country.

A strong prejudice against factory-made *beer* (*cerveza*) exists in Moche. There is a brewery in Trujillo which produces both light beer and dark beer, which experts say are of good quality and which sell for about 50 centavos (7½ cents in United States money) per liter in bottles. This price compares with 10 to 15 centavos per bottle for *chicha* and may have something to do with the prejudice, which in the main, however, seems to be a matter of taste reinforced by traditional beliefs. As a sign of ostentatious spending and to humor a *forastero* friend, a Mochero will order some beer from the shop and will drink it, but he actually does not like it as well as *chicha*. Not only is beer felt to be tasteless or disagreeable, but it is believed to be dangerous. Many ailments are said to be brought on by light beer, colds and other respiratory troubles in particular. Added to this is the general belief that brewery beer contains arsenic as a preservative.

When one sees a Mochero friend and discovers that he is not feeling well that day, the Mochero will frequently say that he believes the cause was that he was "in Trujillo yesterday and drank a bottle of beer." Everyone knows that such a lapse is sufficient cause for illness. I had a persistent cold and cough during the month of June in Moche, and no one ever tired of warning me not to touch any light beer. Dark beer for some reason is not regarded as so dangerous. This attitude toward light beer also seems to be tied up with the general classification of all foods into "cold" and "warm" categories. Beer is among the "cold" substances, but light beer is colder than dark beer.

OTHER DRUGS AND NARCOTICS

Aside from brewed and distilled alcohol the Mocheros are very little addicted to the use of other drugs, except occasionally as medicines.

Coca is available in the shops, costing 5 centavos the handful, but no Mocheros are habitual coca users in the sense that they have a cud in the cheek all of the time. Many men buy a handful of coca which they chew with lime (a pinch is thrown in with the purchase as a form of "yapa" or good-will extra) to keep them awake when they have to stay up all night. Coca leaves are also used for making a tea which is said to be good for aches and pains, but is not drunk habitually as a beverage. No lime gourds, spatulas, or other implements are used in the consumption of coca. A man merely carries his purchase in the paper in which the shopkeeper wraps it.

Tobacco is used only in the form of cigarettes, and there are practically no heavy smokers among the Mocheros. Many men do not smoke at all, others usually only when relaxing. A cigarette is a special treat rather than a daily or hourly necessity. Women do not smoke at all, except as a joke or when drunk. The resistance to the tobacco habit at present is easily explainable superficially by its cost. Tobacco is a Government monopoly, and the cheapest package of cigarettes available costs 45 centavos, a high price for Mocheros. It is illegal to roll cigarettes by hand.

Aside from considerations involved in the psychosocial structure of Moche life, which will be discussed later, the resistance to coca and tobacco seems to be supported by historical tradition. There is no clear evidence that the habitual use of either narcotic was widespread in the Mochica or Chimu cultures; in fact, it is doubtful that the use of tobacco was general even under Inca domination, and the extent to which the Inca introduced the use of coca on the coast remains to be studied.

PREPARATION OF FOOD AND DRINK

In the preparation of food, the following items are used.

Fireplaces of two types.—(1) Fireplace consisting of three or more stones for supporting the cooking pot on the ground or floor of the kitchen (pl. 14, *lower* (*left*)). (2) "Stove" of adobe about 36 to 40 inches high off the ground. Two parallel ridges of adobe run perpendicular to the front of the stove on its top; between them the fire is laid and on them, or on iron straps or other supports laid across them, stand the cooking pots (pl. 14, *middle* (*left*)).

Fuel of three types.—Wood obtained from the areas near the river and from trees growing on the plot and alongside the irrigation ditches, charcoal, and manure of domestic animals.

No ovens are used in household cookery. Bread is not invariably eaten, yuca being the "bread" of Moche. All of those who have acquired a taste for bread buy it in the *tiendas*, from peddlers who visit the houses, or from the households which bake it.

Cooking pots (callanas) of various types and shapes (pl. 14, *middle and lower* (*left*)).—Made of earthenware by Indians of the Sierra or of the region about Chiclayo. No pots are made by hand in Moche.

Water storage jars (olla manca).—Large earthenware pots (pl. 13, *middle* (*left*)), dug up from the Moche ruins.

Gourd vessels of four general types.—Mates, the plate-shaped gourds; *potos*, the bowl-shaped gourds (small-sized bowls or drinking cups are called *cojoditos*); and *porongos*, the bottle-shaped gourds. All of these are made to some extent in Moche, but the better specimens come from the region of Chiclayo. The latter carry fairly elaborate, if crude, external designs etched with hot irons or (a new introduction) with nitric acid and black and red inks.

Fans (abanicos) for blowing up kitchen fire.—Made of *carrizo* woven to give the fan a diamond shape and a handle of *carrizo* ends about 6 inches long.

Hand mills or grinding stones.—These consist of two parts, the *mano*, or movable part, and the *batán*, or base. Neither is shaped in a regular pattern. The *batán* is a flat-topped stone of variable shape, but usually approximating 18 inches in diameter; it may be worn into a shallow depression by use, but does not have a raised rim about the edge as do the Mochica specimens. The *mano* is a stone of variable shape which has a smooth rubbing surface along one side about two handbreadths in length. Some are cylindrical, but others are hump-backed, brick-shaped, etc. In modern times, they are selected (like the *batanes*) for their shape, rather than being worked into shape (pl. 13, *middle* (*center*)).

Wooden spoons.

Chicha containers (botijas).—These have already been described.

The foregoing is a list of the essential items used in food and *chicha* preparation and eating. To this list, which is more or less aboriginal and characteristic of the stabilized native-colonial culture, have been added items of more recent introduction, e.g.: Gasoline cans as containers for liquids; oil drums as water containers and cooking utensils; iron and enamelware pots and pans of various types, of which the metal frying pan is perhaps the most radical innovation (there is considerable doubt that the aborigines of this region fried food); tin cans and glass bottles of all types and shapes; glass tumblers; china drinking cups; knives, forks, and spoons of metal, for eating and for handling the food on the fire.

As with all other aspects of Moche material culture, it is notable that most of the introductions are substitutions for less efficient older items, but that there has been no tendency to adopt new-fangled mechanical devices. For example, the primus stove would be a useful item, and likewise the hand-cranked coffee grinder. Both are within the economic means of many Mocheros, and, while there may be a family here or there which possesses these contrivances, I have not seen them, nor have my informants located any.

The one mechanical improvement, involving the principle of the wheel, which has had wide acceptance in Moche is the sewing machine.

MIDDAY IN A MOCHE HOUSEHOLD

Before presenting more details it may be of interest to set down a description of Moche kitchen management and the noonday household events of a typical menage as seen through the eyes of a North American woman, who is a good cook (in North America), but not an ethnologist. The following notes have been contributed by Helen Norgord Gillin. They cover a household in the pueblo. The señora mentioned is a pure Mochera.

I arrived in Moche at the house of Señora P. about 10 a. m. According to our plan she was going to show me how to prepare the meal which the two families were to enjoy together about noon. She was all ready and had collected in the kitchen: *cabrito, yuca,* potatoes (white and yellow), beans, lemon, fish, and rice.

Her kitchen is a large dirt-floored, mat-walled room at the back of the house. A large door opens into the *sala* (main room). A roof of mats covered the kitchen, but various large uncovered patches in the roof and walls allowed ample light to enter. In one corner was a good adobe stove. Underneath the top on which the fire was laid was a hollow space used for storage of pots and pans, with a few rags put down as a bed for the hairless "Chinese" dog she owns. She claims the dog was given to her by one of the Chinese in town and that the Chinese eat these dogs. The top of the stove, made of wood, but thickly covered with adobe, was used for making the fire, and two ridges of adobe ran down each side from the front to the back of the top. Stretched across these were various pieces of old iron which held the pots over the fire. In the wood supports of the mats of the wall beside the stove, nails had been driven where the wooden cooking spoons were hung.

In front of the stove was a large flat-topped stone (*batán*) with a stone grinder on it. A large old wooden table stood against the farther end of the wall. In the corner next to it was a wooden cupboard with doors on it in which were stored dishes, food, etc. A wooden bench at the side of the cupboard held a wash pan and a bar of soap. Toward the opposite side of the room, as one enters it, was a long wooden table covered with a wornout oilcloth. On either side were benches, and three chairs were grouped around the ends. This is the dining table and the place for drinking in this house. In addition to the *sala*, two enclosures opened off the kitchen, one a poultry yard, and the other a small storage room for *chicha*. The latter formed a small adobe addition to the house proper.

After the older daughter had pinned a large, much-patched apron on me, I was first taught how to grind *ají*. The large red pods are put on the grinding stone and the grinder (*mano*) is moved rapidly and heavily over them, with a sort of rocking motion. Also treated this way were onions and garlic. The *ají* was made into a sort of paste in this fashion. Salt had been brought from the store in the form of large crystals and these also were ground on the *batán*. Meanwhile the *cabrito* was cut up into small pieces and placed in an earthenware pot on the stove to boil in water seasoned with ground salt. Later vegetables were mixed with it. When all was ready the table with the oilcloth was set.

A small drawer in the table held assorted knives, forks, spoons, and two lavender napkins. A place was set for me with knife, fork, spoon, and napkin. The younger daughter took out of the corner cupboard five large spoons which she cleaned by rubbing them with salt, then put them around the table. Six soup plates were then produced from the cupboard and wiped off with a dirty towel before the soup was served in them. After the soup we had the *cabrito*, rice and beans, very *picante*. (For recipes, see below.) The two daughters started to eat with us, then the señora's nephew came in, and finally the señora sat down. While we were eating, Sra. P.'s next-door neighbor and comadre came in. Her husband, she said, was dying of a toothache and had the left side of his face all swollen up. Naturally, it was a neighborly gesture to relieve her of getting lunch while he was ill. Sra. P. said that she would go over to put hot compresses on his face after lunch. Meanwhile the comadre sat down and partook of some nourishment with us, while Sra. P. scolded her for not making her husband have his tooth extracted.

About 10:30, while we were preparing the meal, Sra. P.'s sister, a most attractive woman somewhat younger than Sra. P., had dropped in with a friend to grind some rice on the grinding stone, so that she could make *pepián de arroz*, which she promised to send over for our lunch, also. Now, while we were eating, she came in with the *pepián* in a large gourd plate (*mate*). She was dressed in an embroidered white blouse with a full dark-blue skirt, with an embroidered petticoat of muslin under it, and she had yarns of brown cotton braided into her hair which was twisted around her head in a sort of crown. She was barefoot. The two ladies had to drink a glass of *chicha* with each of us in turn.

After we had finished eating, the plates and spoons and glasses were washed in a little cold water poured out into a shallow gourd (*mate*) and then they were dried with the same dirty towel. The pots and pans were not washed. The remaining food was just left in them.

The Sra. P. and her comadre went next door to attend to the ailing husband, so they brought over the 2-month-old baby for me to play with. It was a fat, smiling, apparently bright child, but dirtier than any I have ever seen. In her ears the dirt was in great cakes, her face was black, and her head was covered with scales. The ladies told me that a baby should never be bathed during its first year. During the second year it is never wise to bathe it in the winter. This one had had one bath about a week before, and, so they said, nearly caught pneumonia, so they would wait until warmer weather or an older age. Its clothes were comparatively clean, but the child was filthy.

About 1:30 in the afternoon Sra. P.'s husband and my husband returned. They brought with them Don V. The señora said that she must immediately prepare a *causa,* which consisted of fish with onions (*pescado encebollado*). I helped her, and, as a contribution to the entertainment, we sent one of the daughters out for six bottles of beer. Before long, three other men, all compadres of the family, of course, wandered in and were invited to *causear.* By this time the party consisted of the señora and me, her two daughters, her sister, her comadre from next door and the baby, and the three compadres who had dropped in. In addition to the beer, I noticed that the bowl of *chicha* on the table was filled four times before we left. Don V., who probably had a few *copitas* before, was slightly drunk and started making mock-serious speeches making fun of various people. We managed to get away about 3:30, by which time the *causa* was going strong and everyone was very merry indeed.

BUTCHERING

All meat is supposed to be slaughtered and dressed in the local slaughterhouse, called the *camal.*[40] The slaughterhouse is owned by the municipality, which employs a municipal butcher (*camalero*). A fee of 3 soles is charged for slaughtering and dressing a beef, 1 sol for a full-grown pig, and 40 centavos each for sheep. There is a cement floor with a drain running through the middle. Sheep are unceremoniously held with their heads hanging over this drain, and the throat is slit. Blood is collected in tin cans and used to feed ducks as well as to make certain kinds of blood pudding. Blood sausage is unknown here, I am told.

A beef is tied with a rope around the horns to an iron ring set into the cement floor. The butcher sticks it with the point of a sharp knife just behind the horns, as in a method of despatching bulls in bull rings. This seems to paralyze the animal, but does not kill it. The killing is done by slitting the arteries of the neck allowing the animal to bleed to death, while the blood is collected in tin cans. Sheep make no noise when their throats are cut, other than three or four very profound sighs as the air leaves the lungs. Pigs are hamstrung before their throats are slit.

Carcasses are immediately skinned and hung up. The meat not needed in the owner's household is sold to the local meat shops (*carnecerías*) and to vendors in the markets. In both cases it is displayed, hung from hooks over head, or laid out on wooden tables.

Nothing is thrown away. Even the intestines are sold for soup and meat (*mondongo*). The intestines are frequently cut into thin slices or shreds and fried, somewhat after the manner of making chitterlings. A local meat seller said that bull's penis is particularly good to eat if the animal is young, not when it is old. When from a young animal it is *"puro nervio,"* and gives one strength if he is run down or nervous. This is a curious belief in the realm of contagious magic, which, however, is not completely diffused throughout the community. Some persons had never heard of it. Beef penis is, however, generally eaten, regardless of its alleged powers, and most frequently appears in *sancochado.* Bulls' testicles are much prized in *sancochado* as well.

In Moche—and this is true in most of Peru—there is little attention given to butcher's cuts of meat. It is generally cut or hacked into hunks, regardless of the part of the carcass from which it is taken. Chops or cutlets are unknown as such in Moche. *Lomo* is practically the only recognized "cut," but it is only a flat piece of meat which can be fried or broiled like a beefsteak. It may be taken from any part of the animal, from the rump to the shoulders, and it may represent either a cut across the fibers or along them. Most meat is prepared either *guizado* or *sancochado.* Both processes make use of hunks or cubes of meat, regardless of cut. Thin slices of meat (*carne mechada*) are cut from boiled joints and served cold in sandwiches.

So far as I know, there is no manufacture of ham or bacon in Moche and no consumption of these products. Sausage is made, by a local *forastero* butcher, for sale in Trujillo, but little is consumed by Mocheros. The only means of preserving meat of

---

[40] This word is a widely used term in the country and appears to be a Peruvianism. See Arona (1938, p. 113). The Mocheros know the word *matadero,* but do not use it except when explaining to a *gringo* what a *camal* is.

which I am aware—if they can be considered in this category—are the customs of frying long strips of meat in fat, after which they may be hung up in the kitchen for some days to be eaten at the convenience of the household; the boiling of joints to be preserved for some days cold; and the drying of small lizards.

Despite the fact that all animals are supposed to be butchered in the municipal slaughterhouse, private butchering takes place as well, especially in the *campiña.* So far as I know, the methods are essentially the same. Animals are never struck on the head with an ax or club, but are always either held down or tied down, and their throats are cut. Poultry are also killed by slitting the throat. Poultry blood is not collected. At the present time no explanation of this method of slaughtering is given, other than the desire to use the blood of larger animals. What its true historical origin or basis is I am unable to say.

MISCELLANEOUS DISHES

In this section is presented a short and partial checklist of foods or dishes not necessarily familiar even to those who know Spanish, if their experience has not included Moche or the north Peruvian coast.

Sancochado.—This is a dish, or at least a term, common, I believe, to the whole Peruvian coast. In Lima, it often appears to resemble something like a "New England boiled dinner," consisting of various vegetables and beef boiled separately and placed separately on the plate. In Moche, however, the *sancochado* is more like "pepper pot." It always contains meat of some kind, yuca, and, usually, boiled corn on the cob. Frequently other vegetables are included. All are boiled together in the pot with a plentiful seasoning of *ají.*

Pepián de choclo.—A thick soup or mash is made of green corn kernels mashed up, strained, and cooked with meat. *Pepián* is also made of rice.

Panes con mecha.—These are actually small sandwiches, made of bunlike "breads" bought in the shops and slices of cold meat (*carne mechada*) cut from a joint boiled with spices and cut cold.

Frijoles entreverados.—Hard beans mixed with meat cut into small cubes and made into a sort of stew.

Arroz fogoso.—Boiled rice, not wet, not dry, of "just the right consistency."

Chochoca.—A sort of mush or soup made from meal of a special yellow maize which is imported from the Sierra.

Tajadas de yuca.—Pieces of boiled yuca cut into lengths of about 2 inches and split in half or four ways. The *tajada* is picked up in the hand and eaten as bread. *"La yuca es el pan de Moche."*

Arroz con cebolla.—A mixture of rice boiled with onions and *picante.*

Lenteja serrana.—Small lentils grown only in the Sierra, but imported and used commonly in Moche. Not to be con-fused with the *lenteja bocona,* also called the *lenteja mochica* or *lenteja mochera,* said to be native to Moche.

Cañanes.—Small lizards. These animals are caught as previously described and disemboweled, after which they are dried in the sun and kept in bundles of a dozen or so. They are cut into short pieces and eaten (heads, feet, tail, and all) in *seviches* and *sancochados,* and are also boiled with vegetables (*ajiaco.*)

A FEW RECIPES [41]

Cabrito Encebollado

1. Cut *cabrito* (kid) meat into pieces about 1 inch square or cube (depending on the piece you are working with) and wash. This recipe is based on about 2 pounds of kid meat (1 kilo).
2. Put meat in earthenware jar and cover with *manteca* (lard).
3. Grind *ají* (chile peppers), both *colorado* (red) and *amarillo* (yellow), one of each, and add paste to pot; stir.
4. Cut up four green onions into small slices, but do not use green stems; add to pot.
5. Chop up *culantro* with a knife and add to pot.
6. Grind salt and black pepper seeds; add to pot, according to taste.
7. Cut up two tomatoes in small pieces and add to pot.
8. Put in a bit of *orégano.*
9. Place on fire and stir occasionally until done.

Arroz con Frijoles

1. Grind four *ajos* (garlics) on batán. Place in earthenware cooking pot (*callana*).
2. Add four wooden spoonfuls of *manteca* (lard). Cook until garlic turns yellow.
3. Add double handful of dry hard kidney beans and salt to taste.
4. Add 1½ Quaker oats cans of water, or according to experience.
5. Wash double handful of rice two times, in shallow gourds (*mates*), pouring from one to the other through the fingers.
6. When the beans, etc., in the pot are boiling, add rice. If the wooden spoon stands upright in the mixture without support, there is just the proper amount of water. If it falls over, there is too much.

Pepián de Arroz

1. Grind two yellow *ajís.* Place in cooking pot.
2. Add two cooking spoonfuls of *manteca* and cook until well mixed.
3. Grind double handful of rice lightly, to break each grain into two or three pieces, but not into a powder or flour.
4. Add water and boil. This mixture should not be quite so "stiff" as previous.
5. After rice has come to a boil, add meat in small pieces, if available.

Pescado Encebollado

1. Put cut-up onions, yellow and red *ají,* and lard into pot. Cook slowly for a few minutes.

---
[41] Collected by Helen Norgord Gillin.

2. Add cut-up washed pieces of fish.
3. Pour *chicha* over all sufficient to moisten well.
4. Cook for about 10 minutes.

Sopa Teóloga

This "theological soup" is an essential dish for special occasions, such as birthdays, baptisms, marriages, births, etc. It is also known as *sopa de fiesta*.

1. Bread is cut into pieces and moistened, allowed to stand for half an hour.
2. Place in cooking pot with water.
3. In the meantime prepare a thick chicken soup or broth.
4. Pour this over the bread pap, boiling.
5. Red and yellow *ají* (ground) added.
6. *Azafrán* rubbed between the hands and dropped into the pot.

La Boda

"Theological soup" is usually served on festive occasions as part of a dish called *"La Boda"* (the wedding). This feast is served in one large plate or shallow gourd and consists of the following ingredients:

1. *Sopa teóloga.*
2. *Maíz tostado molido,* ground roasted corn kernels, often called *máchica.*
3. *Pepián de cancha,* a stiff mush made of ground roasted corn.
4. *Jeta* or *geta,* a sort of sauce made of dry lentils (*lenteja bocona*) cooked to a mush, and beaten.
5. *Yuca machada,* boiled, mashed yuca.
6. A piece of chicken or duck.
7. A piece of kid.

The soup occupies the bottom and center of the plate with the other items ranged about the edges. The piece of chicken is placed in the soup and the piece of kid rests atop the *pepián de cancha*. All are well flavored with *ají*, onions, salt, black pepper, *culantro, azafrán,* etc. It is the management of the seasoning which distinguishes an expert Moche cook from an ordinary one.

Chicha

Chicha may be made from a variety of grains or kernels, other than maize, e. g., peanuts, barley, wheat, etc. In Moche it is always made of maize, although sometimes wheat grains are mixed with the maize. It is boiled directly over the fire either in large 50-gallon oil drums or in earthenware pots. In Monsefú (near Chiclayo) a *chicha*-making arrangement was observed which consisted of four large pots set into the ground close together but at the four points of a small rectangle. The earth was tamped well up around their outer sides, while a fire was placed in the center and blown with a fan so as to circulate between the pots. This pattern is said to have been used in former times in Moche, but

has now completely disappeared. The following is a standard recipe.

1. Prepare the mass of sprouted maize (*chuño de maíz nacido*). Mature maize kernels are laid out on a damp cloth, usually gunny sacking, in a shaded place. Then they are covered with moist leaves or with a second damp cloth. The kernels are sufficiently sprouted in 6 to 8 days.
p. Make the *jora* (*chuño* with water), placing the *chuño* in the boiler, then adding water.
3. Boil for 24 hours or longer, up to 48 hours. At one house where the writer observed the process, the *jora* was being boiled in a 50-gallon oil drum over a cow-dung fire. The woman in charge said that the *chuño* involved in this batch amounted to 1½ arrobas (37.5 lbs.) and that she expected to get "slightly less" than two *botijas* (200 bottles) of drinkable *chicha* after discarding the dregs. During the boiling a plentiful scum accumulated on the surface and was flicked off with a rough branch from time to time. During the boiling process more water is added to compensate for that lost by evaporation.
4. Allow to cool.
5. Strain the *jora* through cotton cloth and/or a basket into the *botija* or other container.
6. Add *chancaca* (a type of brown sugar in cakes), sirup, molasses, or cane juice. *Chancaca* is most frequently used, and the amount depends upon the experience of the maker. Up to a point, the more sugar used, the more alcohol will result.
7. Allow to stand 4 to 6 days until it has finished "working." Chicha made in this way will last about a month without turning to vinegar.

"HOT" AND "COLD" FOODS

All foods are classified as hot (*caliente*) and cold or cool (*fresco*). The classification seems to an outsider to have nothing to do with the physical properties of the foods themselves or the physical state they happen to be in at the moment, i. e., cooked or uncooked, just off the fire or standing cold, etc. In Moche the classification seems to be based upon obscure beliefs concerning the effects which the various foods have upon the human organism in certain states of illness or uneasy physiological equilibrium. Beliefs concerning illness will be discussed extensively in a later section, but, among others, there are two types of sickness in the view of the Mocheros: (1) the illnesses which produce a cold feeling (including colds themselves, *resfríos, catarros, constipados,* etc.); and (2) the illnesses which produce a hot feeling (fever). If one is suffering from or is susceptible to a "hot" sickness, he should avoid "hot" foods, and vice versa.

Common people are not always sure where a given item is classified and seek the advice of *curanderos* (healers) and old women in general, when in doubt.

The matter is not an obsession with the ordinary man or woman, unless he is feeling ill.

There may well be a magical background for this belief, something embedded in the matrix of curative magic. If so, it is my notion that the magical interpretations have been lost. As we shall see later, the corpus of curative magic is not a completely organized and consistent whole. It either represents a collection of incompletely assimilated accretions from various sources, or an older system now broken into a number of more or less unhinged parts, or perhaps it is both. At any rate, I was able to unearth no hints of deeper meanings in the question of the food classification, although, as with all other aspects of this report, I would be the first to grant that the period of field work was insufficient to be certain.

When one is well there is no harm in mixing "hot" and "cold" foods in the same meal, but this is believed to be dangerous when the individual is ill.

There follows a partial listing of foods in each category, upon which four supposedly authoritative informants agreed. The informants consisted of a professional curing woman (*curandera* or *curiosa*, not a witch or *bruja*), a family matriarch, and two men in their forties. None of these persons are recognized relatives or close friends. Various other food items which I tried to check produced disagreement or uncertainty.

COLD FOODS

Carnero (mutton).
Pescado (fish in general).
Corbina (a large sea fish).
Mishito (another type of fish).
Cangrejos (crabs).
Maíz (maize).
Arroz (rice).
Papa (potato).
Tomate (tomato).
Chocolate (chocolate, cocoa).
Té (tea, but not including tea made from *yerba luiza*).
Mantequilla (butter).
Pan (bread).
Azucar (sugar, in all forms).
Dulces (sweets, candies).
Conservas (jellies, canned fruit).
Queso (cheese).
Leche (milk).
Palta (alligator pear).
Guanábano (a native fruit).
Carne de chancho (pork).
Frijol panamito (small beans).
Cebada (barley; because barley is "cold," so is beer).
Cerveza (beer).
Cola (bottled soft drinks).

Plátano de la isla (a bland plantain).
Trigo (wheat).
Quaker (rolled oats).
Avena (oats).
Choclo (green corn on cob).

HOT FOODS

Canela (cinnamon).
Yerba luiza (a common herb for tea).
Frijoles corrientes (most of the common beans).
Naranja (orange, but especially the peel, *cáscara*).
Carne de res (beef).
Carne de gallina o pollo (chicken meat).
Cabrito (kid).
Pavo (turkey).
Camote (sweetpotato).
Limón (lemon, lime).
Sal (salt).
Ají (red and yellow peppers).
Café (coffee).
Pisco (native Peruvian brandy).
Cañaso (drinking alcohol of sugarcane).
Coca (sometimes made into tea).
Mango (a fruit).
Cuy (flesh of the guinea pig).
Plátano (banana, except the variety called *"de la isla"*).
Garbanzos (chickpeas).
Vino (wine).
Chicha.

STATISTICAL STUDY OF FOODS CONSUMED

In an attempt to obtain a more objective idea of foods actually eaten throughout a typical day than could be obtained from a merely impressionistic account and also in order to discover whether or not there were actual differences in the diets or menus of Mocheros as distinguished from *forasteros,* the help of the local public schools was enlisted. A survey was made during three successive week days of the first week of July 1944 during which there were no fiestas or general celebrations. The method followed was similar to that employed in a Guatemalan town in 1942.[42] Through the kind cooperation of Señor Rafael Casteñada, director of the Government-supported boys' school, the Señorita, directress of the Government-supported girls' school, and their associated teachers, a contest was carried out in both institutions on the same 3 days. The contest was explained to the students as one in observation, composition, and penmanship. The students were instructed to write an essay each day on the subject, "What I ate yesterday" (*Lo que comí ayer*). They were to

---

[49] Gillin, 1943, vol. 1, particularly pp. 352–359. The similarity in method does not imply detailed similarity in the two situations of San Luis Jilotepeque (Guatemala) and Moche (Peru).

describe each meal of the day before, listing specifically all types of food consumed, with quantities of each in conventional terms (spoonfuls, cupfuls, pieces of conventional size, etc.). At the head of each paper the student was required to state his name, age, place of birth, sex, school year, and "Mochero" or *forastero.*" Care was taken in issuing instructions to the students to avoid any suggestion that our primary interest was the diet as such, and to avoid implications of invidious comparisons or prestige values which might be involved. The contest was open to all members of the third, fourth, fifth, and sixth years in both schools. Four prizes were offered in each school and a consolation award of 10 centavos for each pupil who turned in his three essays in complete form eligible for the prizes, whether he won a prize or not. The teachers examined the papers and excluded those which were incomplete. They also graded them according to the scholastic objectives set forth for the contest, and the prizes were awarded on that basis. The whole idea was to obtain a naive report from the pupils themselves.

After the returns were in, the papers were turned over to me, and I checked all doubtful cases for their social status, i. e., Mochero or *forastero.* Then, with considerable labor the results which appear in tables 4, 5, and 6 were tabulated. (Anyone who believes that Spanish cannot be misspelled should try reading a collection of school children's papers sometime.) The material was also tabulated by sex, but since the differences between the sexes on the whole did not appear to be highly significant in either group, these tables were omitted. Once the material had been tabulated, the results were used for further checking against observations of food habits, and results of these checks appear in the descriptive section on food and drink.

A similar attempt was made to obtain the same type of data for the *campiña* by instituting a contest in the rural school at Sun, but the director of this school reported that he was unable to secure the cooperation of the pupils on the project. Whatever the difficulty, I was unable to press the matter under the circumstances and with the time available, so it is necessary to confine my analysis to the *pueblo* data.

A detailed discussion will not be attempted, but for those who enjoy the juice which can be squeezed from "statistics" the following drops are offered. The usual warning should be issued to the reader, that is, not to be too impressed with the appearance of precision conveyed by numerals and percentages

set in columns. Very small values, in particular, have no statistical validity as such, but they are included to complete the record and they also serve the purpose of showing the range of variety in the menus. Several other cautions and explanations should be mentioned. (1) Although it is not customary for children to drink *chicha* for all thirst-quenching purposes as do adults, checking showed that a good many children had consumed *chicha* during the period of survey, but had omitted to include it in their essays because the hygiene lectures by the teachers had taught them that *chicha* drinking is considered officially undesirable. (2) Although only the specific reports concerning seasoning items, such as onions, have been recorded, it will be noted that no students specifically reported *aji*, salt, black pepper, and the whole range of *picante* seasonings. Checking showed that invariably the cooked food had been prepared and eaten with *picante*, but that it never occurred to the pupils to consider seasoning "food." For this reason, there is no worthwhile statistical comparison of the seasoning of the dishes consumed between Mocheros and *forasteros.* (3) The same is true in some degree of sugar. Warm drinks, such as tea and coffee, are normally drunk with sugar, but it did not occur to the students as a whole that this was to be considered a separate item. The sugar which was recorded was specifically mentioned by the students, but checking showed that many more had used sugar. (4) It must be remembered that the food consumed during 3 days in July will not necessarily conform in all details to that consumed during some other period of 3 days. The actual details depend to some extent upon what is available in the markets during the period in question. Thus, beef was plentifully available at this particular time and mutton was not, so the low figures for mutton are not as significant actually as they might appear to be statistically. Nevertheless, some kind of meat or fish is eaten every day, and this is the important fact when considering the food patterns. (5) It is for this reason that, although the items themselves are those written down by the students, I have grouped them roughly into categories: beverages, soups, meat, fish, cheese and eggs (animal proteins), vegetables and grains, fruits, sweets, and miscellaneous. These categories cannot be defended in strict terms from the point of view of the science of nutrition, but rather conform to the local ways of grouping food and talking about it. "Tea" includes both herb tea and true commercial tea. Individual checking showed that it is probable that proportionately more *forastero* households use commercial tea, but the majority use herb tea because of taste and price. (6) It should be borne in mind that I have no control of the accuracy of these reports, other than that obtained by the usual ethnological techniques of interview and recheck with informants. Therefore, I have attempted no elaborate statistical manipulation of the data, have not reduced them to constants, other than percentages, and have not employed the standard statistical measures of error. (7) Finally, no attempt has been. made to measure or tabulate quantities of food consumed, either in bulk terms or in terms of nutritional values. Although the subjects were asked to state quantities in their reports, this was for the purpose of focusing their attention upon the food objects themselves, and they stated the quantities in unstandardized conventional terms.

The purpose, in short, was to broaden the base of the usual impressionistic ethnological report. Some quantitative guide to the differences in patterns and trends in food preferences as between the Mochero and *forastero* groups was needed, and the procedure used was the best that seemed available under the circumstances. A more accurate statistical study of these cultural phases of the food problem, as well as of nutritional phases, could certainly be obtained in Moche if one had the time to pursue such questions exclusively for a period of months.

Except for the fact that children do not drink *chicha* as much as adults, and that children do drink milk, which adults disdain, the differences between the meals of school children and their parents are negligible. The three main meals, *desayuno* (breakfast), *almuerzo* (midday meal), and *comida* (evening meal) are eaten in the same house and "from the same pot" as the parents' food, and there is no pattern of preparing separate diets for the children of the age range of our subjects. The after-school lunch (*lonche*), on the other hand, may involve a few centavos' worth of sweets or bread purchased at a shop on the way home from school, a feature which would not appear in the adult menu of the day. Except for *lonche*, then, we may consider these reports as reflecting the menus of adults as well as children.

If the limitations of the tabulations have been sufficiently well set forth, we may proceed to consider briefly a few points of significance which seem to emerge from the material.

The total sample consists of 111 pupils, of whom 83, or 74.8 percent, were Mocheros and 28, or 25.2 percent, were *forasteros*. In the Mochero group, 59 were boys and 24 were girls; among the *forasteros*, 18 were boys and 10 were girls. The age range was 8 to 16. Altogether, the reports covered 789 separate meals of Mocheros and 305 separate meals of *forasteros* over a period of 3 days.

Summing up all of the items of food consumed which were reported for all of these meals, we find that the Mocheros consumed 2,451 items and the *forasteros* 1,171. It thus appears that the *forasteros* had more variety in their menus, for they had an average of 3.83 items per meal in comparison with the Mocheros' 3.10 items, or 23.5 percent more variety.

Now let us consider the incidence of food items, grouped into broad categories. In table 6, columns 1 and 4 show the absolute frequency of food items by category, for Mocheros and *forasteros*, respectively. In columns 2 and 5 these frequencies are expressed as percentages of the total number of meals. Thus, for example, the Mocheros reported 789 meals, and therefore had that many opportunities to report items from any one of the categories, but actually only 51.8 percent of the meals contained beverages, according to the reports, whereas in the case of the *forasteros* 82.6 percent of the meals reported contained beverages. If we divide 51.8 into 82.6, we obtain 1.556. On this basis, then, *forastero* meals contain beverages 55.6 percent more frequently than Mochero meals. In fact, the *forasteros* lead in all categories except meat and fish. They have 27.4 percent more soups per meal, 16.9 percent more vegetables and grains, 115.9 percent more fruits, 115.9 percent more sweets, and 119.0 percent more miscellaneous dishes. The Mocheros, on the other hand, enjoy 22.1 percent more meats per meal than the *forasteros*. Although the *forasteros* seem to have greater variety of foods *per meal,* they do trail slightly in the total number of distinguishable menu items reported. Thus a count of the items in tables 4 and 5 respectively demonstrates that the total *forastero* group reported 65 different menu items, whereas the Mocheros reported 69. The total range is governed by availability in market, garden, and field, and is about equal for both groups. The significant difference lies in the fact that the average *forastero* meal presents more types of food on the table or in the plate, than does the average Mochero meal. Also, the chances of a food item from a given category turning up in a given meal are better for the *forasteros* in all categories except meat and fish.

Let us now turn to the over-all preferences of Mochero as compared with *forastero* menus. In table 6, columns 3 and 6, respectively, will be found the absolute frequencies of columns 1 and 4, respectively, expressed as percentages of the total number of food items appearing in the reports of each group, respectively. For example, the absolute number of beverages consumed by Mocheros was reported as 409, out of a total of 2,451 menu items reported. In column 3, we see that beverages constituted 16.6 percent of all items reported. Thus we have an indication of the proportions in which foods of various categories appear in the over-all food consumption. It appears at once that the Mochero menus are more concentrated in the two categories of meat, fish, etc., and vegetables and grains. The two social groups are about equal in their liking for soups, whereas the *forasteros* prefer proportionately more beverages, fruits, sweets, and miscellaneous dishes. If we lump together the two categories of meat, fish, etc., and vegetables and grains, we find that 68.3 percent of the diet of the Mocheros and only 58.0 percent of the diet of the *forasteros* fall into these two categories; or, in other words, the Mochero diet is 15.9 percent more concentrated in these two categories. On the other hand the *forasteros* lead the Mocheros in beverages by 29.4 percent, in fruits by 71.4 percent, in sweets by 60 percent, and in miscellaneous dishes by 81.8 percent.

Thus we see that not only is the average *forastero* meal richer in variety but also the over-all diet shows less proportionate concentration on staple food categories. The slight place taken by fruit in the diet is in part explained by the fact that the survey took place in July, early winter, at which season little local fruit is available. Even so, appreciably more fruit was consumed on *forastero* tables in proportion to their numbers.

We may mention a few differences indicated by scanning the individual items in tables 4 and 5. Milk, for example, is a much more important drink among the *forasteros* than among Mocheros. It appears 63 percent of the time among them for breakfast and appears in only 35.3 percent of the Mochero breakfasts. Coffee as a breakfast drink appears nearly twice as often on *forastero* tables as on those of Mocheros (33.3 percent and 17.2 percent), whereas "tea" is twice as popular among Mocheros as among *forasteros* (34.5 percent and 16.6 percent, respectively). Fish is much more popular among Mocheros

than among *forasteros*. It appears in one form or another in 21.2 percent of the Mochero midday meals (compared with 11.9 percent for *forasteros*) and in 18 percent of their evening meals (compared with 5.6 percent for *forasteros*). Both groups like other meats about equally well.

Rice is the most popular starchy vegetable food for both groups, being preferred slightly more often by *forasteros*. Potatoes, although much less important than rice for both groups, are much more popular among *forasteros*. Mocheros, on the other hand, show much more fondness for yuca than do *forasteros*. Modern innovations, like rolled oats and prepared cornstarch, play little part in the diet of either group, but appear twice as often among *forasteros* as among Mocheros. Both groups are well converted to bread for breakfast and afternoon lunch. Greens are several times more popular among *forasteros*, who also show much more interest in almost all the green vegetables.

Dessert of sweets or fruit is seen not to be a standard feature of either Mochero or *forastero* meals, although items from both categories are consumed proportionately more frequently by *forasteros*.

"*Lonche*" in the afternoon is a more firmly established custom among *forasteros* than among Mocheros. Among the *forasteros* 74.9 of the children reported had *lonche* at least once during the 3 days in question, whereas only 28.9 of the Mochero children so reported. This snack meal was taken on the average 63 percent as often as other meals by the *forasteros*, only 16.8 percent as often by Mocheros.

The outstanding differences between Mocheros and *forasteros* as indicated by the data may be summarized as follows:

1. The *forasteros* enjoy more variety of foods per average meal than the Mocheros.

2. The total diet of the *forasteros* tends to show more diversification and less concentration in a few categories.

3. In respect to specific items or categories of food, among the beverages *forasteros* show preference for milk and coffee, whereas the Mocheros prefer herb tea. Mocheros eat proportionately more fish than *forasteros*. Both groups like rice, but *forasteros* prefer potatoes, among the other starchy vegetables, whereas the Mocheros prefer yuca. *Forasteros* eat more sweets and fruits than Mocheros.

4. No major menu item of one group is tabooed by the other group, and the differences noted are

statistical preferences or trends of taste, rather than exclusive preferences reflecting rigid patterns of custom.

The *forasteros* may be considered as representing a broader and more varied cultural background than the Mocheros. The *forasteros* are carriers of the so-called *criollo* culture, the general culture of Peru, which is a composite of highland, jungle, and coastal aboriginal elements, compounded with colonial Spanish, modern European, and North American patterns. If these people show somewhat more catholicity in their eating habits than the relatively conservative Mocheros, it is not surprising. It also will not be surprising to see the Mocheros trend gradually toward *criollo* patterns in food as well as in other aspects of their culture, as time goes by.

TABLE 4.—*Foods, classified by meal, category, and menu item, reported as consumed by Mocheros of both sexes for a 3-day period*

Individuals, meals, and menu items	Desayuno (breakfast)		Almuerzo (midday meal)		Lonche (lunch)		Comida (evening meal)		Total or average
	No.	Pct.	No.	Pct.	No.	Pct.	No.	Pct.	No.
Individuals reporting	83	100	83	100	24	28.9	83	100	83
Meals reported	249	100	249	100	42	16.9	249	100	789
Menu items consumed:									
Beverages:									
Café (coffee)	43	17.2	1	.4	6	14.2	1	.4	....
Té (tea)	86	34.5	6	2.4	10	23.8	42	16.8	....
Leche (milk)	88	35.3	....	....	4	9.5	1	.4	....
Chocolate (cocoa)	56	22.4	....	....	1	2.3	3	1.2	....
Chicha	....	....	2	.8	....	....	2	.8	....
Limonada (lemonade)	....	....	3	1.2	....	....	1	.8	....
Agua (water)	23	9.2	15	6.0	....	....	2	1.2	....
Agua de cebada (barley water)	12	4.8	1	.4	....	....	....	....	....
Total	308	123.6	28	11.2	21	50.0	52	20.8	409
Soups:									
Sopa (vegetable soup)	....	....	37	14.8	....	....	58	23.2	....
Caldo (meat soup)	....	....	108	43.3	....	....	25	10.0	....
Total	....	....	145	58.2	....	....	83	33.3	228
Meat, fish, eggs, cheese:									
Carne (meat, unspecified)	4	1.6	115	46.1	2	4.7	118	47.3	....
Carne de res (beef)	....	....	25	10.0	....	....	11	4.4	....
Carne de chancho	2	1.2	4	1.6	....	....	10	4.0	....
Lomo (beefsteak)	6	2.4	....	....	....	....	6	2.4	....
Carnero (mutton)	....	....	4	1.6	....	....	5	2.0	....
Mondongo (intestines)	....	....	6	2.4	....	....	3	1.2	....
Cabrito (kid)	....	....	1	.4	....	....	....	....	....
Pollo (chicken)	....	....	1	.4	....	....	1	.4	....
Pescado (fish, unspecified)	....	....	41	16.4	....	....	38	15.2	....
Marisco (shrimp, crab)	....	....	1	.4	....	....	....	....	....
Cangrejo (crab)	....	....	2	.8	....	....	1	.4	....
Corvina (a fish name)	....	....	2	.8	....	....	1	.4	....
Seviche (raw fish preparation)	....	....	7	2.8	1	2.3	2	.8	....
Huevo (egg)	2	.8	1	.4	19	45.2	3	1.2	....
Queso (cheese)	2	.8	....	....	....	....	....	....	....
Total	12	6.8	210	84.3	23	53.7	199	79.9	449
Vegetables and grains:									
Pan (bread)	236	94.7	6	2.4	19	45.2	10	4.0	....
Biscocho (biscuit)	4	1.6	....	....	4	9.5	2	.8	....
Rosca (sweet bread twist)	2	.8	....	....	1	2.3	2	.8	....
Trigo (cracked wheat)	....	....	1	.4	1	2.3	1	.4	....
Arroz (rice)	....	....	208	83.4	....	....	225	90.3	....
Quaker (rolled oats)	4	1.6	....	....	....	....	....	....	....
Maizena (cornstarch)	1	.8	....	....	....	....	....	....	....
Cereales (mixed cereals)	....	....	3	1.2	....	....	....	....	....
Chochoca (corn-meal mush)	....	....	3	1.2	....	....	6	2.4	....
Tallarines (noodles)	....	....	8	3.2	....	....	1	.4	....
Fideos (vermicelli)	....	....	....	....	....	....	35	14.0	....
Papas (potatoes)	....	....	5	2.0	....	....	4	1.6	....
Garbanzos (chickpeas)	....	....	24	9.6	....	....	19	7.6	....
Alverjas (vetches)	....	....	3	1.2	....	....	52	30.8	....
Frijoles (kidney beans)	....	....	37	14.8	....	....	10	4.0	....
Lantejas (lentils)	....	....	14	5.6	....	....	3	1.2	....
Pallares (large beans)	....	....	17	6.8	....	....	....	....	....
Olluco	....	....	3	1.2	....	....	14	5.6	....
Zanahorias (carrots)	....	....	6	2.4	....	....	1	.4	....
Repollo (cabbage)	....	....	5	2.0	....	....	3	1.2	....
Zapallo (squash)	....	....	14	5.6	....	....	21	8.4	....
Caigua	....	....	....	....	....	....	2	.8	....
Camotes	....	....	9	3.6	....	....	6	2.4	....
Frijol verde (green beans)	....	....	1	.4	....	....	1	.4	....
Lechuga (lettuce)	....	....	1	.4	....	....	....	....	....
Verduras (greens)	....	....	26	10.4	....	....	1	.4	....
Yuca	3	1.2	92	36.9	2	4.7	28	11.2	....
Choclo (corn on cob)	....	....	4	7.6	....	....	4	1.6	....

TABLE 4.—*Foods classified by meal, category, and menu item, reported as consumed by Mocheros of both sexes for a 3-day period*—Continued

Individuals, meals, and menu items	Desayuno (breakfast)		Almuerzo (midday meal)		Lonche (lunch)		Comida (evening meal)		Total or average
	No.	Pct.	No.	Pct.	No.	Pct.	No.	Pct.	No.
Cebolla (onion)			5	2.0			7	2.8	
Mote (green corn kernels)							1	.4	
Total	250	100.3	495	198.7	28	66.6	453	181.9	1,226
Fruits:									
Plátano (banana)	3	1.2	4	1.6	10	23.8			
Naranja (orange)	3	1.2	3	1.2	3	7.4	1	.4	
Chirimoya			3	1.2					
Sandía (watermelon)			1	.4					
Granadilla					1	2.3			
Fruta (fruit, unspecified)			1	.4	2	4.7			
Total	6	2.4	12	4.8	16	38.0	1	.4	35
Sweets:									
Dulce (dessert, unspecified)					5	11.9	1	.4	
Chocolates (chocolate candy)							1	.4	
Azucre (sugar)	25	10.0					5	2.0	
Total	25	10.0			5	11.9	7	2.8	37
Miscellaneous:									
Aceitunas (olives)	10	4.8							
Maní (peanuts)	8	3.2					1	.4	
Mantequilla (butter)	15	6.0			2	4.7	1	.4	
Manteca (lard)			1	.4			1	.4	
Sancochado	1	.4	24	9.6			3	1.2	
Total	34	13.6	25	10.0	2	4.7	6	2.4	67
Grand total									2,451
Average per meal									3.10

TABLE 5.—*Foods, classified by meal, category, and menu item, reported as consumed by forasteros of both sexes for a 3-day period*

Individuals, meals, and menu items	Desayuno (breakfast)		Almuerzo (midday meal)		Lonche (lunch)		Comida (evening meal)		Total or average
	No.	Pct.	No.	Pct.	No.	Pct.	No.	Pct.	No.
Individuals reporting	28	100	28	100	21	74.9	28	100	28
Meals reported	84	100	84	100	53	63.0	84	100	305
Menu items consumed:									
Beverages:									
Café (coffee)	28	33.3	3	3.5	17	32.0	6	7.1	
Té (tea)	14	16.6	8	9.5	15	28.9	22	26.1	
Leche (milk)	53	63.0	3	3.5	14	26.4	4	4.7	
Chocolate (cocoa)	25	29.7			3	5.6	3	3.5	
Soda (soda water, soft drinks)			1	1.1			1	1.1	
Limonada (lemonade)									
Agua (water)	12	14.2	7	8.3	7	13.2	4	4.7	
Agua de cebada (barley water)			1	1.8			1	1.1	
Total	132	157.1	23	27.3	56	105.6	41	48.8	252
Soups:									
Sopa (vegetable soup)			15	17.8			45		
Caldo (meat soup)			41	48.8			11	13.0	
Total			56	66.6			56	66.6	112
Meat, fish, eggs, and cheese:									
Carne (meat, unspecified)	2	2.3	38	45.2			36	42.8	
Carne de res (beef)			4	4.7					
Carne de chancho	1	1.1							
Lomo (beefsteak)	1	1.1	8	9.5			9	10.7	
Mondongo (intestines)							2	2.3	
Cabrito (kid)			3	3.5			2	2.3	
Pollo (chicken)			2	2.3					
Pescado (fish, unspecified)	2	2.3	5	5.9	3	5.6	3	3.5	
Seviche (raw fish preparation)			5	5.9					
Huevo (egg)	1	1.1	1	1.1			5	5.9	
Queso (cheese)	3	5.6			1	1.8	1	1.1	
Total	10	11.9	66	78.5	4	7.5	58	69.0	138
Vegetables and grains:									
Pan (bread)	82	97.6	3	3.5	41	48.8	16		
Biscocho (biscuit)					1	1.8	1	1.1	
Rosca (sweet bread twist)	2	2.3					1	1.1	
Trigo (cracked wheat)			1	1.1	1	1.8			
Arroz (rice)	1	1.1	78	92.8			75	89.2	
Quaker (rolled oats)	7	8.3			1	1.8	2	2.3	
Maizena (cornstarch)			2	2.3					
Cereales (mixed cereals)									
Chochoca (corn-meal mush)			2	2.3	5	9.4	1	1.1	

TABLE 5.—*Foods, classified by meal, category, and menu item, reported as consumed by forasteros of both sexes for a 3-day period*—Continued

Individuals, meals, and menu items	Desayuno (breakfast) No.	Pct.	Almuerzo (midday meal) No.	Pct.	Lonche (lunch) No.	Pct.	Comida (evening meal) No.	Pct.	Total or average No.
Tallarines (noodles)			3	3.5	1	1.8	5	5.9	
Fideos (vermicelli)			12	14.2			21	25.0	
Papas (potatoes)			14	16.6			9	10.7	
Garbanzos (chickpeas)			2	2.3			5	5.9	
Alverjas (vetches)			8	9.5			7	8.3	
Frijoles (kidney beans)			13	15.4			15	17.8	
Lentejas (lentils)			5	5.9			8	9.5	
Habas (broadbeans)			2	2.3					
Olluco			9	10.7			3	3.5	
Zanahorias (carrots)			9	10.7			3	3.5	
Repollo (cabbage)			4	4.7			1	1.1	
Zapallo (squash)			3	3.5					
Caigua			4	4.7					
Camote (sweetpotato)			4	4.7			1	1.1	
Frijol verde (green beans)							2	2.3	
Lechuga (lettuce)			1	1.1			1	1.1	
Verduras (greens)			21	25.0			5	5.9	
Yuca			24	28.5			3	3.5	
Choclo (corn on cob)							1	1.1	
Cebolla (onion)			7	8.3			5	5.9	
Tomate (tomato)							2	2.3	
Espinaca (spinach)							1	1.1	
Total	92	109.5	231	275.0	50	59.5	181	215.4	554
Fruits:									
Plátano (banana)			8	9.5	9	17.0	1	1.1	
Naranja (orange)			6	7.1	2	3.7			
Granadilla			2	2.3					
Palta (alligator pear)			1	1.1					
Fruta (fruit, unspecified)			1	1.1					
Total			17	20.2	11	20.7	1	1.1	29
Sweets:									
Dulce (dessert, unspecified)					1	1.8			
Azucre (sugar)	19	22.6			7	13.2	2	2.3	
Total	19	22.6	17	20.2	8	15.0	2	2.3	29
Miscellaneous:									
Aceitunas (olives)	13	15.3	1	1.1	1	1.8			
Maní (peanuts)	2	2.3					1	1.1	
Mantequilla (butter)	8	9.5			1	1.8			
Manteca (lard)	1	1.1	2	2.3	1	1.8	4	4.7	
Sancochado			18	21.4			1	1.1	
Sandwiches	2	2.3			1	1.8			
Total	26	30.9	21	25.0	4	7.5	6	7.1	57
Grand total									1,171
Average per meal									3.83

TABLE 6.—*Comparison of Mocheros and Foresteros by food categories*

Category	Mocheros			Forasteros		
	1	2	3	4	5	6
	Number	Percentage of total meals	Percentage of total menu items	Number	Percentage of total meals	Percentage of total menu items
Total meals reported	789	100.0		305	100.0	
Total menu items reported	2,451		100.0	1,171		100.0
Ratio between totals	3.10			3.83		
Beverages	409	51.8	16.6	252	82.6	21.5
Soups	228	28.8	9.3	112	36.7	9.7
Meats, etc.	449	56.9	18.3	138	45.2	11.7
Vegetables, etc.	1,226	155.3	50.0	554	181.6	47.3
Fruits, etc.	35	4.4	1.4	29	9.5	2.4
Sweets, etc.	37	4.4	1.5	29	9.5	2.4
Miscellaneous	67	8.5	2.7	57	18.6	4.8

DRESS AND ORNAMENT

Although the costume of the men of Moche might excite some mild interest on Fifth Avenue, it is essentially "modern" in all details (except for the fact that men prefer to go barefoot) and so far as I can see is of the general pattern in use for males throughout the Peruvian coastal region. The costume and ornament of women, on the other hand, does not on the whole conform to modern modes, and until fairly recently the majority of women wore garments which clearly set them apart from cholo women of Trujillo and other cities of the coast. The use of one-piece gingham dresses and other changes are creeping into the women's costume, however, and it is doubtful how long the "picturesqueness" which still lingers will last.

It is unnecessary to describe male dress in detail. A study of the photographs will be sufficient for the curious reader. Suffice it to say that the general pattern is a pair of under shorts and under singlet, a collar-attached shirt without necktie, conventional trousers reaching to the ankles, and a jacket of conventional modern design with two buttons and lapels. This combination is completed at the nether end with bare feet or sandals (llanquis) and at the upper end by a high-crowned straw hat with broad rolled-up brim. Some men omit one or the other or both of the undergarments. The long trousers and jacket are usually made of white or light-colored drill or other cotton material, although a very few men have woolen suits. A certain variety is to be seen in cut and material; lightweight jerseys sometimes take the place of shirts; an occasional man wears overalls with bib instead of trousers held up with a belt; etc. Most trousers are held up by leather belts of European type or rope. Some men wear sashes. When working about his farm a man often appears in rags of his former good clothes, but everyone has an outfit in which to "dress up" for fiestas and on Sundays. Some men also have a pair of shoes which are used for extremely formal occasions, and this is true of all the young Mocheros who go to Trujillo to the university or to high school (colegio). Only the latter, among Mocheros netos, have felt hats, and they practically never wear them in Moche. The felt hat is the class mark of the forastero or cholo man in the Moche community. Overcoats are unknown in Moche, so far as I am aware. Some men have ponchos made in the Sierra, but the use of ponchos is not universal or typical.

The remarkable feature of the men's dress in Moche is its lack of protection from the cold during the winter months. Nights and cold dreary mornings during June, July, and August are distinctly uncomfortable without woolen clothing, and during this season many of the natives of Trujillo wear woolen suits and topcoats. The "palm beach" garments of the Mocheros are ill adapted to the cool season, and this is the more curious in view of the fact that their women's older costume includes woolen skirt and shawl.

Men's garments are made by tailors, of which there were two leading ones and four secondary ones in the community during my stay. They use both hand needles and machines. Their methods were not studied, but it was understood that they are typical of those followed throughout the country. One Mochero has a tailor shop in Trujillo and lives there.

Women's costumes may be roughly classified into three general types: (1) The old costume (vestido antiguo), (2) the modified costume, and (3) the cotton-dress costume. The terms for the second two are my own. The three are illustrated in plates 15 and 16.

The old costume (pls. 15, lower (right and left); 16, lower (right)) is habitually worn at present by only a handful of older and more conservative women. It is said to have been universal up to 1912. In this year a certain chief of police is said to have collected all the women in the market during an epidemic of bubonic plague. He ordered them to strip off their old costumes, which were burned. The women had to reclothe themselves with cotton cloth because of inability to replace the old quickly. This, at least, is the local explanation of the loss of the old costume. It consists of one or more white cotton petticoats as undergarments, a dark-blue coarse woolen (bayeta) wrap-around skirt with the split in front, held up by a woven woolen belt with red and blue woven designs. The upper body is covered by a white blouse with a wide neck, either square or rounded in cut, and with short sleeves ending 2 to 4 inches above the elbow; the blouse is made with a "yoke" over the shoulders and is shirred below the yoke; it is worn tucked into the belt which supports the skirt. Over the blouse, when the temperature is low, a blue shawl of the same type of dark-blue bayeta material as the skirt is worn. This is called a rebozo. Rebozos vary in size, but a convenient measurement is 8 feet in length and about 36 inches in breadth. One end is placed over the right shoulder; the *rebozo* is drawn across the front of the chest over the left shoulder around the back, over the right shoulder and chest again, and the loose end is finally thrown over the left shoulder to hang down in back (pls. 15, *lower* (*right*); 16, *lower* (*right*)).

The essential features of the "modified costume" (pl. 15, *upper* (*right*) and *lower* (*center*)) consist of a skirt, sometimes of *bayeta* but more often of cotton, attached to a sewn-on tapelike belt with loose ends which can be tied in back. The skirt is a complete tube, except for a slit over the hips at one side, which enables the wearer to step into it. Over this skirt is worn a waist. These waists differ among themselves as regards the details of decoration, but they all show the following basic features which set this garment off from the blouse of the old costume: they have high neck lines, the sleeves extend *below* the elbow, and the lower border of the waist hangs outside over the skirt. I do not know the technical dress-making term for this type of waist, but those who do can doubtless identify it from the photographs.

The cotton-dress costume is very simple. It consists of a single garment of printed cotton cloth. A variety of details occur, but the basic model of 1944 had a waistline effect, that is, consisted of a skirt and bodice sewed together, rather than a simple tubelike or sacklike effect. Although the other two types of costumes usually feature skirts modestly near the ankles, the cotton dress often shows a higher hemline.

Young ladies of marriageable age in 1944 appeared in all three of these types of costumes, but they also seemed to have a considerable variety of "modish" dresses (in Trujillo terms) whose patterns had been derived ultimately from North America and Europe. I am incompetent to discuss how far these creations lag behind the current modes of New York, Buenos Aires, or other accepted style centers. Here is a thesis project for a lady Ph. D. candidate. (See pl. 16, *lower* (*left*), for a picture of the leading "younger set.")

Women almost always appear barefoot, even when going into the city for marketing purposes and in church, although the more advanced young women have shoes of modern style (pl. 16, *lower* (*left*)). The woman's hat is also of straw and follows a single pattern. It has a proportionately higher crown than the

man's hat and a narrower brim, which is turned down rather than being rolled up as in its masculine counterpart. A fringed shawl of wool or wool and cotton, made in a factory, replaces the *rebozo* with most women. This is a feature of cholo feminine dress throughout Peru.

A majority of the women seem to know how to sew, but only a minority have sewing machines. It was surprising, however, to run across a large number of women who did not know sewing, other than the simplest patching. The general tendency is to have women's dresses and blouses made by specialist dressmakers (*cosereras*). There are 17 of these specialists who have been identified to me, and there may well be more. In at least one household two sewing machines are operated and the men of the family do not disdain to make women's dresses. An unspecialized housewife will make her own or children's clothes for economic reasons, but sewing is not a general female occupation. One does not see the women of the house sitting about with their needlework as a common thing.

No weaving of textiles is practiced at present (with one doubtful exception) and the *bayeta* used in the old costume is purchased from traveling merchants or in the market in Trujillo or other centers. It is all hand-woven by the natives of the Sierra. The woven belts are hand-made in the Sierra and in Monsefú. The straw hats come from the region of Chiclayo, where the neighboring towns of Monsefú and Lambayeque are highly renowned for their hatmakers; another source of supply is Celendín, in the highlands northeast of Cajamarca. They are made from the fibers of a palm leaf imported from the jungle areas of the Marañón. In Celendín, bundles of this leaf fiber were selling in 1944 at 1.5 to 2 soles. In 1944 a single Mochero had recently started in business as a hat maker and was selling his product in the community.

Sandals are worn by men when doing heavy work, traveling over rough ground, or when they happen to have them. Many men have none at all. The material for the sole is either untanned hide with hair removed or automobile tire casing. The sandal tie is shown in the sketch in figure 5. It is common to the coastal region of Peru. Although it is said that women occasionally wear sandals of this type, it is apparently very rare, for I did not observe a woman so shod in 5½ months' contact with the community. Apparently no kind of sandal was worn by the Mochicas. The sandal first appears in Chimu horizons. Neither the Chimu nor the Inca sandals used the tie that is in use in Moche today.

FIGURE 5.—Type of sandal worn in Moche.

Space does not permit a thoroughgoing comparison of the distribution of costumes in Peru in order to shed light on the origin of the women's "old costume." Two suggestions may be made in passing. One is that it shows no resemblance to the everyday costume of women during Mochica times, as depicted on the vases, other than the short sleeves and the wide cut of the neck of the blouse; Mochica women seemed to have been garbed in a one-piece dress of tubular or sacklike characteristics, reaching from shoulders to ankles, with (sometimes) short sleeves above the elbows and a wide neckline. The second is that the Moche skirt is suggestive of those worn in certain parts of the Sierra.

Babies wear diapers of cotton cloth, dresses, and tight-fitting cotton bonnets of European style. The diaper is a longer piece of cloth than is customary in North America, and, after passing between the infant's legs, is wrapped several times tightly about the stomach with the ends tied together in front.

Toddlers and children up to about 6 years of age (up to school age) are provided with a short shirt or dress and nothing more for everyday wear (pl. 15, *upper* (*left*)); pants are not regarded as necessary at this age except for status purposes. Each child in all but the poorest families, however, has a complete outfit of underpants and suit or dress (according to sex), acquired usually at the time it has its first haircut (if a boy) or when its ears are pierced (if a girl). The child is dressed up in this outfit on subsequent occasions when it may be the center of attention or appear publicly as a representative of its family's status. These children's outfits follow modern North American patterns for the most part. Little boys at this age usually have knee-length shorts.

Children are fully clothed, except for shoes and stockings, after the age of about 6 years. A considerable variety exists in their dress, which is governed mainly by the finances, taste, shopping ability, and frugality of the mother and the availability of cast-offs. Boys wear shirts usually without tails, long trousers, overalls; some, but few, wear knee-length shorts. Young girls wear cotton dresses. I have never seen one in a miniature replica of the "old costume."

About the age of puberty the children begin to take more interest in their clothes, as among ourselves, and new-fangled and faddish excrescences appear—shoes, fancy fabrics, an occasional necktie, an occasional felt hat for a boy, etc. I have been told that most of these innovations disappear after marriage, although this may not be true of the coming generation.

Ornament for men is practically nil. The short haircut is favored by the majority, although some individuals with enough white (?) blood to have curly hair affect a longer cut. Only the minority attempt to maintain a part. My estimate is that the majority of the men do not have sufficient beard to require shaving more than once a week. Most men have shaving instruments, however. The straight razor is rare; this is because of its cost and the difficulty of keeping it honed, according to some informants. The complete safety razor is rare also. Many men shave with the safety razor blade held in the hand (without the holder), while others use a pocket knife. The razor blade is a general utility implement about the Moche household. My impression is, however, that the majority of men with beards of any significance visit a barber shop about once every week on the average. There are four full-time barber shops in town, two of them operated by Japanese, where a steady customer can get shaved for 10 centavos. A haircut is 20 centavos. (The barbers will, of course, charge more if they can get it. The rate in the "first-class" shops in Trujillo, however, is only 20 centavos for a shave and 40 centavos for a haircut, all prices as of June–November 1944.) Adolescent boys use vaseline and pomades on their hair.

The distinctive hairdress of the Moche women is apparently disappearing, but is more persistent than the women's old costume in clothes. The hair is parted in the middle and is braided into two strands in back (pl. 16, *upper* (*right*)). Into the ends of these strands are braided homespun yarns of *algodón pardo* (brown cotton) to increase the length of each braid by a few inches. The braids are then crossed over each other and encircle the dome of the head from opposite sides; the ends of the braids with the strings of brown cotton are then knotted together in front, above the forehead. A small knot of colored ribbon and/or a flower may grace this knot. When a woman does not have time or inclination to put her hair up in this fashion, she allows the braids to hang down her back, but usually tied together at the ends. In former times, the women of Moche were said to be famous for their gold ornaments (*alhajas*). Gold palm leaves were inserted in the crownlike arrangement of the hair-do just described and gold ornaments in the shape of heads of wheat were inserted in the hair above and in front of the ears. Heavy gold collars and chains were worn about the neck and elaborate pendant earrings of gold were common. These ornaments were regarded as important family heirlooms and symbols of status. A woman received a set of them when she married. A few of these ornaments are still in existence, but the elaborate displays at the fiestas and masses of

yesteryear are no longer seen. It is said that most of them have been pawned or sold for money. (At a fiesta in Monsefú near Chiclayo, I saw a considerable number of women wearing sets of this type of ornament, indicating, along with other traits, the greater conservatism of this northern Mochica village.) One of the men of Moche has an oil painting of his mother (painted by a Mochero artist) which shows her decked out in a complete set of this finery.

All women wear earrings on festive occasions. Hand-worked gold earrings are still owned by a number of women, although one would judge that they are on the average less elaborate than the enormous pendants of former times; but the majority of women wear cheaper earrings of silver, gilt, nickel, as well as plastic innovations peddled in the Trujillo market. Earrings are not worn every day, as a general rule, but only for religious and family festivals of first magnitude.

INDUSTRIES

Aside from agriculture and fishing, and service specialties which have already been mentioned, the manufacturing industries of Moche are few and poorly developed. Moche is poor in this respect in comparison with the northern "Mochica" village of Monsefú, where weaving, hat making, and the manufacture and decoration of gourd vessels are well-developed and well-preserved folk industries.

The fact has already been mentioned that gourd containers are made in Moche, but as a rule not on a specialized basis nor for sale outside the community.

The making of fireworks and firecrackers (*cohetes*) is a specialty practiced by three men in the community. These explosive products are used in all religious celebrations and in many other types of festivity. During the recital of the mass in the church on an important religious feast day, such as that of SS. Pedro y Pablo, one can believe that the plaza is under bombardment, because the faithful members of the *hermandad* in charge of the affair are stationed on the plaza just outside the church door and enthusiastically let off a barrage of rockets at each pause in the service. The use of noise-makers and fireworks in connection with religious and other festivals is, of course, common throughout Peru, especially along the north coast. I am told that in

the region about Chiclayo the profession of *cohetero* has achieved the status of an art, with renowned masters who are entrusted with the planning and construction of elaborate and prolonged narrative fireworks "effects." In Moche the two effects most in use are relatively simple. They are ordinary rockets and rockets mounted on a pinwheel which whirls around on a vertical axis while the attached rockets are shot into the air (pl. 17, *lower (right)*). Other effects occasionally produced by the local artists are *La Vaca Loca* (the crazy cow) and *Rabos de Zorro* (foxtails).

The rocket maker must secure a license from the police in order to secure the saltpeter, sulfur chlorate, and antimony which he uses in his trade. Since the police are wary of the manufacture of explosives by irresponsible persons, the number of *coheteros* in a given community is rigidly limited. Otherwise there would probably be more than three of them in Moche, since the trade is regarded as a lucrative one. The rocket maker grinds his materials on a flat stone, using a *mano* consisting of a rocker-shaped river stone about 18 inches long (pl. 17, *middle (right)*). The ingredients of the explosive consist of charcoal, saltpeter (*salitre*), sulfur chlorate (*clorato de azufre*), and antimony (*antimonio*). If one has a license, these materials are obtainable from the drug stores in Trujillo. The rockets, known as *cohetes* and also as *savillanas*, consist of the following parts. The noise-making or bomb part is a ball of explosive wrapped in leaves, with a fuse protruding. The rocket charge consists of explosive powder. Both bomb and charge are stuffed into a cylinder consisting of a leaf-wrapped section of cane in such a way that the fuse of the bomb protrudes backward into the rocket charge. The rear end of the cylinder is stopped with leaves through which a fuse projects. The cylinder in turn is bound to a handle of split cane or bamboo. When the contraption is shot off, one holds the handle in the left hand, pointing upward, and touches a light to the fuse, which starts the rocket charge. The whole thing, handle and all, shoots up 80 to 100 feet into the air. By the time it reaches the top of its flight, the fuse of the bomb is supposed to have burned through and the bomb bursts high in the air, shattering the bamboo or cane cylinder. The light handle falls to the ground. It is said to require considerable skill and experience to be able to mix and place the charges correctly so that all this happens as planned. Ordinary rockets of this sort sell for 3 soles a dozen.

In connection with this chemical industry, mention may be made of a fire-making custom. It is said that when matches are not available in the *campiña*, the people go to the mountains and obtain a certain white stone; there is a good deal of this on the Cerro Blanco back of the Huacas. One rubs this against his pants until it glows, then holds it against a piece of manure and blows on it until the manure is glowing. I have not seen this procedure.

Basketry is made in several households for sale. There are at least a dozen households regarded as specialists in this industry. The material is *carrizo*, which grows wild and is also planted as cuttings in some fields. The stems are split and smoothed down with a wooden-handled kitchen or butcher knife (pl. 17, *upper (left)*) into thin strips. All baskets made in Moche are ovaloid or globular in shape, often with stiff loop handles over the top, but without lids. Trays, rectangular or cubical baskets, either simple, or the telescoping type, are not made. Sizes range from small arm baskets about the size of a gallon container to large storage baskets 4 feet high by 3½ feet in diameter. All baskets have flat bases of a discoid pattern. In making a basket, either three or four sets of stiffening elements ("warps") are crossed at a single central point, as shown in plate 17, *upper (right)*, to give the effect of six or eight radiations from the central base point. Each stiffening element consists of a group of four split canes, somewhat thicker than the strips which are used for weaving the wickerwork. The base is then started by weaving the crosswise element over and under the stiffening elements, around the central crossing point in simple spiral fashion. The weaving is done with the hands while one stands on the stiffening elements with his bare feet to hold them in position. After a base a foot or so in diameter has been woven, the ends of the stiffening elements are tied upright to a cord passing about them, as shown in plate 17, *middle (left)*, to give the approximate shape of the finished basket, after which the spiral weaving continues. The rim is made by a continuous strip of thin material bound in spiral fashion round and round the two uppermost weaving elements and tucked in on itself when the rim is finished.

It seems that textile weaving has fairly recently disappeared in Moche, although it has not been generally practiced during the past 45 years. One old lady living in the *campiña* has a belt loom, but she says that she seldom weaves any more. Most women formerly wove *bayeta* for the old costume; it is said that, since the old trade pattern with the Sierra villages has disappeared (p. 80), it is difficult to obtain wool and dyes, and it is more economical to buy ready-woven material in the markets. Quite a number of the older women still spin, however. The purpose is to make the yarn of brown cotton which is used in the Mocheras' hairdress, as described above. The spindles I have seen have whorls of calabash and a pointed, but hookless, end. They are spun with the fingers and hang free when spinning.

The two types of mats, *esteras* and *petates*, previously mentioned as being extensively used in house construction and furnishing are also made for sale. The *petate* is a simple checkerboard or twilled (two-jump) mat made of split canes or *carrizos;* the elements are stiffer than the *totora* reeds used for making *esteras*. The latter consist of reeds laid side by side and tied together by crosswise running double cords into small bundles of four to six reeds each. The crosswise binder may be of cotton cord or of thinly split *totora* itself. Two methods of binding are used. One is the continuous double cord which is twined and often knotted on itself between each bundle; the other method is the single tie, as follows: Bundles of reeds lie side by side, A, B, C, D, etc.; first a tie is made around A and B, and the cord is knotted and cut off; then another cord is used to make a similar tie around B and C; the next tie will include C and D, and so on. A *totora* mat usually has three horizontal (crosswise) sets of ties, whatever the method used.

A few minor industries or specialities should be mentioned, all intrusive in the community. There is one tinsmith; there are two shoe cobblers; there are five bakeries, or, more properly, households, in the pueblo which bake bread for sale; there is one blacksmith, who seldom shoes a horse but whose work is concerned with the repair of plows and other iron work. One man is a diploma-holding embroiderer and specializes on spangled velvet and silk cloths given by the pious to their favorite saints. We have already mentioned the carpenters, masons, adobe makers, dressmakers, tailors, barbers, midwives, curers, witches.

The so-called industries of Moche are of minor importance in the over-all income of the community. Only mats and baskets are sold outside the community on any appreciable scale, and even that is small. The remainder of the industries are actually service specialties whose product is for local consumption.

ECONOMICS

SPECIALIZATION AND DIVISION OF LABOR

Because of the trends of change present in the situation, it is difficult to speak of the economic "system" of Moche in general terms. For almost any general statement made either there are exceptions in the behavior of individuals or there may well be within a year or two. The following remarks, therefore, are to be understood as depicting the outlines of the situation as it existed, according to my information, in the year 1944. A more precise measure of tendencies of change and deviations from general patterns could perhaps have been obtained by means of a systematic collection of statistical information. But this, for reasons mentioned in the Introduction, was impossible to carry out on a large scale with the facilities at my command.

DIVISION OF ECONOMIC ACTIVITIES ON A SEXUAL BASIS

In general, men do the hard and heavy work, while women are concerned primarily with house and child care and financial affairs. With respect to the latter, the women handle most of the commercial transactions and also handle, if they do not entirely control, the household funds. Although the situation is not actually phrased that way in Moche, many a superficial observer has come away with the impression that the man is culturally regarded as the fellow "with the strong back but the weak mind."

Men are primarily concerned with the following activities: Plowing, planting, cultivating, harvesting, supervision of livestock, milking cows, digging, cleaning, and watching of irrigation ditches, fishing and the making of nets and tackle, and building houses and fences. In the agricultural work, women sometimes assist with the lighter tasks of planting, harvesting, and weeding. The following specialties are exclusively male: Carpentry, masonry, adobe making, tailoring, barbering, fireworks making, shoe cobbling, tinsmithing, butchering (women sometimes kill animals for home use), blacksmithing, hat making (one man). Only men are professional musicians (playing in the bands and singing in the church). Men also serve as *mayordomos* of religious fiestas which are mechanisms of potential economic gain as well as of religious satisfaction. Only men hold political offices and serve as public scribes.

Women are primarily concerned with the following activities: Harvesting of light garden crops for home use; preparation and serving of food, including baking for sale; manufacture of *chicha*; care of the house; clothes washing; care of the children; such spinning as is done; weaving (formerly); repair of clothes and dressmaking, both for the family and on order; transportation of salable goods to market, selling such goods and handling the money or other economic returns; professional midwifery. Unmarried girls and women occasionally help with the lighter field work, but a married woman is not expected to work in the fields.

Both sexes take part in the following activities: Light agricultural and horticultural work; cutting wood for sale; house building (women may carry bags of earth in *tapia* making, while men do the heavy digging and lifting); making gourd containers; basket and mat making, although these activities on a commercial basis tend to be men's work; dressmaking on a commercial basis tends to be women's work, but there are a few men who take part; both sexes can be curers and witches, although there is a tendency for women to preempt the former specialty and men the latter. Both men and women serve as teachers in the schools; in the pueblo, men teach boys and women teach girls.

Children begin to do chores about the age of 6. Girls are given tasks about the house, such as carrying water or sweeping out the sleeping room. Boys help with weeding, watching the cows, and with the irrigation. I have seen no young children doing or trying to do hard labor.

GEOGRAPHICAL SPECIALIZATION

It has already been noted that the *playa* tends to specialize in sea fishing, while the *campiña* specializes in agriculture and horticulture.

SPECIALTIES

The specialties will be listed once more: Carpentry, masonry, adobe making, tailoring, dress making, barbering, cobbling, blacksmithing, tinsmithing, fireworks making, baking bread, basketry and mat making, playing musical instruments, singing professionally, embroidering, butchering, keeping shop, reading and writing (serving as a professional scribe), sea fishing, hat making, midwifery, curing, witchcraft.

All of these specialties require special talents, training, or economic resources. As already indicated, few of them are sufficiently well represented in the community to constitute distinct groups large enough to be recognized and organized as group units in the society. The only exceptions are the carpenters, the masons, the fishermen, and the professional musicians. The carpenters and masons are not recognized as groups. The fishermen are set off from the remainder of the community, but are not organized among themselves. Only the professional musicians who play instruments in the bands are organized, but this organization is only that required by the nature of band music and does not extend into social life in general. There is only one blacksmith (perhaps iron worker would be the better term), two tinsmiths (both are Japanese at present), one hat maker, and one cobbler. Two of the barbers are Japanese. The scribes are not registered by the Government, but work on an informal basis for fees; they cannot be regarded as professional, and their services are part-time—when some illiterate

Mochero needs help; the two most active scribes are *forasteros*.

The curers and witches who operate on a professional or commercial basis number perhaps a dozen in all, but, far from being organized, they regard each other with mutual suspicion and rivalry. The *brujo's* (witch's) calling is phrased in terms of aggression and counter-aggression between *brujos*.

Division of labor and specialization exist in Moche, but the specialties occupy no positions in the organization of groups within the society. This may be partially due to the attitude of individualism which dominates many aspects of life and which must be discussed later. Also, it must be recognized that Moche is still a predominantly rural peasant society in which one should not expect to find highly organized and compact groups of specialists in economic activities. There is still the tendency for every man to be a jack-of-all-trades. As one of my informants said, quoting a proverb of Lambayeque origin,

> De brujo, de cohetero, u tinterillo, no hay cholo que no entienda su poquillo.
> (Of [being a] *brujo*, a rocket maker, or shyster lawyer there is no *cholo* [i. e., man] who doesn't know his bit.)

In other words, everyone knows something about all the specialties.

DISTRIBUTION OF MALE LABOR FORCE

Up to the time I left Peru in November 1944, detailed reports of the age and sex composition of the population of the District of Moche had not been worked up by the Department of the Census. However, we may make a rough calculation which, in round numbers at least, may be fairly near the truth. The Department has already published age and sex figures from the census of 1940 for the Department of La Libertad, of which Moche is a part. For the Department as a whole, males of the age group 20 to 59 inclusive constitute 21 percent of the total population of the Department.[43] The total population of Moche is given by the census of 1940 as 3,773. We have subtracted 500 from this figure as representing the *forasteros*, and we have subtracted 135 individuals counted on the Haciendita and the "Hacienda Moche" (students and staff of the Agricultural School), leaving a total of 3,138 true Mocheros. Twenty-one percent of this figure is 659, which, if our other

---

[43] Censo Nacional, 1941, unnumbered table following p. 52, "Población Nominalmente Censada de Cada Departamento en los Grupos de edad de 20 a 59 . . ."

assumptions [44] and calculations are correct, represents the number of Mochero men between the ages of 19 and 60 and therefore a group which might be considered the adult male labor force available in Moche. We shall take 650 as a usable round number. Of this number 92 were definitely known to be working outside of the community on a more or less permanent basis in 1944. Taking into account 12 others said to be working outside, but whom I could not identify by name, we may assume that 100 is a safe figure for the number of men who gain the major part of their livelihood outside the community, while still maintaining their homes within it. This does not take into account Mocheros who have moved their homes and families to other localities. The outside workers are distributed as follows: 17 work as stevedores and cargo handlers in the port of Salaverry; 40 work as road laborers for the Government, being shifted about to various parts of the Department; 20 work as masons, masons' helpers, and carpenters for private constructors in Trujillo; 8 are employed as masons and laborers on the Government building project, the Barrio Obrero (Workers' Housing Project) in Trujillo; 2 are peons on the Haciendita and 2 are chauffeurs for the same establishment; 3 are professional *arrieros* (pack-animal drivers); and the occupations of the others are unknown to me.

In other words, at the time of this investigation about 15 percent of the resident true Mocheros of working age were employed outside the community. Some of them are landless men, but most have a small plot of ground or a small interest in a piece of Moche land (usually through inheritance), but too small to support themselves and their families. The number of outside workers fluctuates and those that have land sometime have time to work it. If they are busy on their jobs, however, they hire stay-at-home Mocheros to do the work for them. Work for the Government on the roads and building projects is the best paid and steadiest. During 1944 the men working in the port of Salaverry were said to average only 10 to 12 soles per week, owing to the scarcity of ships calling during wartime. The Salaverry workers are required to be on hand every day, but are paid on a piece-work basis. The work is regarded as good and the pay desirable when

there is steady movement of ships, as in normal times. The work consists of handling bags of sugar shipped to the port from the haciendas by railroad. Since Salaverry is an open roadstead, the sugar must be lightered aboard ship, and when the traffic is heavy additional recruits are brought in from Moche.

It would be interesting to have more precise data of a statistical nature concerning the actual land holdings and average amount of land worked per man. On the basis of the above calculations it would appear that about 550 men between 19 and 60 are left to devote their time to 976 hectares of cultivated land (after subtracting the Haciendita holdings). There are about 50 Mochero specialists in the community, but we leave them out of account since they devote part of their time to agriculture and the portion of their time devoted to specialties may be regarded in a rough way as balancing with the occasional agricultural activities of the outside workers. On this basis then, we would have the labor of one man available for each 1.77 hectares (about 4.37 acres). If we subtract the areas occupied by house lots and for other unproductive uses, this figure might well be reduced to about 1.60 hectares. It should be emphasized that these calculations are at best only tentative. It must be left to agricultural scientists to say authoritatively whether or not this represents an oversupply of labor, taking into account the methods used, the emphasis on dairying, and the fact that a considerable amount of labor is forthcoming from women, children, and men over 60 years of age. To me it appears to be excessive.

The primary interest of an anthropologist in a matter of this sort is to gage the situation from the point of view of cultural adaptation and probable future changes. Unless the irrigated area of Moche is considerably increased by the construction of new irrigation ditches which would water the desert to the southeast (and this is unlikely in view of the present shortage of water in the Río Moche), it would seem that an increasingly large proportion of the economically active elements of the population will have to seek livelihood outside the community.

Flourishing handicraft industries—weaving, hat making, calabash working—bring in a sizable income to the people of the northern Mochica village of Monsefú and seem to have protected that community from the results of land hunger. But, as we have seen, the native industries of Moche have practically all died out—completely so from the export point of view—and show no signs of revival. Whether or

---

[44] The unknowns are: (1) The exact number of *forasteros;* our figure, as explained on p. 8, is based on a count of households, not of individuals; (2) the exact proportion of the total population which is aged 20 to 59 inclusive and which is male; we are assuming that this proportion in Moche is the same as in the Department of La Libertad as a whole, namely, 21 percent.

not the official vital statistics quoted on page 9 are accurate in detail, it seems certain that the rate of natural increase is high. This pressure of population upon the fixed land area, already too restricted, will doubtless lead either to population shifts or to cultural changes of a radical nature. There are only a few apparent possibilities: (1) The excess population may be squeezed out of the community, disinherited, as it were, and forced to settle elsewhere. The large haciendas of the Chicama Valley with their chronic labor shortages are glad to accept the Mocheros into the barrack life. This eventuality would make it possible for the remainder of the population to carry on a small-scale farming life as at present, although the repercussions of intrafamily and interpersonal antagonism might be serious. (2) The bulk of the Mocheros would continue to maintain their homes in the community, while an increasing proportion earned its livelihood by outside effort. (3) The whole of the irrigated land, with its inhabitants, might be absorbed into some large hacienda which would then redistribute the population throughout its lands and, probably, destroy the whole structure of Moche life as known at present.

Other possibilities, involving developments in community organization, might well avoid or change any of these rather stark pictures, but these aspects of the matter must be discussed in a later section.

MOCHEROS IN THE PROFESSIONS OUTSIDE OF MOCHE

An increasing number of Mocheros are seeking higher education and entering the professions, often to practice outside of the community. In 1944 there were about 10 Mocheros enrolled in the University in Trujillo, 1 in Mexico, and 1 in Lima, and it is said that there is a colony of about 30 Moche families in Lima. This tendency to enter the so-called liberal professions, provided the candidates are successful, also relieves the economic pressure inside Moche, and it may be expected to increase unless some block is placed in the way of successful careers by Mocheros. Insofar as the young men become lawyers, the trend has certain disruptive features in the sense that the tendency seems to lead to increased litigation, which will be discussed later in the consideration of property matters.

As a sample of the sons and daughters of Moche who have made successful professional careers outside the community, I give the following list, culled from various informants. Except for a few, I do not know the individuals personally. In Moche, at least, they are regarded as distinguished personages.

A doctor of laws, accountant, and professor of mathematics in the Colegio Nacional de San Juan and proprietor of the Colegio de Renacimiento, both of Trujillo.

A doctor of medicine (surgeon), practices in Lima and is on the staff of the Hospital 2 de Mayo of Lima.

A professor in the Colegio Nacional de Nuestra Señora de Guadelupe in Lima.

A doctor of laws and *catedrático* in the Universidad Nacional de Trujillo.

A doctor of laws, practicing in Lima.

An accountant employed by the customshouse in Ica.

A lawyer, accountant, auxiliary *catedrático* in the Universidad Nacional de Trujillo, and professor in the Colegio Nacional de San Juan in Trujillo.

Two lawyers.

A lawyer practicing in Lima.

A professor in the normal school.

A school teacher and professor.

A professor of domestic sciences in the Colegio Renacimiento, Trujillo.

Pedro Azabache, perhaps the most famous of all, is a distinguished young painter who had a successful one-man show in Lima in 1944; he studied in the Escuela de Bellas Artes in Lima and was a pupil of the famous Peruvian painter, José Sabogal. He has maintained his headquarters in Lima, but plans to open a studio and school in Moche.

PROPERTY

We are often accustomed to think of a "primitive," "peasant," or "folk" economy as predominantly cooperative in economic activities and property concepts, although various studies have shown that cooperation is not invariably characteristic of both of these aspects of economics, even on the primitive level (Mead, 1937). However, all the evidence seems to indicate that cooperation in work and a communistic or socialistic attitude toward property, whether voluntary or forced, were characteristic of the aboriginal communities of ancient Peru (Valcárcel, 1943, p. 143 ff.; Baudin, 1943, chs. 6–10), at all events was insisted upon by the Inca conquerors. Moche is in many respects a "peasant" or "folk" community (Redfield, 1941, pp. 338–370), as well as being an heir of the ancient cultures of Peru, but cultural concepts regarding property, particularly land, are definitely individualistic. Even relatives of the closest degree do not hesitate to engage in feuds and litigations with each other over questions of land rights. This matter deserves a rather extended discussion because it is the source of many of Moche's troubles and upon the form of its solution depends much of Moche's future.

Formal definitions of property and its management all conform to Peruvian law, which is governed by the principle of the right of private property, individual and corporative. The Peruvian law also contains provisions for collective and cooperative property holding and management in the cases of legally recognized *"communidades indigenas"* (indigenous communities), and it furthermore permits and protects the formation and operation of producers' and consumers' cooperatives. The Mocheros have not taken advantage of either the corporative, communal, or cooperative features of the law, but operate exclusively under its individualistic aspects.

At first glance the situation appears the more strange because the intensely individualistic attitude toward land is combined with a cooperative attitude toward labor. The shared-work pattern in agriculture, house building, and irrigation (formerly it was on a completely democratic basis) operates side by side with an apparently rather childish jealousy regarding lands, houses, crops, clothing, tools, animals, money and all other forms of property, but particularly land. Thus it might be said that a tendency toward communism in labor exists side by side with individual ownership and management of tangible property. The idea that one's labor is a commodity which can be sold in exchange for property (or its symbols, e.g., money) is an innovation in Moche, and even yet perhaps only 15 percent of the labor force, as we have seen, sell their labor abroad. Under the older work-sharing pattern, labor was and is traded, reciprocally to be sure, but in exchange for labor and hospitality, not for money or goods. One obvious explanation for this superficial paradox might well be that, considering the realities of the Moche situation, labor has always been plentiful, but landed property and other forms of property derived directly or indirectly from it have been distinctly limited and scarce for generations. There are many hands, but few lands.

Land is the most important type of property in Moche and, in truth, is the most important fact in human life throughout the whole desert coast of Peru. By land, I mean irrigated terrain, capable of producing subsistence and/or commercially valuable crops, for no other type of land has any meaning in this region, other than in terms of barren distances to be traveled and the chances of death in doing so.

Practically every adult Mochero man and woman possesses a bundle or so of legal papers stored away in a trunk in the house or, in some cases, it is said, buried on his land for safe keeping. These papers are supposed to prove the individual's right by inheritance, purchase, or transfer to the land which he claims to own. Their effectiveness in protecting land rights in Moche is, however, affected by two facts.

(1) Many, probably the majority, of landowners are unable to read and write, which leaves them ill-equipped to contend with cases of litigation. (2) The majority of the documents do not and under the circumstances probably cannot establish property rights in land beyond any possibility of successful contrary legal action, so that an unethical lawyer can always try "to make a case." Lawyers tell me that clearing titles, particularly of small parcels of land which have passed through many hands during the last 400 years, is at the present time a most uncertain proposition and is almost always exposed to attack provided the opposition can dig up countervailing documents, which, particularly in the case of small holdings, can hardly ever be ruled out of possibility.

It is perhaps not generally understood in North America that the Spanish colonial system saddled Latin America with a tradition of intricate red tape and required documents and reports and that certain of these procedures are still followed. Applied to illiterate natives, this system represents a striking form of cultural inconsistency of a type which I have previously termed inconsistency of pattern with pattern (Gillin, 1944, p. 443). In land disputes, it gives literate persons a marked advantage over those who are illiterate (Cornejo Bouroncle, 1935).

Such a set of patterns—documentary legalism and illiteracy—is inconsistent only if both are present in the cultural system at the same time. Education will eliminate illiteracy, but first there must be a transition period, which often is still one of maladjustment. Moche is in such a period at the present time. With the modern emphasis upon education and professional training a number of young men have succeeded in obtaining complete or partial training as lawyers in the University of Trujillo or elsewhere. Many of these have followed a successful career in the law, but some, unable to obtain a place in an established office or to create a practice of their own, turn not unnaturally, perhaps, to litigation among their own people. With the increased pressure of population on the available land, their hopes are not long deferred. As heirs and subdivisions of inheritances multiply, so do quarrels.

There is no recognized communal or family

mechanism, other than mutual good will and good sense, for the amicable settlement of such differences in Moche at the present time. Litigation is looked upon as a way out of difficulties, especially if the litigants are stimulated by young lawyers from among their own people. The result is that increased education has brought about more litigation during the present period.

The present generation of children will probably all be literate. In the meantime, however, as many illiterate property holders may be expected to live for 20 to 30 years more to carry on their quarrels, a good share or all of the Moche land may be alienated from the hands of Mocheros. In addition to qualified lawyers there are a few fake lawyers, literate men who have read some law and who pose as lawyers to ignorant or illiterate people. The Peruvian term for this type of gentry is *tinterillo* (little inker, referring to his preoccupation with documents). These parasites are not apparently as numerous in Moche as in many highland regions, but their influence is just as prejudicial to the good interests of Moche as a community.

The intrusion of the legal profession into a situation such as that of Moche not only entails the ill-afforded economic waste involved in hiring lawyers by individuals in a community of Moche's comparatively meager wealth and standard of living, but has two further consequences. (1) The lawyers stimulate conflict within the community and open wedges for the entrance of larger and more powerful interests. (2) Small-time lawyers, who are forced for want of better business to promote litigation among their home-town relatives and friends, become the tools of bigger lawyers serving larger and better organized clients.

Women as well as men own land and inherit it as well as other forms of property. Transfer from the older to the younger generation is made by gift before death, by written testament, and by customary division if the deceased has died intestate. In the latter case, my informants tell me that it has been customary for the spouse to receive half of the property in life trust, as it were, with the remainder divided equally among the children and their mother's share reverting, share and share alike, to them on her death. Inheritances of this sort, however, run into many types of legal complications, I am told, if the heirs are disposed to dispute the estate, and give rise to numerous court battles. Even written wills, of course, may be subject to legal ac-

tion. Another source of difficulty is the fact that the estate frequently is too small to be efficiently divided into shares, as when a man leaves one-half hectare of land to a widow and four children. One method of solving this difficulty is to allow one of the heirs, often the oldest brother, to operate the property as a single enterprise, dividing the proceeds among the other heirs. However, it is not difficult to see how such an arrangement may produce disagreements, when there is a widowed mother and the operating heir's family to support, leaving a residue for the remaining heirs which is almost infinitesimal. Such a situation is complicated by the fact that the average Mochero has no idea whatever of how to keep useful written records of his accounts. Many such younger heirs are forced to seek work as day laborers for their fellows with larger lands or to obtain work outside the community.

Another method in such cases is to sell the land and divide the money between the heirs. This has been done relatively rarely up to the present. If it should happen frequently and the sales were confined to the community, it would tend to create a class division between landed and landless families, which, although it exists in incipient form at present, is not socially recognized as a class division. If the sales are made to *forasteros,* as has happened in a few cases, the landless still remain landless and the steady and much feared encroachment of outsiders upon the Moche scene increases. Old timers say that up to about 1900 there were practically no *forasteros* owning real property in Moche, and that it has been traditional for the Mocheros to refuse to sell to or deal with outsiders. The influx got under way on an appreciable scale only about 15 to 20 years ago. I cannot be sure about these dates, but I am convinced that the resistance and reserve toward *forasteros* shown by Mocheros in their personal relations is rooted in fear for their land.

Without more complete historical data it is difficult to do more than speculate concerning the influence of land scarcity on present-day Moche culture and the character structure of the Mocheros. I know nothing which would indicate that the Moche lands were at any period since early colonial times greatly more extensive than when the recent *forastero* alienations began. The Mocheros have been surrounded by *forasteros* for centuries. It does seem probable, however, that the pressure from the *forasteros* has increased appreciably during the past generation. First the railroad, and then the highways made the Moche lands more accessible to outsiders; then certain of the haciendas gradually grew into large, tightly organized, and impersonal enterprises. Only a short time previous to 1944, one of the haciendas of the Moche Valley, a subsidiary of the largest sugar estate in Peru, succeeded through legal action in establishing claim to a fairly large piece of land, formerly considered to be the communal lands of the municipality.

With respect to landed property, then, the Mocheros are divided within and beset from without. If this is an actuality for only a portion of the Mocheros at present, it is a potentiality for all. Under existing conditions of sugar production for export on the world market, an hacienda must attempt to control as much arable land and as large a labor force as possible, if it is to continue to carry on a profitable business. Especially in the case of those enterprises controlled by foreign or absentee capital, the hacienda's approach to the problem of land and labor tends to become impersonal and grimly efficient. It is this type of hacienda in the Trujillo region which exhibits the strongest expansionist tendencies.

The student of cultural change must recognize that the modern capitalistic hacienda system is a mighty mechanism for alteration of the cultural and social system represented by a small, independent community such as Moche. The hacienda system of the coast is incompatible with individual ownership of small plots of ground independently managed, with the production of crops on a small scale for the internal or regional market, with "inefficient" methods of cultivation which do not involve the use of machinery, with undisciplined hours of labor, with time-consuming bargaining by small producers over the disposal of their product, and with freedom of the laborer to change his occupation at will. The hacienda requires the people under its sway to accept a different set of cultural patterns: the worker and his family are to live in a block of dwellings all exactly alike; he is to labor a definite period of hours each day, set by the clock, under the supervision of bosses; he has nothing to say about the disposal of the product, but is paid a small money wage; he is bound to the job for a definite period by contract; he receives gratis part of his rations and buys the remainder in commissaries and markets under the control of the hacienda; he or his family is not allowed to leave the hacienda without permission. Under the leadership of the Hacienda Chiclín (which has not shown expansionist ten-

dencies) and now under pressure of the Government, many haciendas have instituted "welfare features." These features include free hospitals and medical services, supervised housing conditions that result in more hygienic dwellings, free or nominally priced movies and other entertainments, encouragement of athletics and sports, food furnished through the commissaries at prices much below those of the general markets and supervision of the quality and healthfulness of the food, regular hours of labor and discipline that cut down the consumption of alcohol thereby improving health and morals, and others.

The development of the hacienda systems has created a new set of conditions to which the culture of the "independent" community such as Moche must adapt if it is to survive as a free community with an integral culture. Up to the present moment Moche has developed no effective new cultural patterns for adaptation to this alteration of outside conditions, and, as already pointed out, certain existent internal patterns (documentation of land claims and illiteracy) are seriously inconsistent.

Thus, Moche is faced with "a world it never made," and unless a speedy and successful cultural adaptation takes place, the prospects are good for the destruction of the integrity of the culture and the dispersal of the society itself. At present, there is seemingly no general sense of community responsibility on the part of the people. This attitude extends beyond property matters (although it may be derived from them) to practically all aspects of community life. Other features of the matter will be discussed in a subsequent section. During 1944, however, there appeared two organizations, organized by the younger elements, the stated purposes of which are to stimulate and develop community responsibility and pride and to take practical measures for utilizing such sentiments for the public welfare.

FINANCE AND BUSINESS DEALINGS

Very few Mocheros have bank accounts or insurance policies. Formerly everyone buried his saved money in the ground. Nowadays most of the younger adults keep their money in cash in trunks or boxes in the house. No complaints have been heard by me regarding thievery. One of the richest Moche families apparently owes much of its present affluence to an insurance policy. The head of the house, now dead, was persuaded by his wife to take out and maintain a 20,000 sol life insurance policy payable to his wife. When he died a few years ago, his widow, by that time an old woman, prudently bought land and animals with the proceeds so that she, her children, and grandchildren are now able to live in a good house in the pueblo, hire peons to work the fields, take occasional trips to Lima, and plan to maintain one of the grandsons in the University in Lima for the next 3 or 4 years. This is the only case of life insurance of which I know.

As a general rule, families keep savings in cash only sufficient to cover emergencies, such as funerals, doctor bills, etc. Caches of money are also built up in anticipation of religious festivals and family festivals such as christenings, weddings, and birthdays.

The most profitable form of investment is thought to be cows or female calves. Not only does the investor obtain income from the sale of the milk, but the investment steadily increases through the calves produced, and with luck one does not have to wait too long for a turnover. Cattle are always readily salable, although not always at the desired price, and are thus "liquid assets." Even men without land or with insufficient land invest in cows, which are pastured on other men's land either on a share basis (half the proceeds from the cow) or on a fee basis. It is said that pasturage may be obtained for 10 centavos per day per cow. Some complaint is heard that cows thus boarded out on a cash basis tend to be maltreated by the owner of the pasture.

Land is also a good investment, although difficult to acquire. No sales of land took place during my period in Moche and, in any case, land is sold by the piece after an appropriate amount of bargaining, so that it is difficult to quote prices in terms of standard areas. Several *forastero* men told me that "they would gladly give 2,000 soles ($306) a hectare" for good Moche land; another said he thought it was worth only about 1,500 soles a hectare, while still another claimed one would be lucky to get it for 3,000 soles a hectare. I do not know if these estimates mean anything in practical terms or not, except that scarcely any amount of money will buy his land from a Mochero, unless he be in dire financial straits.

Those who own land as an investment usually rent it on shares (*a partidos*). The owner furnishes the land and pays the water rent; the tenant furnishes his labor, the tools, and the seed. The proceeds are divided equally between owner and tenant. The municipality, however, has several parcels of land, all of which are rented for cash; the income is used for the municipal expenses.

Houses in the pueblo are another field for investment. Houses rented to Mocheros for ordinary dwellings rent for from 3 to 8 soles per month, most of them nearer the lower than the higher figure. I rented one without bargaining for 10 soles to use as an interviewing headquarters. The more profitable type of renting is to *forasteros,* either those who make the pueblo their suburban home or those who come to pass 2 or 3 months during the summer season. I was offered a house with six rooms (not counting various small storage rooms), kitchen, small gardens front and rear, and tile floors for 25 soles per month during the winter. According to local opinion I could have obtained it for about 20 soles on a year-round basis, and would have had to pay about 25 soles for the summer season.

There are various other smaller ways to turn a sum of money into a larger sum. For example, a woman, if astute and lucky, may turn 12 soles into 15 or 20 soles relatively quickly as follows. She buys from a woman who makes *chicha* a *botija* of the brew for 12 soles, the standard "wholesale" price. Then she sells it out retail at 15 centavos a bottle, clearing 3 soles for her trouble. (A *botija* contains 100 bottles of *chicha*). If she can get 20 centavos per bottle, her profit is 8 soles.

Women are engaged in deals of this sort all the time, usually on a small scale. For example, one of the women of my acquaintance operated during 1 day as follows: Her husband milked the cows early in the morning, obtaining 12 l. of milk, which the woman sold to a *revendadora* for 28 centavos a liter, 3.56 soles. She left the 6 centavos in her savings cache and pocketed the 3.50. Then she loaded two donkeys with yucas (the donkey she rode carried only a partial load) and set off for the market in Trujillo, arriving at her assigned stall about 7 a. m. By 10:30 she had disposed of the yucas for 4.10 soles. She began to shop around the market, looking for left-over fruit. The bulk of the retail selling in the market is over by 11 a. m. and usually some of the women have not succeeded in disposing of all their produce and are willing to sell off the remainder at reduced prices. My friend is a shrewd bargainer and succeeded in getting her donkeys loaded with assorted fruit in good condition for 4.50 soles, although it took her until about noon to do so. She then set out for Moche, arriving about 2 p. m. at her house in the town. She set up a table just inside the front door and spread out the fruit for display. She is known as a seller of items from the market, and customers soon began to come in. By about 5 p. m. she had sold three-fourths of the fruit for 5.30 soles—she says it was not a very good day. She took a few items for home use and made a deal with her final woman customer to exchange the remainder of the fruit for 2 kilos of shelled beans, which she took to market with her next day and sold for 70 centavos. Thus her total visible "take" for the day was 9.16 soles—3.56 for milk, 4.10 for yuca, and a total profit of 1.50 on the fruit deal. Expenses were 30 centavos for lunch and *chicha* at the market, leaving a gain of 8.86 soles in cash. She was involved in a number of other barters in the market of which I could get no clear picture in terms of the profit and loss. It will be noticed that the 3.56 soles for the milk represents no effort to speak of on the part of my friend and represents value produced by her husband. The value of the yuca is mainly produced by her husband, although she provides transportation to market, time, and salesmanship. The 1.50 soles gained on the fruit represents true commercial profit on the transactions involved. In this day's work my friend spent 12 hours and traveled 16 km. by donkey.

This case in terms of money values represents the median of the few cases which I was able to follow through, but my series is so small that I do not wish to suggest that the money values involved are in any way typical of the "average woman's" daily income. In the absence of an adequate statistical sample and check, I can say with practical certainty that this represents "a very good day indeed." Certainly, the data on family incomes I was able· to secure do not indicate that 8.86 soles per day in cash is a usual average. This case does illustrate, however, the Mocheras' way of doing business. The woman is constantly on the lookout for propositions which promise a small profit. Part of the transactions are in cash, part by barter, and many of them involve a whole series of trades sometimes running over several days. No books are kept and practically all deals are on a face-to-face basis with goods exchanged physically and immediately rather than being taken out of stock.

Each Moche married couple is a sort of business partnership in which the man is responsible for the production of the agricultural and dairy produce and the woman handles its sale and handles all finances. Those men who work outside the community bring home their wages to their wives who act as guardians. Even funds for production expenses such as the hire of a plow, the purchase of tools, etc., have to be obtained by the husband from the wife. She also provides him with spending money upon his request. Some husbands working for wages hold out a certain sum per week for their personal expenses, but in most cases, I believe, with the knowledge of their wives. When asked why they do not conceal some of their money from their wives, men say that "You can't expect a woman to run a household if she doesn't have the money," or something similar. My impression is that, far from feeling henpecked under this arrangement, most men feel well satisfied to leave financial matters to their wives. Personalities differ, of course, but even when the husband thoroughly dominates the wife as a person, he seems to be content to allow the woman to handle the money. To sum up, the arrangement as culturally defined does not seem to involve difference in prestige or invidious comparisons between individuals or between sexes. It is rather a form of division of labor or function. Women are supposed to do some things in this life and men other things, and among the responsibilities of women is the handling of money and finances. This is a cultural tradition in Moche, and from the average man or woman's point of view, that is all there is to it.

It is obvious that this cultural definition of functions may change, particularly if men's work for cash wages becomes an increasingly important element in family incomes.

The partnership arrangement between husband and wife does not necessarily interfere with their individual ownership of property. Thus, if a woman has inherited a plot of land, she has a perfect right to allow her husband to work it or to rent it to someone else, as she pleases. Both arrangements occur. However, the income is used by the wife for household expenses as a general rule. When cash savings of a married couple are turned into tangible assets, as in the purchase of a cow, I believe that they are usually purchased in the husband's name, i.e., regarded for formal purposes as his property. Customarily the husband's property passes to the wife and children after his death.

Although the women, as I have indicated, are commercially active in such fields as *chicha*, vegetables, milk, etc., they do not enter shop keeping. All of the shops (*tiendas*) are operated by *forasteros*.

So far as I know, there is no borrowing of funds from banks by Mocheros. Needed funds are obtained from friends or relatives within the community. Also, there is comparatively little use of credit in the local shops, which make most of their sales for cash.

ECONOMIC ASPECTS OF CERTAIN RELIGIOUS ORGANIZATIONS

In the section on religion will be found a discussion of certain religious groups called *mayordomías* and *hermandades* (brotherhoods). Similar organizations are found throughout most of Roman Catholic Latin America, sometimes being called *cofradías* or *confraternidades*. In Moche there is a difference between a *mayordomía* and an *hermandad*, which will be discussed later, but, although both are phrased in terms of devotion to a saint or other religious object or objective, these organizations have certain economic aspects which cannot be overlooked. The economic aspect appears as follows. A *mayordomía*, let us say, is organized by a leader (always a man) who is known as the *mayordomo*. He goes to perhaps eight of his friends and says that he would like to show his devotion to San Fulano on that saint's day. He asks the men if they would also like to show their devotion to the saint and to the church in general by joining with him in a *mayordomía*. Some men do not feel that they can afford the time, the cash outlay, etc., but in time the *mayordomo* organizes a group which undertakes the responsibility of carrying out the celebration of the day of San Fulano. Each one has to make a contribution in order to carry the preliminary expenses. Five soles each is common. Arrangements are made to pay for a mass (if the saint's day does not have an obligatory one), to hire a band, to buy the rockets and fireworks, and to provide the food and drink for the feast. Then, some days or even weeks previous to the big day, the *mayordomía* starts canvassing the population for contributions. The members go from house to house asking people if they do not wish to show their devotion to the public celebration of San Fulano's day. The people of Moche seldom refuse such a solicitation. Individual amounts vary from 10 centavos up to a couple of soles. A cup of *pisco* is drunk from a bottle carried by the solicitors, and the contributors' names are entered on a list to which publicity is given by word of mouth and, sometimes, by posting the list in the church entrance. The day before the celebration, i. e., the afternoon before vespers, a band is hired and a final public canvassing of the community takes place with a further collection. After the religious solemnities and parade of the saint's image the fol-

lowing day, all contributors and almost anyone else who wishes to come is invited to a large meal, replete with ample liquor and music, usually at the house of the *mayordomo*. Here again it is not rare for guests, especially after feeling the glow of the drink, to make further contributions to the good saint. A plate is conspicuously provided for this purpose.

It is most unusual that the original contributions of the members of the *mayordomía* are not covered by the solicited contributions. A good *mayordomo* usually manages the affair so that all expenses are taken care of and there is a comfortable surplus. The church and the priest take no official interest in these funds, and the members of the organizing group have no obligation to turn the surplus over to the church. It is usually divided equally between the members of the group after all have been reimbursed for their original outlay and their contributions to the feast. The proceeds are frequently not inconsiderable in Moche terms; two or three hundred soles is a not unusual "profit." This is one of the few opportunities within the culture itself for men to make cash profits directly through their own activities. It is also considered highly honorable, and the members of such a group enjoy high prestige in the community. To be sure, considerable time and some financial risk is involved, and many men can afford neither.

The *hermandades* are more permanent organizations than the *mayordomías*, which are organized on the temporary basis. They have now practically died out in Moche. But until a few years ago, at least one *hermandad* operated a sort of insurance scheme. A certain amount of the proceeds from its activities was kept apart, usually invested in cattle, and from this fund the burial expenses of the members were paid. The organization, however, did not renew its membership, and finally all the members but one died off and the group folded up. The surviving member, I understand, was left with one calf from the "funds" of the group.

DISTRIBUTION

The mechanisms for the distribution of economic goods in the community are as follows: (1) Borrowing and lending; (2) the public market and stores of Moche; (3) the shops and saloons (*salones*); (4) Trujillo and other markets; and (5) ambulatory peddlers.

A great deal of informal borrowing and lending

between friends and relatives takes place, particularly in foodstuffs, *chicha,* and the like. This is on a strictly reciprocal basis, i.e., the lender is expected to return the equivalent when he or she is able. Tools and utensils (except plows) are also passed about through borrowing and lending, although this takes place mainly in connection with emergencies or unusual needs. For example, a man may wish to cut a tree and will borrow an ax from another man. In return he will supply some boards when the other man wishes to make *tapia.* A woman may borrow a large pan for making *sopa teólogo* and reciprocate later with an extra container for *chicha* when the original lender has a party. However, everyone is supposed to have a basic set of the utensils or tools used in his work. A man could not get along as a farmer by borrowing all the necessary tools year after year. A woman could not keep house with a complete set of borrowed utensils.

There is a public market belonging to and supervised by the municipality in Moche itself on the Plaza de Armas. It is universally regarded as a poor market (*una plaza muy chicha, no vale la pena*), because the selection of goods available is very small. A few Moche women sell their farm and garden produce here on çertain days of the week and a few meat sellers offer their products. On many a day there will be only three or four persons selling. The market opens at 5 a. m. and is usually over by 9 a. m. Both buyers and sellers will visit the local market to see what is offered in the way of customers and produce, and if things are not to their satisfaction, they go on to Trujillo, where the selection of goods and the number of potential customers are much larger. Many people of Moche never bother to visit the local market, because they know before hand that the variety is poor. The best days in the local market are Thursday and Sunday.

There are eight shops in the town, as shown on the plan in map 1. All of these are operated by *forasteros,* seven by Chinese, and one by a Peruvian. The stock of these shops is small and consists mainly of staples (salt, sugar), cigarettes, soft drinks, bottled liquor and wine, coca, dry grains (rice, olluco, wheat, etc.), bread flour, a small selection of cloth, shelled maize, china dishes, and metal pots and pans. They also sell bread. All bread has to be bought ready-made (except for the few households which bake it for sale). It is provided exclusively in the form of small buns or biscuits which sell two for 5 centavos. The five saloons (*salones*) offer mainly

refreshments—coffee and bread to eat on the premises, sweets, drinks, cigarettes, etc. Cooked meals are obtainable, but only if ordered in advance. This occurs seldom, because the normal way to obtain a meal outside one's own home is to eat a *causa* prepared at the house of a Mochera. Each has a counter and a few tables with chairs. Two have booths or private rooms with oilcloth-covered tables and chairs for parties. Four have hard-packed floors of earth, and the other has a front room with tile floor. Of the five *salones,* two are operated by Peruvians, one by a Peruvian married to a Chinese, a third by a Chinese, and the fourth by a Peruvian woman married to a Russian who works outside Moche. The shops and saloons make a practice of giving a *yapa* (a little something extra) for any purchase of consideration. I have seen *yapa* given to a small boy purchasing 10 centavos worth of sweets. The shops serve mainly the hour-to-hour needs of housewives in the pueblo. Principal purchases are made in the Trujillo market or stores.

Trujillo has a large and active public market where products and handicraft goods from other parts of the country (particularly the Chiclayo region and the Sierra) are available in quantity and variety, as well as manufactured goods. A good many exchanges between members of the Moche community itself take place in Trujillo. In addition, the city has a great many shops or stores. All purchases, even those made in the stores and shops, are accompanied by bargaining, although in this region one does not see the prolonged haggling and gesticulating sometimes visible in other parts of Latin America. Many of the Trujillo stores post signs that they sell only at fixed prices. No one pays attention to this, however, and the proprietors are usually willing to shave the price, especially for country people like the Mocheros, who usually will not buy unless some ostensible concession is made. Generally speaking, in Peru, as well as the Trujillo region, the seller will quote a price. The buyer will say that it is too high. The seller will ask the buyer to "make an offer." The offer is usually too low, whereupon the buyer will ask the seller to make a concession usually accompanying his request with derogatory remarks concerning the goods under discussion and tales about how he can obtain the same for much less at some other place. This goes on for a time until agreement has been reached, but the discussion does not become noisy. In most cases a concession of no more than 10 to 20 percent of the quoted price is made (I am not speaking of prices quoted to tourists, foreigners, and strangers, which are often twice their accepted value). The technique of the buyer walking away in a huff is not generally used. It is not customary for the seller to come running after the buyer with a new concession in an attempt to make the sale. Such conduct is regarded as beneath the dignity and honor of a Peruvian.

A few ambulatory peddlers come to Trujillo. There is a bread man who comes every morning with two donkeys. Each donkey has two large wooden boxes tied on either side, holding the bread. The peddler delivers to some small shops and also sells from house to house. An iceman appears occasionally on Sundays and feast days. He pushes his two-wheeled cart on foot from Trujillo. The cart contains a chunk of ice in a large chest, some bottles of colored flavoring matter in racks on top of the chest, an ice-shaving apparatus consisting of a blade set in a block of wood, and a couple of glass tumblers. His business consists of selling shaved ice colored and flavored with liquid from the bottles, a tumblerful at a time. Children gather around and pay 5 centavos per tumbler for this refreshment.

It is said that the day before Christmas and the day of the fiesta of San Isidro a *feria* takes place in the plaza of Moche, with booths set up by local and outside vendors. These *ferias,* or fairs, are important mechanisms for exchange in many communities of the Sierra and even on the coast. I visited one in Monsefú in September to which people came from all over the northern part of Peru. However, no *feria* took place in Moche during the 5½ months that I knew it, and the entire complex of *ferias* seems to have practically died out in the community. Probably, the good roads and ready bus transportation which have oriented the people toward Trujillo, so far as buying and selling is concerned, have also killed the old fair and local market patterns. Mocheros speak regretfully of the loss of the old institutions of exchange and distribution, but say that no one takes an interest, it is not worth the trouble, when Trujillo is so near and so accessible.

COST OF LIVING AND FAMILY BUDGETS

It is very difficult to be precise about incomes and cost of living in money terms without a long period of intensive investigation, for the following reasons.

(1) Mocheros do not keep written accounts and do not have good memories for figures, especially expenditures. (2) A good part of the subsistence expenses of the Mocheros costs them nothing in terms of money. Most pay out nothing in cash for houses, a large part of their food, etc. (3) Barter and reciprocal borrowing constitute income and outgo, but often are not translated into money at all; in other instances these profits and/or losses emerge in the form of money ultimately, but only after a prolonged and half-forgotten train of intervening transactions. (4) The Mocheros are close-mouthed about their financial affairs.

It is generally considered that an average of 15 centavos per head per day is a necessary minimum daily cash expenditure for articles of diet and drink not produced in the household and considered essential for the maintenance of life in Moche terms. This presumes, of course, that other items of subsistence are produced by the family. This, for a family of five, is a minimum monthly cash requirement of 22.50 soles and for the year, 273.75 soles ($40.06).

The richest Mochero living in the community is said to be worth 50,000 soles. I have no way of knowing how near the truth this may be, except that he does have a fairly well-made town house and several parcels of land. Since he and his wife are childless, there is a good deal of speculation among his contemporaries as to what is going to happen to his fortune after his death. The poorest man in town is said to be the victim of one of the common family feuds over land. It is said that his sister managed to get his land away from him in a legal scrape. He gets a bare subsistence by carrying water from the public hydrants to private houses and appears on the streets a pitiful object in rags.

It is doubtful whether the actual cash income of the average family of Moche exceeds 45 soles per month.

I have collected a number of family budgets which are given herewith. These are based upon the memory and estimates of the families involved and are no more than suggestive. I had mimeographed a simple weekly schedule of expenditures and receipts which had been distributed to about a dozen families, but I was suddenly called away from Moche before they were completed, and I have no hope of receiving them by mail in time for this publication, if ever.

Basic yearly expenditures of family living on a chacra (man, wife, 3 children in school)

	Soles
Clothing	70
Alcoholic drinks	50
Religious contributions	5
School expenses	15
Total	140

Monthly budget of another family living on a chacra (man, wife, 3 children, 1 in school)

	Soles
Estimated monthly income	80
Estimated monthly expense for food (consume ¾ kilo of rice per day, 30 centavos of salt meat; some cheese; 10 centavos of manteca; yucas and camotes; buy 20 centavos of *chicha* per day)	55
Estimated monthly expense for clothing and school	25

This family has ¼ fanegada of ground. They grow yucas and vegetables for their own use and for sale. They have chickens and 2 donkeys, no cows.

Monthly budget of a town-dwelling family (man, wife, and 5 children)

Income:

	Soles
Wife sells wood and charcoal, earning about	15.00
Wife sells *chicha* and earns about	20.00
Man is foreman in Salaverry and earns	150.00
Total monthly income	185.00

Expenditure:

	Soles
House rent	5.20
Pay to water carrier	1.60
Wood and charcoal	15.00
Meat	22.50
Rice	19.80
Milk	4.50
Bread	9.00
Lard	9.00
Salt	.70
Miscellaneous food and drink	40.00
Tuition for 2 children in *colegio*	3.00
Clothes and shoes for the children (estimated 84 soles annually)	7.00
Clothes and shoes for the wife (60 soles annually)	5.00
Clothes and shoes for the father (96 soles annually)	8.00
Total monthly expenditure	150.30

This family enjoys a relatively high expenditure for Mocheros. Another family of five, without land, the father working as a stevedore in Salaverry, get along on 70 soles per month, or a little less than 2.50 soles per day. They pay 3 soles per month for their house.

I asked my friend, Don Victor Rázuri, to write out his estimate of family incomes. Señor Rázuri is a *forastero* who has lived in Moche for the past 25 years and is one of the few outsiders who enjoy the complete confidence, goodwill, and respect of the Mocheros. He has shown himself their friend on many occasions and has never shown any tendency to acquire their land. He is in intimate contact with many families and may be expected to know something of their affairs. His estimates, however, I believe, are somewhat optimistic, if taken to refer to the statistically average family. On the basis of such information as I have, it would seem that he describes the more properous families. He also figures as cash the work of the man in the work-sharing arrangement. His report, in translation, follows.

My small knowledge related to the utilization of labor in this place does not qualify me to have my data taken with complete certainty, but rather they may serve as orientation to direct attention to the ancient development which still persists among the inhabitants, making them a people in their mode of life distinct from many other valleys.

It is known by all that this valley is subdivided into small properties among the agricultural population, so that each farmer is usually owner of his parcel of ground, which he has inherited from his ancestors. Thus it is that somewhat more than two-thirds of the men may be considered *peones* [servants] of their own interests. Naturally they preserve their primitive method of working their lands, that is, with the intelligent use of work-sharing (*préstamos de brazos*). For example, Don Fulano decides to plant his small plot. Then he invites the presence of two or three more workers (*brazos*), and, accompanied by food and drink, according to his economic situation, the planting is accomplished. Of course, when he is invited to return the labor to the others, he is obligated to do so. Thus, one after another, the necessary tasks are performed. But, of course, not all men have the same amount of land; so it is, that among themselves it is customary to give their labor in return for daily wages in cases where this is necessary. Here in Moche the agricultural work is not hard and most men are content to earn a modest living. Added to this is the fact that the major part of this rich *campiña* has been converted into cattle raising, so that each individual has at least two milking cows, which should produce as a minimum 10 liters per day, not taking into account the value of the calves, etc., or let us say, 3 soles daily. Now let us evaluate the work of the Señora (or woman of the house). She frequently dedicates herself to the business of the *chicha* and the *causa*, which can be considered a matter of 15 days per month, with a minimum intake of 2 soles per day. And when she is not doing this she buys certain products, like yuca, *camote, alberja, lenteja*, etc., at a low price and resells them at the market in Trujillo, obtaining more or less the same average profit (2 soles) per day. The labor of the children is absorbed in the production of milk and crops, but occasionally they may obtain a few centavos for running errands for neighbors, in which case they are allowed to spend it for sweets or to keep it for their own. We also must consider that the Moche people raise poultry, the sale of which could be figured as bringing in about 20 soles per month. Finally, we may calculate that the sale of agricultural products other than milk and poultry should bring in about 15 soles per month. Thus we have the following list of income per month.

	Soles
Work of the man	30
Work of the woman (selling *chicha, causa,* reselling vegetables)	30
Sale of milk	90
Sale of vegetable products	15
Sale of poultry	20
	185

Let us now consider the expenses of a household with 3 or 4 children. Nothing is paid for the house, for if the family does not have one in the town, they have one on the *chacra.* For food is spent conservatively 2.5 soles per day. Clothing may be calculated at 10 soles per month. *Chicha* and strong drink would cost about 1 sol per day. For other diversions, 0.5 sol per day; cigarettes, 0.2 sol per day; school expenses, 0.2 sol per day; religious contributions, 0.2 sol per month; taxes to the government, 1 sol per month. We should also add a contingency fund, as when the family celebrates a Saint's day or other festival, makes contributions as *padrinos* at baptisms, diverse gifts, expenses in temporary illnesses, etc. For all this we may consider 25 soles per month. We may now make up the following table of expenses, per month.

	Soles
Food at 2.5 soles per day	75
Clothing	10
Chicha and hard liquor	30
Other diversions	15
Cigarettes, occasional coca, etc.	6
School expenses	6
Religious contributions	2
Contingency expenses	25
Government taxes	1
Total	170
Monthly balance for saving	15

To this small balance saved each month we must add the value of the calves, donkeys, and poultry which each year adds to the reserve and which in case of serious illnesses or deaths serves to save the situation.

Let us now consider the type of family which has some land, but which also enjoys an income from a trade or other outside labor. Income may be calculated as follows. Pay of the man, 60 soles per month. Earning of the woman of the house, selling *chicha* and *causa* and trading in vegetable products, 60 soles per month; in this sum is included the labor, if any, of her minor children. Sale of agricultural products, milk, maize, poultry, etc., 120 soles.

	Soles
Man's work	60
Woman's work	60
Sale of products	120
Total	240

As expenses, we calculate the following:

Food	90
Clothing	15
Chicha and hard liquor	36
Other diversions	15
Cigarettes, etc.	6
School expenses	6
Religious contributions	2
Government taxes	1
Contingency expenses	35
Total	206
Monthly balance	34

If we make a disinterested examination of the situation we may conclude that the standard of living of this community is relatively satisfactory in comparison with that of the *peon* who works in large cities or on plantations, whose income frequently is insufficient to cover the high cost of living.

Our workers have never suffered the pain of a strike or a stoppage of work, because in reality they have no employer (*patrón*). Therefore, it seems to me that our people are privileged to Providence, and they have ample time and opportunity to celebrate fiestas, etc.

In summary, we may say that, whatever an "average" figure might be exactly, the cost of living and the amount of cash needed to maintain life and a family are, in terms of North American values, very small in Moche. It is also obvious that the standard of living, especially in clothing, house furnishings, reading matter, etc., is different and cheaper in money terms from that of even the poorer categories of North American society. One can live in Moche and maintain a family of five not too uncomfortably, according to Moche standards, for 40 to 50 soles cash per month (roughly $6 to $7). It is doubtful that any Moche family has a cash budget exceeding about $30 per month, and such a family would be among the minority.

TRANSPORTATION, COMMUNICATION, AND THE EXPANSION
OF THE MOCHE WORLD

THE OLD WAY

The importance of the human foot and the donkey as a means of transportation in Moche have already been mentioned (pp. 24-25). The use of wheeled vehicles by Mocheros within the community is, so far as I know, totally absent. Not even the wheelbarrow is used.

In carrying loads afoot the principal apparatus is the *alforja,* a woven shoulder bag of cotton or wool, with two large square pockets separated by an unpocketed strip of equal width by which the contrivance is slung over the shoulder, one pocket in front and the other behind. These bags are also carried in the hand in a similar manner, and are likewise used as saddle bags, being slung over the back of a donkey with one pocket on each side. No straps or ties are provided. The bags and their contents are kept in place by gravity. The *alforjas* vary in size, according to the use for which they are designed. They are obtained in trade from the Sierra and from the region of Chiclayo. Those from the Sierra are usually of wool, while those from Monsefú (near Chiclayo) are often of cotton with very elaborate floral designs of Spanish colonial provenience. The tumpline arrangement, which was apparently universal during Mochica times, does not appear in modern Moche at all. Babies are carried in the arms or against the mother's side or hip, but not astride it.

People carry heavy loads only for short distances and the donkey seems to have displaced the human pack animal almost entirely. Horses, as already mentioned, are little used by the Mocheros, and mostly for riding rather than packing.

From the reminiscences of old residents it appears that modern developments in communication and transportation have constituted one of the most important factors in the change of patterns and orientations of the Moche culture. In the old days, up to about the first of the century or a little later, it appears that a regular system of exchange between Sierra and Moche, employing donkey transportation, was in operation. Simbal, one of the so-called Mochica towns, which lies in the coastal foothills of the Andes, served as contact for commercial exchanges from the two regions. Regular trips were made by the Mocheros with donkey trains to this town. The trip required about 3 days, and *tambos,* or rest houses, were located along the road, providing food, *chicha,* and rest for the night. In Simbal the Mocheros came in direct contact with people from the Sierra with whom they did their trading. These contacts, together with the goods exchanged, would seem to explain the presence of many Sierra traits in Moche today. It would seem that something similar to this pattern of exchange between coast and Sierra goes back into antiquity, undoubtedly previous even to the Inca conquest of the Chimu region. In the Mochica material may be seen Sierra plants, animals, and other traits whose presence on the coast can only mean regular contact between the two areas.

Moche, of course, was not unique among the coastal villages in maintaining this commerce with the Sierra during colonial times and the last century, although some informants would have it that Moche did most of the trading and carrying for the communities of the region, such as Virú, Huamán, Guiñape, etc.

In the exchange carried on in this manner, the following seemed to have been the principal products. Moche provided dried and salted fish, *ají, cañanes,* salt, cords of brown cotton for hairdressing and weaving. In return Moche received from the Sierra wool for weaving, maize, potatoes, wheat, *quinoa* (which was formerly much eaten in Moche), *chochoca* (maize flour), hams, and live sheep. Through these contacts a good many intermarriages took place, particularly involving Sierra men who came to Moche, married, and settled down. There seems to have been some arrangement of trade friendships and a certain amount of specialization on both sides, but I have insufficient information to expound the details.

This system of trade must have broken down fairly recently, because its existence, if not the details, remains in the memory of many persons. It is possible that the opening of hard-surfaced highways and the development of bus and truck transportation wrought the change, or at least destroyed the donkey-train pattern. The railroad from Salaverry via Trujillo to the Valley of Chicama has been in operation since the 1870's (Paz Soldán, 1877, p. 858).

MODERN MEANS OF CONTACT WITH THE OUTSIDE WORLD

The railroad, connecting Salaverry with Trujillo and points beyond, a narrow gage line of 0.914 m., passes along the east edge of town, as shown in map 1. At the present time it runs no passenger cars or trains and therefore exercises no appreciable influence in the life of the Mocheros. Until a few years ago, however, it was a principal means of mechanical transportation for trips outside of Moche. A station and siding stood beside the line just opposite from the *plazuela* where the windmill now stands, and a branch line turned off here, passed westward on Calle Alfonso Ugarte to Calle Inclán, where it turned southward and continued to Las Delicias on the shore. This branch line was torn up and abandoned less than 10 years ago. Discarded rails are to be found as uprights in a few houses. The autobuses and the shortages of wartime have conspired to suppress the passenger business of the railroad.

The town of Moche lies in a Y formed by two first-class highways, each two lanes in width and smoothly asphalted. Final work on the surfacing was completed only 3 or 4 years ago. To the north of town the Pan-American Highway (Carretera Panamericana) passes southeastward on its way to Lima. Along the west side of town runs the highway from Trujillo to the port of Salaverry. Only the latter is important for Moche. The busses running between the port and the city turn off the highway and proceed to the Moche plaza, sounding their horns loudly as they enter the town, so that passengers may come running from their houses to the plaza. The trip between Moche and Trujillo requires 20 to 25 minutes and one-way fare is 20 centavos, having been raised from 15 centavos in 1944. According to the posted schedule, Moche is served by 48 trips per day in each direction, an average of one every half-hour, with a couple extra during hours of heavy traffic. In 1944 the first bus was supposed to leave Moche at 5:05 p. m. for Trujillo, and the last bus was supposed to leave at 12 midnight, arriving in Trujillo about 12:20 a. m. The last bus out from Trujillo to Moche left about 11:40 p. m. Although there is some complaint about the high cost of the fare, the majority of Mocheros use the bus, because of its convenience and speed. It is prepared to carry the bundles of agricultural produce (except alfalfa and other excessively bulky bundles) and the cans of milk on its roof. The busses also deliver the papers and mail early in the morning.

The surfacing of the highways also brings some trucks to Moche. A delivery truck from the Panificadora, a large Trujillo bakery, comes every day. Mocheros, both men and women, catch rides on these vehicles and also on trucks passing along the highways, as a further means of mobility.

There is a telephone "central" in the town of Moche on the Calle Espinar. It belongs to the Compañía Nacional de Teléfonos, but its facilities are little used by the general public because it has only one branch line, that to the police station. The instrument in the "central" itself is used, however, in emergencies, and one may call a person in Moche from Trujillo by long distance with some hope that a messenger will be sent out to bring him to the central office. A post office is maintained in the town, also on the Calle Espinar, which also theoretically receives and accepts telegrams. There is no house delivery of mail. The postmistress calculates that an average of about 15 pieces of incoming mail are handled daily.

According to my count, there are eight radio receiving sets, all in the pueblo; five of them belong to *forasteros* and three belong to Mocheros. None of the Government agencies has a receiver with loudspeaker for the benefit of the public, as is the case in many Peruvian towns. One of the radios is in a *salon* (drink parlor) and thus available to the public, as it were, and the others, in private homes, can be listened to by friends. There is not much interest in radio, however, and the extant sets exert practically no influence on opinion or custom. All are battery sets, owing to the fact that Moche has no electric power, so they are turned on only for a few minutes or an hour a day, and several of them are usually out of order at any given time for want of batteries. No gasoline or oil motors for the generation of electricity are in operation in Moche, so far as I know.

The lack of electricity, together with the general orientations of the culture, probably contributes to a relatively low interest in reading, or may be expected to retard its growth, although the dim, flickering light available in many a small Peruvian town which does have electricity is as discouraging to reading as the most primitive candle or oil lamp. Newspapers have a surprisingly large circulation for so rural a community, but they are read in daylight by those who can read. The Lima papers, especially the "Comercio," were printing in 1944 a total of 20 to 25 full columns of news of all types daily, but the Trujillo papers, especially the "Industria," carry much less reading material. All informants agree that the total circulation of daily papers in Moche cannot be less than 200. The following figures were obtained by me from the respective circulation managers and agents. "La Nación" of Trujillo reported for June, 1944, 49 paid subscriptions in Moche and estimated a street sale by newsboys of about 15 daily. "La Industria" reported paid subscriptions in Moche for July 1944 as 79, with no sale by newsboy. The agents for the distribution of the Lima papers report a sale of "about 25" papers daily to customers in Moche. This gives a total of 168, to which must be added an unknown number bought by the *plazeras* (women who go to market) in Trujillo in the early morning. All informants agree that this unknown figure would be at least 32, making a total of 200. I did not have the time to trace down these recipients of newspapers to get a figure showing the precise proportion of the total who were Mocheros, as distinguished from *forasteros*. However, the cream of the news, so far as it is available in the papers, circulates widely among the Mocheros, even in the *campiña,* and the average native was usually quite well informed of the latest battles of the war, governmental decisions in Lima, and outstanding doings of the Prefectura in Trujillo. All of the *salones,* shops, and barber shops, as well as the municipal office, take at least one paper, which is read or glanced over without charge by customers and loafers.

As previously mentioned, a large proportion of the Mocheros, especially those above the age of 50, are illiterate, and of course do not read the newspapers. I have been surprised on several occasions, however, by the interest with which these people follow the news purveyed to them verbally by their literate friends and relatives.

A biweekly newspaper was started in Moche itself in October 1944 under the name of "Inti" (Quechua, "sun"), published and edited by the organization of young men called Moche en Marcha. It is a four-page, four-column sheet printed in Trujillo, but edited in Moche, and is devoted entirely to Moche affairs. The mere fact that a Quechua word was chosen for the title is another indication, I felt, of how deeply is the Mochica tradition buried in the past.

Aside from newspapers, there is no regular inflow of reading matter. An occasional magazine is purchased in Trujillo, but irregularly and at long intervals. The preference seems to be for picture magazines printed in Chile, Argentina, or Cuba, although "Selecciones del Reader's Digest" seemed to be arousing some interest in 1944. Most of the literate Mocheros do not have the habit of reading as a means of cultivating the mind or even as a means of passing the time, while many cannot read at all. On the other hand, there are exceptions here, as in all communities, and quite a number of young men who are in *colegio* or university in Trujillo, take themselves somewhat seriously as intellectuals. A number of these individuals have fairly large collections of books (20 to 30) and magazines.

All of these media of transportation and communication tend to break down the cultural isolation of Moche. Of all of them, the good highways and frequent bus transportation are probably the most important at present. These media serve to place the Mocheros in contact with other cultural currents, but, of course, such contact does not necessarily guarantee that the outside cultural elements in question are or will be adopted by the Mocheros. A discussion of these matters will be postponed to a later section (p. 159).

RECREATION AND ART

DRINKING AND EATING

To eat, drink, and be merry is the customary idea of the proper way to relax and enjoy oneself in Moche. As indicated in the section on the etiquette of food and drink, the Mocheros are prone to recreation of this informal type about the house even on ordinary weekday afternoons, whereas the consumption of elaborate meals and prodigious amounts of *chicha* and cane alcohol is a standard feature of all holidays, religious or secular.

In order to give some idea of the atmosphere of the informal weekday affairs which somehow get started without much planning or intention, I quote from my notes concerning an episode in which I was involved during my first days in Moche. Incidentally, it should not be assumed that either disapproval or approval of a moralistic type on my part is implied in this description or in other recording of Moche customs.

[On this afternoon] I was going down the street in the pueblo with one of my Moche friends, looking for an old lady said to be able to give me details about the former customs of the community. As we passed a certain house, my friend R., said "There's C. A. Let's go in and see what's going on." We entered the house and went out toward the back, where we found an old man, named C. A., drinking *chicha* with some friends, and already in a state of considerable enthusiasm. The house was that of S. R., a middle-aged woman, who is his *compañera* (mistress). Also present was M. A. J., *viuda de S.,* who, it turned out, enjoys the distinction of having had, in addition to the late S., three other "husbands," namely P. R., J. R., and Q., whose first name she does not remember. Another guest was one P. N., a protestant (*evangelista*) who lives in the *campiña*. Although he was dressed in the usual white suit, straw hat, and bare feet of a Moche man, C. A. insisted jokingly that he was a *doctor en derecho* (doctor of law). It later appeared that instead of being a doctor at laws, he had actualy finished only the *primaria* (primary school), but was a serious-minded chap given to reading and to the Seventh Day Adventist doctrine. Another guest was B. de N., an aunt of S. R., the lady of the house. Also present was a woman named M. A. and another man whose name I did not catch at the time.

The affair was taking place in a rather dark back halfroom which opened onto a small and mean back yard containing a kitchen, but not large enough for an outdoor arbor and garden. As soon as we entered, the lady of the house rushed out to boil a couple of eggs for my companion and me, in place of the *causa* which the others had already consumed. I was welcomed heartily by C. A., whose mind was dominated by the fact that, although he was 75 years of age, he was only awaiting a call to take a rifle and begin operations against the Japs, Germans, and all other attackers of *La Unidad de las Américas*. He and I would go forth to battle together, according to him. In the intervals when C. A. was occupied with drinking or going out to the back yard to relieve himself (in plain view of the assemblage), the talk revolved about two other topics. We discussed colds and the family relationships of those present. I had a bad cough and inquired what to do for it. I was overwhelmed with suggestions. Each woman had her own remedy which was chattered at me at the top of her voice at the same time all the other women were doing likewise. This bedlam was punctuated by C. A.'s giggles, and interspersed with his speeches in favor of American unity. Occasionally he would lean over to me and say, "Don't pay any attention to this advice. Rub some kerosene on your chest tonight. Tomorrow you will be cured and we'll go out together to shoot Japanese." When the medical topic played itself out, all the guests started telling me at once their genealogies, since they had heard that I was interested in such matters. If one person managed to go along understandably for as much as a minute, she would be invariably interrupted by someone else who would tell her that so-and-so's grandfather's second mistress was B., not A., etc. At one point the Seventh Day Adventist made a speech in the usual Peruvian flowery style, in favor of the great ideals of North America. I replied in an imitation of the same style, thanking him profoundly and pointing out that we appreciated the confidence of our friends, the Peruvians. This speech was greeted with many cheers and renewed quaffing from the gourd cup. Shortly thereafter a man came in with a guitar and, after a few drinks of *chicha,* started playing, while some of those present started to sing and dance.

About 5 p. m., C. A. insisted on taking me and my friend R., who had brought me to this house in the first place, out to the *salon* of Don Juan Olímpico, for a "*copita.*" We took a booth and he ordered a *cuarto* (quarter of a liter) of *cañaso* and some sandwiches made of buns with two black olives in each. His talk continued in the same way, inviting me to come to his *chacra* whenever convenient, proposing a Jap-hunting expedition on the morrow, etc. He also had a sad period during which he expatiated on being all alone, for his wife had died several years before and his mistress did not take her place.

Recovering from his melancholy, C. A. insisted on ordering a second *cuarto,* which, however, by means of a few winks and whispered words I managed to have the proprietor dilute considerably. However, old C. A. was not to be deceived, and complained loudly that he would never come to this place again, because the *cañaso* was nothing but water. He sent the bottle back and had a new one brought. After C. A. had disposed of most of the second bottle, I had to order a third to respond to his hospitality (*corresponder*), so that he would not feel insulted. By this time, however, he was very drunk and knew it. He insisted on taking his leave, after having one short drink from the third bottle and effusively thanking me for my hospitality. One of the most comical aspects of the afternoon was the process of getting him out of the place.

We were sitting in a booth with something like beaverboard walls, around a table covered with oilcloth. C. A. was very polite and still enthusiastic about my proposed visit to his *chacra* and about inter-American unity, but he was not very well oriented. He put on his straw hat, which had a leather lining, and pushed it back on his head. As he did this, the leather lining came loose and remained as a sort of skullcap down over his eyebrows, while the hat fell off. There was an interval during which C. A. angrily claimed that he had been blinded by the foul liquor purveyed by this place and apologized profusely for having brought his dear ally who was going to hunt Japs with him to such a den. Finally he got his hat on again, but the lining stayed down over his eyes. We all shook hands as C. A. once more took ceremonious leave, and, turning purposefully, tried to walk through the beaverboard wall. He was quite obstinate about it and attempted to continue nonchalantly with legs working steadily, but face pushed up against the wall. R. would say, "No, man, the exit is over here, man," to which C. A. would reply, "Don't tell me that R. I know perfectly well where the door is. Do you think I am drunk?" This dialogue took place several times, with C. A. all the time leaning against the wall with his leather skullcap down over his forehead and the straw hat on the back of his neck, trying to walk through the wall. Finally we got him out through the door, staggering, but still polite.

Later acquaintance with C. A. showed him to be normally a most reserved and rather melancholy man, whose expansiveness and aggressiveness appeared only when released by alcohol.

This episode illustrates several features of the typical *chicha*-and-*causa* relaxation complex. (1) The affairs are impromptu and guests may attend without prior invitation, although strangers without an introduction by a recognized friend would not be admitted. (2) The ordinarily quiet, if not taciturn, natives of Moche become voluble. Inhibitions are released and utterance is sometimes given to statements which it is extremely difficult to pry out of a Mochero when sober. A certain jocularity appears, which is seldom attempted during sobriety. Singing and dancing are indulged in freely, whereas, when sober, the typical individual feels embarrassed by activity which draws attention to himself. (3) The removal of inhibitions leads to expression of suppressed aggressions, as in the case of C. A.'s remarks about his mistress and his eagerness to shoot Japs. Overt physical scuffles sometimes occur during these affairs, and the aftermath of every large fiesta usually includes several persons in the local jail for fighting. Conversely, expression is given to friendly and sympathetic feelings which otherwise are not demonstratively expressed. In fact, it seems that the typical Mochero does not know how "to be himself" without the help of *chicha*. When sober he may be personally pleasant, but he is either reserved and noncommittal, or taciturn, or on the defensive. Of course, a stranger and a foreigner such as myself would receive this impression more forcibly, but as confidence in me developed and my acquaintance deepened, I was even more convinced that *chicha* provided a welcome release from anxieties or other tensions among and within the Mocheros. Strangely, only one person in his cups expressed dislike and aggression toward me personally during my time in Moche. Fortunately, after a tussle between us one day, he became a great friend who thereafter annoyed me almost as much with his effusive *abrazos* (a form of embrace when men greet each other) as he had previously with his insults. His first antagonism toward me was at least in part based upon a long-standing grudge against *gringos*, apparently dating from an unfortunate experience with an employee of the railroad in his boyhood. (4) The pattern is to get drunk, but not "dead drunk." One drinks and eats *causa* with his friends to enjoy himself, not to "pass out." C. A.'s

insistence on leaving when he felt that he was in danger of not being able to walk is fairly typical. A "passed out" drunk is a rare sight in Moche. Individuals usually go home when they cannot hold more. There are exceptions, to be sure, but the Moche pattern is not that of an orgy in which the participants seemingly wish to blot out all consciousness save that of the high-keyed nervous pleasure of the dissipation itself. One might say that the Mocheros unconsciously wish to submerge, by means of drink, the consciousness of certain restraints which prevent them from fully expressing and enjoying their own potentialities; but once the state is achieved, they wish to prolong it, not to blot it out also.

The comparative rarity of quick and stupefying drunkenness is, of course, reinforced by the pattern itself; *chicha* rather than hard liquor customarily forms the major part of the drink; it is always consumed with food; and one drinks in the stimulating atmosphere of the presence of others. Nevertheless, there is no acquired cultural drive leading one to quick drunken oblivion. I believe that I am safe in characterizing the Moche drinking-and-eating pattern's cultural goal as relaxation, relaxation of psychosocial restraints, rather than debauchery.

Another feature of possible significance is the comparative moderation of language at Moche drinking bouts. Although people become voluble and loud, the standard tension-releasing words of Spanish are not very much employed and the obsessive interest in sexual, scatological, blasphemous, and obscene topics displayed by many Mestizos in other parts of the country, even when sober, seldom appears in the Mocheros, even when in their cups. Sex matters may be discussed a little more freely, but not with unusual affect, for sex and bodily functions are common topics of conversation in mixed company at any time. The sonorous oaths and obscenities in which the Spanish language is so rich are not perhaps as much used in Peru as in certain other Latin American countries; but Peru has an ample, if comparatively restricted, fund of them in common use. Yet I have seldom heard much of the standard Peruvian swearing in Moche.

SPORTS

Modern team sports make an appeal primarily to the younger generation.

Football (of the type called "soccer" in North America) is played enthusiastically on Sunday afternoons, usually before an audience of at least 40 or

50 onlookers. The sport is handicapped by the lack of a permanent field, and play and practice have to take place on fields which happen to be out of cultivation at a given moment, such as cornfields awaiting the next plowing, and the like. The sport owes a good deal of its impetus to one of the *forasteros,* a player of some regional renown in his younger days. At present he is the operator of one of the *salones* in the town. Six football clubs are in existence and are named as follows: Atenas, Olímpico, Once Amigos, Alianza Moche, Esport Boys, Santa Cruz de Chorobal. The expenses for shoes, uniforms, footballs, and the like, are paid from the membership dues and contributions. Games are played among the Moche clubs and also with teams from the haciendas of the region.

Basketball (usually called simply "*basquet*") is played by only one team, representing the Club Atlético Espartano (Spartan Athletic Club). It is said to be played on the court which exists in the patio of the Government school for boys, the only one available. During my stay in Moche this court had only one basket in position and no games were played.

Tejos is thought of as the distinctive Moche sport, and in its present form, at least, is claimed to have been invented and elaborated in Moche itself. The prime stimulus of the *tejos* movement has been Don Manuel L. Briceño y Vázquez. Don Manuel is a man of many and real talents, who, with Don Víctor Rázuri and Don José Eulogio Garrido, is one of the three *forasteros* who have lived for many years in Moche, have taken a hearty and sympathetic interest in the community, and have won the complete confidence of the true Mocheros. Señor Briceño is a water-colorist of recognized accomplishment, an architectural engineer, and a practical archeologist. For many years he has been employed by the Larcos of Chiclín and, among his other accomplishments, has made a definitive study of Mochica architecture, which has been embodied in a large portfolio of all the known types of Mochica constructions, shown in floor plan, elevation, and also reconstructed in the form of water-color paintings in perspective. These documents, if the money and opportunity to publish them can ever be found, will doubtless prove to be of immense value to the entire public interested in the north coast of Peru.

Señor Briceño has written a monograph embodying his evidence concerning the origin of the *tejos* game and setting forth the rules as standardized by himself. Although this work has not been printed, it is circulated in typed form among the various *tejos* clubs of the region.

The word *tejos* means "quoits," and the game is played with brass disks 2 cm. in diameter which are supposed to weigh 80 gm. Señor Briceño suggests that certain unperforated disks found in the Mochica and Chimu archeological material may show that a similar game was played in ancient times. Various games involving the throwing of small disks are played throughout modern Peru, but, except for the Trujillo region, in my own travels in provincial parts of the country I do not happen to have discovered any conforming to the Moche game in details. The most common quoits game throughout Peru is that sometimes called *sapo,* which consists of throwing a disk about the size of a silver dollar at a brass frog sitting with his mouth open on a box top that is perforated with a number of holes slightly larger than the disk. The player scores according to the hole into which his quoit falls. The highest scoring play is to throw the disk into the frog's mouth. This apparatus is found in *chicherías* and loafing places in almost all parts of the country.

In Moche the *tejos* game is played on the ground, and it is a sport well adapted to shady arbors with

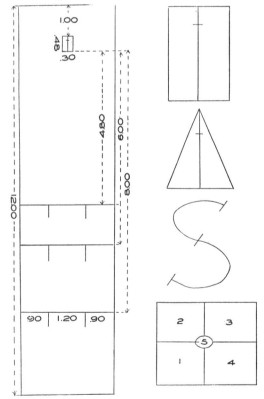

FIGURE 6.—*Left,* scale diagram of standard quoits court *(tejos); right,* three additional designs of targets.

causa and *chicha* near at hand. The standard court is laid out on smooth, hard-packed earth and conforms to the measurements shown in figure 6. The court is 12 m. long by 3 m. wide and the player throws his quoit at a target area, made of adobe set flush with the ground surface, whose closest point is 8 m. from the throwing line. The target (*raya*) itself may take one of four forms, shown in figure 6. The most common is that appearing in the plan of the court. It consists of a longitudinal line bisecting the target area, with a cross line 10 cm. from the farther end. If the disk lands within the target area without touching its borders, the player scores one point; if it lands on the longitudinal line, he scores two points; and if it lands on the cross of the two lines, he scores four points. Each player has two disks, and part of the game is to prevent one's opponent from scoring by knocking his disk out of the target area while landing one's own disk in scoring position. The game is much more difficult than it appears at first glance. As in other sports, there are many theories and usages regarding techniques: the stance, the wrist motion, the arm motion, and so on, are analyzed in detail by the experts. Individuals may play, each winning his own score, or the game may be played between teams of partners.

Moche has its *tejos* club, which has been granted official recognition by the Prefectura in Trujillo, and has organized a sort of league of clubs in haciendas and communities in the Moche and Chicama Valleys. Tournaments are played and the Moche club possesses a collection of loving cups, diplomas, and other trophies won in these tournaments (pl. 18, *middle* (*right*)). Considerable pride is shown in the successes of the team, because this is the one activity in which the community possesses recognized leadership and prestige throughout the region. During the Peruvian national holidays of 1944, the Moche team accepted a challenge from the team of the Hacienda of Laredo. The preliminaries took on somewhat more solemnity than one would have thought necessary, not knowing the importance of *tejos* in Moche. The challenge was received in writing, signed and sealed with a rubber stamp by the secretary of the Laredo club. A meeting of the executive committee of the Moche club was called, at which I happened to be present, to discuss the matter; and the acceptance was finally sent off, inscribed on the printed letterhead of the Moche club, formally signed and sealed.

Small boys play marbles, using round *choloque* seeds or factory-made glass marbles. Top spinning is also popular among the very young. The tops are either bought or made at home; they are of wood with an iron point, and are spun by first winding them around with a length of string, then throwing the top to the ground while holding onto the end of the string. Climbing trees, wrestling, playing on rope swings hung from tree branches, etc., are also among the childish amusements.

Only males engage in sports. Women do not even play *tejos*.

Making string figures on the fingers is a favorite past-time of children. Small girls have dolls, but not invariably. There are probably other childish games which I have not noted. After they are able to walk, most small boys and girls are occupied part of the time with baby watching. They carry the babies about from one part of the arbor or garden to another, using their arms, but one does not see small nurses with babies tied to their backs in blankets walking or standing about for hours at a time as in the Sierra. (See pl. 14, *upper* (*left*), for a group of children eating their midday meal together on the ground under the trees.)

THE CINEMA

The town has a motion picture theater located one-half block off the central plaza. It is served by a traveling apparatus which comes to Moche about once a month and gives shows every night for a week, carrying its own electrical generating outfit. The theater building is owned by a *forastero*. It is a plastered adobe building furnished with wooden benches and chairs, and a booth for the projector. Capacity is about 150 seated patrons. The hall is also used for meetings. The screen is of white cotton sheeting, torn and spotted in several places, and the projector is said to be capable of improvement. Perhaps more interest would be aroused in the movies by better equipment, but at the present time Mocheros are not "movie fans," generally speaking.

MUSIC AND DANCING

Music appears in the following forms, to consider the instrumental types first. (1) There are two brass bands in the community, composed of the typical European instruments, such as cornets, tubas, bass drum, etc. These organizations are hired by *mayordomías* to lead the parade on saints' days when the image is paraded through the streets, and they also furnish alleged music during the mass in the church. (2) A couple of fiddling orchestras, consisting of violins, piano, and drums, are available for occasional fox-trot dances. (3) Several men play the "old-time" instruments in certain costumed dances and parades. These old-time instruments in Moche consist of the reed flageolet (*quena*) and the hand-made skin-covered drum. The only costumed feast day which occurred during my stay was the fiesta of Cristo Rey or Nuestro Señor de la Misericordia. A woman of the community has provided a set of "Indian" costumes for the men and a set of "angels'" costumes for the young girls. The Indians are dressed in a mixture of the North American wildwest movie version of red Indians, with feathered war bonnets, etc., and certain modern additions, such as colored goggles, mirrors, and toy pistols (pl. 18, *lower* (*left*)). An unformalized allegorical dance takes place while the image is being paraded. The burden of the "plot" is a sort of contest between the bad "Indians," or *diablos* (devils) as they are usually called, and the angels. The parade is led by a couple of flageolet players and drummers. One man dressed as an "Indian devil" was playing both the flageolet and the drum at the same time. The brass band participates likewise. The woman who is patron of this fiesta keeps the costumes put away in trunks between the festival days when they are used. (4) Guitar music is very popular, especially for the informally arranged dances which develop along with drinking and eating in the households. The guitars use steel strings and seem to be played mostly by younger men. There is one man in town who repairs and tunes the instruments, on a semiamateur basis. (5) One household in the pueblo has an old and badly tuned piano, which the owner of the house bought second-hand some years ago for 200 soles (about $30.60). The owner's son has become an efficient pianist, considering the instrument he has to work with, and fiestas in this house are popular on this account. As of the present, this young man has not turned his talent into commercial channels, but he is now organizing an orchestra with some of his friends. The pianist for the fox-trot orchestra which occasionally performs is a *forastero*.

Vocal music is not much developed as an art, but rather as a form of recreation. During a drinking spree, when the guitars have become well warmed up, almost everyone will sing, or emit sounds said to be singing. There is one professional vocalist among the Mocheros. He has a good bass voice, and earns money singing in the church as cantor, and also in Salaverry and Trujillo. He happens to be the owner of the piano and the father of the young pianist. His old father, now 93 years of age, tells me that he was a professional cantor in his prime, and his father before him. Thus we may speak of a family musical by tradition, but, of course, the musical forms employed are native neither to Moche nor to Peru. This man is also leader of the church choir, which, however, is a comparatively small and unstable group consisting mainly of young boys whose attendance is not as regular as desired.

There is no original composition in music of which I am aware.

Dancing appears in the following forms: (1) Allegorical dancing of the type indicated above in referring to the "devils" and "angels" is characteristic of certain religious festivals. (2) Occasionally, on the day of a special fiesta, the public market, which has a cement floor, is turned into a dance hall for modern dancing by couples. This type of dance is called "fox trot," regardless of the fact that it may include tangos, two-steps, waltzes, etc., as well as fox trots. Only the younger and more sophisticated natives of the Moche undertake this type of dancing, and at these affairs the majority of couples are *forasteros*. (3) The typical folk dance of the Mocheros, the dance which characterizes household fiestas and drinking parties, is the *marinera*. This type of social dancing is common to Sierra and coast alike, throughout Peru, and hundreds of pieces of special music have been composed for it (not in Moche, however). The dance involves both sexes but does not permit bodily contact between men and women. Without going into a prolonged description, the movements consist of the male partner's doing a sort of two-step on the floor around his woman partner while he waves a handkerchief in one or both hands. He makes sudden turns, lunges, and approaches—which she coyly and rhythmically avoids. The dance is very energetic for both partners and they usually perspire copiously during its performance. The usual pattern is several couples dancing on the floor, while the rest of the party looks on from the side lines, yelling encouragement and making boisterous remarks.

ART

In the realm of pictorial art the stranger is impressed by the general interest in an attempt at painting. It is tempting to see this as a cultural heritage from the Mochicas, who, for their time and place, produced excellent work in the medium of painting on vases and other ceramic objects. Moche has produced one painter whose work has been nationally recognized artistically and in the form of financial awards. This is Pedro Azabache, 26 years of age in 1944, whose one-man show at the "Insula" in Lima in June of that year earned him critical acclaim and the sale of 14 of his canvases. It is rare that an ethnologist finds a competent artistic interpreter of the culture of the people he is studying among the people themselves. Therefore, by special permission of Señor Azabache, a number of his paintings are reproduced herein (pls. 19–21). Azabache was a pupil of the internationally renowned Peruvian painter, José Sabogal, who has done so much to turn artistic interest in Peru toward the interpretation of the native scene, and who has led somewhat of a revolt against the colonial tradition of servile copying of classical themes and compositions. Azabache paints his own people almost exclusively, and, although influence of Sabogal is readily discernible in his style and technique, he is gradually developing a manner of his own. He is unmarried and, when in Moche, lives with his parents in the *campiña*, where one room of the adobe house has been arranged as a studio. He received his technical training in the Escuela de Bellas Artes in Lima. Although I do not attempt to predict his future course, it is worth remarking that his present success is doubly remarkable because of the cultural climate of Peru. An artist who paints "Indian" subjects and themes has a difficult time getting a showing and a hearing in Peru because intellectual and artistic circles are still dominated in large part by the spirit of *hispanismo* which sees everything that is good as coming from Spain and the "glorious Spanish tradition" of colonial times, and disparages *criollismo* and *indigenismo* (interest in Peruvian native and aboriginal subjects). Insofar as there is no active prejudice against native subjects and Indians themselves, the attitude is often that they are best ignored. Therefore, an "Indian" painter who paints "Indian" subject matter has a doubly difficult task, if he is to achieve any sort of recognition.

In addition to Azabache, Moche has three other Mochero professional painters, namely, Teofilo Rosales, Nicolas Asmat, and Juan Manuel Rodriguez. None of these men have had Azabache's training, nor do they apparently possess his talent. However, they each sell a few paintings within the community and the region and do some professional work in the decoration of churches and the like.

Many persons who do not pretend to be professional artists seem to have an impulse to paint or draw. I have no statistical measure of the extent of this tendency, but a considerable number of houses possess inside walls decorated, often rather crudely to be sure, with painted scenes and designs. Although many of these efforts are crude from the point of view of the higher art criticism, nevertheless they are not childish scratchings, but show respectable technical competence in the use of perspective, shading, foreshortening, and so on.

Among the *forasteros* mention has already been made of Señor Manuel L. Briceño y Vázquez, who is an accomplished water-colorist, whose works are even now collectors' items among those who know them. Señor Briceño, however, has painted for his own pleasure and his work has been turned out for his own amusement. Señor José Eulogio Garrido, who is the Government-appointed mayor (*alcalde*) of the town, maintains a permanent art collection in his private house in Moche. For years he has been closely associated with many national artists who, from time to time, have presented him with samples of their works. Señor Garrido is also a writer in his own right and has recently been appointed National Curator of Folklore of the North. Among his other posts he is editor in chief of the Trujillo daily, "La Industria." Up to the present his considerable corpus of writings has been published only as articles in provincial and Lima newspapers, but he is understood to be collecting and preparing for publication a goodly part of this material in more permanent form. He is said to have three volumes of material on Moche itself which, when published, should make a valuable contribution to our knowledge. I have not had the opportunity of seeing the latter material.

Two organizations of younger Mocheros of both sexes have appeared recently, having among their stated purposes the stimulation of artistic and cultural interests. They are Moche en Marcha and La Asociación Mochera Cultural. The membership of each is exclusively, or almost exclusively, composed of true Mocheros, most of them under the age of 25. Moche en Marcha has begun, as previously mentioned, the publication of a biweekly newspaper, "Inti," which affords an outlet for a certain amount of writing in the form of poems and essays, while both organizations hold regular meetings in which the members recite their literary compositions and listen to musical performances.

FIESTAS

Latin America is a land of fiestas and holidays. Peru has 20 official holidays throughout the year in addition to Sundays, and Moche adds at least 7 semiofficial local holidays to this list, not to mention fiestas organized sporadically by *mayordomías* for the celebration of certain saints' days. These are all fiestas involving the entire community. Family celebrations must also be taken into account. In a later section I discuss in more detail the *rites de passage*. For example, there are 11 types of *padrinazgo* (godfather or godmother relationship) in Moche. The establishment of any one of these is the occasion for a fiesta.

It is more illuminating to discuss the details of the various fiestas in connection with their functional relationships with specific aspects of the culture, and to make here the general observation that the fiesta is the institutionalized form in which appear almost all the other types of recreation and art mentioned above, except the actual production of pictorial and literary art. Even modern sports have a place in most of the community fiestas.

All of the officially recognized fiestas have a serious purpose (or I may say, are parts of fundamental orientations of the culture), such as the commemoration of a personage or event, religious or patriotic, as the case may be. This aspect of the fiesta pattern must not be overlooked or minimized, but to the individual the performance of a fiesta brings relief from daily strain and monotony and a certain exaltation. Thus, the fiesta furnishes both relaxation and recreation to the individual and the group.

MISCELLANEOUS ITEMS OF LORE AND LEARNING

The symbolic patterns common in Moche are mentioned at appropriate points throughout this report, and in the following section merely a few miscellaneous items are recorded. A good part of what is ordinarily considered lore and learning will be found in the sections on agriculture, fishing, and medicine, as well as elsewhere.

FORMAL EDUCATION

Instruction is provided by two Government-supported schools, one for boys and one for girls. Each gives instruction through the sixth year. Each school is manned by teachers, including a director, all of whom are *forasteros*. The staff of the boys' school is male, and the staff of the girls' school is female. The fact that there are only four teachers for six grades in each school means that there is a doubling up in the classes. I have made no thorough investigation of the instruction, but the plan of the boys' school, at least, is modern and, on the whole, the equipment seems to be good. The director of the boys' school recently established a school library with a gift from the manager of one of the haciendas. In addition to the public schools, there are two *"colegios"* in the *pueblo*. These are merely private elementary schools, conducted in a private house by the housewife, often while she spends part of her time in her household tasks. Tuition in the private schools is 2 soles per month, and some parents prefer to send their children to these teachers because they believe the children receive more individual attention than in the public schools. A public rural school exists in the small settlement, called Sun, in the midst of the northern *campiña*. It is coeducational and is manned by a male director (who at the same time is a student at the University in Trujillo) and two female teachers. This school offers instruction only up to the fifth year.

On the whole, the people of Moche seem to be anxious to have their children learn the basic skills of literacy, and attendance in school is said to be good. There is, therefore, reason to believe that the coming generation of Mocheros will be completely literate. In addition to the elementary instruction offered in the community, intermediate and high school instruction is available in both public and private institutions in the nearby city of Trujillo, as well as the public university offerings.

PROVERBS AND EPIGRAMS

The use of the proverbial saying and the epigrammatic turn of phrase is much appreciated in Moche. The following I heard frequently enough to remember and to jot down, but I do not suggest that they indicate the extent of the Moche repertoire nor that many of them are native to Moche. On the contrary, my impression is that the Mocheros are not adept at the invention of the bon mot, but rather depend upon stock phrases when they engage in repartee. Some of the following are so overworked as to have almost the standing of cliches. A few examples, however, may be of interest in order to show the patterns of thought transfer, metaphor, and phraseology which have some currency in Moche. Drinking toasts are found on page 48.

Zorro que atreviesa,
Pronto estarás tiesa.
("Fox which meddles, soon you will be stiff."—Play on words in *tiesa,* which also may mean "stuck up".)

La mordidura del perro,
Con la misma lana se sana.
(The Peruvian version of, "I need some of the hair of the dog that bit me." More or less literally: "The bite of the dog is cured with the same wool." This is said to be based on a Sierra custom of clapping a tuft of sheep or llama wool on a wound to stop bleeding).

Tanto tienes, tanto sales;
nada tienes, nada vales.
("You come out in this world according to what you have. If you don't have anything, you're not worth anything," or, more literally, "As you have, so you make out; having nothing, you are worth nothing.")

El hombre propone, Dios dispone,
llega la mujer y todo lo descompone.
("Man proposes, God disposes; comes a woman and upsets it all.")

Quien con lobos anda
a aullar se enseña.
("He who goes with wolves, is taught to howl.")

Lo que fué buen vino es buen vinagre.
("Good wine makes good vinegar," i. e., a good young man is a good old man.)

Más vale morir debiendo que vivir para pagar.
("It is better to die in debt than to live only to pay.")

Lo mismo que di por verte,
diera por no haberte visto.
("The same that I gave to see you, I would give for not having seen you." Used in situations which would be appropriate for the restrained and icy use of the American expression, "If I never see you again, it will be too soon.")

Quien con lo ajeno se viste,
en la calle lo desvisten.
(He who masquerades as another will be unmasked by the public.)

---

[45] The unpolished English translations attempt to convey the sense in the North American idiom, but no endeavor is made to convert the rhythm, rhyme, assonance, or play on words into English.

Gallina no tiene agua para tomar
convida pato a nadar.
("Chicken doesn't have water to drink, she invites the duck to go swimming.")

Aguja sabe lo que cose,
dedal, lo que empuja.
("The needle knows what it is sewing and the thimble what it is pushing.")

Más vale llegar a tiempo
que ser convidado.
("It is more important that you arrive in time for the fun than that you are invited.")

Más pesa una libra atrás
que un quintal al hombro.
("A pound weighs more when you are pulling it than do a hundred pounds on your shoulders," i. e., it's easier in the long run to do the job right.)

Todo hombre debe de tener
nueve concubinas, diez con la mujer.
("Every man should have nine mistresses, ten counting his wife.")

Nada debe decir
de esta agua, no he de beber.
(Literally, "You should not say anything about this water, you don't have to drink it," usually in the sense of, "If you don't like what I'm doing, mind your own business.")

These pithy epitomes of folk wisdom may be compared with a few examples picked up in other localities known to the Mocheros.

The following were recorded in Huamachuco, in the Sierra, directly inland from Moche.[46]

Que sabe el burro el freno.
("The donkey must learn to know the bridle," a way of saying that a certain person must learn to know who is boss.)

El gallinazo no canta en puna,
y si canta, es por fortuna.
("The black buzzard"—referring to Negroes—"does not crow in the *puna*"—high plateau of the Andes—"and if he does, it is only to make his fortune.")

Solo lo falta, que lo pongan jáquima y
capachos para rebuznar.
(As with a donkey, all he needs is that they put the halter and hampers on him to start him braying, i. e., some men start complaining as soon as they have work to do.)

Abril, aguas mil,
Si no, cabe un barril.
(In April there is usually no end of rain—in Huamachuco—but if there is not a lot, a barrel will hold it all.)

---

[46] Rafael Larco Hoyle, my genial host on the short trip to Huamachuco, introduced me to several residents of that town.

Quite a number of proverbs and epigrams which might appear to be "indecent" in English translation are also current in Moche, even in mixed company.

TIME

Modern Moche operates on clock-measured time and this seems to be no recent innovation. The clock in the church has a loud bell which strikes the hours, the quarter, and half hours, and its striking can usually be heard all over town and in most parts of the *campiña*. It was shown in the section "Background of Moche" that the community had a church bell as far back as the beginning of the 17th century, which, according to the records of the Cathedral chapter in Trujillo, had been cast in Moche itself. A considerable number of persons possess watches and cheap alarm clocks, as well. As previously mentioned, a number of cultural activities are operated on measured time: irrigation, hired labor, transportation to and from Trujillo, school hours, etc. Cows must be milked at a certain time, for example, if the lady of the house is to catch the early bus to Trujillo. Children must eat breakfast at a certain time if they are not to be penalized at school. Men who work in Trujillo and Salaverry must leave home at a regular hour. And so on.

Another time indicator is the service of the Compañía Faucett de Aviación (Faucett Aviation Co.) whose airplanes fly up and down the north coast. They fly fairly low over the Moche District to and from the landing field in Trujillo. The plane from Lima and the south crosses the *campiña* at just about 11 o'clock every day, 7 days per week, and the plane from the north crosses in the opposite direction en route to Lima about 15 minutes later.

The fact that the Mocheros usually know the time of day does not mean that they are always punctual in terms of the North American ideal patterns. In the community itself a meal, for example, scheduled to begin at 1 p. m. frequently does not actually get under way until an hour or two later. Even the masses in the church are sometimes delayed as much as an hour after the announced time, because the priest is late in arriving from Salaverry where he has conducted the early mass. The parade of a saint may be announced for 9:30 a. m., but does not start until about 11. In cases of this kind, however, there is not necessarily an inconsistency between the representational pattern (dinner will be at 1 o'clock) and the actional patterns[47] (sitting down to eat at 2:30). It is generally

---

[47] Gillin, 1944.

understood that "1 o'clock" means "about 2:30." The maladjustment which a foreigner feels at first is due to a semantic difficulty arising from the fact that his experience in the local situation has not equipped him to understand the meaning of the verbal symbols in use. Among the Mocheros, then, there is one type of situation, usually of a social or recreational nature, in which a verbal statement of a given hour actually means an hour to 2 hours later than that stated. There are other types of situations, however, usually involving obligations between individuals, appointments of a business nature, school hours, etc., in which there is a close correspondence between the verbal pattern in its literal meaning and the action pattern correlated with it. In other words, the Mocheros have learned to keep appointments punctually when they stand to lose by not doing so. For example, informants who promised to meet me at a certain time and place were seldom late. Men working outside the community arrive promptly at their posts in time to begin work. The responsible parties are always on hand at the time when water is supposed to be turned into their irrigation ditches, etc.

MEASURES

The metric system of weights and measures is in use and fairly well understood by the Mocheros, although apparently it is not as firmly bedded in their thinking as the older Spanish colonial system. For example, the people prefer to talk of land areas in terms of *fanegadas* instead of hectares. The *legua* (league) as a measure of distance is frequently used rather than the kilometer. In weights, it is more common to use the *arroba,* the *quintal,* and the *carga* than to speak in terms of kilograms. In liquid measure, the *botella* is most commonly used, and is assumed to be equivalent to a liter, although the large beer bottles under reference actually hold slightly less than a liter. For small weights, *onzas* (ounces) and *libras* (pounds) appear in conversation almost exclusively. I have never heard a Mochero spontaneously use the term *centigramo* or *miligramo.* On the other hand, the *kilo* (kilogram) is a standard measure of weight.

This preference for the Spanish colonial system is characteristic of all of coastal Peru. The practical use of the Inca land measure, the *topo,* is unknown in Moche.

HISTORICAL TRADITION

A striking negative aspect of "lore and learning" is the lack of historical traditions. There is no time-worn body of tales or legends concerning the past of the community or the region.[48] This is apparently correlated with the lack of community pride and solidarity. There is, to be sure, a certain vague feeling that the people are descended from an important culture of ancient times, but no details have been elaborated, and the distinction between the Incas, the Chimus, and the Mochicas, for example, is not evident in the thinking of the people, even in disguised form. One family named Azabache (there are a large number of Azabache families) speak halfheartedly of the fact that they are descended from the "*curacas*" of ancient times. Other families are willing to admit this in conversation, in part at least, because it means nothing to the community as a whole. The Azabaches are willing to derive some prestige from their allegedly noble descent, but they have no impressive details with which to bolster the hazy tradition. Of course, they have no explanation of the fact that they now

[48] A considerably richer body of traditional material, partly aboriginal, seems to exist in Lambayeque. See Barandarián, n. d.

have a Spanish name. (Azabache means "jet," the black stone).

The ruins are regarded on the whole by the Mocheros as something as curious and foreign to themselves as they are to foreigners and all other persons. The ancient inhabitants are usually spoken of as *gentiles* (heathen) whereas the Mocheros are distinguished from them as *cristianos*. As for the traditional history of colonial times, it is conceivable that prolonged dredging of the memories of the older people would bring up something coherent, but in 5 months I was unable to obtain anything of significance. The two important historical events most often spoken of are the Chilean invasion of 1879 and the floods of 1925.

One cannot escape the conclusion that a community which has no strong solidarity and pride in itself as a group at present cannot be expected to have pride and interest in traditions concerning its past.

SOCIAL FORMS AND ORGANIZATION

POLITICAL CONTROLS

It was not my business to make a study of the Peruvian Government agencies in Moche, other than to consider their relation with the local culture and social situation. Therefore, no elaborate analysis will be attempted, and the following remarks have to do mainly with the functional aspects of the local government as seen from the point of view of an anthropologist, not that of a political scientist. The situation is described as of 1944.

In brief, the political controls in Moche are as follows. The town is the seat of the Municipalidad de Moche (Municipality of Moche), which is included within the Distrito de Moche (District of Moche) which also has its seat in the town. The District of Moche is a subdivision of the Province of Trujillo, which is one of the 7 Provinces composing the Department of La Libertad, which, in turn, is one of the 23 Departments composing the Republic of Peru. The Prefect, whose headquarters are in Trujillo, is the deputy of the central government and supreme political authority for the Department of La Libertad. He appoints political officers for the various municipalities and districts with the advice of his staff and the approval of the central government in Lima. The Department is repre-

sented in the National Congress by three elected senators and several deputies, but there are no elected representatives of districts or municipalities as such.

The appointed political officers in Moche are as follows. The District is presided over by a *gobernador*, who has an assistant and deputy called a *teniente gobernador*. They appoint a number of informal assistants, known as *tenientes del campo*, who carry out errands pertaining to their own neighborhoods. The municipality is in charge of an *alcalde* (mayor), who has a deputy, the *vice-alcalde*, and who is advised by a group of appointed *consejales* (councilors). The only constituted judicial authority is a justice of the peace (*juez de paz*). There is a police post (puesto de la guardia civil) composed of five men under the orders of a corporal. They are directly responsible to the departmental comandant of police in Trujillo, but may be called in by the political officials when needed. With the exception of the police personnel, none of the political officials is paid for his services.

The municipal government is supposed to govern the town and certain surrounding territory and the District government governs the remaining territory of the District. Economic support is understood to be derived mainly from income from municipal lands plus a few fees. The two governments have offices side by side on the main plaza of Moche. During my time, the municipal office was seldom open, except for the occasional meetings of the council. The District office, on the other hand, maintained a secretary who was paid a salary of 60 soles per month. Usually the *gobernador* or the *vice-goberna-dor* was also present during the morning.

The central government has shown discretion in its choice of officials, and the incumbents of the various offices were personally well liked. The *gobernador* was a tailor by profession, a *forastero* linked by marriage to Mochero families. The *teniente gobernador* was a respected true Mochero. The mayor was one of the most trusted *forasteros,* and the vice mayor was a true Mochero.

Public services maintained by the municipality include the garbage collections (one man with a two-wheeled cart and horse), the water system (a windmill and tank, with pipes leading to six public outlets in various parts of town), and the street lights (square kerosene lamps hung or perched on brackets fixed in house walls at street corners). The District seems to concern itself mostly with the issuance of required documents and the registry of vital statistics, etc.

The local irrigation administration has been previously mentioned. During a part of my stay a commission of sanitary engineers was working in the District on the problem of malaria control. During a period of perhaps 2 months the commission entrusted with the surveys for the new land register (*catastro*) was also present. Finally, the Government agricultural school maintains a staff of four to six employees.

In summary it is impossible to speak of a unified or unifying political organization for Moche as a whole, which has roots either functionally or historically in its own culture. Such unity as exists is imposed from the outside, and follows the pattern of local administration prevalent throughout Peru in 1944. There are various arguments advanced in favor of this system, most of which seem to boil down to the basic fear of the national administration that "revolutionary" elements would get out of hand if local self-government were permitted. And it can rightly be claimed that surface order and tranquillity, at least, prevail under the system. On the other hand, there is nothing explicit in the attitude of the Government

which would prevent community organization for nonpolitical purposes.

In Moche individuals are not molested in their daily private activities (unless they are suspected of belonging to the suppressed Aprista party), but they are definitely discouraged from attempting to participate on their own initiative in any way in decisions affecting the community as a whole, although as individuals they are legally allowed to make complaints by means of written depositions made out in proper form. The governmental policy in Moche in 1944 was not that of a rigid dictatorship, but rather a fairly tolerant and enlightened paternalism.

A considerable amount of grumbling is current, however, and the complaint is common that "Moche is neglected" and has no effective way of making its wants and needs known to the higher administrative centers. The governmental system has no social mechanism pertaining to the community as a whole for the settlement of those disputes and complaints whose importance have been previously discussed, no mechanism, that is, other than formal legal proceedings. I am not aware that the law specifically prohibits the formation of an informal community council, or something similar, but the fact is that Moche has not organized one, and the present set-up affords neither encouragement nor training in nonlegal means of settling disputes amicably. In Moche, as elsewhere in Peru, no public meeting may legally take place without the previous issuance of a police permit, which is obtainable only after full explanation of the purposes and expected constituency of the gathering, its place, time, and program. The objective of this regulation is to prevent the formation of disorderly mobs or subversive organizations.

FAMILIAL AND PSEUDOFAMILIAL RELATIONSHIPS

Although Moche as a community lacks solidarity and organization, each person is supported by three nets of relationships, as it were, of a familial or pseudofamilial type: (1) his blood relationships, (2) his marriage relationships, and (3) his ceremonial kinship relationships. If Moche were a primitive tribe we should probably follow the ethnological habit of calling the whole complex the kinship system.

SEX[49]

A boy begins to have sexual relations when he is about 12 or 13, but such relations are restricted.

[49] Most of my information on this topic came from male informants.

Seduction of adolescent boys by mature women was not reported. Most boys seem to have their first experience with girls of about their own age or somewhat older. The more common practice seems to be for a boy to waylay a girl as she passes alone through the *campiña*. Sometimes a group of boys waylays a group of girls. As a general rule, either type of seduction is preceded by verbal plans or hints and certainly by prior acquaintance. I have heard of no cases of violent rape.

By the age of 15 or 16 a boy makes dates with a girl to meet him at a given place in the *campiña* when she is supposed to be coming home from market or is out on errands. Another opportunity is during drinking bouts, when the parents are too occupied to pay attention to the young folk.

There is a belief that a boy who has robbed a girl of her virginity and is apprehended will be brought before her parents. He has the choice either of paying 500 soles (approximately $76) or of marrying her. Some informants said it is the law; others, that it is only a custom. None, however, was able to point out an instance in which such compensation had been paid. To judge by my observations, it would seem that most parents ignore the matter if the couple is not caught in the act and unless the boy is a "good catch" for their daughter. Indeed, there is little else that they could do, for a young adolescent boy is able neither to pay 500 soles, which is a small fortune in Moche, nor to set up a household for himself and the girl. There is a pose taken by most adults that premarital intercourse by girls is reprehensible, but the typical Mochero really takes it for granted in both sexes. The boy and girl receive a beating if apprehended in the act, and the parents may insist on at least a customary "marriage." Generally, however, it is more convenient to hush the matter up.

The modern Peruvian lower-class pattern is followed in requiring that a girl be accompanied by another girl, by a group of boys and girls, or by her parents or brother when she is in public. Actually, she is not very strictly guarded, and there are opportunities for arranging trysts. The Mocheros are, however, neither promiscuous nor obsessed with sex. To the contrary, sex is not an emotion-laden topic, and it has no great interest to them. Although many individuals are somewhat promiscuous during the first year or two of experimentation, a man and a girl usually form an attachment which lasts for months or years before either of them is old enough

to think of marrying or settling down. Mistresses show great fidelity, and men do not circulate promiscuously. Furthermore, the chaperonage system somewhat restricts promiscuity.

With respect to perversions, there seems to be no bestiality with animals. Several informants had never heard of such a thing; a couple of others had heard some jokes about it, but these referred to the Sierra and the informants were not very interested. Two men have been identified as male transvestites (*maricones*). One, a Mochero, is obsessed with religion, dresses like a monk part of the time, and is said to have avoided relations with women. The other is a *forastero*. Neither has been attributed homosexual tendencies. There are some women who are said to have no interest in men. They are spoken of in whispers as homosexuals (*mariconas*), but I do not know if they actually practice perversions. On the whole, Moche seems to be remarkably free of unnatural sex practices.

There were no professional prostitutes living in Moche during the period of study. It is said that some appear during the big fiestas at New Year's and San Isidro, but they do most of their business with *forasteros* and visitors. Four married women have been mentioned as willing to add to their earnings furtively, and there may be more. I am under the impression, however, that prostitution for gain is very little practiced or patronized by Mocheros. Comparatively few Mocheros seem to have an interest in or even knowledge of the brothels in the nearby city.

The modeled vases of the ancient Mochica depict a large variety of heterosexual positions and perversions, and a good many of these motifs linger on in Chimu art. Modern Moche seems to have lost most or all of these. Sexual relations are accomplished in the so-called normal manner.

In the household, the adult pair try to have a sleeping room to themselves. Separate rooms, however, are not possible in many cases. The parents occasionally go outside the house for their relations or send the children out. Perhaps the majority of children, however, have seen intercourse at an early age, and practically all children know about it in a vague way by the time they are 8 or 9 years old, though they fail to understand its details or biological purpose. There is no puritanical attitude about it, and there is no effort to withhold knowledge from children, though privacy is preferred in the act. Intercourse during menstruation is tabooed, but there are no restrictions when a woman is nursing a child.

Mechanical and chemical means of birth control are unknown, and pregnancy is not uncommon among unmarried women. Means are known, however, of producing abortions. One method explained to me by a respected *curandera* is the following (reference to some other methods will be found in the chapter on medicine). A plant called *zavarriala,* which comes from the Sierra but which can be obtained from herb sellers in the Trujillo market, is used. After about a quart of water has been brought to a boil, a handful of *zavarriala* is put into it and allowed to steep. The resulting tea is mixed with bees' honey and all of it is swallowed by the patient. This is alleged to "make the period come when it is stopped" and will produce abortions up to the fifth month, after which any method is unsafe. Quinine is said by this source to be too strong. "It breaks up the child inside the mother" (*Sancocha la criatura dentro de la mujer*). This woman says she is consulted quite frequently in these matters and that many women and girls know the techniques themselves. If abortion is practiced, it seems to be kept secret from the men, for the latter profess to know little about its methods or the extent to which it occurs.

There are various indications of the accretion of European attitudes on a simpler, perhaps older cultural complex having to do with sex. For example, the disapproval of masturbation seems to be more half-hearted than real. People do not talk about it with the affect so often displayed by Europeans and North Americans. The basic attitude seems to be that it is natural if no other release for the sex drive is present, and informants said it was common among boys under 6 and over 12, the latter sometimes performing in groups. Children are not corrected for acts evidencing autoeroticism, but a concession is made to Europeans mores. "Of course it is bad," they say, but children are not lectured on its baleful effects nor hounded to desist. The official attitude is negative, but the basic attitude is one of indifference. The same is true regarding premarital intercourse. Officially, it is disapproved by married people, and there are certain forms of behavior that are supposed to guard against it. But very few parents think that an affair will ruin their daughter's life. As a result of these affairs not a few girls have children, called *niños de la calle,* "children of the street." They are not thrown out of the house or disowned by outraged fathers, nor, in fact, is any serious obstacle put in the

way of their continued normal social development. If the father of the child is economically suitable to the girl, her parents will try to force the pair into setting up a household together; if not, the girl and her child continue to live with her parents. Practically all such girls eventually settle down with some man and form a family without any great social stigma attached either to them or to the child. Men do not disdain to marry or set up a household with an unmarried mother. The main bar to illicit unions is Church disapproval. The guilt felt on this score, however, is somewhat assuaged by having illegitimate children properly baptized in the church.

LOVE MAGIC

There are methods in use for attracting a member of the opposite sex. This procedure is spoken of as *enguayanchar,* or simply as *brujar.* A professional witch (*brujo*) may be employed either to attract the love or desire of a given person to his client, or in cases of unrequited love and jealousy to cause harm to befall the faithless or indifferent lover. I am not completely acquainted with the methods used for attraction, because the *curanderos* and *brujos* with whom I established good contact claimed not to practice it. The baleful love magic uses the same general techniques used to cause harm to anyone, described in the section "Native Medicine and Magical Curing." It is said, however, that one can *enguayanchar* a piece of clothing of the beloved or other intimate article and thereby arouse his or her desire. A plant called *yerba de la señorita* is said to be used in this process.[50] Further reference to love magic and similar matters will be found in the section on medicine.

The standard aphrodisiac in use in Moche and the whole north coast is *huanarpo* (*Jatropha macrantha*).[51] I have been shown specimens a few times in Moche, but believe that it is relatively little used here. In the general market of Chiclayo I saw several specimens on sale. I do not know what this plant looks like in nature, but the specimens kept in houses or for sale look like a species of dried mushroom. There are two kinds, male and female (*macho* and *hembra*). The male type has a rather shriveled stalk with a penislike head. The female type has a very short stalk and a large soft head with a fold in the middle, suggestive of a vulva. The

[50] See Camino Calderón (1942, p. 202, and passim) for reference to this matter in the region of Lambayeque. The plot of this novel turns on love magic whereby a jealous stepmother induces her husband's son to commit incest with his half-sister.

[51] Identification given by Valdizán and Maldonado, 1922, vol. 2.

plant is made into a fine powder and a pinch is administered in wine or other drink. The male type is administered to men and the female type to women. If one wishes to excite a lover, the administration is done by stealth. However, it may also be self-administered to increase one's sexual power and desire. I believe that, in Moche, the latter use is even less common than the former. No chemical analysis of this material is known to me which would show whether it possesses any actual physiological effect, or whether the alleged results claimed for its use are merely psychological. However, overdosage is said to be harmful and even fatal. For this reason the *huanarpo* is also known as *"la muerte dulce"* (the sweet death).

Another aphrodisiac mentioned, which I have not seen, is called *achuni-hullu*,[52] also said to be administered in drink in the form of a powder.

ABERRANT INCEST AND BRUJERÍA

Although it is regarded as incestuous and tabooed to have sexual relations with or to marry a person of the same family name, and certainly one who is a first cousin, the following aberrant case came to my attention. An old lady named J. has a sister named F. who in turn has three daughters by her dead husband, C. J. These daughters we shall call X., Y., and Z. J. had a son named P., now 32 years old, but still a "soltero," i. e., not officially married. Nevertheless, for a time he lived with and had sex relations with his cousin X. Later he had sex relations for more than a year with her sister Y. Y. is now ill and under treatment by a curing witch. While these intrigues were going on, Z. fell ill of a mysterious ailment and died. F. accuses her sister J. of bewitching her daughters, first because two of them committed incest with their first cousin; second, because one of those who did so is now sick; and finally she accuses the sister of having caused the death of the third daughter by witchcraft. J. insists that these accusations are baseless, but admits that the so-called incest took place. It is known as an open scandal in the community and the general public believes that someone was bewitched, otherwise the behavior would not have taken place, but opinion is divided regarding who did the bewitching to whom.

[52] According to Camino Calderón, 1942, p. 193, *achuni* is the Amazonian otter or nutria (*Nasua socialis*) and *hullu* is a corruption of Quechua "tullu," meaning bone. *Achuni-hullu* is, according to this source, the penis bone of the Amazonian otter.

COURTSHIP

Young people of opposite sexes become acquainted in each other's homes when they and their parents go visiting, especially during drinking sprees, in school, in church, during the community religious and patriotic fiestas, and through chance meetings and arranged appointments in the *campiña* and the village.

When a couple decides to set up housekeeping together, the boy is supposed to ask the girl's parents for permission. The proper way to do so is as in the following case, which actually occurred during the period of investigation. The brother of one of my friends, M., is regarded as a correct young man in these matters, and his request for his intended's hand followed these lines. The whole process is called *"intencionamiento."* The brother, or *novio*, came to M. and to M.'s uncle, Tío Pedro, and asked if they would intervene. They arranged to go with him to the girl's house at 5 a. m. one morning, carrying with them a bottle of *pisco, si por acaso* (just in case). M. says that his brother had previously had nothing but words with the girl, and that he would not sleep with her until they were married, even after the betrothal had been formally announced by exchange of rings. This, if true, is atypical of the majority, but nonetheless is regarded as the ideal pattern. Tío Pedro knocked at the door of the girl's house. After some time, the father came and acted very surprised to see them there and asked what he could do for them. First Tío Pedro told what was on their minds, then M. The *novio* kept discreetly silent. The father expressed surprise and said he had never heard of such a thing, but he invited them into the outdoor arbor of the house to hear more. He turned to the *novio* and asked if it were true that the latter had a *compromiso* with the daughter. The *novio* replied in the affirmative. The father asked how long this had been going on and accused the *novio* of being a sly and underhanded character to be able to reach this stage without the father's knowing anything about it. He, of course, had been aware of the whole business for some months, as the couple had made no secret of their affection and the young man had been at the house and at other houses for *chicha* and *causa* with the girl various times in the presence of her father. The father next called in the girl and in a tone of incredulity asked her if she had a *compromiso de amor* with this—this mere boy. (The *novio* was 24 years old.) The girl admitted that it was true and that she wished to marry the *novio*. Tío Pedro and M. chimed in assuring the father that it was true and that everything had been done on a strictly honorable basis. The father, enjoying his position, proceeded to harangue them for their secretive methods, their lack of frankness and confidence with him, etc. After he had held forth in this wise for some time, it was next up to Tío Pedro to inquire whether he perceived any objections to the proposed union. The father called in the mother, and they retired into the house for private conversation, leaving the young couple and their agents in an embarrassed silence. Finally the father came back, looking doubtful and annoyed. The girl and her mother withdrew. There followed a long discussion in which Tío Pedro and M. presented the fine points of the *novio*, his prospects, and the advantages to be expected from so suitable a union, while the father interposed objections and doubts. Finally, there was an agreement on the general proposition, involving also the practical arrangements concerning presents to be made from both families to the couple. The *novio* was pinned down to commitments regarding his circumstances, plans, and projects. After everything had been agreed, Tío Pedro and M. brought forth their *pisco* and everyone drank a *copita* to seal the agreement. The atmosphere immediately changed to one of complete good will and affability, the bottle was finished off, and the meeting broke up about 7:30 a. m.

This is said to be the only decent way to get a woman, although some couples merely set up housekeeping without consulting the parents of the bride. There is no formal dowry pattern, but the girl's parents, if properly approached, usually expect to contribute something to the impedimenta of the house, and the boy's parents expect to contribute something to the stock of tools needed. The question of land and house site is also worked out. The interventors for the groom may include his father, another blood relative, or one of his *compadres* or *padrinos*. Relatives are preferred, because only they usually have authority to speak of economic arrangements involving the boy's family.

Properly, such a proposal is followed by a formal engagement fiesta with *padrinos*, as described in the section on ceremonial kinship (p. 111), and ultimately it is followed by a church marriage ceremony. In many cases the betrothal and wedding ceremonies are simply omitted or postponed and the couple proceeds to set up housekeeping and to live together at once. Until their own house is ready, they may live with either the boy's or the girl's parents, depending on arrangements in each case.

MARRIAGE

An informal type of marriage, more common than the formal, is accomplished by the couple simply starting to live together, as previously mentioned.

"Marriage" and its derivatives (*casamiento, casar, casado,* etc.) have the technical meaning in Moche of a union formally sanctified by the Church. This terminology is often difficult for a North American to grasp at first. He may inquire if Don Fulano is married; Fulano will reply that he is not married, that he is a *soltero*. Later the North American finds that Fulano has lived in the same house with María for the past 20 years and that they have eight children. He begins to wonder whether he heard correctly in the first place or whether his Spanish is failing him. If, after Fulano had said that he was not married, the North American or anyone else had asked, "Do you have a *compañera?*" Fulano would have replied readily in the affirmative and would have shown no hesitation in supplying further details. This technical purity in the use of the word "marriage" is, of course, quite common throughout Latin America, and, having passed through the stage of bewilderment in Ecuador and Guatemala, I was prepared for something similar in Moche.

For sociological purposes, *compañeros* publicly living together on a permanent basis are married, and in the following section "Family and Household" I call this type of arrangement "customary marriage," and discuss the relation of the various types of marriage to the family structure. Here I shall consider only briefly the formal marriage with benefit of clergy, as follows.

First the couple must announce their intentions in the *gobernación,* await the period of the banns, pay a small fee, and secure a certificate properly signed and sealed. From the civil or legal point of view, they are now married. Although some advanced persons in other parts of Peru are satisfied with this, no one in Moche is. The advantage of merely a legal marriage is that one can be divorced, but in Moche a marriage without the Church ceremony carries with it no prestige and is not satisfying to the bride or her family. The groom is obligated to buy the wedding garments for both himself and the bride, as well as another set of new clothes for the following fiestas. He also pays the priest's fee, which is 12 to 14 soles plus whatever the groom is inclined to add. The groom chooses a *padrino* and the bride a *madrina,* who act as their sponsors at the church, and who are often older persons. They usually give presents to the couple. After the ceremony in the church, there is a fiesta the first day in the house of the groom's parents. The next day there is a fiesta in the house of the bride's parents. The third day the fiesta continues wherever convenient, sometimes in the house of the *padrino.* Late at night on the third day the couple go to their own house to live. There is no ceremony of crossing the threshold nor any fiesta in the form of a housewarming. If the house has been recently built, the housewarming fiesta may take place later. The heaviest expense of these celebrations falls on the groom or his family. The feast at their house should include the slaughter of a bullock. This and expenses of clothes, feasts, and priest's fees amount to at least 350 soles, while 500 soles is said to be closer to the average. The economic requirements are sufficient to encourage the postponement of many a marriage.

Following is an account of an atypical marriage, which may serve to illustrate some of the attitudes and motivations surrounding marriage.

I did not get married in the regular way myself. I had lived seven or eight years with my *compañera* and had five children, when a sudden epidemic of pneumonia carried two of them off suddenly. My woman at the time was pregnant. She felt very sorrowful about the loss of the children, and one day she fainted in the *chacra,* the result of which was that the fetus (*feto*) died inside her. She had to be rushed to the hospital in Trujillo, where the doctors opened her stomach and womb and extracted the dead baby. It looked to me as if she were going to die and I wished to visit her and be with her in the hospital. But the nursing mothers would not allow me to enter because I was not married to her. They told me that, if we got married, I could come to see her. It is said to be improper in the sight of God for a man to visit the mother of his children, even when she is on the point of death, if he is not married to her. (This was said with emotion.) I told them that I would be married then and there. That was about 10 a. m. I had to go out and get two witnesses (*testigos*) and a *padrino* and *madrina.* The mothers got the certificate for me and the banns were waived. I got my uncle for *padrino* because I had no time. The priest married us at the side of my wife's bed that afternoon at 2 o'clock, with the regular service with ring and coins. It did not cost me anything, as it would have in church. Why didn't I get married before this? Well, I was always ashamed of being married in the church, and having all my friends laugh at me as I marched in all dressed up. Then there was the question of expense as well. You have to have two sets of new clothes, one for the ceremony and the other into which you change after you leave the church. And the man is supposed to buy the outfits for himself and the bride both. Then there is the question of the fiesta, the *pisco,* the *chicha,* the bullock to be killed, and so on. Since I was left an orphan when I was three years old, I never had any money.

Marriage, of whatever variety, of course, increases a man's or woman's social resources. In time of trouble or need the "in-laws" will usually do what they can to aid. An individual always is respectful toward his or her parents-in-law but real intimacy of a cooperative type also often develops between the individual and his in-laws.

No cases of formal annulment or divorce in Moche are known to me. Effective divorce is accomplished by one or other partner leaving the common dwelling and refusing to come back to it. Attempts are usually made by the respective families and by the ceremonial relatives, especially the marriage *padrinos,* to effect a reconciliation. If this cannot be accomplished, the estranged spouses usually form another household with other partners in the course of time.

FAMILY AND HOUSEHOLD

The Moche household normally consists only of a pair of spouses and their unmarried children, who constitute the family (or immediate family). This family group is the only universal functioning group in Moche which is based on blood relationship (actual, potential, or putative). Although some households exist, composed of an older couple or a widowed parent and married children, they are distinctly in the minority and will be discussed below. The woman, as previously mentioned, has effective control of the finances, but the man is always spoken of as "chief of the house" (*jefe de la casa*). However, there is no tendency toward patriarchal control by the man, and his formal position as head of the house seems to be in the nature of a concession to Spanish customs. On the contrary, if any tendency of dominance is to be noted, it is in favor of the woman, since she controls the finances and the operations of the dwelling itself. Both parents discipline the children, although infants are handled almost exclusively by women. Physical punishment by slapping with the palm of the hand or light switching is used, but not extensively. My data on the everyday details of Moche family life are not as complete as desired because I did not live day in and day out, around the clock, with a Moche family. However, informants and personal observation lead to the impression that the typical family life is tranquil, at least so far as surface manifestations are concerned. There is generally an absence of loud scolding of the children, and discipline would seem to be relatively light. Nursing infants are usually near the mother constantly and are given the breast whenever they cry, although between nursing they are often carried about and amused by older small children.

Quarrels between man and woman do occur, of course, and even lead to physical violence between the partners. However, both spouses seem on the whole to take a more or less equal part, and violence is most likely after one or both have been drinking. Wife beating is not any more common than husband beating, and I know of several cases of husbands who have been driven out of their homes by their wives. Jealousy and the aggressions released by drink, or both combined, seem to be the most frequent causes of violent outbreaks. Both partners may leave the house if fighting takes place. Women tend to go back to their parents' house, but men tend to hide out with a ceremonial relative or to leave the community temporarily, if the matter is serious and especially if the man is embarrassed (*tiene vergüenza*). Persistent quarreling usually leads to break-up of the household.

The details of division of labor and function in the household have been previously described. Those families which can do so have at least two sleeping rooms, one for the children and the other for the parents, because the children are very inquisitive about sexual intercourse (*los chicos son muy curiosos*).

The immediate family as a social structure shows certain inconsistencies which seem to be the result of the fact that it is a combination of a folk institution, a legal institution, and a religious institution. On the one hand, we may see the Moche family as a primary group composed of father, mother, and children performing certain functions, such as economic production, training of children in crafts, techniques, and attitudes, proferring relaxation and recreation, providing shelter, maintenance, and employment for its members, furnishing some religious training, and offering an opportunity and a background for making friends and social contacts. In fact, the family in this sense fulfills all the functions normally expected of a family in a folk society and would show no cultural inconsistencies were it not that the Spanish legal and social system has imposed certain forms upon it, and the Church likewise. Let us try to elucidate this situation as follows.

A family is established *de´ facto* simply by a man and woman living together publicly in the same quarters—setting up housekeeping together, in other words. A family is established *de jure* by filling out certain forms in a Government office (civil marriage). Finally, a family is established *de religio* by participating in a sacrament of the Church administered by a qualified priest. We may speak of these, respectively, as the customary, the legal, and the religious family. A specific family group however, may be only customary, without the legal and religious sanctions. Or it may combine the customary, legal, and religious institutions. (Legal marriage without the church ceremony is practically unknown in Moche.)

We should not overlook the distinction between family and household. At any given time a house is usually occupied by a family and this unit forms the household. Households, however, may be broken up by separation or death of the spouses. Such an event does not break up the family in the legal sense. That is, the members of the former household may still be members of the family in the sense that they may have claims against the persons or property of other members. Thus, although households seem to be characterized by tranquility and lack of disputes, families in the legal and kinship sense are less so. Most of the quarreling over property which occurs between siblings takes place after their common household has been broken up or after they have left it.

As regards the status of the members of a family, there is no cultural difficulty so long as the customary aspects alone are considered. Complications arise when we (and the Mocheros) begin to consider the legal and religious aspects.

First, to consider the religious aspect, a union sanctioned by the Church may not for practical purposes in Moche be dissolved in the eyes of the Church. The training behind this attitude and the solemnities of the religious wedding ceremonies are such as to invest the status of religious marriage with a heavy charge of emotionalism. Although such marriages are occasionally dissolved by the partners simply breaking up the home and going to live with other partners, the guilt feelings involved and the community pressures brought to bear are disquieting, to say the least, to the individuals. Rather than face the responsibilities which a church wedding lays upon them, many a couple elects to dispense with it as well as the preceding legal formalities. The man must take the initiative in arranging a church wedding, and some men apparently are reluctant because the lack of this solemn seal upon their family life gives them a certain hold over their partners. If the woman does not behave, the man can break up the partnership without being damned for breaking his solemn religious vows. Doubtless some women look at the matter in the same way, although none of my female informants have said so.

From the legal point of view, unless a woman is legally married to a man, she may have difficulty obtaining a share of the inheritance unless expressly provided for in a written will or by voluntary acquiescence of the legal heirs. The same is true of children born out of legal wedlock who are not legally recognized by their father. Also, they do not inherit his name. A man may, on the other hand, recognize his children, even when not married to their mother, by a relatively simple procedure in one of the Government offices.

Let us now consider the statuses of individuals as they actually may occur in the Moche family.

The couple under consideration may be married or unmarried at the moment, or they may marry later. The woman, not uncommonly, may have one or more previous children by another man who may or may not have been married to her. Some of the children of the present union may have been born before the couple was married, others after. A child may be in any one of the following statuses. (1) He may be the product of a clandestine affair of his mother before she "settled down" with anyone, and at present has not been recognized as the child of any man. In this case he bears his mother's maiden family name. (2) He may be the child of a former unsolemnized union of his mother, but has been recognized by his mother's former partner. In this case he carries the man's family name. (3) He may be the child of a former marriage of his mother, in which case he carries her former husband's name. (4) He may be the product of a former unsanctioned union of his mother, but has been recognized by her present partner (adopted) and now carries the present partner's family name. (5) He may be the product of the present union which has not been sanctioned by Church or State and remains legally unrecognized by his father, in which case he has his mother's maiden family name. (6) He may be recognized by his father, the present partner of his mother, although they are not officially married. In this case he carries the present partner's name. (7) He may be the offspring of a fully recognized marriage of his mother and father who are now in union, and, of course, he carries his father's name.

Normally there is no stigma attached to being illegitimate in the strict sense of the word. The word is, in fact, little used. The general tendency is for the young children of the mother by previous unions to be taken into the household of her new husband or companion, and arrangements to this effect are usually made before the partners decide to live together. Such children form a regular part of the new household and there does not seem to be any tendency for the man to grow emotional about their presence. He may even legally adopt them. As for his own "illegitimate" children, a man tends to recognize them, if at all, after they have reached the age of adolescence, particularly if they turn out to his liking. The main practical importance of such recognition is that they may share his name and his property.

It should not be supposed that the typical Moche household is notably unstable as a result of these somewhat conflicting patterns of the family institution. As previously indicated, a few liaisons are expected by both sexes before settling down into the customary family. But changes are not frequent thereafter. Of a sample consisting of 46 couples now living together, all over 45 years of age, the average number of permanent relationships including the present one, was 1.30 for men and 1.19 for the women. Forty of the women had been married or partner of a man only once, 5 twice, and 1 three times. Twenty-four men had been married or partner of a woman only once, 10 twice, and 2 three times. Of the 46 present unions, only 27, or 59 percent, claimed to be legally and religiously married.

LOVE MAGIC IN MARITAL SITUATIONS

Magic, or *brujería,* can be and is used in marriage as in most other situations of life. The case of the wandering spouse is not unknown, and magical means may be used both to break up the home and to recapture the affection of a wayward partner. The techniques are essentially the same as those used in courtship magic. Following is a case, translated from the words of one of my informants but omitting names, as taken down in Spanish.

It was not many years ago that I first knew a couple to whom I was united by a certain degree of friendship. They were people of a certain grade of education and of regular economic position . . . My friend, the man, not content with the good spouse which he had in his home, elected to take up with another woman, or sweetheart (*querida*), of whom he was also fond and whom he supported. All right. With the passage of two years or so, the sweetheart, being completely convinced of the affection of her lover, wished to be mistress of his heart (*dueña*) forever, but her ambition would be realized only if she could eliminate from this life the true spouse, who was a model woman of the house. She had to have recourse to crime, by means of *la brujería y el mal*. All this she had to do without the intervention of her lover, because he felt a true affection for his legitimate woman. From this arose the fatal drama of the sweetheart. On various occasions, when the adulterous husband visited her, she insisted that he bring her some bread from his other house. The innocent husband, whether by lack of attention or forgetfulness, failed to do this and his sweetheart pretended to be angry and would not permit the caresses which he had previously enjoyed. He could not understand what motive pursued his sweetheart and said to himself, "Every day she asks me to bring bread to the house. To save trouble I shall just take some of her own bread from her kitchen as I come to visit her the next time." This he did, presenting the sweetheart with some partly eaten bread which he had found in her kitchen when she was otherwise occupied. Great was her satisfaction to see in her hands the desired bread and many were the caresses which she lavished on her lover. Repeatedly she asked him if the bread was from his house, to which he replied, "*Sí, sí, sí, hijita*," not having any presentiment of the cruel denouement. As soon as the bread was in her power, the sweetheart ran and delivered it into the hands of a *brujo* (witch), who had been previously advised to produce certain desired effects in the innocent victim [the man's wife]. But the opposite took place. A short time thereafter the second woman fell ill; she was completely incapacitated and the *médicos* could not diagnose the sickness, until finally the crisis arrived. In her delirium and the pain which she suffered, she could do nothing but call to her bed the husband and invoke his pardon for the wicked act which she had wished to do to his legitimate *señora*. And at the same time she told him, "If you wish to save my life, go to the back yard of my house and in a corner there is a small barrel with a large stone on its top. Take away the stone carefully and inside the barrel there is a toad with the bread in its mouth. Take the bread out of the toad's mouth and throw it in water." The man, bewildered and not accustomed to performing these offices, did the wrong thing. He took the top off the barrel, and without intention, dropped the stone on the toad, killing it. When he arrived at the side of his sweetheart, her condition was hopeless and he could understand only these words, "Now you have killed me. You never really loved me." She died almost immediately, only shortly after the death of her nefarious friend the toad.

My informant says that his friend, the man involved, told him the whole story because he himself was not involved in any magical plot against his wife. The man is now said to be reconciled with his wife, and both regard the experience as a good lesson. It would seem, however, that the wandering husband's preoccupation with the matter is not his sexual infidelity to his wife, but the possibility that he might have been implicated unwittingly in a magical attack upon her. He felt no profound guilt over his "betrayal" of her in the sexual relationship, but he would have been seriously disturbed had he been involved in a magical assault upon her health or life.

LARGER FAMILY RELATIONSHIPS

By means of genealogies, I "placed" 206 adult Mocheros with respect to their blood relationships. I was obsessed at the time with the notion that there must be some structurally recognizable type of extended family or kinship grouping. Now, however, I am convinced that such is not the case.

Although an individual's blood relatives beyond the immediate family are recognized as such, they are not recognized, either by the individuals involved or by others, as a group with internal functional organization or with recognized status relations vis-a-vis other groups. Extended families or kinship groups are not among the constituent units of Moche society. So far as its structural features are concerned, the Moche family and kin are very much like those of North America, except that they and the individuals involved are less mobile, both physically and socially. As a result of the latter circumstance, the average Mochero has more face to face contacts with a large number of his relatives than is perhaps the case with the average North American.

There are a few exceptions in which a group of siblings and other kinsmen maintains a certain solidarity and unity. In all cases the unity seems to be imposed by the personal influence of a "matriarch," an old woman, usually the mother of the siblings. In one of these cases, the brothers consulted with and took orders from their mother, a strong-willed widow in her seventies with a sense of family pride. Each of the brothers, however, maintained his own household for his family of procreation. It is also worth noting that this old lady, who was sometimes spoken of as the "*curaca*" (chieftainess) of the *campiña*, exerted a somewhat similar influence over the actions of other persons not her relatives who were in the habit of approaching her for advice and counsel and who often obeyed her suggestions even when the latter were not solicited. Another "matriarch" of this type is the old lady, previously mentioned, who inherited the proceeds of an insurance policy with which she acquired considerable property. Several of her children and grandchildren live with her in her house and she effectively controls this group. Formerly, one of her sisters, likewise an elderly widow, also lived with her. Another elderly widowed sister, however, is not on speaking terms with her, and a public feud is known to exist between them.

Old people, particularly parents, are always treated with respect and gentleness, which together with the prominent position of the woman in the household, to some extent accounts for the influence of old women, such as those mentioned above. However, the cases in which they have succeeded in holding a group together under their orders or influence are the result of personality factors rather than social status.

FAMILY NAMES

Detailed discussion of the facts emerging from a study of the genealogical material must be postponed to another publication, but we may note that the family name identifies individuals in a limited way, i. e., only with the immediate family and closer relatives, not with an extended group. For example, there are many immediate families named Asmat, but all the Asmats do not consider themselves a group. Although the chances are that all individuals named Asmat are blood relatives (actually or putatively), it is typically impossible for a member of Asmat family No. I to tell one how he is related to Asmat family No. X. Usually he will not suggest spontaneously that he is related to family No. X, family No. XII, or whatnot. It is only after one says, "You must be related, you have the same name," that he will say, "Yes, I suppose we are."

There are two reasons for this state of affairs. (1) Without written records the people have difficulty in remembering the names of relatives beyond the grandparents' generation, so that many collateral lines of relationship, the junctures of which must be sought several generations back, are lost. (2) The extended family or group of relatives has no importance in the social system, so that there is no drive to keep a reckoning of distant relationships in mind, even in the absence of records.

What are found, then, are loose informal groups, each composed of several immediate families, within the larger aggregation of those bearing the same family name. These are immediate families descended from a known, identified ancestor. Thus, we may speak of group A of the Asmats, all of whom are Asmats descended from a man still living or recently dead, named Asmat$_1$. Then there is the

group B of Asmats, all descended from Asmat$_2$, and so on. The same will be found in the cases of all the other widespread family names. Even these groups are not socially recognized as discrete entities; we call them groups merely because they usually define the limits within which an individual can accurately describe his blood relationships.

The inheritance of names theoretically follows the Spanish pattern, i. e., one inherits his father's and his mother's family names, but one passes on to the next generation only his father's name. The mother's name is commonly used only on documents and formal occasions, not in conversation. Thus a man might be named José Federico *Fulano* y Sutano:[53] Fulano is his father's name, Sutano, his mother's. He may marry a girl named María Cristina Mengano (father's name) y Piedra (mother's name). After her marriage, her full name is María Cristina Mengano y Piedra de *Fulano*. And after her husband's death, her full name is María Cristina Mengano y Piedra viuda de *Fulano*. Her son might have the baptismal name of Juan, and would be Juan *Fulano* y Mengano; her daughter, Juanita, would be Juanita *Fulano* y Mengano. It is thus clear that this system is patronymic and that family names persist for more than two generations only through the male line. The principal surface difference between this system and the "Anglo-Saxon" North American system, is that the mother's maiden family name is added to the official cognomen of the child, and that the husband's family name is added to the wife's maiden family names.

In Moche, a woman does not add her husband's family name to her own unless she is formally married to him. She may have lived with a man for 30 years and have 11 children by him, but will still call herself María Cristina Mengano, without adding her husband's name of Fulano. This, of course, adds to the difficulty of genealogical reckoning. There is a simple legal process whereby a father may "recognize" his children, even though he is not married to the mother, in which case the children carry his family name without that of the mother. If the father does not recognize the children either by marrying the mother or by the other type of recognition, they carry their mother's family name only.

Perhaps because relatively so many mothers are

---

[53] As most readers will know, Fulano, Sutano, Mengano are words used in Spanish in the same sense as "Doe, Roe, and Poe," "Smith, Jones, and Brown," or "Tom, Dick, and Harry." No one in Moche, or anywhere else, actually has such names.

legally unmarried to the fathers of their children, it is customary for most women to be known by their maiden family names, although the courtesy title, "*Señora*," is used in polite address, whether they are married or not.

The family name, in addition to identifying family lines of a limited range, serves as a symbol of incest taboo. Although bearers of the same family name do not typically recognize functional membership in an extended kinship group, unless closely related, it is regarded as "bad" to marry or set up a household with a person bearing the same family name. This is borne out in fact by the showing that among the 206 persons in my genealogical material not one has married or set up housekeeping with another of the same family name.

The family names of persons rated as true Mocheros are the following:

Angahuamán.	Ipanaque.
Asahuache.	Jacobo.
Asma.	La Rosa.
Asmad.	Melgar.
Asmat.	Mendoza.
Azabache.	Navarro.
Bracamonte.	Nique.
Bustemonte.	Ñique.
Cafo.	Pumayaga.
Calasán.	Ramirez.
Calderón.	Ramos.
Cedeño.	Rodriguez.
Celestino.	Rojas.
Colisán.	Rosales.
Cornelio.	Sachún.
Delgado.	Sánchez.
Fernandez.	Sicche.
Fuentes.	Suysuy.
García.	Valverde.
Gutierrez.	Variado.
Huamán.	Vega.
Huamanchumo.	Vergara.

Of these 44 family names borne by Mocheros, it will be seen that 30 are unquestionably Spanish. The remaining 14 may be Indian: Angahuamán, Asahuache, Cafo, Calasán, Colisán, Huamán, Huamanchumo, Ipanaque, Nique, Ñique, Pumayaga, Sicche, Suysuy. Of these Angahuamán, Asahuache, Huamán, Huamanchumo, Ipanaque, and Pumayaga seem to be definitely Quechua. I am uncertain as to Cafo, Calasán, and Colisán.

Among the list of Mochero family names only five stand a chance of being Mochica in origin, namely, Nique, Ñique (these must originally have been the same name), Sachún, Sicche, and Suysuy, although all of these may be Quechua or derived therefrom as

well. (In a personal letter to the author, dated October 30, 1944, Dr. J. M. B. Farfán suggests that Sicche may be Aymara (*seqchi*, "ragged").)

SUMMARY REMARKS ON KINSHIP

The usual Spanish terms are used for kinship. These differ from the apposite English terms only in the fact that sex distinction of relative is recognized for grandchildren and cousins. First cousins are always called "*primos hermanos*" or "*primas hermanas*." The terms for "son" and "daughter" (*hijo, hija*) are commonly extended in address to nonrelatives who are on intimate terms with the speaker. The terms for "uncle," "aunt," and "grandfather" (*tío, tía, abuelo*), on the other hand, are not usually extended to nonrelatives, as they are in some Latin American communities, nor are other terms thus generalized. The use of the affectionate diminutive is common both in address and when speaking in the third person, if the individual thus referred to is actually in close and frequent social contact with the speaker. Thus people frequently speak of "*papacito*," "*mamacita*," "*abuelito*," etc. "*Padre*" is never used as a kinship term; the male parent is always "*papá*" or a diminutive of it, while "*padre*" is used only in referring to a priest. "*Padres*," on the other hand, is generally used to mean "parents." "*Madre*" is usually used as a relationship term only in the third person, and then but rarely, in solemn or formal discourse. The usual term for "mother" is "*mamá*", or a diminutive of it.

Among 20 adults from whom I was able to get complete kinship records, the average man or woman could without difficulty call the names of about 45 blood relatives and about 18 affinal relatives. Others were recalled only after hesitation, a period of cogitation, or consultation with some other relative. Time was not sufficient to study these cases in great enough detail to determine the degree of interaction between each individual and his "relatives," but the fact that one can call by name without difficulty a certain number of relatives may be taken as a rough indication that his social relationships with the individuals named are fairly frequent and meaningful to him. To be on the conservative side, we may reduce these figures to 35 and 14, respectively. To this number may be added a very conservative figure for the average number of fully functioning ceremonial kinship relationships, which can hardly be less than 20. These figures would eliminate occasional duplications.

On this basis, it is probably safe to say that the

average adult individual is supported by and helps to support a "net" of at least 69 relationships connecting him by socially significant ties to as many different individuals in the society. He may expect help from and must be ready to give help to any one of these individuals. The relationships are distributed as follows: 35 blood relationships, 14 affinal relationships, and 20 ceremonial relationships. Of the 3 types, the ceremonial relationships are the most permanent and least likely to be broken in times of stress.

It is this network of kinship relationships, rather than a structure of organized groups, which forms a basis for the security of the individual in Moche. The affinal strands may be broken by separation or effective divorce, and the blood lines show a tendency to burst under stress of inheritance disputes, but the strong and abiding fabric is composed of the ceremonial kinship bonds. Two apparent reasons for this are that ceremonial bonds are not normally subject to the strains of cooling "love," sexual jealousy, and other emotional factors, on the one hand, nor to the strains involved in property division and inheritance, on the other hand.

CEREMONIAL KINSHIP OR COMPADRAZGO

The system of relationships called the *compadrazgo* or *padrinazgo* (co-godparenthood and god-parenthood) is perhaps the most important body of interpersonal relationships in Moche. It is also the most foreign to North American customs and ways of thinking, for even that minority of North Americans who possess or are "godparents" find themselves enmeshed in no such web of relationships as do the Mocheros. It is strange that this type of linkage between persons and families has not received more extensive treatment in the sociological and ethnological literature. Its presence constitutes one of the outstanding differences between the basic social organizations of "Anglo-Saxon" North America and those of Latin America.[54]

The essence of the system in Moche is an "artificial" bond, resembling a kinship relationship, which is established between persons by means of a ceremony. The ceremony usually involves a sponsorship of a person or material object by one or more of the persons involved, and the ceremony itself may

be relatively informal. However, in Moche it seems to be placing the wrong emphasis to label the whole system, in Spicer's terms, "ceremonial sponsorship." In many cases the sponsorship is secondary in importance and is merely the mechanism whereby the social relationships are set up. The emphasis in Moche is upon the relations between sponsors (*padrinos, madrinas*) of an individual or thing, and between them and other persons (the parents of the godchild or the owners of the thing sponsored)—in other words, relations between adults rather than between adults and children or things. Sponsors and other unsponsored persons so linked together are *compadres* and *comadres* to each other, and the relationship involved is *compadrazgo*, whereas the relationship between a sponsor and a child is that of *padrinazgo*. However, human beings may also be sponsors to inanimate objects, such as houses, *botijas* of *chicha*, and altars, in which case no social bond exists between the "godparent" and the object, but only the bond between the "godparent" and the owner or proprietor of the object, who are mutually known as *compadres* or *comadres*. Not only in this formal aspect, but also in everyday behavior, the emphasis is placed upon the relationship between adults who are linked by *compadrazgo*. Finally, there is one type of *compadrazgo* which involves no sponsorship whatever. There are no persons in Moche who do not have *compadres*, and some persons stand in this relationship to scores of other persons. It is the nature of the system that, for every godchild an individual may have, he will have several *compadres* and *comadres*.

The whole idea of this type of relationship has been carried to extremes in Moche. There are more types of *padrinazgo* in this community than in any other concerning which I have seen reports. This fact may be linked with the absence of spontaneous community organization and solidarity. The ceremonial kinship system provides security for individuals which is not provided otherwise. It would seem that the ceremonial kinship ties are even stronger in some respects than the relationship ties of blood and marriage. Although various cases of quarrels over property between blood and affinal relatives are known to me, I have been unable to find a single case of such feuds involving *compadres, comadres, padrinos* or *madrinas* and *ahijados* or *ahijadas*. One may speak sharply and with relative impunity to one's blood relatives or in-laws, but it is a cause for

---

[54] The only analyses of a system of this sort of which I am aware are in Spicer (1940, pp. 91–116) and Beals (1946, pp. 102–104). See also Redfield, 1931, passim; 1941, pp. 122–125, 192; Parsons, 1936, passim; see also Rojas Gonzáles, 1943, for aboriginal antecedents in Mexico.

widespread comment if any cross word passes between persons linked by ceremonial kinship.

The following types of ceremonial kinship are recognized in Moche at present. In order to simplify the terminology, I shall speak in terms of the types of godparents and it will be understood that, except as noted, females as well as males may be involved.

A. Spiritual *padrinos*. (They sponsor persons.)

1. Godmother of birth (*madrina de alumbramiento*). The midwife who delivers a child stands thereafter in relation of *comadre* to the parents of the child.
2. Godparents of baptism or christening (*padrinos de pila* or *de bautismo*). The child has one such godparent of each sex.
3. Nail-cutting godmother (*de quitar uñas*), when the child's nails are first cut, usually a woman only (*madrina*) serves as sponsor.
4. Water of succor godparents (*del agua de socorro*) when an unbaptized child is in danger of death and is baptized with holy water by someone who is not in holy orders.
5. Haircutting godparents (*del corte de pelo*), when the male child has his first haircut.
6. Ear-piercing godmother (*de la apertura de orejas,* or *de abrir oídos*) when the girl child has her ears pierced for earrings; followed at age 10 to 12 by ceremonial presentation of earrings.
7. Confirmation godparents (*de confirmación*).
8. Scapular godmother (*de escapularios*), when scapulars are hung on the child; usually a woman only (*madrina*) serves as sponsor.
9. Engagement godparents (*del cambio de arcos*), when a couple exchange rings as a sign of betrothal.
10. Marriage godparents (*de matrimonio*), when a couple is married.

B. Friendship *padrinos*. (They sponsor things.)

11. Altar-lowering *padrinos* (*de bajar altares*). They sponsor the ceremony of taking down the altars and crosses erected by individuals, families, or groups for certain religious feasts. The most important of these is:
    a. *Padrino* of the lowering of the Altar of the Nativity (*Altar del Nacimiento del Hijo de Dios*) on January 6.
12. House-warming *padrinos* (*de la casa*), when a new house is opened for the first time.
13. *Chicha padrinos* (*de la botija de chicha*), when a new container of maize drink is ceremonially broached.
14. Carnival *compadres* (*compadres de la cinta*). No sponsorship is involved here. During *carneval,* several days of festivities preceding Lent, it is customary that men and women be tied together with strips of paper or thread in a mood of fun while dancing. Either the man or the woman may make the advances, and if the other accepts, the two become *compadres de la cinta.* The relationship is extended to their respective spouses.

The ceremonies and relationships involved vary in importance. In the above list they have been classified into two categories, "spiritual" and "friendship," which are the terms used by the Mocheros in speaking of them. The "spiritual" *padrinos* sponsor persons, and the "friendship" *padrinos* (*de amistad*) sponsor things. (Actually the *padrino* helps out or assists the owner or proprietor of the thing.) All those ceremonies in the first category celebrate recognized "life crises" or transition states in the life history of the individual who is being sponsored, whereas those in the second category celebrate an event of importance only to the owner or proprietor of the material object involved (although the material object may have certain religious or animistic aspects).

Another classification might be made. It will be noted that certain types of *padrinos* are established in connection with crisis rites of the Roman Catholic Church, namely, *padrinos* of baptism, water of succor (which is an approved emergency substitute for baptism), confirmation, and marriage. In the establishment of this type of *padrinazgo* and *compadrazgo*, the ceremonial kinsmen participate in Roman rites. Certain other types of ceremonial kinship, on the other hand, are also set up in connection with individual life crises, but bear marks of being derived from an aboriginal or "pagan" context. They are the relationships involved in haircutting, ear piercing, nail cutting, and scapular hanging (although the scapulars now in use are church medals or at least are blessed). Possibly the engagement ceremony should be included in this category as well, although it may possibly be derived from European or North American cultural sources.

In the "friendship" type of sponsorship, the *padrino* is said to sponsor a thing, but he is actually sponsoring or aiding the thing's owner or proprietor. The word or relationship of *ahijado* (godchild) does not appear in this type of ceremonial kinship, and the only relationship between human beings involved is between *compadres* and *comadres*. In this category, the lowering of altars is the most serious type of ceremony and involves Catholic religious beliefs, although it is not enjoined by the church. Whatever may have been the spiritual or animistic background of the house warming, *chicha*, and carnival ceremonies in the past, at present they are merely mechanisms for creating social relationships between individuals.

The most important of all the types of ceremonial kinship is that based on baptism. The child is baptized by the priest according to the usual ritual of the Church, and actual baptism takes place at the font to the right and just inside the main entrance to the church. Children are baptized at almost any age under 6, depending upon when their parents feel financially capable of organizing the fiesta and the ceremony, and there is no feeling of compulsion, as in some North American Catholic families or communities, that the child must be baptized within 8 days after birth. Following the church ceremony a large meal accompanied by copious drinking—in short, the typical Moche drinking-and-eating household fiesta—takes place with all friends of the family invited. (In these affairs, noninvitees are not encouraged "just to drop in.")

The statuses involved in a system of baptism relationships are illustrated in the diagram in figure 7. They may be described as follows: (1) The child being baptized, who is the *ahijado* of the godparents; (2) the godfather; (3) the godmother; (4) the nurse (*ama de pila*) who carries the child in her arms from the house to the church and return (pl. 25, *middle (right)*); (5) the child's father; (6) the child's mother; (7) the godfather's wife; (8) the godmother's husband; (9) the nurse's father; and (10) the nurse's mother. The

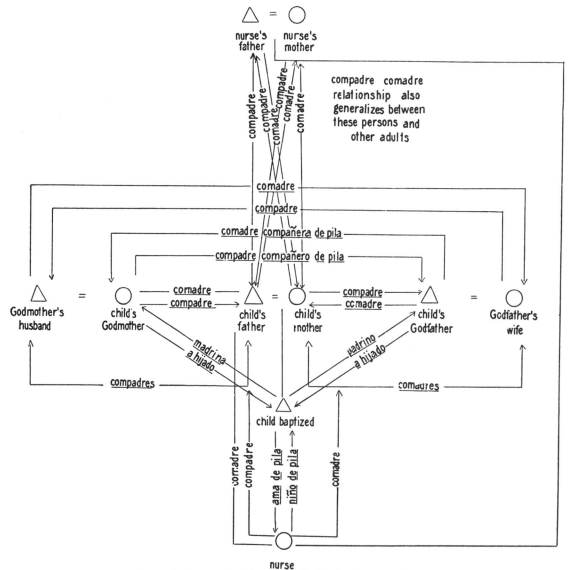

FIGURE 7.—System of relationships involved in baptism *compadrazgo*.

nurse is usually an unmarried woman or girl. Except for herself and the child, all the other statuses in the system are occupied by adults. The relationships of all to one another are signalized by the use of terminology. Thus to the child, the nurse is *ama de pila*, and to the nurse the child is *niño de pila*. The godfather is *padrino* to the child and the godmother is *madrina*. To both godparents the child is *ahijado* (*ahijada*, if female). To the godfather, the godmother is *comadre compañera de pila*, and to the godmother, the godfather is *compadre compañero de pila*. In everyday address these terms are sometimes shortened to *compadre* and *comadre*, but the fact is made plain that this is a special type of *compadrazgo*. A joking relationship exists between these two statuses. The jokes turn on the fact that the two persons can "almost" be considered husband and wife. *"Compañero"* and *"compañera"* mean not only "companion," but in local usage mean "lover" and "mistress" respectively.

In addition to this *compadre* and this *comadre*, the system contains a number of other relationships recognized by the ordinary, unadorned terms, *comadre* and *compadre*. Thus the godfather and the father are *compadres* to each other; the godmother and the mother are *comadres* to each other; the godfather is *compadre* to the mother, and she is *comadre* to him; the godmother is *comadre* to the father and he is *compadre* to her. The same terms, sex differences considered, then extend to include the godmother's husband, the godfather's wife, and the parents of the nurse. The nurse herself is *comadre* to the parents of the child, but her *comadre* relationship does not extend to other statuses in the system. It will be noted that the child is *ahijado* only to the actual godparents, not to their spouses or to other statuses of the system. The godfather's wife, when speaking of the child, will usually say, "He is my husband's (or my companion's) godchild (*ahijado*)," but will not attempt to claim the status for herself.

Finally, the *compadrazgo* terms generalize to blood relatives of the parents and of the godparents. Thus, brothers and sisters of the parents always stand in this relationship to the godparents and also to the latters' respective brothers and sisters. The relationship even extends to cousins of the same generation. Some informants say that it also extends to the grandparents of the child, but in testing this I have never heard a godfather spontaneously call his godchild's grandfather, "*compadre*."

We may sum up this matter in our own terms as follows: The baptism of a child creates a sociocultural subsystem which we may think of abstractly as a system of statuses. So far as the patterns and customs are concerned, they fall into three groups.

I. The mental customs consist of the customary ways of "thinking" about the statuses involved, e.g., "what a godparent should be in relation to all the other statuses in the system."

II. The representational aspects of the system consist of a series of ceremonial kinship terms. These terms are used in reciprocal pairs, with sex of the occupant of the status recognized in the terminology. The terms (representational patterns) fall into three general categories, reflecting three types of relationships between the statuses involved: (1) *padrinazgo* terms, referring to the relationship between godparents and godchild; (2) nurse-child terms, referring to the relationship between these two statuses; and (3) *compadrazgo* terms. The latter are divided into several subclasses according to falling degrees of intimacy, right, and obligation: (*a*) first-degree *compadre-comadre* terms are those in use between the godparents and the mother and father of the child; (*b*) second-degree terms refer to the relationships between godfather and godmother; (*c*) in the third degree are *compadre-comadre* terms used between parents and godparents, on the one hand, and other statuses in the "core" of the system as represented in figure 7, except the status of child and nurse; (*d*) fourth-degree terms are those in use between statuses in the core of the system and statuses defined with respect to the core statuses in terms of blood relationship, which latter may be considered the "fringes" of the system.

III. The actional patterns and customs will now be discussed briefly. Individuals are invited to serve as godparents either directly by the father or both parents of the child, or by an intermediary, usually a brother or close cousin of the father. There is no fixed ceremony of invitation, but it is always done solemnly with a sense of responsibility on both sides, and if the godparent accepts, the parties drink a *"copita"* of *pisco* brandy together at the expense of the parents to seal the arrangement. Godparents may be blood relatives, but usually the attempt is made to secure persons who are not relatives of either of the parents. Not only Mocheros, but in these days, trusted *forasteros* are chosen. From the point of view of the parents, it is desirable to choose godparents who are financially responsible, if not rich, and also persons who have "influence" and prestigeful social connections. The real function of godparents is to broaden and, if possible, increase the social and economic resources of the child and his parents and by the same token to lower the anxieties of the parents on this score. It is for this reason that relatives are usually passed over, and *forasteros,* if trusted, are invited. Also, the godparents have certain financial responsibilities with respect to the ceremonies, and if they do not perform properly, the family is "ashamed." Although *padrinazgo* is sometimes abused in certain parts of Peru, this does not seem to be the case in Moche, and it is not usual to attempt to levy more than the customary obligations against the godparents. It is, on the other hand, regarded as an honor to be chosen, if one feels that he can meet the obligations which, on the whole, are not heavy.

The *padrino* and *madrina* are not husband and wife, and usually are not relatives. They have the obligation to provide printed announcement cards which are given to the guests at the feast following the baptism and either pinned on their clothes or tied on with colored ribbons, and afterward stored away as keepsakes. A typical announcement of this sort, consisting of three parts, reads as follows:

[first card]
Flor Victoria Rodriguez Vargas
Nació el 10 de Marzo de 1944
Se bautizó el 5 de Noviembre de 1944
PADRINOS
Luz Yupanqui de Tám
Abraham Díaz y Días

[second card]
FLOR VICTORIA
Nació: el 10 de Marzo de 1944
Se Bautizó el 5 de Noviembre de 1944

[third card]

PADRES:	PADRINOS:
Sr. Carlos Rodriguez	Sra. Luz Yupanque de Tám
Sra. Elena Vargas de Rodriguez	Sr. Abraham Díaz

The *padrinos* are also expected to make a present, of money, clothing, or a toy, to their godchild at the feast. After the ceremony itself the *padrinos* have the obligation to bury the child if it should die before its twelfth or fifteenth year (informants are vague on the year) and to render help to the child upon demand. Usually a good *padrino* will make an occasional present to his *ahijado,* especially on the latter's birthday, and will always be available for advice and counsel. The godchild, on the other hand, has the obligation to pay respect to his godparent at all times, and for this reason does not trouble the latter with trivial matters. Also, a good godchild should be willing to offer assistance to his godparent when the latter needs it. The *padrino's* responsibilities and rights extend only to the godchild, not to other brothers or sisters. It appears that a number of lawyers, interested in fomenting litigation over land, have taken advantage of this fact by installing themselves as godparents, and are quite ready and willing to contest wills and claims of other siblings, ostensibly on behalf of their godchildren (and, of course, for a fee). At the feast of baptism, the godparents also frequently contribute a bottle of *pisco* or some other delicacy to the parents.

The nurse (*ama*) carries the child in her arms to the baptismal font, where she turns it over to the father. After the church ceremony has terminated, the father gives the child to the nurse once more and she carries it back to the house. She also is supposed to look after it during the subsequent festivities. A respect relationship continues between the child and the nurse. This is the only ceremony in which an *ama* appears.

The parents themselves are obligated to provide as elaborate a party in their house as their circumstances will permit. Weeks before, they start collecting poultry and make plans to get meat. In this, as at all other times when help is needed, their *compadres* assist and on the day of the feast the *comadres* of the family are usually in the kitchen helping to prepare and to serve the viands. (These are *comadres* and *compadres* previously established, not those established in the present ceremony.) *Chicha* and hard liquor are provided, as well as music and a place to dance the *marinera.* During the feast numerous toasts are drunk to the health of the child, its parents, and to the newly established *compadres.* Aside from its recreational aspects, the feast, in short, serves as a public recognition of the newly established ceremonial kinship relationships.

In after years the *compadres* and *comadres* continue in a special relationship of mutual respect, friendship, and disposition to aid each other. The closest relationship exists between the parents and the godparents, and so far as obligations between these two pairs are concerned, the heaviest falls on the parents, for they are under obligation to the godparents for the obligations which the latter in turn have undertaken toward the child. Thus, if a man is in need of assistance, he will tend first to turn to his *compadre de pila,* meaning the father of his god-child, before turning to another type of *compadre.*

The two godparents, who are *compadres compañeros* with each other, share the mutual responsibilities of the announcements and other matters previously mentioned as concerned with the feast, and stand up beside the parents and answer for them during the church ceremony. After the ceremony and feast, they continue without formal obligations to each other, although in a relationship of special friendliness which, as already mentioned, usually involves a joking pattern with sexual overtones. At the feast itself, the two godparents are usually supposed to start the dancing, by performing alone the first dance, and the godfather frequently makes a show of mock courting behavior toward the godmother. This is especially true if the two godparents are Mocheros. If one is a Mochero and the other a *forastero,* especially if the latter is from outside the community, their mutual behavior is usually more restrained and respectful.

As a rather pallid imitation of this joking behavior, the spouses of the two godparents will also sometimes engage in playful courting activity. All such joking behavior is, of course, supposed to be performed strictly in public and accompanied by the laughter of the other members of the assemblage. The two families of godparents now enter into a relationship of special friendliness, the *compadrazgo.* All the other persons who call each other *compadre* and/or *comadre* as a result of this occasion are from now on united into this type of bond. In general terms, it means that one may approach his *comadre* or *compadre* with less timidity or shame (*vergüenza*) than he would feel with other persons. One may call on his *compadres* for help in social obligations, work and emergencies, and one has the obligation to respond to such appeals and even to offer aid and assistance without appeal, as at times of sickness and death. The work-sharing groups, for example, usually are composed of *compadres.* Pallbearers are frequently *compadres* of the deceased. However, the rights and the obligations are graded more or less according to the degrees which we have indicated in discussing the terminology of the *compadrazgo.* When in need, one goes to a *compadre* or *comadre* of the first degree first, and so on down the line.

Aside from the drinking of toasts and the practice of newly established *compadres* and *comadres* dancing together, there is no formal ceremony involved in the establishment of this relationship. No one lectures the participants on their new obligations or reads a ritual solemnizing their status. Godparents are, of course, registered as such in the baptismal records by the priest.

Perhaps the foregoing discussion will make clear the basis of the view that, although the ostensibly central social feature of the baptism, aside from its religious features, is the establishment of a bond between godparents and godchild, actually the most important goal is the establishment of a group of *compadres.* At least, this aspect has more far-reaching social results than the godparent-godchild relationship. First, the latter relationship in itself has reduced social importance, because, regardless of the godparents' behavior, the child is functionally incapable of effective social interaction until it has passed its infancy; after that, the formal social and economic obligations of the godparents continue only until the child has reached adolescence and is supposed thereafter to be capable of fending for itself in case of need. Second, the largest number of relationships in the system established by a baptism are relationships between *compadres.* By playing a role in such a system an individual increases his range of intimate friends, creates a net of relationships for himself, as it were. From the individual's point of view, one might think of these relationships as something like the ropes attached to mountain climbers, if such ropes were spread from climber to climber in a number of directions, instead of in a continuous line. The individual may get along all right by his own efforts, but, if he slips or falls or has difficulty, he may lean on his connecting ropes and be supported or pulled out of the abyss. Conversely, if some other member of the group slips or falls, our individual has to stand fast and pull on his end of the rope to assist or rescue his fellow. In the baptismal system, the individuals who have the most "ropes" attached to them are the parents of the child, not the child himself, and all the other *compadres* and *comadres* are better linked up by the system than is the child.

Although adults, by entering such a system of *compadrazgo,* form a group of *compadres,* it must be recognized that this is not an organized group with status in the society as a whole. The relationships are phrased in terms of social connections between individual statuses and the individuals who occupy them. Although the child might be considered the symbol of the group, there is no leadership, no group activity, no right or obligation pertaining to the group as a whole, and no internal organization. Furthermore, there is no word in use in Moche referring to groups of this sort as discrete, functioning entities, occupying a place in the social organization. In short, there are no symbolic, representational, or actional patterns in the Moche culture which would lead us to see these aggregations as status groups.

With this somewhat lengthy discussion of the system set up by baptism, we may pass to a briefer mention of the other types of ceremonial kinship establishment. All of them establish *compadre* relationships and extensions of them, although the baptismal *compadres* usually outrank other types in importance.

If a child falls seriously ill before it has been baptized, the father and mother seek a *padrino* and a *madrina* and ask them to perform the ceremony of the *Aguas de Socorro*. This is a simple emergency affair and involves no fiesta. The *madrina* holds the child, while the *padrino* baptizes it with holy water (Agua Bendita), a bottle of which is always kept in the house. He simply says, "I baptize you"—giving the child a name suggested by the parents—"in the name of the Father, Son, and Holy Ghost. Amen." The only requirement is that the *padrinos* themselves be baptized Christians. The purpose of this ceremony is to prevent the child's dying without benefit of the church's blessing (conveyed through the blessed water). If the child recovers, it goes through the regular baptism ceremony, but remains a godchild of the godparents of *Aguas de Socorro,* although the formal godfather-godchild relationship usually takes precedence. In any case, the parents and the godparents are *compadres.*

Usually when the baby is about 2 months old, its nails are cut for the first time. A small fiesta (*de quitar uñas*) is organized and there is usually only a *madrina,* no *padrino,* whether the baby is male or female. The *madrina* has to buy a new pair of small nail scissors with which she performs the operation and which are later given to the child. Other persons present may make small presents.

Between the ages of 2 and 3 years, boy children are supposed to have their first ceremonial haircutting. A *padrino* and a *madrina* are chosen. They provide colored ribbons with which the child's hair is tied into small tufts. A fiesta is organized at the expense of the parents, and in the midst of the assembled guests the child, dressed in its best clothes, is set on a stool or chair in front of which is another stool holding a

plate or *mate.* Although there are some variations, the *padrino* is supposed to deposit a *propina* (gift or tip) of money in the container, after which he takes the scissors provided by the parents and clips off the first tuft of hair below the knot of ribbon, so that it remains a loose lock of hair tied with ribbon. He is followed by the *madrina,* who deposits a similar or smaller gift, and also cuts a tuft of hair (pl. 25, *middle (center)*). Then all the guests do likewise, although they are not expected to deposit such large gifts. The *padrinos* are expected to deposit something sizable— 5 to 10 soles—the others 50 centavos or 1 sol. In theory, this is supposed to be the child's money to be used for purchase of childhood clothing, now that it has passed from helpless infancy. The theory, at least, is respected, and if the child wishes to play with the money after the haircutting is over the parents, at least in front of the guests, do not prevent it from spilling coins on the floor, bouncing them against the wall, and the like. By the time everyone has sheared a lock of hair, the child has a complete, if uneven haircut. The *padrinos* and guests pin the ribbon-tied locks to their clothes during the fiesta and are supposed to take them home as souvenirs.

The ear-piercing ceremony for girl children takes place at the earliest at the age of about 3 months and sometimes as late as 2 years. Frequently only a *madrina* is involved, although some parents ask a *padrino* as well. In the midst of the usual fiesta with guests, the *madrina* opens the ears with a needle and puts a loop of red thread through each lobe. No tips or gifts are involved in this ceremony. About 10 or 12 years later the little girl receives her first earrings from the same *madrina,* an event which is celebrated by another fiesta during which the guests often present the girl with small presents of clothing or ornament. This second ceremony, which is called the *fiesta de aretes* (celebration of earrings), might be considered as signalizing the social recognition of the beginning of the status of adolescence for girls.

Not all children are confirmed in church, but when they are they have a *padrino* and *madrina* who accompany them to church. The usual type of fiesta takes place after church, although it often involves a combination of several families, each of which is celebrating confirmation of children. The *padrinos* have the obligation of providing part of the confirmation costume.

A scapular is usually a small bag of cotton containing a sacred medal or a relic and provided with a string from which it can be hung from the neck.

The type for which *madrinas* serve are blessed and are bought from the Carmelite monastery in Trujillo. People may be sitting around talking and one of the women will notice a child of the house playing about. She will say, "*Voy a ser madrina de escapularios, porque quiero echar escapularios a este chico.*" She then goes to Trujillo, returns with the scapulars, and in a small fiesta drapes them around the child's neck. There are usually two or more and they are supposed to ward off various types of misfortune.

Betrothals are announced at a fiesta at which the couple exchange rings, and publicly plight their troth, usually with the announcement of the date on which the church ceremony will take place. The man chooses the *padrino* and the girl chooses the *madrina* who act as sponsors before the guests. The *padrinos* are usually older than the betrothed couple. Even when this ceremony is not followed by the church ritual, the couple are regarded as having done the honorable thing by thus publicly announcing their intentions.

A wedding performed by the priest is a serious business because it is permanent and because it is expensive. The groom chooses a *padrino* and the bride a *madrina*, who function respectively somewhat as do best man and bridesmaid or matron of honor in North America. They have no obligations other than to give presents to the couple and in case of subsequent marital difficulty to try to patch matters up. The latter function, however, is apparently often evaded.

May is "the month of the crosses" during which the crosses set up in the countryside for the past year are taken down and renewed. Some crosses are cared for by an individual and others by a small group or *mayordomía*, but in either case a *padrino* and *madrina* are required to supervise the lowering of the cross. The man in charge (*dueño*) places a plate or *mate* before the cross, in which the *padrino* deposits his contribution, followed by the *madrina* and the other guests. After the lowering of the cross, a party takes place at the house and at the expense of the *dueño* or of him and his group. The funds collected are supposed to be used for the refurbishing of the cross.

At Christmas time some houses set up small altars in the house in front of which is laid out a miniature tableau of the Nativity, composed of toy animals, figures, a manger, etc., either made at home or, more usually, bought in the Trujillo stores. This is called the *Altar del Nacimiento del Hijo de Dios* (Altar

of the Nativity). On January 6 these altars are taken down (*bajan los altares*) and put away for the next year. *Padrinos* and fiestas are required.

The *padrinos* of the housewarming fiesta are usually expected to furnish *chicha* or a piece of furniture for the house. Other guests likewise bring small gifts.

Occasionally a family wishes to have a party without having to pay for it. They get a *botija* full of *chicha* and cover the mouth with paper or cloth. Then the husband goes out to find a *padrino* or *madrina* or both, and to gather in their friends. The *padrino* pays a *propina* of a sol or two for the privilege of broaching the *botija*, after which everyone else present lays some change on the collection plate and the party proceeds to become inebriated. Anyone who serves as *padrino* becomes *compadre* with the husband and wife of the house, but is usually referred to expressly as *compadre de botija* and with a laugh of pleasant reminiscence.

In the carnival type of *compadres*, there are no *padrinos*.

It should not be supposed that every individual of proper age in Moche has *padrinos*, *ahijados*, and *compadres* of all the types mentioned above. Although it confers great prestige to be a *padrino* often, it costs money and time. Likewise, many families cannot afford to put all their children through all the crisis ceremonies. The solution is to drop out some of the ceremonies (baptism is, however, never omitted) and to double up on others, i.e., to have 1 set of *padrinos* and 1 fiesta for 2 or more children at the same time. However, everyone has passed through some of these ceremonies, and through the extension of the terminology and behavior characteristic of the system he is provided with a sizable group of ceremonial kinsmen. One of my informants is a poor man. He is an orphan without land or other inheritance, and he works in Salaverry as a stevedore. Yet he is able to call the names of 27 living *compadres* and *comadres* without difficulty, and by thinking a while can recall 11 others. He also has 7 *padrinos* and *madrinas*. Among all his *comadres* and *compadres*, only 2 are blood relatives (2 aunts) and none are affinal relatives. Among his *padrinos* none are blood relatives, and only 1 *madrina* (a godmother of baptism) is a blood relative (an aunt). Among his *comadres* and *compadres* are: The 2 midwives (*parteras*) who delivered his 7 children; 13 *compadres-comadres de bautizo* (several of the children were baptized in pairs to save money, the same *padrinos* serving both); 3

comadres of ear piercing for his girls; 5 *comadres* and 4 *compadres de cinta;* and the others are extensions of these relationships. His children have not yet been confirmed, for lack of funds, but when they are, new sets of ceremonial relatives will be added to his collection. Among his *padrinos,* he counts 1 *padrino* and 1 *madrina* of baptism; 1 *padrino* of confirmation (the *madrina* is dead); 1 *madrina* of scapulars; 1 *madrina* and 1 *padrino* of marriage; and a *madrina* of nail cutting.

Another man, somewhat more comfortably fixed economically, named 67 *comadres* and *compadres* and 15 godchildren. He claims that he has many more. The ceremonial relationships which function best are, of course, those which are kept bright with use, that is, those in which contact between the individuals involved is frequent and meaningful. Many of the half-forgotten *compadres* occupy statuses, to be sure, but the individuals in these cases have not practiced the customs linking them sufficiently recently to maintain the occupants of the status fresh in memory.

About 2 weeks before we had to leave Moche my wife became a *madrina de bautismo,* and I became a *padrino de corte de pelo.* The 2 children involved were brother and sister in the same family, but there were 2 other godparents in addition to us. Between us we were immediately recognized as *compadre* or *comadre* by 47 persons, according to the count we kept, and the counted number of our recognizable *compadres* and *comadres* would probably have increased considerably had we had more time to fix in mind and celebrate socially the extensions to other relatives of the families involved.

NAMESAKES

Two persons who happen to have the same name call each other *tocayo* or *tocayito,* and there is supposed to be a mystical or a "spiritual" bond between them. It is easier for one to become acquainted with such a person and, once acquainted, two namesakes tend to feel closer to each other than to other persons, unrelated in any way. The namesake bond, however, is not as strong as either the blood or ceremonial kinship ties.

THE FORASTERO ELEMENT

Among the *forasteros* settled in the community, there are 96 family names represented (counting the Chinese and Japanese). Only 4 of these family names are found in the list of Mochero family names:

Bracamonte, Rodriguez, Sánchez, and Vergara. This would seem to indicate that the present *forasteros* have had little to do with bestowing the Spanish names which occur among the *Mocheros.* Also, the large number of distinct family names (96 compared with 44 for the Mocheros) among the *forasteros* seems to be an indication in itself that the *forastero* families are relatively recently established in the community; in fact, it indicates either that the great majority of *forasteros* are of the first generation in Moche, or that their descendants do not multiply, marry, and settle in Moche. We know both facts to be true from other evidence, but the great majority of the strangers are comparative newcomers as residents in the community. Marriage and sex relations between the *forasteros* and Mocheros are very rare.

Speaking in general, the *forasteros* do not form a part of the community world of the Mocheros. Except for about five families, they are ignored by the true Mocheros and, at least subconsciously, resented. One *forastero* who owns land in Moche, who has lived in Moche for the last 7 years, and hires Mocheros as peons from time to time told me that in all that time he had never been invited to a Mochero house or had any approach of a friendly nature made to him. Mocheros will speak to him civilly, but when he tries to engage them in conversation, they shut up like clams. So far as I could discover, this man is guilty of nothing more than being a *forastero* landowner in Moche. His experience is typical of that of the other *forastero* landowners.

On the other hand, certain *forasteros* fulfill useful functions in the community. The Chinese are all shopkeepers, the Japanese are barbers and tinsmiths, several of the Peruvians are engaged in shopkeeping and saloonkeeping. These strangers have more contact with the Mocheros, and some of them seem to be liked by the natives, although only a few are on terms approaching intimacy.

Among the foreigners (non-Peruvians) only the Chinese are known to be organized. If the five Japanese have an organization, they keep it quiet. The Chinese have a "Chinese colony," of which the leading shopkeeper, whose place of business is on the plaza, is president. The Chinese are a familiar element in this part of the coast. Considerable numbers of their countrymen were brought into the country during the past century as bonded laborers for the haciendas. The usual term of bond was 12 years, during which time it is said that they were often treated for practical purposes like slaves. It is said that at the present time there is no Chinese laborer on any of the haciendas of the north coast. Practically all of the Chinese have gone into shopkeeping and into other types of business, and throughout the region most of them have reached at least the level of a lower middle-class standard of living, and some are comparatively wealthy. This seems to be an interesting demonstration of what persistence, thrift, and hard work will do, even under conditions which many a local Peruvian claims offer no opportunities for advancement. For the Chinese had neither wealth nor influence behind them in their rise, and their economic situation at the start was about as hopeless as could be imagined.

One of the Japanese, who has lived in Moche some years, is married to a Peruvian woman and is said to have become an ardent Catholic. This man has ceremonial kinship relationships with several of the Mocheros.

If all the *forasteros* together as a group are considered, with a few exceptions, it must be concluded that they do not form a functioning element of the society. They are an element of the population, and that is all. Many of the families are actually Trujillo suburbanites and their social position and function are to be found in the circle of Trujillo society rather than in that of Moche, and in the city they belong to varying social levels and interest groups, a fact which robs the Moche *forastero* population of functional cohesiveness. The *forasteros* as a group have not attempted to define a position for themselves within the Moche social scheme. There is no prestige in being a *forastero*, which is recognized by both *forasteros* and Mocheros. Although certain *forastero* individuals may consider themselves "better" than Mocheros, there is no general claim made out to this effect. Thus one cannot view the *forasteros* as a castelike group with generally recognized rights and obligations vis-a-vis the "Indian" group in the community, as is the case in some parts of Guatemala, for example (Gillin, 1943). Also, within the group the interests of individuals are too varied to permit us to consider the total aggregation as a social class within Moche society. In short, the *forasteros* are physically present [55] and are tolerated, but under present conditions, they are a rather undefined, although disturbing, element in the society.

The patterns of relationship between the *forasteros* and the Mocheros are characterized by avoidance and their effect is to maintain maximum social distance on the "horizontal" plane. It is for this reason that the *forasteros* are not as effective in the acculturation of the Mocheros as they might be expected to be from a superficial consideration of their numbers and physical proximity.

CLASS

There is no evidence of true social classes in Moche at the present time. The following bases of differentiation exist on which class distinctions and structures might be reared in the future: (1) Differences of wealth; (2) differences of residence, e. g., town, *campiña*, and *playa;* also the three neighborhoods of the *campiña;* (3) differences between *forasteros* and Mocheros; (4) differences in education.

I have already pointed out the bases of my view that the *forasteros* do not compose a class or caste in the community at present. So far as the other differences are concerned, there are no symbols, privileges, obligations, or internal cohesiveness which set off individuals who might otherwise be considered members of one class from possible members of another. The anthropologist or sociologist can classify the population of the community according to the differences mentioned above, but the society itself has not reached agreement on the matter.

PRESTIGE

In the present situation, which may be one of transition, such prestige as is generally recognized in Moche attaches to individuals rather than to groups, and is based upon what is considered valuable in individuals. Although one Azabache family, as previously mentioned, vaguely promotes the idea that they are descendants of the former *curacas* or chiefs of the area, no visible or practical benefits to their social position accrue thereby. One does not achieve prestige, in general, because he belongs to a certain family.

A man may achieve prestige and honor among his fellows by his work in *mayordomías* and other religious functions, by the successful management of his lands (thereby acquiring a respected position as a good farmer), by having wealth (provided this is combined with agreeable personal characteristics), by being a generous entertainer (frequently inviting

---

[55] The black dots on the plan of the pueblo (map 1) show the location of *forastero* dwellings, which will be seen fairly well scattered throughout the town without evidencing a pattern of concentration of or choice of location of social significance.

other persons to his house for eating and drinking), and by personal characteristics which render him agreeable and respected in the eyes of others. Among the personal characteristics admired are geniality, capacity for food and drink, honesty in dealing with others, and a disposition to mind one's own business. Anyone who achieves distinction outside the community by becoming a successful professional man also enjoys prestige among his fellows, although he usually is no longer a functioning member of the society. Ability to read and write and to acquire "influence" with the powers that be is gradually becoming a most important prestige-giving characteristic, and therewith is developing a powerful "acquired drive" (Gillin, 1942) within the culture which should produce an increasing rate of acculturation.

Women acquire prestige by their beauty and sex appeal while young. Once settled down, a woman is valued for her housekeeping and child-raising qualities (ability to perform woman's tasks efficiently), by her success in marketing, trading, and financial operations (providing she does not habitually cheat the other women), by being a good entertainer and providing good food and drink for household guests, and by personal qualities of affability, virtue (i. e., not being a man chaser once she has formed a household), and capacity for food and drink. Literacy for women is likewise acquiring an increasing value, and certain girls who have secured positions of a clerical nature or as teachers outside the community are highly regarded.

A man or woman who is a *brujo* (witch) or a *curandero* (curer) has prestige because of power and knowledge. The attitude toward such individuals is mainly one of respect, mixed with a certain amount of fear and awe. Since their profession is illegal, the *brujos* are not publicly advertised or overtly recognized. The prestige which a "bad *brujo*" (*malero*) enjoys is something like that of a malevolent, but powerful underworld character among North Americans, while that of a "good *brujo*" who specializes in counteracting black witchcraft is something like that of a North American lawyer who "fixes" the difficulties of people, although he has to operate on the quiet and according to legally shady methods.

Thus it is that prestige in the community itself is rather loosely defined, and practically all of the prestige statuses are of the "acquired" type.

SUMMARY OF SOCIAL ORGANIZATION

From what has gone before it appears that if I were to portray the social organization of Moche graphically, I could not use one of those neat "organization charts" so common in business organizations and government offices, in which clear lines from top to bottom and side to side connect rectangles representing groups, such as departments X, Y, and Z, all neatly suspended from a higher rectangle representing a group called "Board of Directors" or "Executive Committee," and the like. In social organization in Moche, the only constituent groups are the immediate families, and these, as we have seen, often have a somewhat blurred position from the legal and religious points of view. There are other groupings to be sure, the association of irrigators, the two cultural clubs, the body of Government officials, the amorphous group of *forasteros* set off from the group of Mocheros, the neighborhood or regional groups in the *campiña*, the *pueblo* as set off from the *campiña* and *playa*, etc. But at the present time the relations of these groups to each other are indistinct and "unorganized", i. e., no clear-cut general pattern of relationships has been worked out. This situation may well represent a phase of development and change in the community and in the course of time patterns of group and social organizations could be expected to emerge.

As the case now stands, however, a diagram showing the socially significant relationships in Moche would depict individuals, each with a varying number of lines radiating from him. Most adult individuals could be enclosed in rectangles representing the limits of their respective household groups, but even so the majority of the significant relationships burgeon from the individuals within the household groups leading to specific individual relatives, "in-laws," ceremonial kinsmen, and so forth.

Certain of these individuals would be placed on a slightly higher prestige level than others because they happen to be relatively wealthy farmers, or are ardent and successful organizers of religious devotions and celebrations, or because they are lavish entertainers, etc. However, their status would not appear as a function of the family groups to which they belong. If we may use the metaphor, we might say that outstanding individuals in Moche are those who have the most lines of functioning social relationships radiating from them; as a result of the more numerous and more tightly drawn lines connecting them with other individuals, they are raised higher, they are "better supported" socially than those of their fellows with a paucity of social connections. Thus they are raised above the multitude.

It would not be fair to suggest that in social organization Moche is necessarily typical of all the small rural communities of Peru. Its proximity to a city, its rapid and recently established communications with the outside world, its peculiar land problems, and probably certain imperfectly known features of its cultural development are all factors which combine to form a configuration the details of which may be unique to Moche. The vegetative type of life and a certain lack of development of community enterprise and organization are not unknown, however, in other parts of Peru.

NATIVE MEDICINE AND MAGICAL CURING

GENERAL ORIENTATION

The complex of customs concerned with the curing of physical and mental ailments in Moche exhibits perhaps the greatest range of "primitive" elements of any aspect of the culture, and also illustrates most vividly the mixture. of old and new which is so striking and sometimes so confusing a feature of Moche in general. Characteristic of the latter is the following incident.

One afternoon I was enjoying a leisurely *causa* (typical Moche lunch) at the house of one of my friends in the *campiña* near the Huaca del Sol. One of the "accepted *forasteros*" was with me, but otherwise the gathering was composed exclusively of Mocheros *netos*—six men and their female *compañeras* and *señoras*. While the women were disposing of the remains of the food in the outdoor kitchen, we men continued sitting around the table, trading anecdotes and drinking *chicha*. One of the men told a story concerning a discovery he had made in a *chichería* in Ascope, where, during his residence in that community, he had for some years been in the habit of eating *cuy* (guinea pig) and *picante* once or twice a week. One day, when the proprietress stepped out of the establishment to obtain some rice from a nearby *tienda*, our friend slipped into the kitchen and, to his surprise, found that the "guinea pigs" which the good *señora* had been in the course of preparing were actually large, fat rats. The discovery took away his appetite.

This story stimulated a pseudophilosophical discussion of the sources and preparation of meats. Except for the "idea of it," everyone agreed that there was no reason why people should not eat dogs, horses, and a series of other familiar animals not actually used for meat in Moche. But rats were different, because they lived in filthy conditions and fed on garbage and offal. Then someone asked, "How about pigs? Aren't they just as filthy?"

One of the Mocheros replied, "Yes," and went on to point out that pork must be thoroughly cooked before eating, because it often contains "trichinosis." The actual word was used. Discussion continued as to whether or not cooking actually kills the trichina, with everyone using the words and the concepts in what struck me as a most educated and modern manner. At the same time, however, that my Mochero friends were learnedly bandying about words and theories of modern medicine, the single *chicha* glass was making the rounds in the usual fashion. None of the men paid any attention to the slime and the lip marks on the common glass, which, to me, were only too visible.

This tendency to use both the modern and the old together, often in the same situation, but in what one might call a dissociated manner,[56] occurs in practically all aspects of Moche culture, but is especially evident in curing beliefs and practices.

First of all, the Mocheros are acquainted with modern medicine and with drug stores, called *boticas*. Although there is neither a physician nor a drug store in Moche itself, those of nearby Trujillo are available and are used. The general attitude toward physicians is a mixture of respect and lack of confidence, and this is true of Mocheros, old and young. Although I have discussed these matters both directly and indirectly with many Mocheros, including some who are attending the university and who hold professional positions in Trujillo, I have yet to find one who seems to have wholehearted and complete confidence in the *médicos*. Yet most Mocheros agree that in certain conditions if anything at all can be done, only a *médico* can do it. For example, even the *curanderas* and midwives agree that a case of complicated childbirth, such as a breech presentation, must be immediately taken to the hos-

---

[56] This is an example of a violation of the principle of consistency in culture, or of a cultural inconsistency as between representational patterns and actional patterns, as discussed in Gillin, 1944.

pital in Trujillo if the lives of mother and child are not to be lost. It is likewise agreed that all cases of major surgical intervention must be handled by *médicos* and, in fact, there are, so far as I know, no "native" techniques of major surgery in practice in Moche. However, the ordinary Mochero will usually either express skepticism that surgery is necessary in a given case or attribute the need for it to non-scientific causes. For example, the great-aunt of one of my informants died last year of cancer. At least this was the medical diagnosis, and the family is willing to admit that she had cancer. However, they are firmly convinced that it was originally caused by the fact that she had been *brujada* (bewitched). At first she was treated by *brujería* (curative witchcraft). When she got worse, she was turned over to a *médico* and, finally, at considerable expense, was taken to Lima for an operation. The hospital care and surgery were actually supervised by the then Minister of Public Health, who took a personal interest in the case, by reason of being a friend of a friend of the family. The family, in short, was convinced that the best of scientific medical care had been provided for the old lady. However, after the operation she was returned to Moche and, as is often the case with postoperative cancer conditions, continued to decline after a short period of improvement. Finally, as a last desperate resort, she was taken to Salas, the great center of the north coast *brujería,* where, after a short period of treatment by the best *brujos,* she died. Her body was brought back to Moche in a truck for burial, and when the box was opened after the journey, it is said that she had turned over during the trip and was found to be lying on her face—the final insulting result of the original *brujería* which had caused the sickness. Although this case is slightly more spectacular than the average, it is typical of many with which I was familiar personally or through reliable accounts. In the treatment of illness, however serious, the modern Mochero oscillates between folkloristic methods of treatment and modern scientific medicine (i. e., that version of it which exists in this region), with the balance usually tipped in favor of the folkloristic. The Mochero takes the stand that he will try the *médico,* but if satisfactory results are not forthcoming, he will seek out a *brujo* or *curandero.* A common comment is, "Perhaps the *médicos* know some things, but, among us people here, there are a lot of things which they can't cure. Take *susto,* for

example. The *médicos* don't know anything about it."

As we go on with a description of the folkloristic cures, it will be noticed that "modern" elements appear, even in the most esoteric parts of the *brujería* and *curandismo.* One "modern" institution appears to be indispensable to folkloristic medicine in its present form, namely, the drug store or *botica.*[57] Without the *botica,* neither the *curanderos* nor the *brujos* could carry on their present practices, since certain products which play a central role in their manipulations are obtainable only from these institutions.

To sum up, the treatment of sickness among the present-day Mocheros is handled by three general classes of specialists: (1) Physicians, i.e., practitioners of modern medicine; (2) *brujos* (witches), and (3) *curanderos* or curers.

In addition, every adult person is acquainted with a number of first-aid practices and the uses of certain herbs and other remedies. This may be called the unspecialized, household medicine. As in rural communities in the United States, certain individuals, usually older persons, have a wider knowledge of these household remedies than others, without pretending to be specialists or making a profession of their knowledge.

Since the present section is not a treatise on modern medicine, we shall leave the practitioners of this science among the Mocheros to their own devices, mentioning them and their arts only as they enter in-

---

[57] Neither in the Sierra nor the coastal cultures of prehistoric times do we find clear evidence of pharmacists or pharmacies, although, as Valdizán says, we may see an antique parallel in the persons still found in most markets dedicated to the sale of medicinal products. Such specialists seem to date from prehistoric times. True pharmacists were introduced by the Spaniards, but not for some time after the Conquest. "In the first years of the conquest there was neither *médico,* nor surgeon, nor farmacist." The first mention of pharmacies occurs in the year 1537 (Libro de Cabildos). "The *boticas* of the colonial period . . . must have had some similarity to the present stands of herbalists, since herbs and vegetable simples composed the principal part of the therapeutic arsenal of those times, when the pharmacists had to store up a quantity of leaves, roots, woods, flowers which served as the base for the preparation of ptsans and potions . . . . The pharmacists kept a large quantity of lards, greases, viscera of certain animals (the omentum of the hog, for example), etc. To the Spanish system of weights and measures there was added another, completely conventional, not only in Colonial Peru, but in the whole world. We refer to the bits [*pocos* or *pocas*], handfuls, knife pointsful, papers." Lickers (persons who lick the skin, *lamedores*) and *seringueros* (persons who specialized in giving enemas) were other colonial medical specialists. Mustard plasters were much employed. The training of pharmacists during the colonial period was by apprenticeship and practice, and it was not until the establishment of the Colegio de San Fernando in Lima in 1808 that formal courses in pharmacy were offered in Peru. More scientific training and supervision of pharmacists began in 1856 with the establishment of the Facultad de Medicina in the University of San Marcos. (See Valdizán, 1938, article "Boticas," vol. 2, pp. 173–186.)

to the customary or folkloristic beliefs and practices of the Mocheros.

The practice of *brujería* is not, of course, confined to Moche. The casting of spells and the curing of them goes back both into Inca culture and into pre-Conquest Spanish tradition. Undoubtedly the Mochicas practiced and believed in something similar. At the present time both *brujería* and *curandismo* are illegal and frowned upon by the authorities, especially the former, a fact which renders their investigation in a situation like that of Moche doubly difficult, because it adds legal sanction to the natural reticence of the practitioner with a vested interest in his knowledge and manipulations. Although these "superstitious" practices are forbidden by law, they are, as previously stated, extensively practiced, and the legal sanction is rather more of a potential than an actual threat. Relatively few arrests and trials have taken place in recent years, and the general practice of the police is to act only upon specific complaint, when a general hulla-balloo or scandal breaks out, or when a person seems to have died as a result of the ministrations. Nevertheless, the practitioners do not take unnecessary chances and are suspicious of any investigation until their confidence has been won, which is a fairly long process in some cases. I myself succeeded in establishing good relations with only one *brujo* and one *curandera*, and for many weeks I despaired of being able to accomplish this. I have personally watched their various ceremonies and have held long discussions with them on all phases of their work. However, each practitioner has specialties of his own; information from the two informants mentioned, therefore, does not necessarily represent the complete range of practices in Moche. Although this has to some extent been supplemented by information and experiences proffered by laymen of the community, I am not by any means sure that my informants have exhausted their knowledge for my benefit. There may be certain special secrets which only years of association with the practitioners would bring out. In this respect, however, the material at hand seems to check well enough with such published data as exists, the best two sources for which are Valdizán and Maldonado (1922), and Camino Calderón's fictionalized presentation of 1942.

It would be possible to write an entire volume on native medicine and magical curing in Moche. The following pages present only the highlights of even that material which I have at hand. A more extended exposition awaits a later opportunity. Much of the unused material at hand should be followed up by longer period of investigation, not only from the anthropological point of view, but also medically and psychiatrically. The "superstitions" of the common people of the Peruvian coast are not mere ethnological curiosities but form a setting for customary action and thought which is extremely important for the interpretation and understanding of Peruvian culture as a whole. It also seems possible that a close study of the native *materia medica* and the techniques of its use might lead to discoveries of therapeutic importance to somatic as well as to psychological medicine, which could be generalized to medical practice in other parts of the world.

BRUJERÍA[58]

In Moche, as in most parts of Peru, there are two kinds of brujería, good and bad, or white and black, with their corresponding practitioners. According to my information, which for reasons mentioned above, may not be complete, there are in the community at least seven persons frequently mentioned as brujos (experts in or practitioners of brujería). Five of these are regarded as bad brujos, usually called *maleros* or *hechiceros*, and only two are good brujos, sometimes called *brujos curanderos*, or *brujos buenos*. Three of the brujos are women, and they are all said to be bad. I had at least a speaking acquaintance with all of these individuals, but I was intimately friendly with only two, and only one of these discussed and demonstrated his brujería to me with freedom. This man is a good brujo, who has studied his craft among the great experts of the art in Salas. My impression is that there are actually only three professional brujos living in Moche itself. All of these are men. Two are good brujos,

[58] We shall use the Spanish word *brujería*, henceforward without italics. It is pronounced, as "Time Magazine" might say, "broo-her-EE-ah," rhyming with English "diarrhea." Although this Spanish word is usually translated as "witchcraft" or "sorcery," these two English words have wider and more uncertain connotations for modern American readers than has "brujería" for residents of Moche. Possibly this is because the witchcraft of North American tradition represented a historical complex (compounded of English and North European elements, involved with Reformation and Puritan formulations) distinct from those which are the historical sources for Peruvian coastal beliefs and practices (derived from aboriginal Indian, Spanish, Arabic antecedents, involved with the Inquisition, etc.). "Magic" in its anthropological connotation would be satisfactory except that the Spanish equivalent, *magia*, is used in a different sense than is "brujería" in Moche. "Shamanism" would likewise be satisfactory except for the fact that it is generally used to refer to usages untouched by so-called higher religions involving belief in God or gods and to usages entirely "primitive," i. e., representative of cultures basically unmodified by literate civilizations. Moche brujería, on the contrary, involves certain aspects of the Catholic region and is also compounded, not only of "primitive" but also of Western elements.

one of them my friend mentioned above, and another who is still in more or less of an apprenticeship status. The "bad brujo" is an old man. Although I was friendly with him, either because of his senility or his slyness I was unable to extract any useful information from him with respect to his art, but everyone I know in the community claims that he is a powerful *malero*. The other four individuals frequently mentioned as brujos (including the three women), I am not inclined to regard as professionals. They are either the victims of slander—and the accusation that one is a brujo is a favorite theme for whispering campaigns—or else they are believed to have accomplished certain feats of spell-casting against their enemies, but without special training or attempting to make a career of it.

When I say that an individual is to be regarded as a "professional" brujo in Moche, I do not imply that he employs all his time in this profession. Nowhere in Peru, so far as I know, does an individual usually devote himself exclusively to one calling, except in agriculture. Just as the university professors of Lima have their law practices, their drug stores, and their haciendas, so the brujos of Moche have their *chacras* and agricultural activities.

The origin of the black and white varieties of brujería is a historical problem, which perhaps cannot yet be definitely solved. According to Guamán Poma, an outstanding authority on many Inca customs, both "good" and "bad" brujos and curers seem to have existed among the galaxy of specialists concerned with such matters in the Sierra under the Inca rule. Guamán Poma, however, makes it sound as if the bulk of the brujos' efforts were devoted to undesirable activities, whereas the counteracting and curing of such business was mainly in the hands of a variety of herbalists and surgeons.[59] Surgical intervention seems to have been much more highly developed in the "medicine" of the Sierra than on the coast.[60] On the other hand, Guamán Poma

makes no mention whatever of the diagnostic use of the guinea pig rubbed over the body of the patient.

The curing *brujo* with whom I worked was a native of Virú, although he made his home in Moche many years ago and has raised a family of Mocheritos. He has more white blood than many Mocheros, however. He himself is a man of serious mien, about 60 years of age, with large, "piercing," bloodshot eyes. He is somewhat reserved in manner, but after a basis of confidence has been established, talks in a frank way. His conversation is sprinkled with quiet jokes and he speaks freely. With me, at least, he made no great show of omniscience, eccentricity, or of supernatural powers. He admitted frankly that there are some things he does not know and some conditions which he cannot cure, but he showed a quiet confidence in those powers and that knowledge which he believes he possesses. He himself got into brujería when he went to Salas in his early youth to be cured of a "case of worms in the leg." One of the great masters of Salas cured him, but since he had no money to pay the fee, required him to stay 6 months and work out the payment of the treatment as an *alzador*. In the course of time he became interested in brujería as a profession. The master "tested" him for another year, during which he continued to serve as assistant, living in a room of the master's house with bare subsistence. He says that only those candidates are accepted for final instruction who the master is convinced have the "true spirit." One must have an innate ability to learn the techniques, and to see visions, but above all, the candidate must be absolutely sincere in believing in the power of the herbs. He claims that his own master could detect the slightest faltering in interest or belief, and that he was thrown out of the master's graces several times before his "soul was pure." He says that the emphasis is on spiritual dedication and honesty. Chicanery of all kinds is definitely ruled out.

Although the most which the average Peruvian medical man would admit regarding this is that there may be honor among thieves, I am inclined to believe that brujería, at least the "good" type, does involve a strong spiritual element regarding which its properly trained practitioners are quite sincere. Considered as a professional institution or cultural orientation, its symbolic patterns would seem on the whole to be consistent with its representational patterns. If laymen are "duped" by brujería, so also in most cases

---

[59] Guamán Poma (1936). I have succeeded in obtaining this original source (in the facsimile edition) for only a few hours' study. Consequently I have had to lean heavily, for the present, on Lastres (1941) for a summary of the medical data and methods of curing set forth in the original work. See also Dietschy, 1938. The French facsimile edition of Guamán Poma is apparently out of print at this writing, and another facsimile edition, published in Bolivia, I have been unable to purchase up to the time of going to press.

[60] Although the Mochica ceramics in the Museo Arqueológico "Rafael Larco Herrera" at Chiclín show that punitive surgery was extensively used in the amputation of limbs, nose tips, and sexual organs of presumed criminals, therapeutic surgery occurs very infrequently, both in the ceramics and in the bones recovered from Mochica graves. Trepanation, so common among the Incas, is extremely rare among the Mochicas.

are the practitioners themselves. This does not mean, of course, that the practitioner does not endeavor to acquaint himself with all of the objective facts of a case before he undertakes it, e.g., sickness and symptoms of the patient, his quarrels and other social relations, his state of mind and prominent anxieties, etc. Likewise the brujo does not fail to maintain a certain air of mystery and authority about his treatments and seances, and to guard his secrets from laymen. However, within the framework of brujería, this is, of course, regarded as no more unethical than the practice of scientific physicians looking into the economic and social circumstance of their patients without directly interrogating the patient himself. Likewise, a certain "window dressing" is employed by the medical profession because it gives the physician a position of dominance and authority in relation to his patients—it helps him to "control" the case, which is regarded as an essential part of the treatment. Even the most enlightened modern patient in North America expects his physician to assume an air of certain seriousness when considering his complaints, to wear a white coat or gown when performing surgery if not at other times, to keep his instruments in a compulsively regular although perhaps unnecessary neatness in their cases, and so on. Likewise, the care with which the brujo lays out his *mesa,* the solemnity with which he conducts the divination, etc., are "ethical" accompaniments of the practice of the profession. And, of course, the brujo, just as the modern physician, comes to convince himself that such ritual is an essential part of the cure he is trying to effect. No doubt it is.

I do not wish to appear to defend brujería against modern medicine, but in many parts of America we must face the facts that brujería has existed for a long time and is still firmly imbedded in the culture of many of the common people. To persist in this manner, it must be rewarding in certain ways to its clients. It seems plausible that its *materia medica* does possess real therapeutic value in certain physical conditions, and that its procedures have the effect of lowering personal anxieties in many cases. If any curing system can relieve pain—either physical or psychological—it is rewarding and will persist. Therefore brujería cannot be lightly dismissed as a mere body of superstitions which can be legislated out of existence. Modern medicine makes slow headway against brujería, especially in those conditions in which it takes no account of the cultural factors which

produce certain punishing "acquired drives" [61] from which individuals seek relief. In Moche, for example, the complex of patterns and customs involved in bewitchment or magical attack, in *susto,* in *ojéo* (evil eye), and so on are not purely "imaginary." They exist in the thinking of the people and in the culture of the group and produce ailments which for all practical purposes are quite real. A man's anxiety does not have to be based on the germ theory of disease in order to make him sick.

Only in certain areas of therapeutics has modern medicine as practiced in the region shown itself to the Mocheros to be more rewarding than the native procedures, for example, in surgical intervention, in difficult deliveries, and in violent infections such as certain types of pneumonia and malaria.

THE SÉANCE

A curing brujo operates by means of a séance called the *mesa de brujería* (table of witchcraft). Actually the *mesa* or "table" is laid out on a white cloth spread on the ground (pl. *22, upper and lower (left), upper and middle (right).* It is a sort of altar where the herbs and simples, patron saints' images, and other magical apparatus of the brujo are laid out before him. I attended one séance, after which my friend the *maestro* put on another séance for my benefit alone, in which he went through the actions slowly and carefully with explanations, and on a third occasion he set up the *mesa* for me in daylight so that I could photograph it and note down in detail all the elements composing the collection of working materials. These are listed in the following section.

The general theory of the standard séance is that the operating brujo is carrying out the affair in order to discover who has done magical harm to the patient and how it was done. Once this information, produced by the séance, is obtained by the brujo, he may prescribe remedies for the patient from among the materials on the *mesa.* However, the theory always is held that the patient is sick because some other individual has caused evil magic to be worked against him. Hence, in the séance the brujo is always thought to be working against a rival, *la parte de la contra.* The rival brujo or brujos or their familiar spirits, the *shapingos,* may appear during the séance as shadowy forms with the intent of upsetting the proper course of events, confounding the operating brujo, and confusing the cure of the patient. In other words, the rival evil brujo is constantly at work to prevent the

---
[61] See Gillin, 1942, for a discussion of these matters.

reversal of the evil influence which he has produced in the health of the patient. It is partly for this reason that séances are held at night and in secrecy, so that the rival brujos and the individuals who have employed them to do harm to the patients may not learn that their evil work is about to be undone.

Séances may be held for the benefit of two or more patients, but the following description is in terms of one patient. These affairs can take place only on Tuesday or Friday.

The séance may take place either in the house or in the open. In the former case, the brujo sets up the *mesa* so that he is facing the door which is left wide open, so that he may see the approach of the shadowy forms of the counter influences, and with his back against the wall. In the open the affair takes place in a secluded spot. The brujo is called the *maestro de la mesa* or simply *maestro* (master), and is aided by two assistants, called *alzadores* (literally "raisers"). The latter are sometimes young men "studying" to be brujos themselves. The assistants and the master form a team which always works together, and the assistants each are paid an agreed sum from the fees obtained by the master for the treatment. In the team I know personally, one of the assistants is a man in his fifties who has been working with this master for the past 20 years. The other is his son, about 20 years old, who has been working at this profession for about 3 years and hopes to become a master himself in the course of time. The older assistant is the father of the woman with whom the master lives, but was the master's assistant before this household was set up, and in the affairs of brujería at least, is thoroughly subordinated to the master at all times.

The *mesa* must be set out and ready to operate at 9 p. m. The master kneels on the floor or ground with his back against a wall, if possible. First he says the phrase of invocation in a pious voice, "*Al nombre del Padre, del Hijo y del Espíritu Santo.*" Then he begins the proceedings by laying out the white cloth and sticking the protective dagger (*puñal*) in the ground at the opposite end and with the blade facing outward. Then he proceeds to take the various articles which compose the content of the *mesa* one by one from an *alforja* and to set them out in their proper places on the cloth. The two pictures of the saints are first set up against a bottle of alcohol, and the other articles are then laid out in their proper places. The two assistants stand, crouch, or kneel facing him on the other side of the

mesa. All three members of the team should have been on a diet for 3 days previous to the séance. They cannot eat cow meat during this period, only mutton, *garbanzos*, rice, and vegetables which stand up off the ground, nothing which touches the ground while growing, such as potatoes, sweetpotatoes, etc. They are not to eat bread or pastry made with shortening, or to drink milk. The patient likewise is supposed to have dieted for 3 days during which he eats no meat and partakes only of "cold" foods. (See classification, pp. 53–54). Also, great care must be taken that the patient's food is prepared separately from that of other persons. The pot must be continually watched, for, if any of the contents boils over or spills on the ground or in the fire, the patient will be seriously harmed.

The patient lies or sits facing the master and behind and to one side of the assistants, alone or accompanied by one or two friends or relatives. The affair begins with the light of a candle, and the first step is for the assistants to "raise the table" (*levantar la mesa*). This "raising" procedure is the principal activity of the assistants and recurs at intervals throughout the séance. It consists of snuffing up through the nostrils an alcoholic liquid contained in a flat sea shell. The master takes two of the smooth sea shells (Nos. 30–32; see list, p. 124, and fig. 8) and places them before him. He pours into each about a tablespoonful of *cañaso* from the bottle (No. 3). Then he pours in about a teaspoonful of *agua de florida* (No. 47) and finally adds a few drops of jasmine perfume (No. 50). This process of mixing is repeated each time a "raising" takes place during the séance. The assistants now proceed to "raise the table, one hand to each side." They both kneel on the floor and place their respective shells full of the mixture before them. Then, in unison, each takes his shell in his right hand, bows down with his face to the ground so as to place his nose against the edge and takes a large sniff through the right nostril. Then, in unison, they raise the head and the shells about 6 inches and take another sniff, thus continuing in a slightly higher position each time until they are kneeling upright. Then, each raises his right knee, with his left knee still on the ground, and takes another sniff; then they get to their feet, and so on until they are completely upright and all the liquid has been snuffed into the right nostril and swallowed. The process is then repeated, using the left nostril, the left hand, and raising the left knee before the right knee. This imbibing of a strong alcoholic mixture through the nose produces violent eructations and belches from the stomach and causes tears to run. The theory of this snuffing is that the assistants vicariously purify the situation by so doing. When they "raise" the *mesa* at the start of the séance, they thereby purify it and protect it from evil influences. When they "raise" the patient, the latter is purified and protected. The procedure is said also to "raise the soul." Great care must be taken during this process that no drop of the liquid is spilled, and the procedure should be followed through smoothly without hesitations or time taken out for lengthy belching and eye wiping. If a drop is spilled, the master has to purify the assistant, patient, and *mesa* by blowing white corn powder, chewed in his mouth,[62] over all, and the "raising" must start all over again. If an assistant gets a nostril stopped up, the master uncorks one of the bottles of *seguro* (Nos. 27 and 28) and gives him a whiff to clear it up.

After the *"mesa* has been raised," the lights are blown out and the séance proceeds in darkness. The master now begins by snuffing up the same mixture in the same way, one shellful to each side. All the time he is talking rapidly in an undertone, "Now we'll see. Now let's see. Ha, now it's coming," and so on. Next he takes two or three noisy gulps of the jasmine perfume and twice in succession sprays a mouthful over the *mesa* to make it smell good. This is supposed to keep the *maleros* away. Next he takes a mouthful or two of *agua de florida* and twice in succession sprays the table with this. Next he "sweetens the table" (*endulca la mesa*) by blowing a mouthful of white granulated sugar over it. None of these perfumes or sugar is swallowed. Swallowing a liquid through the mouth during a seance makes the patient weak. Swallowed liquid must always be taken through the nose.

Now the master begins to call the spirits, which are thought to be represented by the functional articles on the *mesa,* by beginning to shake his rattle (No. 49) rhythmically, chanting and whistling a special tune the while (each master has a sacred tune composed by himself). At the start of this process he cuts a piece of *misha negra* (No. 54) about the size of a quarter-inch cube and puts it in his mouth, chewing it slightly and keeping it in the cheek for a while until he swallows it. Calling the spirits continues for about half an hour, provided no counter

spirit (*shapingo*) appears. If this should happen, the calling is stopped at once. Working in a house, the master has to keep his eyes fixed on the door to see the shadowy shapes. In the open he looks about continuously, for they come from all sides. When a counter spirit puts in an appearance, the proceeding stops suddenly. The audience hears the iron magnet crashing to the ground some distance away, accompanied by a few fierce curses from the master. It is said that the magnet flies toward the evil shade of its own power, although on a confidential level the master admits that, of course, he throws it. Since this heavy piece of iron may be flying unannounced through the darkness at any minute, it is advisable for all present to stay quietly in their places during a seance, unless ordered to do otherwise by the master. If the counter spirits do not go away after being attacked by the magnet, one of the assistants, on orders from the master, will seize the long dagger or knife (No. 1) and fight a shadow battle, slashing the air with the knife. If he is unsuccessful, the knife will be seized by the master, who fights the battle himself. It is said that occasionally a brujo is overcome in one of these ghostly contests and falls to the ground in a faint (or possibly from intoxication). This breaks up the séance and is exceedingly dangerous, both for the health of the patient and the reputation of the brujo.

Once the *shapingo* has been routed, all present stand up, the master repeats again the phrase of invocation, and then continues with his calling of the spirits of the herbs. At 11 p. m. the counter spirits begin to come in greatest numbers, and therefore it is advisable to "raise" the patient at this time. This is done by the assistants, each of whom sniffs three shellfuls of liquid in the process, which is divided into three *"manos"* (beginning with the right hand) as follows: (1) Up to the waist on each side; (2) up to the neck on each side; and (3) from neck up to top of head, one assistant in front and the other behind. The patient stands up or is held up, and as the assistants raise themselves sniffing the liquid they press closely against the body of the patient. After the third *"mano"* is finished, each assistant places his shell upside down on the head of the patient and rubs it all over the scalp. Then the patient lies down to rest.

An even more powerful method and one also prescribed for certain conditions of the patient—of which the master must be the judge—is to administer

---

[62] Blowing maize meal from the mouth was used by Inca brujos to nullify the power of rivals. See Lastres (1941, pp. 147–148).

about a gallon of the San Pedro brew (No. 7) to the patient after he has been "raised." The recipe for two patients is as follows: Peel one cactus, but save the skin; the peeled cylinder is then disked and quartered and placed in the gasoline can one-half full of water, together with 16 grains of white maize, and a bit from each herb in the bottle of *seguro* (Nos. 28 and 29). The mixture is heated over the fire, but is cool by the time of the séance. Some brujos administer this brew or something similar to all persons present at the séance. It is said to produce vomiting, diarrhea, and visual hallucinations.

Usually the brujo has divined the cause of the trouble before the patient is "raised" for the second time. While he is calling the spirits, he continues to chew *misha*, replenishing his cud from time to time, and also has usually inhaled several shellfuls of alcohol because of interruptions by contrary spirits. Gradually his singing, whistling, and monologic exclamations increase in tempo and he begins to be more certain. "Now they're coming. Here it is," and so on, he mutters excitedly. Finally, when the possession is full upon him, he stops shaking the rattle and lights a candle. Then he stops and sits motionless as if in a trance, gazing fixedly at the framed pictures of the saints on the *mesa*. Finally he sighs, and says with conviction, "Yes, now I see it. Aha, so that's the way it was," and so on. He calls other members of the company to come and look at the framed photographs. "You see that figure in back there. A man, no? What is he doing?" In the flickering light it is not too difficult to see a ghostlike form in the cloudy backgrounds of the photographs. At the first séance I attended, I was the only one for some time able to "see anything." The *maestro* announced to the others that I was the only one present who had true spiritual sight. The trouble with the others, he said, was that they were letting their minds wander. Members of a séance must concentrate only on the matter at hand. After he has received some agreement that there are forms or figures to be seen, the master then asks certain questions of the patient. "Did a woman visit you on Thursday of last week? Did she have anything in her hand? It was your cousin, wasn't it?" And so on. If he has not completely made up his mind concerning the cause, the identity of the persons involved, and other features of the case, the master puts out the light and continues to call the spirits for a further time.

If he has decided in his own mind the diagnosis of the trouble and how the case should be handled, he tells the patient so, and advises him that he will describe the affair to the patient next day and advise further magical measures to be taken. For the moment, the next thing to do is to relieve the patient of his symptoms. The patient is stood up again and "raised" by the assistants moving closely alongside his body. This time, however, the assistants move over all parts of his body, not just along the two sides, and, whenever they come to a part which hurts, the patient so advises the master. The assistants then finish the contents of the shells, holding their heads closely pressed to the complaining spot, while the master speaks reassuringly to the patient and prepares one of the herbs from the *mesa* to be administered at once and/or to be taken home. Patients usually feel better after this treatment.

The work of the *mesa* usually continues until at least 2 a. m., and often until daybreak, before all matters have been satisfactorily cleared up. Sometimes the brujo requires two or three seances to cure the case.

In this kind of cure, the patient always expects to be told that some specific person has had black magic worked on him. If the divination has been completed, usually the next day the *maestro* visits the patient and relieves his curiosity concerning the identity of the enemy. The herbs are considered to act as neutralizers of this baleful influence.

Without a precise knowledge of the physiological effects of the cures given, we may concede that they perhaps have some therapeutic value. Serious illness in Moche, however, is always accompanied by strong, but diffuse, anxiety feelings. Doubtless this is true of sickness in most human societies, but in the Moche context the patient is certain that his trouble comes from baleful magic wrought against him by some person or persons; the uncertainty is the identity of his persecutor or persecutors and the type of magic which has been used. Once a plausible identification of these elements has been provided by a séance, the individual is able to reintegrate himself. His diffuse anxiety is lowered by identifying its source (channelizing it) and also by the protective or neutralizing measures believed to be taken by the prescriptions of the brujo. By countervailing magic the patient may even transform his anxiety state into aggression aimed at a definite object. This change in the feeling state of the patient which is wrought by the *brujo's* treatment also is apparently therapeutically effective in certain types of somatic complaints. From the point of view of psychosomatic medicine it is not surprising that cures take place under this type of treatment.

If we may grant that the cure may be at least temporarily beneficial to the individual, we nevertheless have to admit that it is unhealthful for the society in which he lives. The results of these divinations often serve to reinforce the aggressions and divisions which, unfortunately, are too frequent in Moche society in any case. Moreover, the *brujo* is in a position to foment various aggressions which otherwise might not exist. This is illustrated in the following case told me by several informants and typical of a number of similar cases. I set it down as told by one informant, in translation.

Our good friend and compadre S. was the only son of his parents and inherited all the goods of his father, some land, house, cattle, yoke of oxen, donkeys, a horse, etc. His wife was completely healthy and robust, weighing about 80 kilos. We must believe that there are in this life envious persons and characters of bad faith, but this case took place in the bosom of a family and involved a person who was receiving favors from that family. All right. The Sra. S. was a person of good humor, loving, amiable with her friends. The couple had been several years married and were educating their children. The Sra. enjoyed life, but with no one more than a female relative of the house, the daughter of one of her sisters whom she had invited to live with her. This niece knew how to make herself prized by preparing good *causas* and food, and, in short, the family was very happy. Suddenly, after New Years the Sra. S. became sick with acute liver colic, which became so bad as to endanger her life. It was at this time that our compadre S. began to dispose of some of his property in order to attend to the serious illness of his woman. Very just of him. The best doctors of Trujillo could do nothing to cure these colics which were frequent and painful. Finally they diagnosed the case as an incurable illness and the Sra. remained sentenced to death. By this time the weight of the Sra. had declined to only 46 kilos, she could not walk, and was bedridden. Then arrived the Angel of her salvation. Our friend C., propagandizer of this art of bujería, visited S., and learned of the illness of his woman. He succeeded in convincing the suffering husband that a brujo was needed and offered to bring one immediately who was his *compadre*. Since the case seemed to S. to be lost, he agreed. Previous to this S. had never believed in the occult science, but the upshot was that he and the brujo agreed on the fee to be paid and the work of cure was begun. They had to go to a secluded part of the *campiña* where a *mesa de brujería* was prepared. Then the human cargo was carried there and the seance took place. The next day the sick woman was better and gave signs of life. It was necessary to prepare a second *mesa*, which started work the night of the following Friday. As luck would have it, this second *mesa* was raided by the police, because, as you know, the brujos are knocked about and persecuted by the authorities, because it is believed that they needlessly take away the money of the poor people. Bueno. But to S., in the midst of his affliction, appeared the Virgin, as they say, for the

chief of the police party turned out to be one of his best friends. S. offered to pay the fine if his friend the chief would allow the brujo to continue and then told the sorrowful story of his wife. The chief reminded S. of the dangers which might ensue, but finally allowed himself to be convinced, if S. would agree to take full responsibility. Pocketing the fine, the police party left. The brujo, relieved of his anxiety over the affair of law, proceeded with his treatment with such success that the Sra. S. was completely restored to health following this second *mesa*. As is usual, the brujo told the Sra. (patient) that in order to be permanently cured she should "see" the person who had caused her the harm (*daño*). Of course, the Sra. was anxious to know. A third *mesa* was organized and during the séance he showed her a form in the glass plate covering the picture of the sacred image and near this image a plate of food which she recognized as one of her favorite dishes prepared by the niece who lived in her house and by means of which the harm had been transmitted to her. The surprise of the Sra. was great to recognize the face of her niece in the glass, she with whom she had shared her moments of pleasure and whom she had befriended economically. This bad friend, this ungrateful niece, upon learning that her plot had been uncovered, fled from the community and is at present in Lima.

No one to whom I talked seemed interested in further evidence regarding the culpability of the unfortunate niece. The evidence of the séance seems to have been sufficient to satisfy all.

MESA DE BRUJERÍA

In plate 22, *upper and lower (left)* and *upper and middle (right)*, the process of setting up a *mesa de brujería* has been photographed, and in figure 8 the

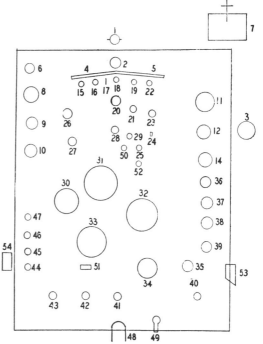

FIGURE 8.—Explanatory diagram of a *mesa de brujería*.

various objects on the *mesa* in question are identified. This, so far as I am aware, is the first time that a brujo or his apparatus has been photographed at work and is the first published account of the details of the apparatus. As previously mentioned, each brujo has specialties and peculiarities of his own and, according to accounts, no two *mesas* are exactly alike. The *mesa* in question is supposed to be for white witchcraft, i. e., for the helping and curing of persons who have been attacked by witchcraft.

The *mesa* itself consists of a rectangle of white muslin, actually a sugar sack, laid out on the floor or on the ground, as shown in the photographs. Before anything else is put down, the *puñal,* a large wooden-handled steel knife, is stuck in the ground at the head of the *mesa* (opposite end from the operator) with its edge facing outward. This is supposed to "cut" the interference of rival brujos and must be of pure steel. The other items may be listed as follows, according to the identifying numbers which appear in the sketch (fig. 8).

1. *Puñal,* or knife.
2. A half bottle of cane alcohol with which to prepare *cañaso.*
3. Bottle of *cañaso,* made from one-half bottle of alcohol, fresh water, and three tablespoonfuls of sugar.
4. Frame containing pictures of La Virgen de los Dolores de Virú, covered with glass.
5. Framed, glass-covered picture of La Virgen de la Puerta de Otuzco. Each brujo has his own favorite saints' pictures. In them appear the visions at a certain point in the seance.
6. A raw piece of San Pedro cactus.
7. Tin 5-gallon gasoline can for making infusion of San Pedro cactus, with a cross made of *carrizo* stuck into it. One-half the contents of the can are given to the patient.
8. Paper-wrapped package of an herb called *flotación.*
9. A bottle of holy water (*agua bendita*).
10. Paper package of white sugar.
11. Paper package of *solimán,* a white powder which is used dry in massage of the skin. It is a counterirritant. It is powdered onto the skin with cotton, then rubbed with the hand.
12. *Yerbas para el aire,* wrapped in paper. Included in the package are five types which are mixed together in an infusion and given to the patient hot: (*a*) *toro* stems, (*b*) *misha negra,* a root, (*c*) *piedra mineral negro,* a black root, (*d*) *piedra mineral blanca,* a root, and (*e*) *cóndor blanco,* a root.
13. A cloth sack containing the following: (*a*) *Mishpingo* fruit, about as big as a walnut, in a hairy shell; (*b*) *piedra imán* (iron pyrites), male and female; the male pieces are covered with long exudations of rust which look like hair and cling by magnetic attraction to the female piece; (*c*) a cube of bone with an incised face; design consists of three squares one within the other,

and seven dots on the face of the inner square; (*d*) metatarsal bones of a human "*cristiano*"; (*e*) three rusty steel needles; (*f*) *haylulito negro,* a stone; (*g*) *aserín,* loose flaky and dusty rust, which is called the food of the pyrites (*alimento del imán*). The contents of this sack are used with the *yerba para el aire* to cure and control "*aire.*" The seven dots on the bone cube indicate that the remedy should be taken every 7 days, on Tuesday or Friday, at 11 a. m. The *piedra de imán* is placed in a glass of cold water for an hour, then taken out and dried with a cloth before putting back in the sack; then the water in which it has been soaked is used for cooking the herbs listed in No. 12. The bones and other articles in the package are considered "food for the *imán.*"

14. *Piedra de ara* ("communion stone"). This is scraped to make a powder which is administered one-half teaspoonful in one-half a glass of cold boiled water for heart troubles.
15. *Piedra de lobo del mar.* Comes from the body of the sea lion. Powder is made from it by scraping, which is mixed with powder of No. 14, and the two administered for heart troubles.
16. *Piedra de huaca del rayo.* Ornament only. All items called "*de huaca*" have been obtained in archeological ruins.
17. *Piedra de huaca del Cerro Blanco.* Ornament.
18. *Piedra de lobo del mar.* More of the same as in No. 15.
19. *Corazón.* Ornament for the "heart of the *mesa.*" It is a heart-shaped piece of chalky stone with *piedra de huaca* set into it.
20. *Caracol blanco de huaca.* Ornamental shell.
21. Blessed image of San Antonio de Padua, *patrón* of the *mesa.* San Antonio de Padua was a brujo before becoming a saint. This image was blessed in the church in Moche.
22. *Piedra de ara oscura.*
23. *Piedra de huaca.*
24. *Piedra de huaca;* quartzite?
25. *Piedra de huaca;* quartzite? These two stones (Nos. 24 and 25) are a part of the defenses of the operator. During the seance, when the opposition influence ("*la parte de la contra*") is nearby, these stones shoot off sparks which warn the operator. He then takes the two stones in his hands and rubs them together vigorously so that more sparks fly out, which forces the rival to go away.
26. Round egg-shaped pebble *de huaca,* for decoration.
27 and 28. "*Los seguros.*" Two small glass bottles containing the most powerful drugs and plants (called *pajas* or *hojas*) of the brujo. These are called "*la fuerza de la mesa.*" The contents of these bottles is as follows: (*a*) *Trenzacia blanca,* small sections of certain plants called *huaringas* found in a large sacred lake inland from Salas among the outliers of the Andes; (*b*) *trenzacia negra;* (*c*) *vira-vira;* (*d*) *botón de oro,* a plant; (*e*) *trenzacia macho;* (*f*) *condor macho;* (*g*) *condor hembra;* (*h*) *simora blanca;* (*i*) *simora negra;* (*j*) *hunguay;* (*k*) *misha blanca;* (*l*) *misha negra;* (*m*) *piedra de ara,* small pieces. All of these remedies are surrounded in the bottles by a liquid composed of the following substances: (*a*) *agua calanga legítima extranjera;* (*b*) *essencia de jasmín extranjera* (foreign-made essence of

jasmine, a cheap perfume) ; (c) *agua de florida extranjera* (a proprietary product made in the United States). The liquid in these bottles is believed to have very strong curative powers. If the patient is seriously ill, he is given some of this liquid by drops in boiled, but tepid, water. After the patient has been "raised" (*alzado*), one of these bottles with contents inside it is rubbed over the head and body. This is called *limpiar al enfermo con la botella.* After this has been done, the bottle must be "refreshed" by placing it next to some pulverized white maize. Otherwise the contents will "burn" with the heat from the patient, and lose its efficacy.

30–32. Three *perlas de nacra blanca.* Large flat sea shells, bivalves, smooth inside and outside. One for each assistant and one for *maestro* for "*alzar*" (imbibing through the nose) as explained in text.

33–35. The *perlas de huaca.* Flat sea shells with pink, serrated edges, one smooth, and two with spiny backs (*Spondylus pictorum*). These are sea shells, but were found in the Moche ruins. Bad brujos use these for imbibing through the nose (*alzar*), but only by left nostril. A good brujo imbibes from them when under attack by rival, a situation which is made evident by "*rumores,*" nearby sounds, like "*ka-ka-ka,*" during the seance.

36–46. Twelve *caracoles* (spirally formed sea shells), for ornament only.

47. One bottle of *agua de florida legítimo,* manufactured by Murray and Lanman, New York.

48. An iron magnet (*imán*). These may be purchased in Chiclayo. This particular one was given to the operator by a colleague in Virú.

49. A gourd rattle (*chingana or macana*) containing white stones of quartzite (?) ; has wooden handle.

50. *Olor.* Bottle of cheap jasmine perfume, manufactured by Laboratorios Maldonado, Lima.

51. A bottle of *agua cananga legítimo.*

52. Ten centavos worth of white maize kernels.

53. Ten centavos worth of white granulated sugar.

54. A head of the drug plant, *misha negra.* I do not know the chemical composition of this substance, but it is chewed in small pieces by the *maestro* and apparently has the property of producing visual hallucinations.

The contents of the *mesa* thus constitute the material equipment of the patterns of brujería practiced by the master, his "stock in trade" from the material point of view. These materials are seen to be in total a strange mixture of the indigenous and the European, of modern and medieval, of pagan and Christian, of coastal, Sierra, jungle, and foreign provenience. Yet each brujo feels that every item is essential to his work. In this publication I have no space to analyze in detail the origins of these various elements. A few passing comments will suffice for the present to indicate the diversity of cultural backgrounds involved in this complex. The purifying properties of white maize, for example, seem to be an Inca trait, if not older. Guamán Poma, in discussing provisions made by the Incas in times of epidemic, says that a diet of nothing but white corn was decreed (Lastres, 1941, p. 132). Many of the allegedly powerful drug plants (often called "*hojas*"—leaves), especially the *huaringas, mishas,* and San Pedro cactus come from the region of Salas, the headquarters of the north coast cult of brujería, and may be in part derived from the pharmacopoeia of the ancient coastal cultures. Other items, such as *mishpingo,* come from the jungle regions. The insistence on a trade-marked foreign-made perfumed alcohol called *agua de florida* alongside these items is a curious touch, as is also the presence of human bones of a baptized Christian alongside the pictures of saints and a bottle of holy water. The importance of the iron magnet and magnetized iron pyrites might be derived from the use of the magnet in 19th-century mesmerism. On the whole, the indigenous elements seem in the majority to be derived from coastal rather than Sierra indigenous cultures.

The treatment with guinea pigs (*limpia con cuy*) is said to be entirely different from "*mesa* work."

OTHER PROCEDURES OF "GOOD WITCHCRAFT"

The type of seance in which a guinea pig (*limpia con cuy*) is used for diagnostic purposes is, according to the brujo with whom I worked, entirely separated from "*mesa* work." I have not personally witnessed this type of session. It is a method of diagnosis used when the patient is apparently suffering from some serious, but undetermined, internal ailment and, in this man's technique at least, is not in itself concerned with discovering the human being who has perpetrated the black magical cause of the illness. He says that this is the view of all properly trained brujos. Some use the guinea pig diagnosis preceding the *mesa* in a single session. My informant uses it, he says, as one of a series of sessions. The session begins with an invocation and by the brujo making the sign of a cross with his forefinger on the head, chest, and stomach of the patient. He then takes a live guinea pig, preferably red, in his hand and starts to rub the entire body of the patient with it carefully. If the patient is in an extremely grave condition, the animal dies immediately. If not, after the entire body of the patient has been massaged, the animal is opened by ventral incision while still alive to see if the circulation is normal. If any part of the viscera is congested, the analogous organ of the patient is the seat of his trouble. If this type of examination is not convincing, after the guinea pig dies, the master grinds white corn kernels on a table with a bottle used like a rolling pin and sprinkles powder over the viscera. Those portions where the white powder darkens are, analogously, the sick portions of the patient's viscera. After this, the animal is buried on its back in a hidden place. First dirt is placed over it, then kitchen ashes, then dirt. If anyone or any animal digs it up, harm is done to the patient.

No *alzadores* or sniffing of alcohol appear in this type of diagnosis.

The work of Valdizán and Maldonado (1922, vol. 1) contains an extensive, although somewhat diffuse, discussion of brujería in various parts of Peru. Miñano, 1942, has reported some interesting laymen's accounts recorded in the town of Chicama, near Chiclín.

The most vivid and detailed account of brujería seances of which I know, occurs in fictionalized form by Camino Calderón (1942, pp. 179–185). I have the pleasure of Señor Camino Calderón's personal acquaintance and I have his word for it that the background material pertaining to brujería in his very successful novel "El Daño" was obtained by him at first hand during a period of a year and a half, during which he lived in Salas and became intimately acquainted with the leading *maestros* of this center of north coast curing. Since his book is practically unknown to readers of the English language, I quote, in translation, several passages bearing upon the subject at hand, with permission of the author, in order to round out the background of the present material recorded in Moche. The brujería of Moche of which I know lacks several features mentioned by Camino Calderón. This may be because it is a somewhat pale and "provincial" reflection of the center of this art described by him or because this account represents a literary synthesis of the work of a number of different brujos.

Speaking of a certain practitioner, he says:

In addition to Spanish—which he spoke somewhat masticated, in truth—he spoke in "lenguaraz," or the Quechua brought from the Sierra by the warriors which Tupac Ypanqui sent to restrain the fierce men of Chota. (P. 176.)

Personality:

Narciso was very educated, very suave in his manners, and belonged to a family in which the practice of the "limpiadura" dated from the ancestors and was practiced as a true profession, with absolute orthodoxy, and with a spirit full of charity and disinterestedness. (P. 176.)

Profession:

A "limpiador" not born in Salas is like a bullfighter not born in Spain. Salas is the matrix of the brujos, the cradle of the diviners, the mastic tree (*almácigo*) of the love magicians, the Lourdes of Peruvian curandismo, the Montesinos cave of everything grand and supernatural.

Whoever does not know Salas, does not know the North. Everything that is most fantastic and marvelous, takes place in Salas. . . The mountains and the lakes, bewitched, provide miraculous *pajas* upon demand if one sings to the rhythm of the chungana:

> *Cerrito encantáu*
> *dá la medicina*
> *que la necesita*
> *tanto desgraciáu*
>
> *Taita San Cipriano*
> *con que Dios trabajas*
> *guíame la mano*
> *pá sacar las pajas* . . .

. . . Every year Narciso Piscoya . . . went up to purify himself and to receive new training at the Gran Guaringa de Huancabamba where Quintín Namuche lived, an almost mythological person who was the Pope of witchcraft and the owner and distributor of the *pajas* which originated there: *the misha rey, the simora, the huachuma* . . . divine plants whose alcoloids awoke supernatural spiritual powers and with which the *curandero* acquires a double sight which extends beyond all scientific notions of time and space. In this chilly *páramo* whither he had had to flee from the Guardia Civil, Quintín Namuche—the repository of the therapeutic tradition of the Incas—uncontaminated by *maleros* and humbugs, led a life of an anchorite, receiving the homage of the neophites, initiating them in the secrets of the *pajas* [herbs] which must be employed for the welfare of mankind and exercising an absolute power over the brujos for 100 leagues around. (P. 177.)

To bring rain, a *curandero* goes to the sea to fill jars with sea water, which is sprinkled on the fields.

"Mal de hombre, the finest brujo cures, *mal de Dios,* no one," said Narciso Piscoya, drawing near to the bed of Don José Miguel. There was no time to lose. This same night he would diagnose (*rastrear*) the patient with a *cui ruco,* in order to find out which organs were affected and what type of *daño* was involved: bad wind, shadow cut with a dagger, or soul lost. Late at night, Piscoya took out of his bag an enormous *cui ruco* [red guinea pig], and whispering mysterious words, began to pass it over the back of the neck and the head of Don José Miguel. Then he passed it over the back, the ribs, and the lumbar region. Then the thorax, and upon being placed over the heart, the animal let out a squeak. "Pain. Pain. The señor has pain in his soul," said Piscoya lowering the *cui* to the abdomen. Upon scraping the knees of the patient, the poor *ruco* had convulsions and died.

As all grave and solemn facts which a *limpiador* has to announce, this also was announced in lenguaraz: Huañolonna, Huañolonna . . .

The diagnosis having been finished, Piscoya opened the *cui* with a knife and examined the entrails carefully. *"Chachu. Chachu,"* he exclaimed, "It is all *chachu* [irritated or congested]." And so it was in fact. The viscera appeared irritated and congested, covered with violet spots. There was not an organ which was not affected. The congestion was general—*todo está chachu.*

Fortunately, it was *mal de hombre,* caused by an *ayahuaira* —bad wind—and could be cured. It all depended upon using the proper *paja* [herb]. Thus said Piscoya as he rubbed the body of the *cui* with vinegar and gave it to be buried, warning that the face not be turned, under threat of the immediate death of the patient. (P. 179.)

Following the diagnosis, a great difficulty developed. Traditional practice required that Don José Miguel be taken to a solitary spot in the campo where at midnight, the *limpiador*— provided with his classic equipment: table, *chonta,* and rattle (*macana*) and accompanied by the *alzadores* who would raise the spirit of the patient, and by the *rastrero* who would direct the treatment—would ask the saints, the mountains and the sacred lakes which herbs Don José Miguel would have to drink there in infusion. Given the prostration of the patient, it was not possible to move his bed . . .

The preparations lasted only a short time. The following night, Piscoya appeared with his bag and his group of assistants: Casimiro Farroñán and Miguel Peche, "sorbedores," and Mateo Sernaqué, "rastrero." Beside the bed . . . the table was set up, consisting of a piece of cloth (*tocuyo*) El Inca, and the instruments were lined up: a rusty sword, various images of saints in *piedra Berenguela,* bits of quartz, sea shells (*perlitas*) and small idols taken from the *huacas.* At the end of the table were the medicines, represented mostly by the vegetable kingdom: sea weed, cactus and verbenaceas of the coastal plains, the *gayas* and perfumed flowers of the mountain *quebradas;* the velvety and resinous plants of the *jalcas* [high plateaus], the liquens charged with metallic oxides and calcareous salts of the cordillera. And together with these vegetables, the egg of the Angelote, against the tuberculosis; the eye of the Gran Bestia, which cures heart trouble; the grease of the Yacumama, without rival in rheumatism. Finally, within a tin of "Bacalao de Noruega sin espinas" were placed three powerful panaceas of the jungles of Jaén: the *ojé* (*Fincus glabrata*), the Chuchuhuasi, and the Ubos (*Spondia momborin*). And, inside a bottle of Spey Royal Whiskey were two lizards and a centipede, drowned in cane alcohol (*cañazo*). (P. 181.)

When the arrangement of the table was finished, Piscoya took his *macana,* made from a dry calabash, and rattling the dry seeds within, opened the affair with an invocation to *San Cipriano, patrón of the brujos:*

> *San Cipriano, milagroso santo,*
> *dáme la virtú*
> *pá la gloria de tus años, y de tu juventú. . .*

"Tirense una perlita." At this word of Piscoya, the "sorbedores" filled the sea shells with a mixture of Agua Florida and tobacco, and sniffed up, part of the contents in their noses. The "rastrero" drank a glass of the infusion of *San Pedro de Cuatro Vientes* (a cactus plant; the flutings of the stem are called *vientos;* its power is thought to increase with the number of flutings; also called *huachuma;*

best grown on the sacred mountain of Chaparri) and the "mestro" began to chew some leaves of *misha.* By means of these terrible narcotics, all aimed to place themselves in a position to be able to "see" the cause of the *"daño"* and to select the herbs which would cure the patient.

Various minutes passed; half an hour; an hour, and nothing. The invocations to San Cipriano, the Cruz de Chalpón, and the sacred lakes and mountains seemed to have no end. Neither the *limpiador* nor his assistants *alcanzaron a ver:*

> *Santo San Cipriano*
> *permítenos ver,*
> *y que tu yerbita*
> *Salga diondesté. . .*

Suddenly the *"rastrero"*—who had never stopped drinking the infusion of San Pedro constantly—began to stagger. "Yerbita, what do you see?" shouted Piscoya, stopping the rattle and going near to the *rastrero.* "I am seeing a *malero* who wishes to do harm to the table," answered the *rastrero,* and getting hold of himself as much as possible, added, "He is going to blow a *remalazo* [bad wind blown by an invidious brujo]. Look out!" Upon hearing what the *yerbita* said by the mouth of the *rastrero,* the *sorbedores* threw themselves face downward, trying to cover the head with the poncho. With a jump, Piscoya placed himself in the middle of the table; and seizing the sword, he started to cut the wind, while he howled:

> *Atrás Atrás sombra mala.*
> *Estoy con Dios, y los santos;*
> *Con el alto Yanahuanga,*
> *Con el ancho Chaparri.*
> *No podrás contra de mí.*

For a good while the sword, agilely wielded by Piscoya, whistled through the air, while the *rastrero* did not tire in "raising the spirit," of the Maestro: *"Crie valor, mestro. Crie valor. Yá está cortáu el ramalazo. Yá se jué. Yá se jué."*

Now that the *remalazo* had passed, Piscoya wiped the sweat off himself; he made the *sorbedores* get up—they were completely stupefied—and replacing the sword with the *chonta,* he started to dance.

There was a long period of singing and dancing:

> *Yerbitas, Yerbitas,*
> *vamas yá viniendo,*
> *porque el enfermito*
> *mucho está padeciendo.*

At this point, one of the *sorbedores*—not being able to restrain himself and inspired by a force greater than his will— got up and placed himself in front of Piscoya, making the same movements as the latter. With his eyes turned inward, his gaze fixed on the maestro and the muscles of his face shaken as by an electric current, the *sorbedor* had a horrible and strange aspect. There was a moment in which, balancing himself on the threshold, he tried to leave; but Piscoya, sure of the hypnotic power which he exercised over the unfortunate man, retained him with a movement of the *chonta;* with another movement he made him return to his place; and with another, he immobilized him. "Yerbita, qué ves?" he demanded. *"Una mujer gorda, con dos moños largos, está dañando a Don Miguel."* Piscoya continued to ask, *"Tiene contra?"* *"Si tiene. Pero no puedo ver tuavía."* Piscoya took up the dance again and the song. But this time, the verses were more emotional and plaintive:

> *Taitito San Cipriano,*
> *caballerito,*
> *con lágrimas te ruego*
> *ese tu yerbita milagrosa.*

Finally, San Cipriano was moved; and the *sorbedor* Miguel Peche, amid hiccups and sobs, communicated to the maestro the happy news: *"Yá vide la yerbita. Yá la vide. . ."* *"Onde está?"* shouted Piscoya. *"En el montoncito, junto a mi Señora del Cármen. . ."*

Rapidly, Piscoya extended his arm toward the indicated place. There were the *pajas* and *yerbas más apreciadas:* the *huachumas,* the *hórnamos,* and the *cóndores* of Yanahuanga; the *hualmis,* the *huamingas,* and the *simoras* of the Gran Guaringa de Huancabamba. He took the first which came to his hand: a small branch musty and spiny, covered with the varnish common to the bushes of the *puna.* Don José Miguel was saved. The medicine which would cure him had been found; it was only necessary to apply it immediately. (P. 185.)

Love magic is practiced by brujos, according to my sources. The brujo with whom I worked sells love potions to unrequited lovers. This business involves no seance. If a husband has left his wife for another woman, the brujo can bring him back, provided the other woman has not been *"segurado"* by another brujo. The brujo desiring to reunite the spouses works with hairs of the wandering husband. My brujo told me one case in which he brought the man back simply by writing him a letter, unknown to the wife, of course. The magical discovery of the whereabouts of a missing lover consists of setting up a *mesa,* but without *alzadores.* Directly under the saints' pictures on the *mesa* is some of the hair or other intimate property of the missing man. After imbibing jasmine perfume and spraying it over the *mesa* and the token of the man, the brujo proceeds to work with his rattle, asking the *mesa* a series of place names where the man might be. If the answer is negative, a road appears in the saints' pictures. When the brujo says the name of the right place, the road disappears and the face of the man appears.

A cure recommended for female infertility is the powdered flowers of a plant named *pacra* infused in water from boiled potatoes, to be taken each morning after breakfast. Nothing can be done about infertility unless menstruation is natural.

EVIL WITCHCRAFT

Whether "good brujos" also practice evil witchcraft and the casting of spells I am unable to say with certainty. The brujos themselves say they do not. Many laymen think they do, or that some do. My data on their operations are all second-hand. It is said that they cause harm to a person by making a doll (*muñeca*) representing the person. Then a stake, a nail, or a pin is stuck through the part of the doll which represents the part of the body of the person which is to become sick. The doll is then buried or hidden away where it cannot be found. Countervailing magic consists of the procedures previously described. In Moche itself I have heard of no systematic procedure for discovering these dolls and destroying them, other than through revelation to the curing brujo in the seance. This does not often occur, however.

The *shapingos* are believed to be the evil spirits at the command of the evil brujos. In Moche they are visualized in the form of the European devil, with horns and tail. They are the shadowy shapes which try to break up the curing seances, and are sent out by their "master," the evil brujo, to do his bidding. They are said to appear to women now and then, nude, and with the intention of having sexual intercourse. If a woman is once conquered by one of these spirits, she becomes the servant or dupe of the evil master; if she resists, there is danger that the evil brujo will cast a spell upon her, and cause her to fall sick.

It is not entirely clear in some informants' minds whether or not the *shapingos* are the same beings as the "messengers of the devil." Properly speaking, the latter apparently represent another concept stemming from medieval Europe. It is they who persuade men to sell their souls for money.

Evil brujos are believed to have the power to change themselves into animals and birds. Thus disguised, they are able to visit farms and houses to work their evil without the knowledge of the residents.

One account, illustrating the supposed power of evil brujos to change themselves into animals, has been given in the section "Sustenance and Basic Economy." Following is another.

C. was renting a piece of his *chacra* to another man and one night about sundown he stopped by to ask his tenant how things were going. The tenant said that everything was all right, except that for the last hour a large hawk had been making a noise in the *chacra,* hopping about, flapping its wings, and that he was on the point of going out to chase it away or kill it. The two of them went out to the field, the tenant with a stick, and they saw a large hawk hopping about and making a commotion. The tenant sneaked around through the bushes on the field border, sprang on the hawk, and struck it with the stick, breaking the left wing. Immediately the bird yelled out, "Don't hurt me, *compadre,* I am A. (one of the known brujos). I am doing nothing to your *chacra."* The two men drew back and the bird scurried into the bushes and disappeared as if by magic. It did not fly away and C. claims that he and his tenant could not find it (although he admits that they were somewhat afraid and not very enthusiastic in the search). At all events, some neighbors found old A. a few hours later in the night at a spot between the site of this event and A.'s house. His left arm was broken, as if by a sharp blow, and it was bleeding. He was taken to his house, speechless, and a short time later died of his wound.

When I ask why brujos, if they have the power to transform themselves into animal shapes, cannot ward off attacks of this sort, or at least cure themselves afterward, my informants say that once a brujo has been surprised and wounded in this way, he is lost. If they see a man about to attack them, they can frequently transform themselves quickly enough to save themselves, but when taken by surprise and real damage is inflicted upon them, there is no hope. Many other anecdotes tell of supposedly personal experiences in which individuals have been about to beat some stray animal and drive it away, when, before they can begin, it disappears and a known human being appears in its place. In some cases this has been the first intimation that the observer has had that the individual in question is a brujo. In order to start a whispering campaign against an individual, all that is necessary is to tell a story of this sort. "Last night I was about to kick a duck out of my garden when it suddenly turned into Fulano. I had no idea that Fulano was a brujo." The persons to whom such a story is told will say, "Oh, so that's it, is it? I thought Fulano was behaving queerly lately. He must have studied to be a brujo." And thereafter everyone will keep a sharp eye out for Fulano and suspect his movements.

Hórgamo is an herb which is ground to a powder and thrown on the doorsteps of a house by evil witches. It is supposed to make everyone therein fall sick. The evil witches likewise are said to possess a full armory of herbs and stones, comparable to those employed by good witches, except that their effects are deleterious to the health and peace of mind of victims. These are given to clients with instructions for slipping them into the food and drink of intended victims. Toads seem to be a favorite spell-casting animal used by the evil brujos or used with their advice.

When an evil witch wishes to ascertain who is working countervailing magic against his spells, it is said that he sets up a *"mesa negra"*—black table. This resembles the *mesa* of the curing brujo except that everything which is white in the latter is black in the evil *mesa.* Thus black bottles are used instead of white, a black cloth instead of a white one, powdered charcoal instead of white maize, etc.

Finally, an evil witch may work harm against his victim by blowing a "bad air" (*mal aire*) at him. I am by no means clear how this is supposed to be done. In the seances of the good brujos the patient is sometimes asked if sometime before falling sick he did not feel a draft or *aire,* followed by a chill. With all due respect, this seems to be a sure-fire question for the diviner, because it is seldom that the patient cannot recall such an occurrence. Of course, the diviner still has to give an answer to the question, "Who did it and why?"

Any cold draft or sudden chill is suspected of being a *mal aire,* and in the list of remedies (pp. 139–142) will be found a number of items used by laymen to ward off the evil effects.

CURANDISMO

A CURANDERA

Most of my information on the practice of *curandismo* in Moche comes from an old lady about 68 years old, acknowledged to be the outstanding curing woman of the community. She is now married to her second husband, who cultivates with her help a small *chacra,* and they live in a small adobe house, not very well kept up, on the outskirts of the *pueblo.* The house has the arbor or *ramada* in front rather than behind and here she receives her patients. Directly behind this is a semiopen room containing the kitchen and the usual large wooden table. There the brews which she uses in her cures are prepared.

When I first visited her, she was sitting on a *petate* on the ground under the front arbor with two *cholo* women who had journeyed to her from outside the community. She was engaged in the cure of *susto* in their respective babies, and the ladies were loud in praise of her knowledge and technique. Nonetheless, her appearance was somewhat forbidding, and, during the following months of our acquaintanceship, I learned to know that this first impression was typical. She was wearing a dark-gray cotton skirt, somewhat patched, very ragged, a once-white blouse, and a straw hat of the Mochero type. Her hair was not cared for, and hung about her head in a somewhat matted mass. She has a heavily pock-marked face with inward slanting eyes with small bags under them and a good many wrinkles and crows' feet around their edges. Her mouth is wide and the upper incisor teeth are worn off at the roots. Her hands were dirty, with long, black-rimmed fingernails. In general, she looks, on first appearance, a good deal like the proverbial "witch" of the fairy tales. But when in a good humor she is capable of a wide, easy smile that transforms this forbidding visage into a map of merriment, and she is ready with a comfortable chuckling laugh when she is convinced one is her friend.

After we had become acquainted on the first day, it was, of course, incumbent upon me to partake of her hospitality in the form of *chicha* and *causa,* and during the refreshment I told her that we had no such methods of curing in the United States and that I was convinced that she probably knew things of which our medical men had never heard. I invited her jokingly to come to New York with me, and told her if she would teach me some of her methods we would set up an office together. To this she agreed readily in high good humor and promised that, at all events, before I went back she would give me a complete course in curing. We discussed various cures superficially and I went away well pleased, because I had been warned on all hands that I would never succeed in getting her "secrets" from her. Then, however, I made a series of mistakes. Not having heard from her, after a week I sent an intermediary to ask if I could visit her and start the "course." The answer was evasive. Then I bethought myself to enlist her professional interest. My young son was ill in Trujillo with what was thought to be rheumatic fever, and I asked her to come and examine him, saying that I thought he might have *susto.* She did not reply positively but said to send for her on the coming Friday. I then asked one of her *compadres* to go on Friday to remind her. When she did not appear in Trujillo, I got in touch with the *compadre* and discovered that she had driven him out of the house, saying that she would not be ordered about by him and that if Don Juan (meaning me) wanted her, he could come personally, bringing the child. I then got in touch with her daughter and son-in-law and we went to see her. She told me to stop fooling around with intermediaries, that she would not be treated that

way, that she knew very well I would not entrust my own child's cure to her, and that anyway she did not want to go to the hotel in Trujillo and have everyone laugh at her. I then told her that she was right and that I had only acted as I had because I did not understand her. Now, I said, if she would talk to me as one "doctor" to another, we would exclude all other persons from our meetings, and I would give her 50 soles as a token of my esteem, provided she was frank with me. If I could find out that she had used a certain method in a cure which she had not told me about, I would deduct 10 soles from the total for each such concealment. She was somewhat taken aback by this approach, but shortly agreed, we drank *chicha* together again, and became friends. For several months thereafter I consulted with her on all matters of *curandismo* and found no reason for deducting anything from her gratuity. Even so, I am sure, of course, that I have not learned all about this art in Moche. The photographs reproduced herewith are, so far as I know, the first published series of photographs of certain of her curing methods.

The following discussion is in terms of locally recognized symptom groups or disease entities.

SUSTO

Susto, an abbreviation of *asustado* (past participle of *asustar,* to frighten), is a term widely used throughout Peru (Valdizán and Maldonado, 1922, vol. 1, pp. 61–90) to refer to a generally and popularly recognized type of syndrome believed to be caused by or associated with soul loss. In some parts the term *"espanto"* is used. The latter term also occurs in Central America, but there the symptoms and alleged etiology differ in some details (Gillin, Ms.). The wide distribution of this complex must be fully studied, but here I can only attempt to deal with it in the local situation. Valdizán states that *susto* was very prevalent among the "ancient inhabitants of Peru" and that it not only represented an individual nervous upset, but also reflected a "true state of collective anxiety." (Valdizán, 1915, 1917; Valdizán and Maldonado, loc. cit.)

In Moche *susto* occurs in the following forms: (1) Adult, of which there are two varieties, (*a*) nearby and (*b*) distant; and (2) infant.

Adult *susto* is always precipitated by a sudden fright of some kind. Frequently the patient is frightened by an animal, sometimes merely by a sudden gust of wind, a reflection in an irrigation ditch, a sudden fall, etc. This is believed to scare the soul out of the body. The difference between the nearby (*de cerca*) and distant (*de lejos*) variety is that the former usually takes place in or near the house, and the soul of the person which has been jarred loose nevertheless remains near him. If the fright has taken place in the field or some distance away, however, the soul stays at the site of the fright and special methods must be used to get it to come back.

No one, even a strong man, is ashamed of being *asustado*. It is regarded as something beyond the control of the individual. Men pride themselves on their physical courage when facing other men or dangerous physical situations, but they do not regard it as childish to be "frightened" in the technical sense of *susto*. Several Moche men have served as conscripts in the armed services in the jungle and during the "incident" with Ecuador, but claim they had never been *asustado* in this sense, although they are willing to admit that on occasion they have been *asustado* (frightened) in the ordinary sense of plain physical fear. Women do not fall ill of *susto* during childbirth nor at the monthly crisis. Although individuals are frightened by nightmares, one does not get *susto* from them. It is thus clear that *susto* involves special psychological complexes which are not well translated by the English words "fright" or "fear" in their ordinary North American contexts.

The symptoms of importance to a *curandera* are as follows. The armpit and lobe of the ear are white and the inside skin of the arm does not show any veins and is often wrinkled. There is a low fever and the patient is "nervous" and hypersensitive to sudden sounds. Physically he is weak, and he often has diarrhea. A man does not lose potency, but he will do harm to a woman if he tries to have intercourse with her. Urine is yellow; when it turns white, the cure is successful. Aside from hypersensitivity to loud noises or interruptions, the patient seems to be in a depressed state, saying little, often with the eyes closed or cast down to the ground. Some patients have an abstracted or dreamy attitude, gazing off into space. I have personally seen only three adult patients in the first stages. All of them were depressed and quiet but contactable and well oriented in time and space. I was able to obtain some detailed history on seven cases in all. I discussed nine other cases from the experiences of my informants. One man in Moche died, allegedly of

susto, during my work there, although the immediate cause of death was recognized as tuberculosis. There were no newly developed cases of adult *susto* handled during my work in Moche, but I had an opportunity to see something of three new cases brought for cure from outside the community and four old cases from the community itself (including the fatal one just mentioned). Full case histories were not obtained from any of these patients, but the following features appeared in all histories: (1) A debilitating illness, usually malaria, had appeared some time before the *susto* attack; (2) all patients seemed to be emaciated or wasted physically; (3) all but one case gave a history of some emotional crisis preceding the fright which had precipitated the *susto* itself. The four women all had a "love" or sex crisis, such as a man leaving them for another; two of the men had had trouble with their sweethearts, while a third had had a row over inheritance rights.

Dr. Pedro F. Castillo Diaz, chief of the women's section of the Trujillo general hospital (Hospital de la Beneficiencia Pública), has handled a good many cases of alleged *susto* in his service. He emphasizes that he is not a psychiatrist, but rather an internist. However, his impression is that *susto* is a hysterical manifestation based on general debility usually caused by malaria or tuberculosis. He says that he has practically never seen an alleged *susto* patient who is not run down; the patient usually has a low fever, is poorly nourished, usually has anemia, and is in a "delicate and irritable frame of mind." He does not rule out the possibility of such cases appearing in families with a history of psycopathology, but has no records which would show this. In Lima I discussed this matter with two young psychiatrists attached to the Hospital Loyaza, Dr. Arnoldo Cano J. and Dr. Valega. They expressed the opinion based on their experience that so-called *susto* usually turns out to be either hysteria or tuberculous meningitis with an underlying history of malnutrition, malaria, or tuberculosis, or all three.

Certainly the medical and psychiatric aspects of this condition should be more thoroughly studied, and I await the opportunity to carry out more intensive investigations of this interesting problem. The present tendency of the medical profession seems to be to pooh-pooh the business, because it does not fit neatly into the textbook definitions of diagnostic symptoms.

It is my tentative opinion that *susto* is somewhat similar to the "nervous break-down" among North

Americans. Both phrases may cover, in their respective cultural contexts, a variety of psychopathic and physically pathological conditions, considered from the strictly diagnostic point of view. Both, however, are culturally defined escapes for the individual from the pressures and tensions of life. When a North American "can't take it any longer," he has a "nervous break-down;" when a Peruvian cholo "can't take it," he gets *susto.* Actually, depending upon the configuration of the case, one patient may have hysteria, another a depression, a third possibly an anxiety attack. *Susto* also becomes a mechanism for calling the group's attention to the individual by his assumption of a culturally patterned configuration of "symptoms." At all events it seems to represent at least a temporary collapse of the psychic organization of the individual and consequently of his ability to deal normally with his life problems.

The treatment of nearby *susto* by the curing woman already mentioned proceeds as follows. Three treatments are required, on Tuesday, Friday, and Tuesday. The materials used are as follows: (1) The seven herbs of *susto—yerba de gallinazo negra, de gallinazo blanca, Santa María, ajenjo, chocha, ruda,* and *campana;* (2) the four waters of *susto—agua de la reina de Hungría, agua de azahar, alcohol de melisa, agua de Buda* (some curers use five "waters," and among them, other types of waters, as indicated in the list of remedies); (3) *San Mério,* an incense powder. The steps in each session of the cure are the following. (1) The curer or the patient, if the latter is able, strips the herbs of their leaves and mixes the leaves together in a pile on the ground. (2) When the *"pajas"* have all been stripped, the pile of leaves is kneaded in the hands. (3) A double *escapulario* is made with needle and thread from unbleached cotton cloth; it consists of two square bags or sacks each about 2 inches square with two cloth connecting strips each about 18 inches long. These are called *almohaditas* (little pillows). The two small sacks are stuffed with the mixed leaves of the herbs, then sewn shut. Then the sacks are well moistened with the mixed *aguas de susto.* The patient puts his head through the two connecting strips so that one sack of leaves hangs over the chest, the other on the back between the upper corners of the shoulder blades. The waters of *susto* have been previously mixed together and are kept in an ordinary pop bottle. (4) An earthen pot of about 2-quart capacity is heated over the fire

and the remainder of the kneaded and mixed herb leaves are placed in it and well sprinkled with the mixed waters of *susto,* and kept on the fire long enough so that the whole mass becomes lukewarm. (5) A retiring room is made by placing an *estera* on the ground or floor and leaning *esteras* against the wall, so that privacy and freedom from drafts are provided. (6) The patient goes into the retiring room and removes his clothing and the *curandera* follows with the pot of lukewarm herbs and a frying pan or plate of hot coals from the kitchen fire. The *curandera* takes a handful of the moist herbs and begins the massage (*frotación*). In the first of the series of three treatments she begins with the feet, in the second with the back of the head, and in the third with the feet again. In any case, with her hand full of herbs, she makes the sign of the cross, muttering an invocation, *"En el nombre de Dios, de la Virgen Santísima y del Rey del Cielo."* If she is beginning with the head, she squeezes some juice into the right ear, then into the left ear, then rubs the back of the head, the scalp, and the face with the wad of moist herbs. Then she works down over the whole body. If she begins with the feet, the massage proceeds in the opposite direction, covering all parts of the body. (7) *San Mério* is sprinkled on the hot coals of the plate or frying pan, producing a sweet-smelling smoke. The patient drapes himself in a sheet and stands up with feet spread apart over the coals, allowing his whole body to be smoked. (8) The patient lies down inside the retiring room, wrapped in a sheet and blanket. Shortly he begins to sweat and goes to sleep. (9) The *curandera* takes in her hand one of the garments removed by the patient. This is used to call the patient's spirit. Waving the garment through the smoke, the *curandera* makes the sign of the cross in the air, then calls out in an animated voice, *"Vámonos, Juancito* [or whatever the patient's name may be]; *vámonos. No te dejas. Vámonos con nosotros; no quedas solito; ven, vámonos."* This calling is repeated three times, after which the article of clothing used is placed under the patient's neck. (10) The *curandera* closes up the retiring room tightly so that drafts cannot enter, leaving the patient inside. (11) She then takes the remains of the herbs and the incense to an isolated spot. First she buries the herbs in a hole, then spreads the ashes of the incense and coals over it and makes the sign of the cross; then she scatters rubbish over the spot, so that it will be unnoticeable. If anyone digs up the herbs, harm will befall the patient. (Pls. 22, *lower (center and right)*), and 23 show various stages in the process of the cure.)

In case the patient has lost his soul at some distant place, e.g., in the field, the curing ceremony just described must be gone through at the site of the fright. Some curers walk through the streets and the lanes, carrying the patient's clothing in hand and calling loudly for the return of the soul. The curing woman with whom I worked disapproves of this, because it may attract the attention of evil brujos and *shapingos* (evil spirits or devils).

After a treatment, the patient must be kept in bed for a day. He is not to take milk, cow meat, plantain or banana, or oranges. The patient can take sheep broth or chicken broth and can eat *plátano de la isla, sancochado.* Tea made from the gratings from the stem of the valeriana should be given frequently. Otherwise he should eat only rice, noodles, and "cold" foods, but plenty of them.

It should be noted that no internal medication is given during the curing session itself.

Some *curanderos* use a cock's comb instead of the herb-stuffed *escapularios* mentioned in step No. 3 of the above-described treatment. The comb is cut off the living bird, and a cross with the blood is made on the forehead and on the base of the neck of the patient with a verbal invocation. Then the patient is rubbed with *agua de florida* sprinkled on brown cotton, after which the comb is strung on a string with a needle and suspended around the neck, hanging down on the chest. This is supposed to be especially good in the treatment of women.

If the patient recovers his normal personality and health, it is believed that the spirit has returned to his body. However, it is sometimes impossible to call back the spirit and the patient dies, for it is believed that it is impossible to live with a permanent *susto* (i. e., to live without one's soul). While I was working in Moche, a young man named H., about 32 years of age, died. It was widely believed that the basis of his trouble was an uncured *susto.* About 4 years previously, he had fallen down and hurt his hand, and in the process had sustained a violent *susto.* Although he received treatment, it was impossible to secure the return of his soul, and he continued to decline until he contracted tuberculosis, which killed him. This case, incidentally, is complicated with brujería. Many persons agreed on the following version. He became enamored of a certain girl, who was said to be very determined (*bien guapa; guapa* here does not mean "good look-

ing" as in some other parts of Latin America, e. g., Guatemala). She became pregnant by him and was resolved that he would marry her. He was working as a collector on a bus, but she persuaded him to give up this job so that he could be with her more. Although other work was offered, such as road work, she would not allow him to take it because he would have to be away from Moche part of the time. He became restless, would not marry her or care for the child she bore him, and had affairs with other women. Therefore she bewitched him or had him bewitched. After this he became much attracted to her and settled down with her, but shortly thereafter fell ill of *susto.* He left her with three small children at his death. It is believed that the bewitchment prevented the return of his soul, which had been captured by his *enamorada* or the brujo she had employed. I cannot vouch for this series of events, of course. The story is only "what people say."

Another case was told me of a woman who fell ill with *susto* and died within a year, "because she did not believe in *curandismo* and would not take the cure."

Susto in children seems to occur most often at about the time the child is beginning to walk and to be weaned, about 1 year of age. The locally recognized symptoms are fretfulness, low fever, "colic," diarrhea, pale shriveled armpit, and bloodless ear lobe. It is of much more frequent occurrence than *susto* in adults. One cannot pass over the suggestion that the difficulty, whatever it may be from the medical standpoint, seems to occur at a period of crisis in the infant's life, i. e., when it is making a readjustment from the complete dependency of its mother's arms to the increased necessity for self-reliance of the toddler. There is no forcible weaning among the Mocheros, but one child is frequently supplanted by a younger one at his mother's breast, so that sibling rivalry may be one of the factors in infantile *susto* as well as dietary readjustment. The treatment session follows exactly the same steps as those outlined above for the adult, including the calling of the spirit, except that the child is usually held in its mother's arms. Plate 24 shows a series of scenes in the treatment of infant *susto.* The condition may also befall older children as well, in which case its onset coincides with a specific "fright."

PHYSIOLOGICAL WEAKNESS

It is believed that the physiological system is at its lowest ebb about midnight, and this is the time when most people are said to die. The reason for this is said to be that the world has revolved on its axis with the effect that at midnight in Moche everyone there is hanging head downward, a position which upsets the normal functions of the body and weakens it. The bodily system is at its best just before dawn, between 3 a. m. and 4 a. m. At this time one can do his best work, especially intellectually, a belief which reinforces the early rising pattern of the Mocheros and coastal *cholos* in general. (It is superfluous to point out that this early morning period is the time when most deaths occur among ourselves and when the body forces are at their lowest.)

UMBILICAL HERNIA OR QUEBRADURA

Quebradura, or umbilical hernia in infants, is regarded as a serious condition which must be corrected before the child is 2 years of age at the oldest. It is believed to be caused if either a pregnant or menstruating visitor to the house picks up the child in her arms. This will produce *"empuje,"* a straining and coughing of a particular type which induces *quebradura.* Treatment may be given any day of the week and proceeds as follows, to describe one of several treatments I have witnessed. The mother brings the child to the house of the *curandera,* bringing along a pad of white surgical cotton previously purchased in a pharmacy. The *curandera* then goes with the mother and child to the house of a woman in whose garden grows a *higarón* tree. This woman charges 50 centavos for the use of the tree. Some twigs are broken so that they exude a white, sticky sap, which turns brown after a period of exposure to the air and which has a strong astringent action on the skin. Curing takes place in the open air in the *huerta* itself. It is also possible for the mother to obtain the twigs previously and for the cure to take place in the house of the curing woman. A flat pad of white cotton about 4 by 6 inches in size is thoroughly moistened on one side with the *higarón* juice. A hole about 2 inches in diameter is made in the center of the pad, which is then placed, moist side down, on the child's abdomen, so that the umbilicus appears through the perforation. Then the curer massages and pushes down the protruding umbilicus with her index finger so that a reflex contraction of the muscles of the abdominal wall is produced and the umbilicus retracts somewhat. Then she pours into the umbilical depression about a tablespoonful of a white powder made from the feces of

the small lizard. This is a secret remedy not made known to the client. Then strips and tufts of moistened cotton are stuck onto the remaining surface of the abdomen in more or less haphazard fashion. Next, a pad of moistened white cotton is placed over the umbilicus itself, but only after it has been thoroughly smoked in the incense of *San Mério,* produced by sprinkling this powder over live coals in a plate. Then a binding of cotton cloth is wrapped around the abdomen two or three times and tied together tightly in front. Usually three treatments are given, one every other day. Then the binding is kept in place for 15 days. When it is removed, if the hernia is not well reduced, a final treatment is given.

INGUINAL HERNIA OR ESTIRADURA

The curing woman cures inguinal hernia, involving descent of the hernia into the testicles, as follows. The condition is called *estiradura,* and treatment may be given any day of the week. A pomade is made of *cebo de macho* and menthol with which the groin is first thoroughly massaged. Then the testicles (*compañones*), with the penis protruding, are placed in a suspensory bandage made of unbleached cotton cloth, together with a paste made of *matica* and *compana.* Next, the testicles are massaged gently until the hernia is drawn up. The suspensory bandage is tightened. Then a pad of white surgical cotton well moistened with *higarón* is placed over the lower abdomen or groin, and another on the small of the back, and the two are bandaged firmly into place with cloth which is also wrapped around the suspensory bandage, with the penis left protruding. The whole produces a fairly firm truss. Several men of the community tell me that they have been cured in this manner. One treatment is said to suffice in some cases, several treatments in others. In the latter case, the bandage is removed and treatment repeated about once a week.

DISLOCATION OF THE RIBS OR TRONCHADURA DEL PECHO

Tronchadura del pecho usually occurs in children or infants. In the cases I have seen a lump appears on the chest near the sternum. One has the impression that it may be bowing or enlargement of the heads of the ribs due, possibly, to rickets, but the local explanation is that the head of a rib has slipped out of its articulation with the sternum.

Treatment may take place on any day of the week. A paste is made from *cebo de macho, agua de caranga, resin,* arnica, menthol, and *paico.* The patient takes a bottle in his mouth and alternately sucks and blows hard according to the directions of the curer. This is supposed to help bring the bone back into place. In the meantime the curer manipulates the swelling with her hands, attempting to reduce it. When she has reduced it ("the bone back into place"), the aforementioned paste is spread over the affected part with a cloth that has been smoked in *San Mério* and a tight cloth bandage is wrapped around the chest and tied in front over the site of the swelling.

Other sprains and dislocations (*tronchadures*) are treated with the same medicaments. The sprain or dislocation is first reduced by massage and manipulation, after which it is bandaged. The curing woman does not believe in reducing such swellings by pulling the joints by force as is done by some *curanderos.*

EVIL EYE OR OJEO

Ojéo, or sickness caused by the evil eye, is practically always a children's ailment. It is caused by a glance given the child by an adult who possesses the power to "*ojear*" children. Some persons have this unfortunate power and others do not; those who do, have it functioning at certain times and not at others. The power is entirely involuntary and the persons possessing it are not held accountable. One of the respected men of the community has this power and he cannot help himself. He is well liked in other respects, and both he and parents take care to keep children out of his way. Some say that this fluctuating power is due to a "bad humor" (*mal humor*) in the body which arises only on certain days. Others say that it is due to "electricity." At any rate if a person thus endowed looks directly into the face of a child, the latter falls ill with *ojéo.* If the adult and the child laugh together when the event takes place, the result is said to be much worse.

The distinctive physical symptom is that the back of the neck and head pulsate (*brincan*); this is not a symptom in *susto.* Also, the child may be hot and feverish and restless. There may also be nausea and vomiting. The diagnosis is made by the *curandera's* placing thumb and forefinger on the back of the head and neck to feel the pulsating.

Medicaments which may be used are brown cotton (*algodón pardo*), willow leaves, a pinch of salt, half of a cigarette, yellow pepper (*ají amarillo*), *cerraja,* fruit of lime, a pinch of white sugar, and water.

The treatment, which may take place only on Tuesdays or Fridays, is as follows. (1) First the seeds are taken out of the cotton, if not already removed, so that they will not scratch the body. A good handful of cotton bolls may be bought from the owner of a cotton bush for 10 centavos. The seeded cotton is made into a pad which is held in the hand, and inside the pad is placed a yellow pepper. (2) The *curandera* takes the child on her lap and says, "*En Nombre de Dios, de Jesucristo, y del Espíritu Santo. Amen.*" Then she begins to massage the back of the head and the nape of the neck with the cotton held in her hand. Then she proceeds to a careful massage of the abdomen, mostly in a circular motion, then the small of the back, then the arms. The child's clothing is not removed, but the massage is given underneath it. The cotton is now stringy and is thrown out. It must be thrown out toward the north. (3) With the heel of the hand the *curandera* next massages the forehead, the back of the head, nape of the neck, and the whole face. (4) If the child is feverish, a small can of menthol is heated on a dish of hot coals and the contents poured into the bare hand of the *curandera* who then uses it to massage the crown of the head, the back of the neck, and the whole body. After this, if there are no other symptoms, the child is wrapped in a blanket and put to sleep. It sleeps, sweats, and loses its fever and fretfulness. (5) If the child is nauseated or is vomiting, a special massage of the abdomen is given. A handful of willow leaves, a pinch of salt, and half of a cigarette are all made into a sort of wad which can be held in the hand. It is first heated in a dish of live coals, then used to massage the abdomen in a circular motion. (6) For nausea a small lime is cut at one end with a knife; the incision has the form of a cross. The lime is not squeezed. It and a handful of *cerraja* leaves, well chopped up with a knife, are boiled together in one-half cup of water. When this mixture cools, a pinch of white sugar is added and the liquid is given to the child internally.

Some curers precede the massage with brown cotton by an egg treatment. An egg is broken into an earthen pot full of water and is beaten alternately with the right hand and the left (bare) foot of the patient, until it coagulates. Then it is thrown out to the north. What the purpose of this procedure is, I am unable to say, unless in terms of homeopathic magic the egg is taken to represent the eye which has caused the *ojéo.* Informants are unable to provide a verbal explanation.

HEART PAIN

Orange flowers, lemon flowers, and *toronjil* are placed in a cup. Boiling water is poured over them, after which white and red carnation petals (*clavel blanco y negro*) are put into the mixture and two drops of *agua de florida* are added. After the mixture has cooled, a pinch of white sugar is added. The liquid is given to the patient every morning for a week.

VENEREAL DISEASE

Syphilis and gonorrhea do not seem to be clearly recognized among the Mocheros, nor have I seen much evidence of them among the people. However, it is recognized that men sometimes get sores (*llagas*) on their sexual organs. As a treatment for this condition oil of canime (*aceite de canime*) and hydrogen peroxide (*agua oxigenada*) are used. First the sore is washed with the peroxide, then the oil is applied and a bandage tied on.

COLIC (CÓLICO)

The symptoms are extreme abdominal pain, sometimes in the lower right quadrant of the abdomen. The idea of appendicitis is not clear either to curers or to lay informants. "Colic" probably covers indigestion, liver and gall bladder trouble, appendicitis, and all abdominal pains. Treatment is as follows. (1) Three stalks of the leaves of the *yerba santa* are washed in a basin of water and wrung out. The water itself, by now green, is thrown away, but the pulpy leaves are placed in a bottle. (2) Two corncobs of the red variety (*tusas negras*) are burned or toasted until they are carbonized. They are then put in a pot with water and boiled, stirred meanwhile with a spoon. The resulting water is then poured into the bottle on top of the *yerba santa* pulp. (3) Then a tablespoonful of sugar—one-half raw, one-half burnt white sugar—is added. (4) About two tablespoonfuls of the liquid is administered to the patient. (5) The first result is vomiting. (6) After the patient has vomited, a whole cupful of the liquid is given; the result is a strong purgative action.

Apparently the Mocheros do not suffer much from infected appendixes. Otherwise I would have heard more about conditions resembling peritonitis as an aftermath of this treatment.

PREGNANCY AND CHILDBIRTH

These matters are not necessarily handled by curers who treat *susto, ojéo,* and the like, although some women who specialize in *curandismo* are also midwives. The profession of midwife (*partera* or *curiosa*) is, however, more generalized and less esoteric than that of *curandera*. Nevertheless it is a speciality in Moche, and it is not customary for women to be delivered by untutored, unspecialized members of their families.

It is well-known among Mocheros that sexual intercourse is the cause of pregnancy and that the stoppage of menstruation is an indication of its onset. It is popularly believed that a male child is born 8 months and 8 days after conception, whereas the term of a female child is 9 months and 9 days. According to a *partera* who explained her calling to me, it is possible to determine the sex of the child after the seventh month. The midwife palpates the head of the foetus in the woman's abdomen; if the head is hard, the child will be a male; if soft, it will be a female. Neither *parteras* or lay informants have any theory of predetermination of sex. This is purely a matter of chance ("*casualidad*"), and there is no other explanation.

I did not witness a delivery in Moche, and the following information concerning midwifely techniques was obtained from midwives and from women who had passed through the experience.

After a woman knows that she is pregnant, or at least after the seventh month, she retains a midwife, who advises her for a period before childbirth. In general, there seem to be no stringent rules for pregnant women. They go about their usual duties, nurse their latest child, and have sexual intercourse, even during the last months. They are not supposed to bend over or lift heavy loads during the last 2 months, and it is advisable, although not required, to eat only "cold foods."

When the labor pains begin, the midwife is called and the patient lies on her back either on a bed or on a mat on the floor. The midwife massages the abdomen from above downward, but does not have the patient sit up. No ropes or poles are provided for the patient to pull on, nor are any instruments used by the midwife, although a tight band is usually bound about the upper abdomen. During labor the midwife palpates the abdomen in order to determine the type of presentation. If it appears that a breech presentation, or some other abnormality is in the making, a member of the family is sent at once to the telephone office to call an ambulance from Trujillo. Some midwives claim to be able to work a transverse foetus around into the proper position with their hands, but all agree that only a hospital can handle a breech presentation. A typical attitude toward antisepsis is reflected by my conversation with one midwife. Since her hands always appeared dirty, I asked her if she washed them before delivering a child. She smiled and tossed her head, saying *"Si, si"* as if it were a matter of small importance. This same midwife claims, however, never to have lost a patient in childbirth and that puerperal fevers are unknown in Moche. The latter claim is doubtful on the basis of lay information. Some cases were mentioned of midwives extracting dead foetuses with their hands, but apparently most such cases are handled in the hospital.

In order to ease the labor pains, *agua de albahaca* and port wine are given by mouth, as much as a glassful. A punch made of port wine and *chicha* is also said to be helpful. Camphor oil is massaged on the stomach to hasten the birth. On the whole, there seem to be few magically colored attitudes involved in childbirth; both patients and midwives proceed in a strictly businesslike and secular manner.

It is said that most women bear relatively easily; midwives say that the average labor of multiparous women is 5 hours. Several cases of primaparas staying in labor for over 20 hours were mentioned to me, however. If labor lasts 24 hours without delivery, the patient is usually taken to the hospital. The midwife seeks to avoid a dry birth by administering by mouth an infusion of *jerania* flowers.

The birth takes place in bed or in a reclining position. To start the child crying and breathing, the midwife picks it up by the feet and pats it on the buttocks. In stubborn cases, she lays it on its stomach and places a newly hatched chick on its buttocks. When the chick pecks the babe invariably comes to life, according to the *parteras*. The umbilical cord is cut with unsterilized scissors the width of four fingers from the child's abdomen and is tied with cotton sewing thread. The mother is then required to stand up, spread her feet out, and shake herself until the placenta is expelled. It must then be buried in the floor of the kitchen by the midwife. If it is touched or dug up by anyone else, "the mother will die." The umbilical cord falls off eventually. No attention is paid to it. The child's abdomen is bound with a bandage of cotton cloth. To clear the eyes of the newborn child, the midwife bathes them with white cotton moistened with drops of boric acid solution. The ears are cleaned with a toothpick and cotton, but very carefully, to avoid breaking the drums.

The newborn is given a cloth nipple to suck for 3 days after birth. This contains a starch compound (*amidón compuesto*) mixed with powdered sugar and is said to have the dual virtue of providing nourishment and cleaning the infant's system. If the child has colic, it is given a few drops of *agua de anís de estrella*.

To stop uterine hemorrhage, *rumilanche* and a few drops of iodine are mixed in boiling water and injected hot into the vagina with a douche bag and nozzle. A preventive of recurring hemorrhages is *tara* boiled in water. To this infusion are added *jerania* flowers well cut up. The liquid is given by mouth. Eight days is the standard lying-in period, although some women habitually get up after 3 days and others lie in as long as 2 weeks. Only "cold" foods should be eaten. *Chicha* helps to increase the mother's milk. A wet nurse is used, if necessary, usually a relative or a *comadre*. This is seldom required.

The Peruvian Ministry of Health has been carrying on a campaign against infant mortality, and attempts to persuade women to have their children delivered in hospitals. This service may be had free or at a nominal charge, and a number of women in Moche have been converted to this method and always go to Trujillo. In cities, certified, registered female midwives, who have passed an officially approved short course are available. As a sidelight on the impression made by these modern facilities, I quote from my notes the substance of a conversation with a woman who is not a Mochera but who has lived years in Moche and is married to a Mochero, whom she met while he was working in Lima. Although she comes from a *cholo* working-class family in Lima, she is well acculturated to Moche ways.

Two men and I dropped into this woman's house for some *chicha* and *causa* one afternoon. The woman received us heartily and told us the news that the woman next door had just given birth to a robust male infant. This provided an opening for the discussion of childbirth customs, and the *señora*, who is the mother of six, was far from bashful. In fact, her frankness in discussing such matters with three men was surprising to a North American. It was as if this were one subject on which she, as a mother, was a clearly recognized authority and concerning which no one present could easily contradict her. We shall skip over her remarks about the technique of childbirth, which have been abstracted, together with information from other informants, in the material which has gone before. She said that the midwives charge about what the traffic will bear within a range of from 3 to 15 soles. She herself has never paid more than 10 soles in Moche. One time in Lima, however, she said she had a terrible experience. She fell into the hands of a *profesora* (an officially qualified midwife). Our friend was scandalized by the requirements and the costs which this expert laid upon her. First and last it cost her about 100 soles ($15.30) to have her baby, and the *profesora* was always coming around before the birth, prescribing clean sheets for the bed, a mountain of paraphernalia for the delivery (which took place in the house), many "useless" medicines, and so on. In the opinion of the *señora* such fussiness is entirely unnecessary and nothing but an affectation and excuse for getting money out of poor women. If she ever allows herself to get involved with a *profesora* again, she knows that she will be ready for the *manicomio* (insane asylum). The Moche midwives are quite good enough for her or for any self-respecting woman, she says.

LAY CURING

Many of the remedies in the list (p. 139) are used by ordinary laymen and women just as North Americans use household or old wives' remedies. We shall omit further description of these therapeutic measures, contenting ourselves with a brief discussion of *chucaque* and *secretos*.

CHUCAQUE

A certain complex of rather vague symptoms is called *chucaque*. In general, it is a feeling of "being out of sorts"; one feels a slight stiffness in the muscles, may have an upset stomach with a feeling of nausea, a slight headache, and the like. It generally appears after a shock of some sort which produces ego deflation or an upset of the emotional balance. For example, one of my informants fell off his horse while riding with me and some other men back from a visit to the *campiña*. This embarrassed him. Next day he felt bad until given the treatment for *chucaque*. Although it is described in the literature as precipitated by "shame" (*vergüenza*),[63] the word was never used in describing or discussing the condition by my friends in Moche.

In Moche all adult men are able to cure *chucaque*, although some are better at it than others. The treatment which might be called the native version of chiropraxis or osteopathy is as follows: (1) The patient is given a general massage of the face, back

of the neck, shoulders, arms and trunk, without removing his clothes. The curer uses only his bare hands. (2) The patient's arms are folded across his diaphragm tightly, so that a hand protrudes on each side. The operator stands behind the patient. With his right hand, he grasps the patient's left, and with his left hand grasps the patient's right hand. Now he pulls hard with both arms so that the patient's folded arms are pulled tightly across his trunk. Then with a swift series of jerks the patient is lifted off his feet and bent backward sharply by the operator. Usually the operator places his knee in the small of the patient's back and continues jerking until there is a cracking sound in the patient's vertebral column. (3) Next the operator, still standing behind the patient, places his right palm open against the lower right jaw of the patient and his left hand is held in position to steady the patient's head while, in a series of quick jerks, the right hand rotates the patient's head sharply several times to the left until a cracking noise comes from the neck. This is repeated in complementary fashion on the other side until the "neck cracks."

Brutal as this treatment may sound, it has a soothing and relaxing effect, as I can personally testify. Psychologically speaking, I can only surmise that the treatment serves to shock the patient out of his feeling of inferiority or anxiety by reducing his internal tensions. Whatever may be the internal neurological and physiological mechanisms involved, the patient usually loses his physical symptoms as well as his anxiety feeling. He drinks a glass or two of *pisco* with his curer and the whole thing is forgotten. Men perform these cures for each other without payment. However, it is believed that *chucaque* must be cured without delay; otherwise it will persist and become worse.

SECRETOS

Secretos are of two types, children's and adults'. They are made of woolen yarn. Small babies have a red yarn tied around the left ankle. It is believed to prevent *empujes*, such as those which produce umbilical hernia. Such strains are caused by a particular type of evil influence which menstruating women, especially, exude, and the *secreto* prevents the entrance of this power into the child's body. Cords of any color are worn by grown persons on the wrist or above the elbow to prevent "cramps" (*calambres*), and it is stoutly maintained that they are very effective.

---

[63] Camino Calderon (1942, p. 201) states: "In Arequipa they call *Trocadura* that which in the north is called *Chucaque*. It consists in the malaise (*malestar*) produced by a feeling of shame (*vergüenza*)." In Lima it is called *pavo* (fear). According to Valdizán and Maldonado (1922, vol. 1, p. 102), *chucaque* is especially widespread in the north, in the Departments of Piura, Lambayeque, La Libertad, and Cajamarca. They speak of it as a syndrome found in a person who has suffered strong shame (*vergüenza*): vomiting, diarrhea, pains in the stomach. They give the treatment as follows. Head is massaged with open palms of the curer. He spits on the hair of the patient several times in several directions. Then he rolls a lock of hair in thumb and index hair and pulls it out with a cracking noise, which "breaks the chucaque." Then both ears are jerked downward. Afterward the patient drinks an infusion of the leaves of *chileno* and the ashes of *tocoyu* dissolved in water.

GENERAL REMEDIES USED IN CURING

Below, I have itemized a selection of the plants, remedies, and apparatus used in curing in Moche. Not being a botanist, I do not vouch for the scientific names, which I give only so that readers unfamiliar with the local terminology may have some clew for identifying the plants or substances mentioned. The scientific names have been determined by comparing the common Moche names with common names given by Valdizán and Maldonado (1922, vol. 2), by following a similar process in certain other literature, and by consulting with Dr. Nicolas Angulo, who, in addition to an extensive medical practice, teaches one course of botany in the University of Trujillo. Dr. Angulo is the favorite *médico* of the Mocheros. He will come at any time of day or night in response to a call, his charges are reasonable, and he does not press for collections. All this, in addition to his skill as a physician and his geniality as a man, has made him the most trusted of the scientific medical men with whom the Mocheros are in contact. Dr. Angulo is also a scientist of wide interests in anthropology and botany, in both of which fields he has published a number of papers. Up to the moment, however, he has not had sufficient time to complete his studies in "popular medicine," a project in which he is much interested. I hereby express my appreciation to Dr. Angulo for his many kindnesses, including his placing at my disposal such information as he possessed concerning botanical identifications of plants used in native curing.

I also wish to express my appreciation to Señor Juan Llontop, proprietor of one of Trujillo's leading drug stores, who furnished the information incorporated in the following notes concerning the pharmaceutical preparation of certain items habitually obtained by the Mocheros from the drug stores of Trujillo. Señor Llontop, although he received his professional training in Lima, was reared in the northern "Mochica" community of Monsefú, and his family name is one of the oldest and most distinguished among the genuine natives of that community.

Except when otherwise noted, scientific botanical names in the list given below are those given by Valdizán and Maldonado (1922, vol. 2).

The bulk of the articles used in the *mesa de brujería* are listed and explained in the section with that title.

In every market in the Sierra there are several stalls or places on the pavement occupied by sellers of herbs and simples, with the various products set out before them in small cloth sacks with their tops open and rolled down. In the Sierra these medicine-sellers are called *callahuayas* and in Arequipa, *arroceros*. There are no such vendors in the Moche market. In the Trujillo market some of these products can often be obtained, but the variety and selection is not as wide as in a typical Sierra market or in the market at Chiclayo. The supplies used by the curers and *brujos* of Moche are mostly obtained in Trujillo, in Chiclayo, and from itinerant peddlers, called *médicos bolivianos*, who visit Moche about once or twice a year.

The following list of remedies can only be considered a set of notes which, haply, may serve to round out the picture of folk medicine in Moche until such time as the material at hand can be more fully studied and until further investigations can take place. It would be very helpful to have a thorough-going pharmaceutical study of the *materia medica*.

Aceite de alcanfor. Camphor oil, used for massage. Obtained in pharmacies.

Aceite de camine. Obtained in pharmacies and used in treatment of sores, particularly venereal lesions.

Agua de azahar. A pharmacy preparation, orange-flower water, one of the "waters of *susto*."

Agua de espanto. A pharmacy preparation, distilled water of rosemary (*romero*). One of the "waters of *susto*."

Agua de la Reina de Hungría. A pharmacy preparation, one of the "waters of *susto*." Distilled water of lavender.

Agua de melisa. A pharmacy preparation, "water of balm," (distilled water of *toronjil*) which is one of the *aguas de susto* (waters of *susto*).

Agua florida. A patent preparation obtainable in the pharmacies; something like eau de cologne, alcoholic and heavily scented. One of the "waters of *susto*" and also essential in the *brujería* seance. Original is manufactured in the United States. A Peruvian imitation is now on the market; *brujos* and *curanderos* claim that the national product does not have the power of the original.

Agua oxigenada. Hydrogen peroxide, obtained in pharmacies.

Ajenjo. Apparently a species of wormwood (*Artemisia* sp.). Some persons grow it in *huertas* for curing purposes. Dried stalks may also be purchased in the pharmacies.

Albahaca. Grown in gardens and used as a pain killer in childbirth.

Angelote, peje perro. A large fish egg, sometimes about the size of a goose egg. Consists of a mass looking like egg yolk enclosed in a tough membranelike covering. Small quantities are given with food. Each specimen sells for 3 to 4 soles, depending on size.

Altamís. When one has "cold bones," leaves of this plant are heated and bound onto the leg or arm where complaint is.

Algodón pardo (*Gossypium* sp. ?; not definitely identified in literature). In Moche this variety of cotton is grown in *huertas* and sometimes along roadsides. Those who own bushes sell the cotton to those who need it. The cotton is light brown in color, streaked or uneven in tone, ranging from almost yellow to dark brown. After being separated from the seeds, it is rolled into strands or loose rolls about as big as the little finger and these in turn are made into a small pad or mass used for massaging the body, in *ojéo*. The cotton is also used by curers and frequently by witches, in other types of curing. It is not moistened or medicated, but is believed to have a special power in removing magically caused ailment.

Amor seco (*Bidens* sp.). In Moche is taken as an infusion to cure inflammation of the stomach and liver, especially after heavy drinking. It is said to reduce "inflammation" of these organs.

Anís estrellado, or **agua de anís de estrella.** A pharmacy preparation, one of the "waters of *susto.*" Anis seeds are mascerated and infused in water.

Arnica. Made in the pharmacies; a tincture of the mascerated flowers steeped in low-grade alcohol for 10 days. Used for sprains, etc.

Bálsamo de Buda. A standard pharmaceutical formula, also known as bálsamo fioravanti. Used in cure of *susto.*

Bórico. Boric acid powder obtained in the pharmacies. Made into solution at home and used as an antiseptic by some curers.

Brocamelia. Flowers made into infusion, which is drunk for cough.

Campana, floribundo. A small tree with lilylike leaves; flowers are rubbed together in the hands and bandaged over an inflammation.

Caraña. Officinal preparation of the pharmacies, composed of essence of turpentine, beeswax, Burgundy pitch (*pez de Borgoña*), and coloring matter. Used as an application for curing umbilical hernia and gumboils.

Cebo de macho. Fat extracted from mules; a pharmacy preparation; used in cure of sprains and bone breaks.

Cebolla, onion (*Allium cepa,* identified by Angulo). An infusion is made for pneumonia, composed of three pieces of ollin and three heads of the white onion, to which is added a cup of cognac. Taken by mouth.

Cerraja (unidentified). Infusion of the stems used in Moche as a cure for colic. Leaves also may be used for making infusion, although they are said not to contain the medicinal element in large quantities.

Clavel, carnation (*Dianthus* sp., identified by Angulo). Flowers as an infusion for cardiac trouble.

Cola de caballo (*Equisetum xylochaetum, E. giganteum*). Given as an infusion for kidney trouble in Moche. In other parts of Peru, according to Valdizán and Maldonado (1922, vol. 2, p. 37), used as follows: As a decoction for washing old rebellious ulcers; decoction used as a collusive in all affections of the mouth and for washing stubborn acne of the face; the infusion enjoys prestige as a constrictor and is used for combating all kinds of hemorrhages; also used as a dissolvent of renal calculus and as a diuretic and emmenagogue, in the Department of Lima. Used as a stimulant and for illnesses of the liver in Ica.

Congona (*Peperomia congona sidro,* identified by Angulo). Given in infusion for heart trouble.

Corpusuay (*Gencianacea* sp.?, according to Angulo). Given by mouth as infusion for malaria and also for kidney trouble.

Culen (*Psoralea glandulosa,* according to Angulo). Used in Moche as a stomachic. Valdizán and Maldonado (ibid., pp. 78–79) give following information concerning medicinal use of *P. lasiostachys* and *P. pubescens:* The ancient Araucanians cured their wounds with culen, according to Guevara; nowadays is given by mouth as an infusion for diarrhea in Ambo, Huancayo, Hualgayoc, and Loreto; reported as a decoction with celery and burned bread administered by mouth for diarrhea in Ambo; reported as a decoction for foot baths in Arequipa; as an infusion by mouth as a carminative and vermifuge in Lima, Cajamarca, and Piura; as a sudorific in Cajamarca and Piura; as an infusion with bread and burned sugar by mouth for indigestion in Cajamarca; as an infusion by mouth in infantile enteritis in Huaylas; in infusion as an astringent and in decoction as a purgative in Santiago de Chuco; in infusion by mouth as a stomachic and carminative in Cailloma.

Cuncuna (*Vallesia dichotoma,* according to Angulo). In Moche said to be used for bubonic plague. Poultices are made with it and salt of ammonia (*sal de amoniaco*) and applied to the buboes, while enemas are administered made of an infusion of the leaves.

Chamico. A weed, the dried leaves of which are smoked in cigarettes as cure for asthma.

Chicoria (*Hypochoeris* sp., according to Angulo). In Moche used in infusion as an antimalarial; in a warm bath as an emollient.

Chilco macho (unidentified). In Moche used in cure of *tronchadura* (dislocation of joint or sprain). Leaves are bound hot onto affected part with bandages. Also bound over a broken bone "to keep out the cold." Sometimes single leaves are stuck on as a form of sticking plaster without bandages. According to Valdizán and Maldonado (1922, vol. 2, p. 394), it is used in Piura in decoction as a bath in cure of tumors and exuberances created by the cold.

Chocho. Unidentified green plant used in curing.

Flor de arena (unidentified). In Moche used in infusion externally as an emollient in inflammations and boils.

Flor muerta. A yellow flower which is cooked into a paste and stuffed into an aching tooth.

Flor de overo (*Cordia rotumbifolia,* according to Angulo). The flowers in an infusion are given internally for liver trouble.

Grama dulce (*Cynodon dactylon,* according to Angulo). Infusion of the leaves administered internally as a diuretic. Valdizán and Maldonado (ibid., p. 45) say it is widely used for same purpose, also that freshly squeezed juice is used in drops to remove "clouds" from the eyes, in Arequipa.

Higerón. White cotton is moistened with the sap after which it is applied to the abdomen of child with umbilical hernia.

Huanarpo (*Jatropha macrantha*). Powder used in wine and other drinks as a love charm and aphrodisiac.

Jerania. Flowers used to prevent hemorrhages.

Llantén (*Plantago major,* and other species). Used externally in decoction for pimples in Moche; also, infusion of leaves mixed with *aceite rosado* is applied to inflammations. According to Valdizán and Maldonado (1922, vol. 2, p. 330), is used in decoction as an astringent wash for wounds in Arequipa; as astringent in ocular affections in Loreto and Huancayo; leaves fried in oil as an analgesic in earache in northern Peru; infusion or maceration of leaves given in enemas for bloody stools; decoction with barley, *yedra* (ivy), *verdolaga* (purslane), and *altea* (mallow) in pulmonary hemoptisis (Arequipa); decoction made with leaves of rosemary, to which, when cool, beaten white of egg is added, taken by mouth to stop bloody vomit (Arequipa); widely used against hemorrhages of all kinds and against inflammations.

Maichill *(Thevetia nerufolia).* In Moche an infusion is used for bathing wounds and pimples. According to Valdizán and Maldonado (1922, vol. 2, p. 283), the seeds are poisonous and are used in some parts for killing dogs; in the jungle regions the stringed nuts are used as cascabels.

Maíz blanco, white corn kernels. Used in setting up a *brujería mesa.* White corn is specified.

Malva real. A roadside green plant, used in enemas.

Marrajudia (unidentified). A drop of the milk is used in the eye to remove film.

Matico, yerba de soldado, cordoncillo *(Piper angustifolium).* Taken as an infusion of the leaves for cough and as a douche for inflammations of the vagina. According to Valdizán and Maldonado (1922, vol. 2, pp. 130–132), the pulverized leaves are widely used to cicatrize the umbilicus of the newborn child and an infusion of the leaves is generally used to bathe wounds. Also reported as a pectoral from Santiago de Chuco.

Menthol. "Mentholatum" or a proprietary imitation of this mentholated salve. Obtained in the Trujillo pharmacies and also in the Moche *tiendas,* usually in small tin cans about the size of a half dollar.

Molle *(Schinus molle).* A small berrylike fruit growing on a bushlike tree native to Peru. In Moche the leaves are bound on sprains, in hot form, so that "cold does not enter the bones." Fruit is sometimes eaten; in other areas *chicha* is made from it, but only rarely in Moche.

Nogal *(Juglans regia, J. neotropica).* The first species was apparently introduced by the Spanish after the time of Padre Cobo, as he does not mention it. Professor Weberbauer has found *J. neotropica* growing wild in the valley of the Utcubamba and the jungles of the Montaña, according to Valdizán and Maldonado (1922, vol. 2, p. 135). In Moche an infusion of the leaves is used internally as a pectoral and in douches for vaginal baths, also as a bath for all types of inflammations. It is also reported as an astringent in uterine baths in Arequipa and Lima, as a wash for wounds in Lima, and as a cough remedy in the Department of Lima and, with boiled milk, for the same purpose in Arequipa. A decoction made of scrapings of the wood is taken internally to reestablish menstruation, in Arequipa. And in the south, leaves are placed under the pillow as a cure for insomnia (Valdizán and Maldonado, *loc. cit.*).

Paico *(Chenopodium ambrosioides).* In Moche the leaves are removed, heated moist, and bound in a poultice on any painful part of the body. According to Valdizán and Maldonado, Cobo gives the following information of aboriginal uses: Leaves were applied in the form of a poultice to any tumor to reduce it; this species was also used to reduce flatulency, for which purpose it was eaten, or cooked with *muña,* drunk hot before breakfast with some *aji;* paico eaten with much salt reduces the swellings of gouty legs. In modern Peru, according to Valdizán and Maldonado (vol. 2, pp. 146–147), the leaves are eaten as seasoning in food; leaves also eaten as a vermifuge; cooked root is applied as an astringent to bleeding wounds; it is given internally as an infusion for *susto* in Huancayo; cooked leaves mixed with *borraja* (*Borago officinalis*) in cure of "*caracha*"; it is said that roasted leaves are eaten to counteract chills and "aire" in Trujillo; also, the juice is taken to stop diarrhea; in Cuervo, an infusion of three hearts of paico, taken 3 mornings successively with a Pater Noster each morning, is believed to increase intelligence.

Pez, resin. Obtainable in the pharmacies.

Pie de perro. In Moche used in infusion as emollient and diuretic.

Polvo de lagartija. Pulverized, dried, white feces of the small lizard; used in cure of umbilical hernia and placed on navel of newborn child to hasten healing and to prevent rupture.

Rabo flaire. Roots are mashed up and used as infusion, mixed with infusions of chicoria and verbena in enemas.

Romero, rosemary (*Rosmarinus officinalis*). In Moche an infusion of the leaves is taken internally for heart trouble; also appears as a pharmaceutical preparation, *agua de espanto,* one of the "waters of *susto.*" For inflammations, especially of the eyes, an infusion of the flowers. According to Valdizán and Maldonado (1922, vol. 2, p. 291), this plant was brought to Peru in 1579 by Alonso Gutierrez from Spain.

Rosa de castilla (*Rosa indica,* according to Angulo). The infusion of the leaves is administered internally as a purgative and in douches for vaginal baths.

Ruda (*Ruta graveolens*). In Moche the plant, minus the roots, is used in raw form to give massages in the cure of *susto.* The stalks which have been used in curing are then placed on the ground under the growing plant. If a *brujo* wishes to do harm to the person who has been cured, he kills the growing plant. This causes the *susto* to return, as well as the appearance of other symptoms. Also used in decoction as an agent to promote menstrual flow and as an abortifacient. Used also against *brujería,* to attract women, and also for good luck and good times. Elsewhere in Peru, say Valdizán and Maldonado (1922, vol. 2, p. 221), the temples are massaged with the leaves for "aire" in Arequipa and Ambo; an infusion or powder of the leaves is used internally for dismenorrhea and as abortifacient; a decoction is administered in enemas as a vermifuge; the stems are used to stop the nosebleed of *serroche* (mountain sickness); infusion of the stems in southern Peru for palpitations, hystèria, and in general as an antispasmodic; infusion of the leaves drunk for epilepsy in Loreto, etc.

Rumilanchi. Used as an infusion to promote menstrual flow and as an emollient.

San Juan. A creeping vine with a yellow flower. Body of an *asustado* is rubbed with the whole raw plant.

San Mério. A type of incense powder obtained from the pharmacy, composition unknown to me. In Moche the smoke is used for magical fumigation in various cures, including that of *susto* and *quebradura*. Sr. Llontop tells me that it is taken internally by the *criollo* public of Trujillo to cure pneumonia, dissolved in weak alcohol and mixed with a small quantity of white kerosene. Also, it is used in the form of plasters on the chest, mixed with boiled onions and lard.

San Pedro (family of the Cactaceae, according to Camino Calderón, 1942, p. 205). Used in Moche in *brujería* seances. It is a fluted cactus stem and must have at least four flutings; the more flutings, the more power.

Santa María (family of Liliaceae, according to Angulo). In Moche the leaves are heated over the fire, and the whole body is massaged with them in cure of *susto*. Also taken internally in infusion for correcting menstruation, according to Angulo. Also, leaves used to make a tea drunk with meals as a beverage.

Sávila (*Aloe vera, A. abyssinica*). In Moche it is believed that when a *brujo* enters the house, the sávila hanging over the door will turn red and even, in some cases, exude drops of blood. According to Valdizán and Maldonado (1922, vol. 2, p. 199), this plant was brought from Spain in the first years of the Conquest. In addition to its power to protect from *brujería*, which is general throughout Peru, these authors say that it is in use as a general antidote for poison.

Sombrerita. A lilylike low-growing ground plant; an infusion is drunk for kidney trouble (*dolores de los riñones*).

Tamarindo. Fruit used as a purgative.

Tara (*Caesalpinia tinctoria*). In Moche an infusion of the vine is used as a vaginal douche to cure white discharge and uterine hemorrhages. Valdizán and Maldonado (1922, vol. 2, pp. 209–210) indicate that it has a general use in Peru as an astringent.

Toronjil (*Melissa officinalis*). In Moche used as a stomachic and in heart trouble; also as a pharmaceutical preparation, one of the "waters of *susto*."

Turre. In Moche a cure for scurvy. The root is mashed up and a bit of bicarbonate of soda and some drops of lemon mixed with it, to which is added boiled water. Taken internally.

Valeriana. Used in *susto* and as a heart remedy.

Veneno. A plant used for curing in Moche. The leaves are mascerated and mixed with or moistened with *agua de florida*. The whole mass is sewn into a cloth scapular and hung around the neck as a protection against *susto*, especially in children.

Verdolaga, purslane (*Portulaca peruviana, P. oleracea*). Infusion of stems as diuretic in Moche. Valdizán and Maldonado (1922, vol. 2, p. 151) report the following uses in various parts of Peru: Applied as a plaster to the abdomen in certain dysenteries, in southern Peru; seeds used as emmenagogues and vermifuges; trunk or stem as infusion for liver trouble in Loreto; decoction given as refreshing enema in burning fevers (Piura); also as cooling agent, sedative, and antiscorbutic (Cuzco).

Verbena (*Verbena littoralis,* according to Angulo; *V. bonariensis,* according to Valdizán and Maldonado). Root only in infusion used as an antimalarial and emollient in Moche. Elsewhere, according to Valdizán and Maldonado (1922, vol. 2, p. 228): Decoction for pernicious ulcers in Arequipa; for malaria in Ayachucho and Loreto; as a poultice of the leaves to relieve pain and superation in the liver (Ica); powder drunk in old wine for liver trouble in Arequipa; decoction taken with salt and lemon as a purgative in the north; decoction taken as mouth wash for toothache in Cajamarca; poultice of leaves as hemostatic in small wounds; decoction in enemas during typhoid fever in Loreto; decoction by mouth for colic in Puno; decoction by mouth as a febrifuge in Huaylas.

Yedra, ivy. Leaves and stems are mascerated and made into an infusion which is used to bathe irritations of the skin. Not mentioned by Valdizán and Maldonado.

Yerba de gallinazo (*Chenopodium opulifolium; C. murale,* according to Angulo). Leaves and stalks in raw form used for massage by *curanderas* in Moche, in cure of *susto*, especially in adults.

Yerba mora. A small plant with long white flowers, used in enemas.

Yerbaliza, yerba Luisa (*Andropogon schoenanthus*). Used as a standard beverage in Moche, also believed to have stomachic properties. Valdizán and Maldonado (1922, vol. 2, p. 113) say that this plant is native to the north and center of India and was unknown in Peru until introduced by the Spanish. They report that it is used as a carminative in Lima, Arequipa, and Loreto.

Yerba santa. Leaves are boiled and bound onto a wound in a poultice, especially good also for boils and pimples.

RELIGION

THE VARIOUS RELIGIONS OF MOCHE

Strictly speaking, the "religious" parts of a cultural system are those complexes—orientations, trends, and objectives—which invariably involve symbolic patterns dealing with the supernatural. In other words, "religion" in cultural anthropology refers to cultural beliefs and practices based upon notions of supernatural or extranatural power and/or beings. In this broad field, Moche culture is a mixture or mosaic as in so many other areas. In the foregoing section on Native Medicine and Magical Curing much of the "religion" of Moche has been described. In this section I shall deal briefly with certain religious beliefs and practices associated with the Roman Catholic Church. Before opening this subject, however, it is worth noting several divergent trends in Moche religious culture and thus in the religious thinking and acting of the typical individual. Underlying all is a common body of rather generalized and amorphous ways of thinking which we might call the substratum of folk magic. These can be classified into the two hackneyed categories of sympathetic and contagious magic. For example, the fact that the aphrodisiac *huanarpo* looks like the human sexual organs is an important fact of sympathetic magic, whatever its pharmaceutical properties may be. The use of a garment of the patient in the cure of *susto* is, on the other hand, based upon concepts of contagious magic. Both of these types of concepts, if not universal, are at least very common among peoples in all parts of the world.

In Moche these basic magical beliefs, together with later accretions and concepts of "higher religion," have been organized into at least two cultural orientations or institutions. These are (1) the institution of witchcraft which has its (*a*) white and (*b*) black subdivisions, related to each other in opposition; and (2) the institution of the Roman Catholic religion which, as we shall see, aside from the central body of approved doctrine, is manifested in a number of subsidiary or peripheral patterns, and which also has its opposition aspect in a number of beliefs surrounding the Devil. Although witchcraft in its "white" aspect, at least, has made some concessions or bows to Christianity (e.g., use of saints' pictures in divining, the invocations, presence of the cross on the *mesa*, etc.), nevertheless witchcraft as a cultural institution is functionally entirely separate from institutionalized Christianity. Thus there are at least two fairly well organized bodies of religious beliefs and practices which function in a "parallel" fashion in Moche and are not functionally interrelated, even in the sense of being opposed to each other. On the whole, witchcraft tends to be individualistic and divisive, socially speaking, and anxiety-raising, psychologically speaking, while Christianity tends to be unifying in its social effects and anxiety-reducing in its psychological results.

Historically each of these systems is in itself derived from various cultural backgrounds. The complexity of Christian history is familiar to all, and in Moche is further heightened by cultural changes wrought in the institution of the church since its importation at the time of the Conquest. The tracing in detail of the various historical components of witchcraft must wait for another publication, but it is obvious that Moche witchcraft at present is a fusion of both coastal and Sierra elements, which originally belonged to entirely separate cultural traditions. The recognition of this historical diversity of the religious orientations of Moche—and other Latin American

communities—is important from a functional point of view, if it prevents us from falling into one of the common errors of identification. We cannot merely dismiss the diverse patterns in this kind of situation by saying without qualification that the Mocheros are "Christians" or that they have "Inca" witchcraft, or "Chimu" magic, or something relatively simple of that sort. In religion as in respect to its cultural system as a whole, Moche is not "European," nor is it "Indian."

ROMAN CATHOLICISM

There are said to be about 30 Protestants ("Evangelistas") among the Mocheros, apparently Seventh Day Adventists. They have no chapel at present, and they hold their meetings in private homes. Otherwise everyone in Moche is nominally Roman Catholic. The Mocheros take pride in being "very religious" and they have this reputation in Trujillo and elsewhere. Specifically, "very religious" and "very devoted" mean that the community makes a good showing in the performance of the various religious fiestas.

The dogma and rituals of the Roman Catholic Church are, so far as I know, faithfully followed by the local priest, who also serves the port town of Salaverry.

Our discussion is limited to certain selected aspects of the religious picture in Moche.

The position of the church in a community is dependent to a large extent upon the methods and manner of approach of its ministers. In Moche in 1944 the active priest was a young Peruvian, trained in a Lima seminary, who had been in charge only a year or two. He lives in the small semiruined former monastery (*convento*) on the plaza, which was apparently erected to house the members of the Mercedarian order who seem to have founded the Moche church. The former priest, a Spaniard, is now retired, but still lives in Moche in a house of his own, and intends to spend the rest of his days there. He is a genial and affable old gentleman with a good many personal contacts among the Mocheros, but he no longer takes an active role in the church, other than to say an occasional mass when the *cura* is absent on some other mission.

INDIVIDUAL PARTICIPATION

Generally speaking, it is only the older men, among the male element, who take an active and continuing interest in the church itself (as distinguished from the fiestas). Most men of adult age take the position that they, of course, are members of the church, but that the devotions are mainly an affair of women. Most men questioned could not remember when they had confessed last or had taken communion. Many men over 35 years of age had confessed only once or twice in their lives. All of them know the Pater Noster (Lord's Prayer), but that is all that many of them know. Strings of rosary beads are possessed by some women and old men, but the average man never uses them. Several men did not know what they were. Apparently, confirmation does not as a rule involve the organized study and memorization of the catechism, and most of my informants report that they have been confirmed without effective examination at about the age of 12 in a body of boys, when the bishop of a "mission" of friars had come to the town for that purpose. Parents are, of course, enjoined to provide religious instruction in the home, but perhaps the majority fail to provide anything effective. I found it quite impossible to obtain a coherent explanation of church doctrine or "what the church stands for" from any Mochero, or, in fact, from the forasteros. One concludes that the church to the typical individual represents not a body of verbal teachings and precepts, but a body of personal and group experiences. The most devout Catholics among men whom I could contact were a few older men, retired from active life, who spent a good deal of their time reciting prayers, taking communion, and confessing. It seemed to me for a time that I must have involuntarily associated with only the very secular-minded or indifferently minded section of the male population, but attendance at services in the church tended to confirm the picture. On ordinary Sundays, it is common to see only a handful of adult Mochero men in the church, amounting to about one-tenth the number of the women present, and very few taking communion. The men are usually at the back of the church, sitting on stone benches along the sides, or standing. They go in and out during the service, indulge in a certain amount of conversation among themselves, and, although respectful in attitude, do not give evidence of strong attention or emotional involvement.

Apparently the true definition of "devotion" in Moche consists in participation in the mayordomías which operate the various fiestas. A man who gives contributions to these organizations is a devoted and respected man, and one who participates is even more so. Many men seem to have an attachment to one of the saints whose days they celebrate. They pray to the saint and believe that he takes a personal interest in their worldly welfare. Many, if not the majority, of persons thus devoted to saints know nothing of the saint as an historical personage, but are devoted to the image itself. In conversation they admit that the image is representative of a saint, not the saint itself, but the ideas of who or what is represented by the image, are vague. On the other hand, an individual takes an active interest in the physical welfare of the image to which he is devoted, helps in keeping it clean, dressing it, refurbishing its paint, and so on. One of the best ways of showing one's devotion to a saint is to provide at one's own expense a sudario or some other ceremonial garment or ornament for the image. There is a qualified embroiderer in the town who makes most of his living from preparing these gifts, usually made of velvet, richly embroidered with gold and silver thread and ornamented with glass brilliants, sequins, and other bright decorations.

Women seem to participate more often and more earnestly in the rituals of the church than do men. They attend confession and take communion, on the average, much more frequently than men. Also, they are organized into groups which meet occasionally in the church in the afternoon or at night to sing novenas for a departed relative and in adoration of various saints. The average woman is better acquainted with the prayers and rituals. For this reason, the priest apparently has more contact with the women than with the men of the community. Women are also devoted to saints, but they do not participate formally in the mayordomías. One of the richer women, as a sign of her devotion, presented one of the images of the Christ with a sudario in October of 1944 which cost 700 soles.

In Moche there is no organization of laymen similar to the Knights of Columbus or the Catholic Action groups which endeavor elsewhere to some extent to interpret and to apply the precepts of the church for the benefit of laymen to the affairs of the world and of the community.

SOME PSYCHOLOGICAL ASPECTS IN MOCHE

From the psychological point of view an important aspect of the church's function in Moche is that it does not create a load of anxieties for the individual. The Mocheros do not have "consciences" of a type with which so many North Americans and North Europeans are equipped and from which they are so continuously suffering.[64] The "conscience" is, of course, a complex of "acquired drives" of a punishing sort [65] which are created within the individual by cultural (frequently religious) training. Such training usually also includes learning of responses (habits or customs) which, if performed by the individual, will lower the anxiety drives and thus relieve him of their punishing effects. In Moche, the "average person" is ignorant of many of the anxieties.

Fear of hell is not a particular obsession with Mocheros. The living worry somewhat about the condition of the souls of their departed relatives in purgatory, an anxiety which is connected with the potential willingness of such souls to intervene on behalf of the living, but such anxieties can be easily lowered by offerings and masses for the repose of the dead. And it is always desirable that burial should be in hallowed ground with benefit of clergy. Finally, many of the problems of everyday life can be referred in a familiar manner to the saint to whom one is devoted.

Although the church offers fairly simple ritualistic means for quieting the anxieties which it creates, most of these rituals cost money in themselves and also for the peripheral expenses. Funerals, for example, are classified into first, second, and third class, each with its set fee. In a first-class funeral, the priest officiates at the church, at the house, and at the cemetery. In a second-class funeral, he officiates only at church and house, and in a third-class burying only at the church door. Because of the inhibition on approaching the priest for a service of this kind without having the fee in hand, several individuals are said to have been buried without the services of the priest, simply because the family could not raise the money.

I have never heard women express verbal aggressive attitudes toward priests, but they are very common among men, to whom the priest does not occupy a generally respected social status, although his status as a religious officer is never questioned.

SOCIALIZING FUNCTIONS

In Moche, religion has certain socializing functions. In the first place, the fact that practically all Mocheros are Catholics provides practically the only generally accepted basis of real, if somewhat vague, unity present in the community.

In the second place, the fiestas celebrated in connection with the various images in the church building itself, are occasions for general community participation as well as for effective organization and group activity in the responsible mayordomías in charge of the respective fiestas.

In the third place, the church looks with a tolerant eye upon the recreational features of the ceremonies—the feasts, parades, dances, drinking, fireworks, and displays—which, with the passing of time, have become as much a part of the life crisis ceremonies and saints' day celebrations as the performance of the holy offices themselves. Puzzled outsiders are often at a loss to understand the hold which the church has over the population of Latin American countries. However, it should not be forgotten that in Moche one may "enjoy himself" at the same time he is "being religious." Devotion and recreation, one might say, are combined, rather than separated into distinct areas of experience. In Moche the religious fiestas are the only activities in which all members of the community may spontaneously participate and are therefore of importance in promoting a certain degree of social unity. And the fact that they are accompanied by a feeling tone of satisfaction and enjoyment accounts, I believe, for much of the strength of the church among the population. In psychological terms, it is more rewarding to be a Catholic than not to be one or than to be a practitioner of puritanical Protestant patterns.

RELIGIOUS FIESTAS

Although there is not a large attendance at Sunday mass, the templo is full of people on the days when the fiestas are celebrated. In general, each fiesta is in charge of a mayordomía, organized as previously explained in the section on Economics (p. 75). A few fiestas, such as that of Nuestro Señor de la Misericordia (which was held on October 20–22), are a charge of a permanent group called an hermandad, although these groups are gradually dying out.

The general pattern of a fiesta is, in outline, as follows. Some days before the central date of the fiesta, the encargados (those in charge, members of the mayordomía or hermandad) pass through the streets, taking up a collection. (See p. 75.) In the night previous to the day of the fiesta, the priest performs the rite of the víspera in the presence of a large crowd. After this the mayordomos, followed by a musical band and carrying paper lanterns, lead a parade out of the church through the streets of the

---

[64] This generalization is based on notes of numerous conversations and discussions.

[65] See Gillin, 1942, and references cited there.

town. At each corner they stop while at least two individuals dance the *marinera,* usually in costume, disguised as Negroes or Indians, while the *mayordomos* set off a few rockets. The parade winds through the town, returning to the central *plaza,* where a barrage of rockets is set off. Then the *mayordomos* and the band go to the house of a *devoto,* who awaits them. They dance and drink *chicha* and hard liquor until about dawn when they return to their own houses. Shortly after sunrise on the day of the fiesta, everyone comes out of his house, shooting off rockets while the band starts up the music at the house of the chief *mayordomo.* Then the *mayordomía* proceeds with the band to the church to prepare for the mass, which is usually supposed to start about 9 a. m., but does not customarily get under way until about 10 a. m. The mass lasts about 2 hours, punctuated by the discharge of rockets just outside the church door and by the rather dissonant music of the band, which has been installed in the choir loft in the back of the church. After mass, the *invitados* go to the house of the chief *mayordomo,* preceded by the band, and a feast takes place. From the house, plates of food are sent to certain *devotos* or contributors who are unable to be present. In the afternoon, the party, well fed and somewhat drunk, goes to the *templo* and takes out on parade the image which is being venerated that day, passing through the streets of the town, preceded by the band, at a pace so slow that it is nightfall before it returns to the church. Another feast usually follows in the evening, accompanied by the usual drinking and dancing. The following Sunday there may be a mass of the Adoración and afterward the *mayordomos* and the contributors go to the house of another *devoto* where the eating and drinking of the previous Sunday are continued. Often during these feasts fights and family arguments develop, which are said to be an invariable accompaniment of a fiesta. The majority of the celebrants, however, enjoy themselves and suffer nothing worse than hangovers and "liver colic" after the fiesta is past. The drinking and merrymaking aspects of the usual fiesta are said to be absent from the fiestas of Holy Week, beginning on Holy Thursday.

The religious fiestas which are most actively celebrated in Moche are the following: Epiphany, with the lowering of the home altars of the Nativity, January 6; Fiesta del Señor de Ramos (Palm Sunday); Semana Santa (Holy Week); San Isidro, patron of agriculture, May 15; Corpus Christi; SS. Pablo y Pedro (SS. Peter and Paul), June 29; Santa Rosa de Lima, August 30; La Exaltación de la Santísma Cruz, September; Señor de la Misericordia (Our Lord of Mercy), October; Fiesta del Cristo Rey (Christ the King), October; Todos los Santos and Todos los Ánimas (All Saints' and All Souls' Days), November 1 and 2; Santa Lucía de Moche, "La Mocherita," patroness of the church of Moche, December 13; La Pascua de la Navidad, December 24 and 25.

In addition, a number of fiestas of various images which adorn the church are celebrated somewhat irregularly, depending upon whether a *mayordomía* is organized or not, during a particular year. The celebration of the fiestas of certain of these images brings out especially clearly the importance of the image cult. Thus, the image of Nuestro Señor del Calvario, celebrated on September 14, 1944, does not represent a historical personage distinct from Nuestro Señor de la Misericordia or Nuestro Señor de Ramos, for example. To be sure, the images in each case represent Jesus, but the attention of the people is fixed on the image itself, and people speak of the images as distinct beings, rather than as representations of the one and only historical and sacred person of Jesus Christ. The same is true of a number of images of Virgins and Señoras, each of which, unless otherwise specifically named, it may be presumed is derived from the historical and holy person of the Mother of Jesus. Yet people have fallen into a way of thinking as if the image were an entity or being in itself. The nearby village of Huamán possesses a famous Señor. Mocheros compare their several Señores with that of Huamán, as if speaking of distinct persons. Certain images have exhibited powers of curing and healing which other images have not shown and are therefore the more venerated, better dressed, and so on. It is perhaps too much to label this "cult of the images" idolatry, because the devotees are usually willing to admit that a vague higher power stands back of the image itself, but it represents a type of cultural orientation in which the material object (the image) has lost much of its function as a mere representation of a character or of a concept in church history and instead has come to represent a power and a goal in itself.

The same is true in many cases of the images of the saints, but with them it is always possible to argue that the image is a mere representation of a historical personage now present in spiritual form on the right hand of God. For example, Santa Rosa de Lima, being the national patron saint of Peru, is still fresh as a historical woman who lived and wrought miracles in Lima. No doubt many individuals are more devoted to her material representation than to her spiritual personality, but the image is not everything. With the other type of images, however, the idea of the image itself as a personality or embodiment of supernatural power seems to overshadow any notion for which it might stand.

New Year's is always celebrated, but not always with a religious observance.

Following is an inadequate translation of the celebration of the Fiesta de Ramos (Palm Sunday) as written for me by a true Mochero, Manuel Ñique, a young man who shows considerable promise as a writer. It portrays one of the outstanding fiestas of the year, as seen through the eyes of a representative of the younger, progressive, and educated element of the Mocheros.

This movable fiesta takes place the Sunday before Holy Week and is an annual event. The narrow streets of the town are filled with people who come from surrounding places. Amid the crowd, which can be counted in the thousands, we can distinguish two types of pilgrims. Some are manifestly Catholics and others only attend the fiesta in order to enjoy the popular diversions. The fiesta begins the previous Saturday. On this day the vespers are celebrated and the day has both a religious and a profane phase. Thus we may note a general activity and a sudden growth in the number of houses serving food and chicha. Also booths for refreshments and amusement are set up in the plaza. Each tries to present the most attractive menu.

When the afternoon is well along, the ancient devotee of the Señor de Ramos, Don Juan Ascencio, is very busy, for the altar of the Señor must be ready by 7 o'clock in the night. The altar where the image will be placed from Saturday night until 4 o'clock the following afternoon is located in the park where the water tower is, near the railway tracks. At 7:30 the bells of the church begin to ring, calling the faithful and announcing to the town that the religious fiesta has begun. Inside the church the liturgical hour proceeds in the midst of a profuse illumination, and the priest makes plain in suggestive form how The Savior entered Jerusalem. Once this ceremony has been terminated, the mayordomos proceed to carry out the Señor de Ramos (a life-sized image of Jesus) in their arms, taking him to the outdoor altar which they have erected for this occasion. The procession moves via the Calle Grau, continues via Espinar and Salaverry, and finally via the Calle Galvez to arrive at the place where is erected the altar. Along the streets, the people give their adoration and with profound devotion prolong the procession. Once the image has been placed in the spot where it will pass the blessed night, those who have not had opportunity to adore it proceed to do so. As the hours of the night advance, the crowd begins to diminish until the only ones left with the Señor are those who pass the night guarding the image, and receiving alms

in the early morning from those who leave early for their chacras to milk their cows. The youth of Moche mixed with forasteros in a compact living mass occupy themselves with the traditional dance which the Junta de Progreso Local or one of the sport clubs has organized in the plaza. The dance continues until nearly 5 o'clock in the morning. How many couples will be from this moment inseparable lovers, how many will have been deceived by illusory promises, and how many will have felt they could have better spent the time preparing for the following day! But the gaiety began on Saturday and will not depart until Holy Monday.

The town arises very early, and with the arising, begins Palm Sunday. The earliest risers have already visited the altar of the image. Amid rustic aromas and surrounded by flowers, the happy image of Christ Triumphant distributes his benedictions to his adorers. Again the bells sound forth their merry tones and groups of people fill the streets. The temple is filled with Christian people from town and campiña, from port and city, from hacienda and chacra. The mass begins with the rituals of the cult. The padre, from the sacred pulpit, begins the sermon, turns his eyes to heaven, and blesses in the name of God the crowd in the temple. A few minutes later the music stops with the distribution of palms and olive branches. Shortly afterward begins the renactment of the entrance of Jesus into Jerusalem. For this the padre, followed by the faithful, goes forth from the temple, and they proceed to cover the streets to the image with palms and olive branches.

After this the people begin to look for a place to eat lunch, some searching among the booths for those with the best dishes and music, while others go to visit the houses of their comadres. In many cases these visits are occasions for household fiestas for hair cutting or ear opening of the small children.

In the afternoon begin the kermes and the dance. There near the booth where they are selling cabrito, yuca, and sweetpotatoes, the people are indulging in criollismo without equal. Here others are eating sopa teóloga and other typical dishes. Over there is a merry party quaffing chicha. In other booths lively maidens offer, in addition to food and drink, the temptation of ruby lips. The orchestra and the band animate the dance and there is no place to sit quietly. Everywhere is movement, agitation, and music. The minutes slip away, the hours. The moment of the procession draws near. The merry throng thins out as people go to the place of the image.

The tradition is displayed in this procession. A white female ass is present in front of the altar. [This white donkey roams the town freely during the rest of the year and is fed and watered by whomever she visits.] The mayordomos divide into committees, one to direct the band of music and the other to put the saddle on the "little donkey of Our Lord." Here is the band of the Maestro Antonio Sachún with his justly famous musicians. The image of The Señor is placed on the ass, and then begins the majestic procession of Palm Sunday to the temple.

The view which this transcendental procession affords is magnificent. Palms and candles, music and faith, confounded together in the most remarkable act of the year in the town of Santa Lucía de Moche. Along the line of this procession have been erected various altars, and the people along the streets have been stirred by the explosions of numerous rockets. The bystanders carpet the pathway of God with flowers they throw from their hands. In front of the temple, the image of Christ Triumphant is lowered from the saddle and carried in the arms of the *mayordomos* to the main altar of the church. After a few words by the priest, the religious fiesta is terminated.

It is 7 o'clock in the evening and almost the entire crowd which took part in the procession begins to dance again. Merriment reigns supreme and there are no sad faces. People dance, they drink, they enjoy themselves and forget their troubles. This dance continues until late in the night. The omnibuses are working overtime until the next dawn carrying home the visitors from other towns, while other visitors accept hospitality in local houses.

Silence begins to enter the town with the beginning of Holy Monday. The village will again sink back into the peacefulness of other days. The streets will be empty and one will no longer meet the strange face. Once again conversation will return to the gossiping of the *comadres* and *compadres*. The gossip will rotate about the events of the fiesta. Palm Sunday and its merriment will not return for another year. Holy Week with its mantle of grief will cover the town with an aching pain, silence, and sadness.

PACTS WITH THE DEVIL

There is a well-developed belief that mortals can and sometimes do make pacts with the Devil or his emissaries. The Devil and his minions are in general considered to be the arch enemies of Christianity. It is said that the Devil or his deputy usually appears in the form of a man to a person who is in difficulties of a worldly sort, needs money, is in trouble with the law, etc. In return for the worldly aid required by the individual, the Devil demands the delivery of the person's soul, and sometimes the souls of other persons under the orders of the individual in question. The Devil is simply called *"El Diablo,"* or *"El Príncipe de Mal."* If one wishes to make a pact of this kind, he invokes the Prince of Evil, by concentrating his mind on it and calling out in private or inaudibly. It is believed that the Devil or one of his minions is always hanging about, waiting for such a call, so that one does not have to shout very loudly. Once one has sold himself to the Devil, there is no way he can renounce his pact nor is there any help which the church can give. The souls of such persons, of course, are believed to reside permanently and inexorably in hell. The case of a certain man is told who repented of his pact with the Devil. He confessed and even went to Spain where he took Holy Orders and later became a missionary father in Peru. However, the Devil kept after him, tormenting him, until he died.

Such beliefs seem to be clearly derived from European sources. The *shapingos*, familiar spirits of evil brujos, are the native analogy of these beliefs, and some individuals tend to confuse the Devil and the *shapingos* in their thinking, but most persons are quite explicit that the Devil is something entirely different. The evil witches and their spirits are not thought to be in competition with God, whereas the Devil is considered to be a competitor of God and the church. Following are some incidents illustrative of the belief in the Devil and his nefarious schemes.

T., the woman of J. A., disappeared from her coffin. The priest, who had been called to say responses over the coffin, surprised the family filling the box with adobes in order to simulate the "weight of a Christian." A few days later the woman's son found the naked body of his mother in the *chacra*. It was buried there secretly so that people would not know. The disappearance of a body from its coffin is, of course, irrefutable proof that the individual had formerly made a pact with the Devil, who has come to foreclose on it; for once a person is buried in hallowed ground, he is beyond the power of the Devil.

Another case is said to be that of A. S. On his death bed a person came to him, in the presence of his family. This person was clothed in white and rode to the house mounted on a white horse. The person said, "Come with me," and disappeared. The moribund man tried to get up and follow him. It was almost impossible to keep him in the bed. He raved and shouted and his tongue swelled up so that he could not talk coherently. He had to be restrained by force. Finally he died. During the night following his death, his body disappeared. It was never found and a coffin filled with adobes had to be buried to avert suspicion. Of course, the mysterious visitor was the Devil, come to claim his own.

M. R. S. had a startling experience with what he takes to be the Devil. Behind the mountain to the east is a valley where, in wintertime, men sometimes take their animals to graze off the short-lived grass. One day M. happened to be in this region and came upon a rock which looked much like a dining table. More surprising was the fact that it was set with a complete silver service, which also included silver plates and cups. M. picked up the silver and took it home with him. He estimates that it was easily worth 5,000 soles. That night, as he was sleeping in his house, he was awakened by a stern voice which commanded him immediately to get up and to return the silver service to the place where he had found it. He lay awake frightened all night, and the first thing in the morning he took the silver back to the table rock. It is supposed that it was a table set by the Devil for the entertainment of someone who was invited to make a pact with him.

The I. house in Trujillo, a large old colonial mansion, is said to have a long subterranean passage in it, connecting the house with the same spot (mentioned above) behind the mountain. Through this passage peons in the old days disappeared, so goes the story, never to be seen again. They were delivered to the Devil in return for silver plate, of which formerly this house possessed a great deal.

Young R. is said to have died after having met the Devil. S. C., his cousin, was in an argument with him about land. Young R. was in the disputed *chacra* on Good Friday. This land he had acquired from S. C., but they were having an argument about it. S. C., unknown to R. at the time the deal was consummated, had previously promised the land to the Devil in return for money which he had received some years previously. On this Good Friday the term of the pact with the Devil was ended and the Devil came to obtain the land from S. C. Instead he found young R. on the land and young R. saw him. He appeared in the form of a well-dressed man. As soon as R. realized who it was who was asking him for the land and why, he fell down with a *susto*. He was sick for a long time thereafter. None of the regular cures for *susto* did him any good, and in the end he died.

G. worked for J. A. as a herder and had taken some animals to the winter pasture on the other side of the Cerros. There is a water hole there which has to be dug out repeatedly. One day G. started to dig for water in a new place, only to find that the ground was solid rock. Suddenly he looked up and saw an elegantly dressed white man before him. G. was ashamed because he was so poorly dressed in comparison with the stranger. The newcomer told G. that he could not expect to find water there, but that if G. would deliver to him his soul, he, the stranger, would arrange ample water and pasture. G. realized that he was talking to the Devil, and immediately rounded up his animals and took them back to the Moche *campiña*.

DEATH IN MOCHE

HARBINGERS OF DEATH

The hooting of an owl near a house is an omen of an impending death. *"Le cantó la pacapaca"* (Quechua, owl) is a way of saying, "His hour has struck." The Spanish word *lechuza* is also used. The firefly (*luciérnaga*) is likewise believed to announce that someone is dying or is about to die. The black cat, the *toledo* bird, the *chichy* bird, and the sparrow are also regarded as harbingers of death or disasters. Apparently the association of the owl with death goes back to Mochica times, according to the material on display in the Museo Arqueológico "Rafael Larco Herrera." Numerous vases with representation of owls associated with what seem to be cadavers are extant.

PREPARATIONS FOR THE FUNERAL

When a person succumbs, there are a number of things to be done at once, and the relatives and *compadres* of the deceased gather at the house to assist. Death is announced by tolling the *doble* from the bells of the church—two short strokes together, repeated over and over for about an hour. Small boys do this without pay. The word runs about the town and countryside that so-and-so has died, and those who feel obligated or wish to help gather at the house. The body must be laid out. It is usually not bathed completely, but the face, feet, and hands are washed. It is laid on a wooden table in one of the interior rooms of the house, on its back, either dressed or wrapped in a blanket, feet together, hands folded on chest, a white cloth over the face. A small cross made of carrizo is placed upright in the folded fingers of the hands. Embalming is not practiced in Moche, and by law the dead must be entombed within 24 hours after death. Next, word must be sent to Don T., one of the local carpenters who specializes in coffins and funeral trappings. He has a supply of black hangings and coffin ornaments. A good coffin in Moche costs about 80 soles. They can be had as cheap as 30 soles. Don T. acts as funeral director, and usually appears in a fresh white ill-fitting cotton suit. As soon as the coffin is brought to the house, a few old clothes are placed in the bottom of it, the body is lifted in, and the coffin is set on the table. It is no longer customary to bury all the deceased's belongings with him as in former times. By this time a fairly large group of friends and relatives has gathered for the *velorio* or wake. A black cloth with silver stars on it hangs on the wall at the head of the coffin and eight candles are set up on the table and lighted, one at each corner of the coffin and one in the center of each side. The female attendants have long since begun a monotonous weeping and wailing. There are no professional mourners (*lloronas*) in Moche, but older women who come to wail will be provided with food and drink.

The next thing to plan is that the male relatives and *compadres* organize themselves in a *minga* to dig the grave or to prepare the tomb, if an adobe or cement tomb belongs to the family. The surviving spouse, or responsible head of the deceased's family, has obtained a burial certificate from the Municipalidad (2 soles for adults, 1 sol for children), and will provide food and drink for the gravediggers. The night following the death the *velorio* is held in the house. The guests speak of the character and personality of the dead person and imbibe *chicha* and food. Sometimes the affair becomes rather animated.

THE FUNERAL

Next day at the hour the procession to the cemetery is to take place, the *doble* is tolled once more for about an hour. If it is a first-class funeral, a coffin and hearse from Trujillo will be involved, and the padre will accompany the procession to the cemetery. If it is a second-class funeral, the coffin will be carried by relatives and ceremonial kinsmen of the deceased. In a second-class funeral the priest, accompanied by a cantor to sing the responses and an altar boy with a censor and a portable holy water font, comes to the house at the appointed time. He annoints the body with holy water dipped from the font with a small wand. He repeats the Latin of the service and the cantor intones the responses. During the whole ceremony the wailing of the women continues, so that the words of the service are usually inaudible. It is bad form for the male mourners to wail; if the dead person is a close relative a man may allow tears to run down his cheeks, but he does not "carry on" as do the women.

The religious service in the house lasts about 10 minutes, after which the padre and his assistants precipitously leave. Then the coffin is lifted to the shoulders of the bearers—usually only four at a time—and they carry it out of the house and up the street, around the plaza to the door of the church, followed by the mourners and those attracted by curiosity. The general wailing ceases when the coffin leaves the house. Frequently there is quite a wait for the priest to come out of his dwelling. During the whole time the sorrowful tolling of the *doble* continues. Finally the padre appears, the right half of the church door is opened, and he reads, book in hand, a few words over the coffin. During the whole time the box has not touched the ground. Then the procession starts off down the street for the long walk to the cemetery. If the person is of ordinary good reputation, there may be a crowd of 150 or more persons. Some people wear their better clothes, others only workaday garments. The older women wear black shawls around their shoulders (nothing on their heads). The cross which will be set up at the head of the grave is carried by relays of small boys at the head of the coffin. It is a wooden cross, painted black; on the upright arm is painted the date of death, and on the cross arm the name of the deceased. Four dots at each point complete the ornament. Various men, relatives and *compadres*, alternate as bearers of the coffin.

In these processions, humble and quiet, one is struck by the humility of manner, a certain stoicism in the face of death, and a lack of expressed emotion, especially by the men. They are simple people following the coffin of one of their companions in life to its final resting place. To be sure, there is usually at least one female relative who keeps up a ritual wailing: "*Mamacita, ay-y-y, q'he perdido mi mamacita,*" or "*Papacita, porque te has ido?*"—a sorrowful phrase repeated over and over again.

At the graveside there is no ceremony, but there is considerable delay while the carpenter removes all the silver and tin *adornos* from the coffin. These usually include a metal crucifix on the top, an embossed tin plate on the side reading, "*Descanses en Paz,*" and 14 or 15 embossed tin plates of angels, doves, and stars, and silver-looking handles on the sides. These are used on other coffins, ad infinitum. This task completed, the coffin is lowered into the grave. Two men stand inside the grave and receive it from the bearers. They cross themselves, set the box on the bottom of the hole, and, with a hand offered from someone along the margin, hoist themselves out. Then everyone moves up and tries to cast a handful of dirt on the coffin from the two piles lying on either side of the excavation. After a few minutes the *compadres* get to work with their shovels and the humble people straggle out of the Campo Santo, which the priest did not visit. Some families have adobe or cement vaults above ground, so that the grave digging part of the sequence is not necessary. The older vaults are in disrepair, with not a few loose bones scattered about. (See pls. 25, *lower (right)*; 26, *center, upper and lower (right)*, *lower (left)*, for pictures of funeral and cemetery.)

AFTER DEATH

Survivors who can afford it usually pay for a mass in the church on the eighth day following death. There are few who pay for masses at regular intervals thereafter, although some do.

On the eve of All Souls' Day, November 1, the survivors of the dead gather in the cemetery at the respective graves to hold a *velorio*. Wreaths of flowers are placed on the graves, candles are set up, and the night is spent in eating, drinking, and recalling the virtues of the departed. Although souls are supposed to go to purgatory after death, in accord with Catholic doctrine, not a few of the Mocheros entertain somewhat hazy beliefs in the persistence of the soul in the neighborhood after death. The house is cleaned out, the walls brushed down or whitewashed, and the intimate articles of the deceased washed or destroyed. Frequently dogs bark inexplicably in the night, a sign that the ghost is returning to its former habitation. Persons out in the dark are occasionally troubled by whisperings, nudgings, and odd sounds, which are attributed to the disembodied spirits still extant in the neighborhood.

THE CULTURAL POSITION OF MOCHE

THE CONCEPT OF THE CREOLE CULTURE

There is a romantic appeal in considering Moche a living museum of the ancient culture of the Mochicas, a culture which was developed in this very region and which, as we have seen, came to an end, according to the most conservative estimates, not less than 900 years ago. It is true that Moche, like every other healthy society, is not a static structure as of today only. Its culture is in part the product of its history. If we consider the historical aspects, the past, we are at once convinced that the present-day culture of Moche is a composite, a conglomerate or fabric, as you wish, composed of elements derived from many sources, some of them now almost unrecognizable. And among the contributions out of the past, those of the Mochicas are undoubtedly of considerable importance.

However, if Moche's culture is a product of its history, it is no less the foundation of its future. It seems that we shall be more realistic if we regard Moche, not as a survival from antiquity, but as one of the seedbeds from which is growing the new Pan-Peruvian or Creole culture, the culture of today and tomorrow, which characterizes a nation of living human beings seeking and finding a place in the world community. I submit that, taken as a whole, the mode and organization of life in Moche at present is more characteristic of this new synthesis than of any of its ancestral sources in their functioning forms.

I do not believe that we are jousting with straw men when we say that one of the reasons for the failure of North Americans to understand completely the Latin Americans is our failure to recognize or identify properly the cultures of Latin America as cultures in their own right. Our tendency and that of most Europeans has been to identify the modern way of life either with some indigenous configuration or with European civilization in one or other of its European national traditions. We have persisted in seeing the Latin Americans either as latter-day Indians with an impoverished native culture or as tainted Iberians fumbling with the traditions of Spain and Portugal. It is as if, since an "angel food" cake contains appreciable amounts both of eggs and of sugar, we should refuse to recognize it as an angel food cake, but insist on considering it either an omelet or a chunk of candy.

The new culture, for want of a better name, may be called Creole (*criollo*). Since the early days of the colonization, this term has signified a mode of life and a type of person of Spanish antecedents, in part, but developed in and as a product of the New World. It seems to be a better term to apply to culture than the word "Mestizo," which implies racial mixture. Although genetic hybridization has everywhere paralleled the development of the Creole culture, it is not a necessary cause for the latter, and the use of the term "Mestizo" tends to confuse biological and cultural processes. At present, some pure Indians on the one hand and some pure whites on the other hand, as well as most Mestizos, participate in the development and performance of the Creole culture, and there is no reason to believe that biological mixture does or will proceed at the same rate as cultural mixture and development. In fact, most of the indications are that the Creole culture, at the present time, is growing toward an integrated configuration more rapidly than the Mestizo race.

The Creole cultures of Spanish America (leaving Brazil out of consideration for the moment) have a common general framework and a common tone which enables them to be spoken of collectively as *the* Creole culture and to be compared with *the* North American culture, for example. The similarities in the cultures are apparently due to the Spanish elements which are common to their composition and which were involved in their development during three centuries or so under Spanish Colonial control. Thus all are nominally Catholic and many of the details of content and organization are those of Iberian Catholicism as distinguished from the North European type. Of course, the Spanish language itself with sundry modifications has become part of the Creole culture. Ideologically, the Creole culture is humanistic, rather than puritanical, if such a contrast is permissible. Intellectually, it is characterized by logic and dialectics, rather than by empiricism and pragmatics; the word is valued more highly than the thing; the manipulation of symbols (as in argument) is more cultivated than the manipulation of natural forces and objects (as in mechanics). Patterns of medieval and 16th century mysticism are strong in the culture, and these patterns show no inconsistency with those of argumentation, for, as with the medieval scholastics, the worth of the logic lies in the manipulation of concepts, not in the empirical investigation of premises. It is partly for this reason, I believe, that ideas have been more readily accepted as part of the content of the Creole culture than artifacts and their associated techniques. The use of modern medical words and the manipulation of verbal legal concepts, even in Moche, for example, are more advanced than the "practical" techniques associated with them in certain other cultures. If we were to analyze the intellectual content of Creole culture as a whole, we would find a vast variety of ideas, derived from numerous sources —ideas from the Enlightenment, from the French and American Revolutions, and, more recently, from Marxism, etc. The content of the ideas themselves is in many cases not Spanish, but the patterns of argumentation probably represent heritages from Spain. In the more mundane level of life, we see other Spanish or Spanish Colonial patterns fixed in the Creole culture—for example, in town planning (the "plaza plan" rather than the "main street" plan), in family organization (official male dominance, double standard, and patterns of ceremonial kinship), in the preeminence of the ox and the ass as traction and transport animals, in certain features of domestic architecture (e.g., the "patio" or courtyard in some form; the barred window; the house front flush with the sidewalk, and the absence of "front yard"), in the broad-brimmed hat either of felt or straw, in the use of a cloth head covering by women (mantilla, head shawl, decorative towel, etc.), in the preference for the one-handled plow in agriculture, in concepts of "personal honor" and emphasis upon form in interpersonal relations, in certain political statuses still persisting from the colonial system, in the patterns of Roman law, etc.

It should be clear that these remarks are not to be taken as a substitute for a formal analysis of the Creole culture, a task which is beyond the limits of this monograph. But they are intended to suggest that Creole culture is a synthesis of elements drawn from various sources and that the Spanish stamp gives to this general mode of a life a certain external uniformity, at least.

Although the Creole culture is to be found in all nations of Spanish America, its areal, regional, and local forms vary and are distinguishable among themselves. This seems to be primarily because the natural environments of the various regions and localities differ among themselves and, even more important perhaps, because the indigenous components of the regional Creole cultures derive from aboriginally distinct configurations. Thus it is, that the Creole cultures of Guatemala and Peru, for example, while sharing a common set of Iberian elements, are nonetheless distinguishable, because the one contains many patterns of Maya origin while the other is colored by its Inca heritage. And within each such area of Creole culture one recognizes present subconfigurations associated respectively with regions and localities. Thus, although the Inca culture of the Empire covered both the coast and the highland of Peru, one recognizes a Creole culture of the coast and of the highland at the present day. On the coast, again, it is possible to distinguish local differences between Moche, for example, and Cañete.

Added to these two historical components, the Creole culture since Independence and, particularly during the present century, has received increasing increments in the form of patterns contributed by the cultures of North America and northern Europe—from the mechanical, industrial, empirical, Protestant, democratic, secular phases of Western Civilization—which Spanish culture was incapable of transmitting or which Spanish policy endeavored to bar from the New World.

In Peru at the present time it is probably correct to say that there are two types of cultures, generally speaking: the Republican Native cultures and the Creole cultures. I use the term "Republican Native culture" in the sense in which Kubler speaks of the Republican Quechua.[66] These cultures, of which the most prominent are those of certain Quechua- and Aymara-speaking groups of the highlands, but which also include various native groups of the Montaña, are not aboriginal as they were before the Conquest. Each has absorbed elements from Western Civilization (if nothing more than dependence on certain types of trade goods, such as factory-made cloth among the Campa of the Montaña, for instance), and the organization of each of these "native" cultures has been affected by the impact of European political and social controls, either directly or indirectly. Nevertheless, the Republican Native cultures are still predominantly indigenous both in content and in

[66] Kubler (1946); this culture is described by Mishkin (1946).

emphasis. Although there is not space to demonstrate this fact in the present paper, it may be appreciated by consultation of published sources (e. g., Kubler, 1946; Tschopik, 1946; Mishkin, 1946). In Peru it is generally recognized by the public that an individual has ceased to practice a Native culture when he no longer lives in a tribe or communally organized group (ayllu, etc.), no longer wears a "native" costume, and when he no longer speaks some indigenous language either exclusively or as his primary language. These are the generally recognized status marks, although, like all symbols, they suggest rather than describe the differences between the cultures which they represent.

The Creole culture in general (ignoring for the moment its regional and local subtypes) is still in process of consolidation. The society which it serves is a class society and the Creole culture manifests itself in various forms that are related to the various categories of the society, as well as in geographical peculiarities. Thus, many members of the "sophisticated," "cosmopolitan" set in Lima might perhaps at first deny any Creole content in their culture, for much of their prestige depends upon their having assimilated the manners and mode of life of such "cultural centers" as New York or Paris. Yet, it is probable that a careful study would reveal the presence in the higher social strata of certain cultural common denominators of the Creole culture of Peru, and that this will become a matter of local pride. For our hypothesis is that the Creole culture, which may some day justly be called Peruvian culture, is not a servile copying of either foreign or indigenous models, but a new and vigorous expression of national life. This is what is actually meant by the word Peruanidad, in addition to its purely nationalistic and political significance. The Peruvian Creole culture is a new synthesis. If it is still in process of integration, it is nevertheless the framework of the future; if it is not yet universal to all citizens of the nation, the chances are that, in one form or another, it will be. It is at least a tenable hypothesis that both the present Republican Native cultures and such importations from abroad as still persist in the country will eventually either be absorbed by the Creole culture or be crowded out of national life.

Moche is merely a case in point. A generation ago it apparently was classifiable as a Native culture, more indigenous than Creole. But by 1944 it had swung over to the other side of the line; it is now more Creole than Native. The same change is taking place every year—subtly, slowly, almost imperceptibly, to be sure—in scores of Peruvian communities throughout the coast and the Sierra, and even in the Montaña (e. g., Tingo María, Pucallpa, Pantoja, etc.).

A number of "movements" have arisen whose object has been to halt this trend of creolization and whose publicity has occasionally confused the foreign observer. Thus, "Indigenismo" believes that the real future of the bulk of Peruvians lies in strengthening and preserving the Republican Native cultures and even in fortifying the indigenous elements thereof. The proponents of Hispanismo see the true cultural future of Peru in a return to the fundamentals of classic Spanish culture.[67] And the partizans of "Modernismo" would do away with indigenous and colonial elements alike, and convert Peru into a Spanish-speaking United States (or a Spanish-speaking version of some European country of their predilection).

It is doubtful that any of these movements will ever completely attain its objective in the sense that any particular set of cultural elements for which the proponents respectively argue will become exclusive in the culture of Peru. But, if they will examine the emerging Creole culture, they will see that something from each of their favorite cultures has been woven into the fabric of Peruvian life.

To turn once again to Moche, it is clear that the Mocheros conform to the common Peruvian definition of a Creole: they have no tribe or organized community, they wear European clothing (except for a few old women), and they speak Spanish exclusively. The style of their clothing and the style of their life may be somewhat "quaint," but they are fundamentally neither aboriginal nor foreign. Yet the indigenous elements, often in modified form, are numerous.

If we attempt to sort out the elements of Moche culture which seem to be derived from indigenous sources, most of those in actual function at the present day appear to be referable to a "Pan-Peruvian" indigenous base rather than specifically to discrete cultures of antiquity known from the chronicles and from archeology. This conclusion must be qualified by the admission that historical and archeological records are too incomplete to permit a more precise tracing of aboriginal antecedents in many cases. Also, we must

[67] The late Dr. José de la Riva-Agüero was a leading exponent of this point of view in some of his historical writings. See particularly the essays, "En el día de la raza" and "Algunas reflexiones sobre la época española en el Perú" (Riva-Argüero, 1938).

acknowledge the general leveling and diffusing influence of the Inca conquest which rubbed out and blurred numerous items of local origin and which had the effect of transforming many cultural features of formerly restricted distribution into "Pan-Peruvian" or "Inca" elements of culture.

MOCHICA ELEMENTS

We may briefly compare the present culture of Moche with that of the Mochicas as we know it from the archeological record. Certain of the basic ways of life current at the present time were undoubtedly characteristic of Mochica culture as well. It seems to me, however, that this merely shows that certain patterns date back to Mochica times (say 1000 A.D.) in this region. Most of them are general to those parts of the coast where they are environmentally suitable, and it is difficult to prove a persistence to modern Moche of the really distinctive features of Mochica culture, features which would lead us to see Moche as a community more "Mochica" in character than other communities.

Then, as now, irrigated agriculture, on the one hand, and fishing, on the other hand, provided the economic bases of life and presumably formed the central core of interests of the society. Some of the irrigation ditches built by the Mochicas, for example, the Mochica, are still in use. Although in the Moche *campiña* the present water gates and dams are of modern construction, the straight ditches, the system of *pozas,* and the meandering ditches (*surcos de caracol*) of Mochica times are still employed.

How does a modern Mochero resemble, in his mode of life, the ancient Mochica? He lives in a house of adobe with a dirt floor, supported by an unsawed wooden framework similar to Mochica. Although the majority of roofs are now low-sloped, they are still made of mud plastered over a framework of cane and *estera* (p. 37). Pitched roofs occur (pl. 12, *upper (left)*), and the use of an inclined roof of *estera* matting as a sunshade is quite common. Open work in the house walls below the roof (pls. 11, *upper (right)*; 12, *lower (left)*) seems to come down from Mochica times, as well as the half wall and broken wall of plastered adobe (pl. 11, *middle (right)*).

Our Moche friend rarely eats a meal without boiled green corn (*choclo*) and yuca, which were two of the stand-bys of the Mochicas. In his field or garden he cultivates the following plants, which were also cultivated by the Mochicas: [68] Maize (*Zea mays*),

chirimoyo (*Annona cherimola*), guanábana (*Annona murcata*), palta (*Persea americana*), beans (*Phaseolus vulgaris*), pallares (*Phaseolus lunatus*), peanuts (*Arachis hypogaea*), pacae or guaba (*Inga feuillei*), yuca (*Manihot utilissima*), cotton (semiwild brown cotton is the only type occurring at present in Moche), papaya (*Carica papaya*), guayaba, red and white (*Psidium guayava*), lúcuma (*Lucuma obovata*), camote or sweetpotato (*Ipomoea batatas*), *ají* pepper (*Capsicum annuum*), small wild tomato which grows half wild around the edges of fields (*Solanum lycopersicum*), potato (*Solanum tuberosum*), although not much cultivated in Moche at present, caigua (*Cyclanthera pedata*), three kinds of pepino (*Solanum muricatum*), zapallo of several varieties (*Cucurbita maxima*), and gourds of various kinds. Coca is not grown here at present, but according to Stiglich,[69] was so grown in the 1890's, and it is chewed by modern Mocheros occasionally and on special occasions.

Of course, our Moche friend also cultivates a long series of subsequently introduced plants, but those mentioned above have come to him from the Mochicas. He uses a modern broad-bladed iron spade for cultivating his fields, but the technique seems to be the same as that employed by the Mochicas with their narrow-bladed copper and bronze spades or metal-tipped digging sticks. Corn is still hilled up (with the spade) by hand, even by many farmers who own plows and oxen. The hooked knife or "calabazo" (pl. 5, *lower (right)*; 6, *center*) also was possibly a Mochica tool.[70]

Our Mochero usually eats his food and drinks his *chicha* from containers made of gourds in various shapes, and with a whittled spoon of wood. Gourd containers, *chicha*, spoon are all Mochica traits. He usually has a good many items on his menu which the ancient Mochicas never heard of, such as rice, coffee, beef, pork, chicken, but a considerable part of his food was also known to the Mochicas. His wife cooks the food in earthen pots, which, to be sure, are no longer made in Moche, but acquired in the market from other Indian potters; but this appears to be a survival of a Mochica, or at least an Indian, custom, because metal and china vessels could be easily, and just about as cheaply, obtained. She still prepares *ají* and green corn kernels on the *batán* and

---

[68] See Larco Hoyle, ms. b, for plants cultivated by Mochicas.

[69] Stiglich, 1922, p. 688: "Desde el año 1891 ha comenzado la prosperidad de este valle donde sólo se cultivaba coca y fruta. La coca siempre es llevada á Trujillo por arrieros."

[70] Several specimens of copper exist in the Museo Arqueológico "Rafael Larco Herrera" which are surely pre-Conquest, but may be Chimu.

mano (grinding stones) and also uses the mortar and pestle of stone. Although the *batán* is now a simple, flat-topped grinding stone (without the rim of Mochica times), the persistence of the custom is worth noting. Although the common adobe stove is probably a later elaboration, faggots and manure (in Mochica times, presumably llama manure) are still used for fuel in place of newfangled possibilities, such as kerosene. Likewise, the fireplace of three or four stones on the ground is not uncommon (pl. 14, *lower (left)*), although such arrangements were found also in the Sierra.

Fish as a prominent article of diet in Moche seems to be derived from the Mochica ancestors. Although seviche (raw fish prepared with lemon or lime juice) in its present form could not have been a Mochica preparation (for lack of limes and lemons), it is entirely probable that raw fish was eaten in some form anciently and that its present prominence is a carry-over. (At present, in the absence of citrus juices, seviche is prepared with *chicha* vinegar.) All deep-sea fish seemingly caught by the Mochicas are fished today and eaten. Of special notice is the still prominent use of shrimps and crabs, by no means common to all fish-eating peoples, even on this coast. The practice of sucking the meat out of the shell of the *muy-muy*, or sea shrimp, seems to be illustrated in several Mochica ceramic paintings. Likewise, the use of this shrimp as bait on hooks may well be a Mochica survival.

Although nothing definite is known of the nets used for fishing by the Mochicas, it is probable that the *chinchorro* type of net was used for sea fishing. Something very similar seems to have been used on land for hunting deer, as illustrated in painting on specimen No. 2054 in the Museo Arqueológico "Rafael Larco Herrera." The use of a globular-shaped gourd as float on the *espinel* (setline) and also as floats on the *chinchorro*, seems to have been a definite Mochica trait (Larco Hoyle, ms. c, ch. 10), likewise the use of large hooks without barbs,[71] although in modern times they are made of iron and imported. The Museo Arqueológico "Rafael Larco Herrera" possesses a large collection of Mochica wooden objects very similar to the netting needles now in use, although without the "eye" and "hook."

The eating of lizards and iguanas seems also to have been a Mochica trait (Larco Hoyle, ms. c, ch. 10), as well as the *totora*-roll trap still used.

The use of gourds (*potos*), not only for drinking and serving *chicha*, but as dishes (*mates*) and bottles, seems to be a well-established Mochica trait. Even younger persons at present claim that the *chicha* tastes better when drunk from a *poto*. The decoration of gourd containers by incisions and fire is practically lost in Moche at present, but is maintained in Monsefú, although new techniques involving acids and inks have also been introduced.

The Mochero prefers to sleep on a mat of *totora* (*estera*); and he uses mats of *carrizo* (*petates*) for sitting on the dirt floor, as roofing for his arbor and even for the houses, and as temporary partitions. The use of these materials, the techniques of manufacture, and the customary uses of the finished article all go back to the Mochicas.

In the field of dress and ornament the Mochero preserves little from his Mochica ancestors. The preference, often shown and put into practice, for going barefoot may well be a survival from the barefoot Mochica culture. The piercing of women's ears and the wearing of long earrings [72] were present among the Mochicas, but the earrings themselves show little influence in detail on the designs current in Moche today.

Spinning of cotton and weaving of coarse cotton cloth (bayeta) are almost extinct in Moche today, but were fairly common until recently. Older women still spin the yarn of *algodón pardo* (brown cotton) which they work into their hairdress, and one doubtful case of full-scale weaving is reported, although I have not seen the loom. The northern village of Monsefú maintains weaving in a well-developed state. The belt loom and the calabash-whorled spindle could be derived, in form, either from Mochica or Sierra cultures.

The binding of babies' arms to their sides may be a Mochica trait, although in the ancient culture it was combined with a cradle of *carrizo*.[73] The scene involving a baby sitting upright on its mother's lap and nursing from her breast hanging over the upper border of her blouse or dress, as illustrated in specimen No. 1054 of the Museo Arqueológico "Rafael Larco Herrera," for example, is frequently seen in present-day Moche.

---

[71] A large collection, unnumbered, exists in the Museo Arqueológico "Rafael Larco Herrera."

[72] Illustrated, for example, is specimen No. 30737 in the Museo Arqueológico "Rafael Larco Herrera"; the piercing of women's ears and the use of earrings were not customary among the Inca, according to Rowe (1946).

[73] Actual cradles and clay models (e. g., No. R–4400) of children bound onto cradleboards exist in the Museo Arqueológico "Rafael Larco Herrera."

Until recently, wooden combs of the Mochica type were in current use in Moche, and the use of cactus spines as thread picks, etc., is still fairly common.

Probably a good many features of modern *curandismo* and *brujería* go back to Mochica times, although later elements have obviously been grafted onto said base. In the Museo Arqueológico "Rafael Larco Herrera" is a modeled vase (No. 340) apparently depicting a curandero massaging the body of a child, as in the modern cure of *susto*. The spiny-backed shells (*Spondylus pictorum*) of the mesa de brujería are found in large quantities in Mochica deposits. Among other herbs used at the present time, Larco Hoyle has identified in the Mochica culture various varieties of cactus, ashango, maichil, habilla. Doubtless, much of the philosophy of curative magic in Moche comes down from the Mochicas. On the other hand, the Mochica surgical techniques seem to have been lost.

The art of making *tapias* and something very similar to *quincha* walls are also Mochica traits. Panpipes, used infrequently in Moche today, and still occasionally made there, were used also in Mochica times. (Vase No. J–356 in the Museo Arqueológico "Rafael Larco Herrera.")

The considerable art talent (most of it uninstructed) which appears in Moche may possibly be a vague inheritance of the more than ordinary talent so successfully exhibited by the Mochicas, although at the present time the forms and the media have changed completely. Interest in depictions of the human face, however, still survives.

Although it is possible that further investigation of the two cultures would reveal a few further similarities between the ancient Mochicas and the modern Mocheros, the review just made of Mochica survivals in Moche is sufficient to indicate, perhaps, that a considerable part of the cultural equipment and customs of the modern community were at least present in the Mochica culture.

LATER ELEMENTS

But we should not fall into the romantic error of seeing modern Moche as an unmodified survivor of Mochica culture. So far as we can tell, for all its similarities, life in Moche today is very much different from that in the same region under the sway of the Mochicas. A few of the aspects of Mochica life which have disappeared are mentioned below.

The archeological documents speak eloquently of an elaborately developed religion, centering about a supreme deity of feline cast, who appears in various incarnations, according to Larco Hoyle's material. Associated with this was a large amount of material equipment in the form of temples, adoratorios, priestly costumes, and the like. Nothing of this remains today, except possibly certain "primitive" elements in religious thinking and beliefs. All of the old-time religion has been superseded by or absorbed into the local version of Catholicism. The image cult in modern Moche Catholicism may well be supported by an age-old symbolic pattern of reverence for images, but image cults are so common in rural Latin American Catholicism [74] that the image cult in Moche cannot be regarded as a specific Mochica survival.

Likewise, all formal governmental patterns of Mochica times have disappeared,[75] and, apparently also, practically all of the social organization, both of graded and kinship types, which, by inference, probably existed formerly. War patterns and artifacts have likewise passed out of the picture. The elaborate and differentiated costumes and headdresses, functionally connected with the religion and the social organization of the Mochicas, have left hardly an echo in Moche. Practically all of the industries and handicrafts of the Mochicas have disappeared, including pottery making, metalworking, weaving (with exception of traces noted above), and wood, stone, and bone working. Burial customs are overlaid with traditions from other cultures. Houses now, in the majority, are Spanish colonial design, despite the Mochica traces noted previously. The llama has disappeared, as well as the use of the tumpline as an aid to human transport. Although the Mochica underlying base is still visible, life has changed in Moche during the last 900 years. And this is as we should expect.

To sum up, Moche still preserves a general orientation of the common man's life and activities, derived possibly from the Mochica civilization. But Moche is not Mochica. It is a composite culture. It is a culture which has passed through numerous periods of change, and one which is undergoing at present probably the heaviest pressure for change in its entire history.

---

[74] Little difference is found in Guatemala. See Gillin (Ms.).

[75] For succinct summaries of Mochica culture, see Larco Hoyle (1946).

TIAHUANACOID AND CHIMU ELEMENTS

It is difficult to place one's finger precisely on elements of contemporary culture which may have been derived from the period of Tiahuanacoid influence revealed in the archeological record. The only trait which stands out clearly is the small balsa, or *caballito del mar,* which, because of its similarity to certain types of reed balsas used on Lake Titicaca, may possibly have been introduced to the coast through Tiahuanaco influence.

The culture of the Chimu which dominated the region until well into the 15th century when the Kingdom of the Grand Chimu was conquered by the Inca was apparently in part glossed over by Inca culture and in part absorbed into what is now known as the culture of the Empire. At all events, the present Moche culture shows little exclusive either to the material culture of the Chimu (as revealed in the numerous museum collections and the nearby ruins, such as those of Chanchan) or of the social, political, and religious culture (as described by Calancha (1638) and other chroniclers). Traditions and lore current under the Chimu seem to have persisted into modern times in the region of Lambayeque (Barandarián, n. d.), but nothing significant of this sort remains in Moche.

SIERRA INFLUENCES

Not a few elements of culture in Moche seem to be ultimately derived from the Sierra. Although most of them were probably remolded and worked over by the Inca culture during the all-pervading dominion of the Empire, some of them doubtless antedate the Inca Empire and even the spread of the Quechua language. It is clear from the archeological material that the coastal region was in contact with the Sierra even during Mochica times, and contacts of one sort or another between the two areas have continued to the present. We lack the information to be able to say with certainty in many cases exactly when a given element was introduced from the Sierra to the coast, and therefore shall merely mention a number of traits seemingly originating in the Sierra. Identification of certain traits is admittedly tentative.

The practice of having an assistant to break the clods turned over in plowing suggests the similar practice in the Sierra (even though the plow itself is animal-drawn in Moche), as well as the *minga* system of work sharing. The cloth saddlebag (*alforja*) is probably derived originally from pack bags used with llamas in the Sierra. Except for maize, the indigenous crops grown in Moche are not those characteristic of the Sierra, because of the environmental factor, but in the diet a few Sierra products, obtained in trade, are eaten when available. *Chicha* is, of course, characteristic of the Sierra, but it was probably also known on the coast during Mochica times, and I have no definite information concerning the region of its origin. Among Sierra food products are "Sierra lentils" (*lentajas de la Sierra*), white potatoes, wheat, chochoca, hams, quínoa, ullucos, guinea pigs. On the whole, however, it does not appear that Sierra elements have entered into either the agriculture or the diet to a large extent. The occasional use of coca is apparently a trait derived ultimately from the Sierra.

In women's costume of the "old" type there are a few suggestions of Sierra influence: the woolen cloth itself is imported from the Sierra or (in former times) woven from imported Sierra wool, and it seems probable that the wrap-around skirt, the rebozo, and the woven belt supporting the skirt are Sierra styles, although their present form was not characteristic in all details of the female costume of the Inca Empire (cf. Rowe, 1946).

The influence of the Quechua language in place and family names is very strong, and seems to have submerged almost completely Mochica or Chimu toponymy and patronymy which may have been present formerly. We have already seen that the word Moche itself may be a corrupted Quechua word. Many Quechua words are in common use, just as they are in the general Spanish of Peru: *huaca, chacra, minga,* and the like. Place names are divided between Quechua, possible coastal languages, and Spanish. For example, *Güerequeque* (an irrigation ditch) is Quechua, *Sun* and *Choc Choc,* possibly coastal, while *Esperanza, Los Muertos,* etc., are Spanish. Nearly 20 percent of the 44 family names studied (p. 102) are definitely Quechua, while one other may be Aymara. In all names, either of places or people, however, Spanish predominates.

The celebration of the child's first haircut and first nail cutting was a standard feature of the Inca culture (Rowe, 1946). In Moche this ceremony has been made into two, they have been robbed of their name-giving function, and the child's uncle has been displaced by a *padrino* as sponsor.

The ultimate sources of the many native elements in brujería and magical curing may never be known. It seems not improbable, however, that most of those now identifiable in Moche derive immediately from the generalized "Inca" culture present in this region at the time of the Spanish Conquest, and several elements seem to have been current in the Sierra during the Empire. The practice of brujería itself, both in "good" and "bad" forms, was well established in the Empire. With the exception of articles previously noted as having been used by the Mochicas, the bulk of the curative herbs and objects seems to have been derived from the Sierra. All non-Spanish names for such articles are Quechua, which would possibly indicate that, whatever their ultimate source, they had been taken into the Inca system. Many individual items used are also to be found in Inca practices, e. g., white maize and white maize meal for purifying, numerous herbal remedies and terms, sacred stones from the huacas, etc. Certain forms of sickness seem to have been similarly recognized in the Inca configuration, especially *susto* and *mal aire*.[76] The concept of soul loss involved in *susto* is probably aboriginal. The practice of evil witchcraft through the employment of homeopathic magic on dolls and images of the victim was current in Europe, but was also definitely practiced among the Inca. The use of amulets for protection against evil influences seems to derive more from the native pattern than from Europe.

Relatively few, if any, specifically identifiable Inca traits are to be found in Moche Catholicism. However, it is probably no accident that the official religion now, as in Inca times, combines worship with features of social relaxation and merrymaking. It appears that about the middle of the 17th century, the church took a more tolerant attitude toward such features as well as to the parallel persistence of "native superstitions," provided they did not violate the doctrinal definition of heresy (Kubler, 1946).

Several remnants of Inca belief seem to survive in the notions of death. For example, the owl was a harbinger of death among the Inca as it is among the Mocheros, and the presence or songs of a number of other birds were regarded as evil omens among the Inca, as in Moche today (Rowe, 1946). The alcoholic and gustatory features of the wake (*velorio*) in Moche remind one of similar practices among the Inca. The wake in the cemetery on the eve of All Souls' Day recalls the interest in the dead manifested in Inca times and nearly coincides with a special ceremony for the dead said by some authori-

[76] The belief that sickness is caused by "bad air" was, of course, also present in European culture, and can be traced back at least to the time of the Greeks.

ties to have occurred at this time in the Inca calendar. The hazy beliefs in ghosts and spirits of the dead may be influenced by the Inca tradition, or, on the other hand, may also derive from European folk belief.

Many of the "Inca" elements also had their parallels in the Spanish culture of the Conquest, and their presence in Moche may indicate a Creole consolidation of these parallel traits.

EUROPEAN ELEMENTS

A complete recapitulation of the European elements in Moche culture will not be attempted in this place, because a reading of the descriptive material of the text will make these sufficiently clear to the modern reader.

However, one point is to be borne in mind in considering the European components of Creole cultures. These components have come from two European or Western contexts, generally speaking: Spain of the Colonial Period and modern Western Civilization. The first type of European cultural element is usually numerous and has an important influence in the coloration and orientation of Creole culture, especially in its rural or peasant phases. Much of the impression of "quaintness" which a modern North American or North European receives from the Creole culture is, I believe, to be explained by the presence of these Colonial Spanish aspects of behavior and belief, with which such an observer is usually quite unfamiliar.

It must be remembered that the Renaissance and the Enlightenment reached Spain much later than other nations of western Europe, and that their Spanish forms were somewhat attenuated when they finally appeared. The Reformation, of course, made no headway in Spain, and modern mercantilism and capitalism have not become dominant influences in Spanish culture even today. In short, the medieval, feudal, Catholic cast of European culture persisted in Spain during most of the Colonial Period in Peru. Furthermore, the monopolistic and restrictive policy followed by the Crown with respect to the Viceroyalty of Peru prohibited the export to the colony of many of the innovations and "modernisms" which finally did take root in the culture of the "mother country." The result is that for nearly 300 years the emerging Creole cultures of the colonies were on the receiving end of a steady inflow of European culture patterns funneled out of Spain, but the funnel, we might say, was equipped with several strainers which served to select only certain elements for transmission to the New World. Spain itself rejected much of the newly developing modern culture of the rest of western Europe, and its official policy restrained the flow to the colonies. Thus it is that the European elements absorbed into the Creole culture were on the whole more characteristic of 16th century Spain or medieval Europe than of 20th century western Europe and North America. The free chance to borrow from the latter cultural sources came only with Independence after 1821, and, for Peru, has been effective only during the past 30 years or so, at the beginning of which period the opening of the Panama Canal first provided relatively rapid and frequent import of shipments, travelers, mail, and cultural influences in general to Peru from Europe and North America. Succeeding development of air communication and radio reception has placed the Creoles in even closer touch with "modern" European and North American culture, while the development of good highway communications within the country itself has served to diffuse these innovations throughout the Nation.

If we consider those aspects of Moche culture which are derived from European sources, we shall find that they are still dominated and outnumbered by the Spanish culture of the Colonial Period. Let us mention only a few—the ox and the ass, the one-handled plow, domestic and public architecture of the pueblo, the preference for old Spanish weights and measures, the town plan, broad hat, women's modified costume, the Spanish language itself, basic ceremonial kinship system, the basic orientation and most details of Catholicism, practically all of the non-indigenous features of the witchcraft and curing complexes (evil eye, for example), etc. Added to tangible traits of culture is a certain trend toward rustic mysticism and animism—a tendency to believe in supernatural experiences (e.g., those involving pacts with the Devil), to see ghosts and spirits in material things, and to discuss on the basis of unverified premises. These tendencies of thought and attitude were, of course, characteristic in some degree of the aboriginal cultures as well, but they are reinforced by the persistence of the Spanish semimedieval Weltanschauung.

Although traits of modern culture are being rapidly introduced to the Mocheros, few have yet become integrated parts of their culture. The machine, for example, has not yet become an essential part of their life, even though, in the form of autobuses, it is regarded as a convenience. The mercantile complex, with bookkeeping, credit, stocks of goods, and all the rest of it, has not yet fastened itself on Moche, despite all the trading activity of the women and the fact that they have become thoroughly familiar with money as a medium of exchange. The constant search for novelty has passed the older Mocheros by. Political democracy, either as a complex of concepts or in practice, is little understood.

However, it seems that the younger generation is responding to the presentation of modern culture. Literacy and the use of the written and printed word should be all but universal within another generation. The motion pictures and the radio are beginning to exert their appeal in their own right and also as purveyors of new ideas and usages. Modern styles in clothing and hats are affected by the younger generation. Factory-made cloth and artifacts of metal and glass are universally accepted. They are organizing cultural and community societies to promote "progress." The church is losing some of its influence over private lives and even the laymen's organizations are declining (hermandades, mayordomías). An increasing number of both men and women are seeking advanced education and seeking employment either in the professions or as wage earners. Lima is no longer another world, but an actual city which may be visited in reality and in which one may live and seek a living. Modern political arguments are beginning to interest even middle-aged persons. Modern sports (European football and North American basketball) have already become part of the culture of the younger set. The news of the outside world is followed with interest.

In short, Moche is becoming a part of the modern world, and judging by the progress of events in the past, this is taking place at a fairly rapid rate. Moche is now a rural or peasant exhibit of the Creole culture of Peru, and it demonstrates many features of creolization characteristic of the country as a whole.

Although Moche is broadening its contacts and "modernizing" its interests, I do not anticipate that it will ever become completely "modern" in terms of North American small-town life, barring a radical upset in the processes of cultural change and reintegration. I venture to predict that as the Creole culture approaches greater stability and integration it will still embody recognizable traces of its indigenous and Spanish Colonial ancestors, interwoven, worked over, and intermingled with contributions from abroad. The time is already at hand when it is practically impossible to take any complex of traits from Moche culture, figuratively nail it to the wall, and label it as an unmodified survival or borrowing from any other culture, indigenous or foreign, ancient or modern. The time is doubtless approaching when most of the foreign and indigenous elements will be so firmly imbedded in the Creole matrix as to resist isolation, even for analytical purposes. Their influence will still be felt, however, and the forms and directions of the Creole culture will remain in their debt.

The *forasteros* who live in Moche at the present time also practice a variety of the Creole culture, although it might be called a provincial urban variety rather than the rustic type of Moche in all its details. The mutual exclusiveness which exists between *forasteros* and Mocheros, as previously shown, is not due to any great cultural gulf which separates them, but rather to economic and social factors which have already been discussed. There is good reason to believe that the two groups will eventually be integrated into one community, although this event may take place on a class basis and with further disruption of Moche patterns.

BIBLIOGRAPHY

ALAYZA PAZ SOLDÁN, LUÍS.
    1939. Mi país. El paso de los libertadores. Lima.
    1940 (?). Mi país. Lecturas peruanas.
APUNTES Y ESTUDIOS . . .
    1935. Apuntes y estudios históricos sobre la fecha de la fundación de la ciudad de Trujillo. (Published by the Junta del Cuarto Centenario de la Fundación de Trujillo). Trujillo. [Includes reproductions of 2 maps by Feijóo, Miguel, showing Moche as of 1760.]
ARONA, JUAN DE (pseudonym of Pedro Paz Soldán y Unánuc).
    1938. Diccionario de peruanismos. Biblioteca de cultura peruana, primera serie, No. 10. Paris.
BARANDARIÁN, A. LEON.
    n. d. Mitos, leyendas y tradiciones lambayecanas. Lima.
BASTIAN, A.
    1878. Die Culturländer des alten Amerikas, vol. 1. Berlin.
BAUDIN, LOUIS.
    1943. El imperio socialista de los Incas. (Trans. by José Antonio Arze from L'empire socialiste des Inka). Santiago de Chile.
BEALS, RALPH L.
    1946. Cherán: A Sierra Tarascan village. Institute of Social Anthropology, Smithsonian Inst., Publ. No. 2.
BENNETT, W. C.
    1937. Chimu archaeology. Sci. Monthly, vol. 45, pp. 35–48.
    1939. Archaeology of the North Coast of Peru: An account of exploration and excavation in Viru and Lambayeque Valleys. Anthrop. Pap. Amer. Mus. Nat. Hist., vol. 37, pp. 1–153. New York.
BETANZOS, JUAN DE.
    1880. Suma y narración de los Incas. (Edited by Marcos Jimenez de la Espada.) Madrid.
BRÜNING, E.
    1922. Estudios monográficos del Departamento de Lambayeque. Chiclayo.
CABROL, ABBOT.
    1934. The Roman missal in Latin and English for every day of the year in conformity with the latest decrees. Ed. 9. New York.
CALANCHA, ANTONIO DE LA.
    1638. Coronica moralizada del Orden de San Augustin en el Peru. Barcelona. [The copy consulted is in the Duke University Library, Durham, N. C.]
CAMINO CALDERÓN, CARLOS.
    1942. El daño. Ed. 3. Lima.
CARRERA, FERNANDO DE LA.
    1644. Arte de la lengua yunga de los valles del obispado de Trujillo. . . . Lima.
        See also VILLAREAL, 1921; and LARCO HOYLE, 1938–39, vol. 2, pp. 48–82.
CENSO NACIONAL.
    1941. Censo nacional de 1940. Resultados generales. Primer informe oficial. República del Perú, Ministerio de Hacienda, Departamento de Censos. Lima.
CORNEJO BOURONCLE, JORGE.
    1935. Las comunidades indígenas. Revista Universitaria, año XXIV, No. 69, pp. 56–114. Cuzco.
DICCIONARIO DE "LA CRÓNICA."
    1918. Diccionario geográfico peruano y alamanaque de "La Crónica." Lima.
DIETSCHY, HANS.
    1938. El médico del tiempo de los incas y sus remedios. Acta Ciba, No. 10. Basel.
ESCOMEL, E.
    1913. Las disenterías en Arequipa. Arequipa.
EXTRACTO ESTADÍSTICO.
    1942. Extracto estadístico del Perú. Ministerio de Hacienda y Comercio. Dirección Nacional de Estadística. Lima.
FARFÁN, J. M. B.
    1940. Clave de la lengua quechua. Lima.
    1941. La clave del lenguaje quechua del Cusco. Sobretiro de la Rev. del Mus. Nac., vol. 10, No. 2, pp. 215–239. Lima.
FEIJÓO, MIGUEL.
    [1763.] Relación descriptiva de la ciudad y provincia de Trujillo del Perú. [Undated reprint.]. Trujillo.

GARCILASO DE LA VEGA.
1918–20. Los comentarios reales de los Incas. (Horacio H. Urteaga, ed.). Colección de historiadores clásicos del Perú. 5 vols. Lima.
GILLIN, JOHN.
1942. Acquired drives in culture contact. Amer. Anthrop. n. s., vol. 44, pp. 545–554.
1943. Houses, food, and the contact of cultures in a Guatemalan town. Acta Americana, vol. 1, pp. 344–359.
1944. Cultural adjustment. Amer. Anthrop., vol. 46, pp. 429–447.
1945. Parallel cultures and the inhibitions to acculturation in a Guatemalan community. Social Forces, vol. 24, pp. 1–14.
Ms. San Luis Jilotepeque, a Guatemalan community in process of change. (In preparation.)
HERRERA, FORTUNATO L.
1942. Etnobotánica. Plantas tropicales cultivadas por los antiguos peruanos. Revista del Museo Nacional, vol. 9, No. 2, pp. 179–195. Lima.
HORKHEIMER, HANS.
1943. Historia del Perú. Epoca prehistórica. Trujillo.
1944. Vistas arqueológicas del noroeste del Perú. Trujillo.
JIMENEZ BORJA, ARTURO.
1937. Moche. Lima.
JUAN, GEORGE, and ULLOA, ANTONIO.
1751. Reise nach Süd-Amerika. Leipzig.
KROEBER, A. L.
1925. The Uhle pottery collections from Moche. Univ. Calif. Publ. Amer. Arch. Ethnol., vol. 21, pp. 191–234. Berkeley.
1926. Archaeological explorations in Peru. Part I: Ancient pottery from Trujillo. Field Mus. Nat. Hist., Anthrop. Mem., vol. 2, No. 1, pp. 1–43. Chicago.
1944. Peruvian archaeology in 1942. Viking Fund Publ. Anthrop., No. 4. New York.
KUBLER, GEORGE.
1946. The Quechua in the Colonial world. In Handbook of South American Indians, Julian H. Steward, Editor. Vol. 2, The Andean Civilizations, pp. 331–410. (Bur. Amer. Ethnol Bull. 143, vol. 2.)
LARCO HOYLE, RAFAEL.
1938–39. Los Mochicas. 2 vols. Lima.
1941. Los Cupisniques. Lima.
Ms. a. Los Mochicas, una sinopsis. Unpublished manuscript in Museo Arqueológico "Rafael Larco Herrera," Chiclín.
Ms. b. Los Mochicas, capítulo IX, "La agricultura." Unpublished manuscript in the Museo Arqueológico "Rafael Larco Herrera," Chiclín.
Ms. c. Los Mochicas, capítulo X, "La casa y la pesca." Unpublished manuscript in the Museo Arqueológico "Rafael Larco Herrera," Chiclín.
1946. A culture sequence for the North Coast of Peru. In Handbook of South American Indians, Julian H. Steward, Editor. Vol. 2, The Andean Civilizations, pp. 149–175. (Bur. Amer. Ethnol. Bull. 143, vol. 2.)
LASTRES, JUAN B.
1941. La medicina en la obra de Guamán Poma de Ayala. Revista del Museo Nacional, vol. 11, No. 1, pp. 113–164. Lima.
MacLEAN Y ESTENÓS, ROBERTO.
1943. Sociología peruana. Lima.
MEAD, MARGARET, ED.
1937. Cooperation and competition among primitive peoples. New York.
MEANS, PHILIP AINSWORTH.
1931. Ancient civilizations of the Andes. New York.
MEDINA, FELIPE DE.
[1650.] Relación del Licenciado Felipe de Medina, Visitador General de las idolatrías del Arzobispado de Lima, inviada al ilustrísimo y reverendísimo Señor Arzobispo della, en que le da cuenta de las que se han descubierto en el pueblo de Huacho, donde ha comenzado a visitar, desde 19 de febrero hasta 23 de marzo de 1650. Colección de libros y documentos referentes a la historia del Peru (Horacio H. Urteaga, ed.), 2d series, vol. 3, pp. 89–104, 1920. Lima.
MIDDENDORF, E. W.
1892. Das Muchik oder die Chimusprache. Leipzig.
1893–95. Peru. 3 vols. Berlin.
MIÑANO G., JOSÉ ANGEL.
1942. Las brujas y shapingos de Chicama. La Nación, June 12, 14, 15, 16. Lima.
MIRO QUESADA S., AURELIO.
1938. Costa, sierra y montaña. Lima.
MISHKIN, BERNARD.
1946. The contemporary Quechua. In Handbook of South American Indians, Julian H. Steward, Editor. Vol. 2, The Andean Civilizations, pp. 411–470. (Bur. Amer. Ethnol. Bull. 143, vol. 2.)
MONOGRAFÍA DE LA DIÓCESIS.
1930–31. Monografía de la Diócesis de Trujillo. 3 vols. Trujillo.
MURDOCK, GEORGE PETER, and OTHERS.
1938. Outline of cultural materials. Yale Univ. New Haven.
ORE, L. J. DE.
1607. Rituale seu manuale peruanum. Napoles.
PARSONS, ELSIE CLEWS.
1936. Mitla, town of the souls. Chicago.
PAZ SOLDÁN, MARIANO FELIPE.
1877. Diccionario geográfico estadístico del Perú. Lima.
PAZ SOLDAN Y UNÁNUE, PEDRO. See ARONA, JUAN DE.
POMA DE AYALA, FELIPE GUAMÁN.
1936. La nueva corónica y bueno gobierno. (Facsimile edition.) Paris.
PRADO, JAVIER.
1941. Estado social del Perú durante la dominación expañola. Colección de libros y documentos referentes a la historia del Perú, 3a. serie. Lima. (Originally published in 1894.)

REDFIELD, ROBERT.
1930. Tepotzlán, a Mexican village. Chicago.
1941. The folk culture of Yucatan. Chicago.
RIVA-AGÜERO, JOSE DE LA.
1938. Por la verdad, la tradición y la patria (opúsculos). Lima.
ROJAS GONZÁLES, FRANCISCO.
1943. La institución del compadrazgo entre los indígenas de México. Revista Mexicana de Sociología, vol. V, pp. 201–214.
ROMERO, CARLOS ALBERTO.
1909. Contribución al estudio del Yunga. Rev. Hist., vol. 4, pp. 169–183. Lima.
ROMERO, EMILIO.
1944. Geografía económica del Perú. Lima.
ROWE, JOHN HOWLAND.
1946. Inca culture at the time of the Spanish Conquest. *In* Handbook of South American Indians, Julian H. Steward, Editor. Vol. 2, The Andean Civilizations, pp. 183-330. (Bur. Amer. Ethnol. Bull. 143, vol. 2.)
SPICER, EDWARD H.
1940. Pascua, a Yaqui village in Arizona. Chicago.
SQUIER, E. GEORGE.
1877. Peru, incidents of travel and exploration in the land of the Incas. London.
STIGLICH, GERMAN.
1922. Diccionario geográfico del Perú. Lima.
TSCHOPIK, JR., HARRY.
1946. The Aymara. *In* Handbook of South American Indians, Julian H. Steward, Editor. Vol. 2, The Andean Civilizations, pp. 501–573. (Bur. Amer. Ethnol. Bull. 143, vol. 2.)
UHLE, MAZ.
1913. Die Ruinen von Moche. Journ. Soc. Amér. Paris, vol. 10, pp. 95–117.
VALCÁRCEL, LUÍS.
1943. Historia de la cultura antigua del Perú, t. 1, vol. 1. Lima.
VALDIZÁN, HERMILIO.
1915. La alienación mental entre los primitivos peruanos. Lima.
1917. Los factores etiológicos de la alienación mental a través de nuestra historia. Lima.
1938. Diccionario de medicina peruana, vol. 2. Lima.
VALDIZÁN, HERMILIO, and MALDONADO, ANGEL.
1922. La medicina popular peruana. 3 vols. Lima.
VILLAGOMES, D. PEDRO DE.
1919. Exortaciones e instrucción acerca de las idolatrías de los indios del Arzobispado de Lima. *In* Colección de libros y documentos referentes a la historia del Perú, t. 12 (Horacio H. Urteaga, ed.). Lima.
VILLAREAL, FEDERICO.
1921. La lengua yunga o mochica según el arte publicado en Lima en 1644 por el licenciado D. Fernando de la Carrera. Lima.
ZEVALLOS QUIÑONES, JORJE.
1941. Una nota sobre el primitivo idioma de la costa norte. Revista Histórica, vol. 15, pp. 376–379. Lima.
1944. Toponimia preincaica en el norte del Perú. Lima.

GLOSSARY

Since practically all Spanish or other non-English words used in the text are defined or synonymized in English at their respective first appearances, only those words which appear repeatedly or those whose sense in Moche differs from that of standard Spanish dictionaries are included in the following list. The glossary is to be regarded primarily as an aid to the reader, and not as final authority for definitions and other matters of linguistic or semantic interest.

Acequia, an irrigation ditch.
Acomodado (a), well-off, well-to-do, financially speaking.
Agua bendita, holy water.
Agua de socorro, holy water used to anoint a child who appears to be about to die without baptism in the church.
Aguardiente, strong liquor, usually made from sugarcane.
Aguja, needle, netting needle for making fish nets.
Ahijado, godchild.
Ají, red and yellow pepper plant and fruit.
Albañil, mason, or adobe layer.
Alcalde, mayor, municipal executive officer.
Alforja, a woven saddlebag or shoulder bag.
Algodón pardo, native brown cotton.
Atarraya, casting net.
Baja policía, garbage collector.

Barranca, ravine or gorge; a section of the Moche countryside.
Barrio, a ward or subdivision of a town; does not exist in Moche.
Barro, bar or club of wood for breaking clods.
Barro de hierro, crow-bar of iron.
Bastón, a roll of material; in Huanchaco, a roll of reeds embodied in the reed raft; scepter of image of San Isidro.
Batán, grinding stone.
Batea, carved one-piece wooden vessel used as a container for liquids, for washing clothes, etc.
Bayeta, coarse-woven cloth.
Bocadita, custom whereby a small morsel of food is passed from mouth to mouth.
Botica, drug store or pharmacy.
Botija, large earthenware container for *chicha*, originally imported from Pisco with native brandy.
Brujería, witchcraft.
Caballito del mar, literally, "little horse of the sea," a small cigar-shaped raft made of a species of reed.
Cabecera, "head," as of a fish net.
Cabo de manila, Manila rope.
Cabresta, colloquial for *cabrestante*, capstan, winch; specifically in Moche, the ropes which are tightened around the boards of the wooden forms in making *tapia*.
Cabrito, young goat, kid.

Cahuan, dip net for catching shrimp, crabs, etc.

Caja, box or hole; in Huanchaco, the place on the reed raft where the operator sits.

Cajón, a large box; the wooden form into which *tapia* walls or fences are molded.

Calabozo, heavy knife with hooked blade, for cutting brush and weeds.

Calcal, fishing net used with reed raft in Huanchaco.

Callana, earthenware cooking pot.

Camal, slaughterhouse, place where animals are slaughtered; also gunny sack or any large coarse sack made of any material.

Camaron, shrimp.

Campiña, irrigated countryside as distinguished from the pueblo or town.

Caña brava, cane or reed.

Caña de azucar, sugarcane.

Caña de Guayaquil, bamboo.

Cañan, small lizard, caught for eating in dried form.

Cañaso, beverage made of flavored sugarcane alcohol.

Carreterra, main highway.

Carrizo, stiff reed or cane.

Casado (a), person married by church ceremony.

Casamiento, marriage formally sanctified by church ceremony.

Catastro, property list or register.

Catedrático, university professor on permanent appointment, one who occupies a *cátedra* ("chair") in a university faculty.

Causa, form of lunch or light meal.

Cerro, mountain; Cerro Blanco, Cerro Cumunero ("White Mountain," "Community Mountain"), near Moche.

Chacra, agricultural landholding or small farm.

Chancaca, unrefined brown cake sugar.

Chicha, native fermented alcoholic beverage.

Chinchorro, two-man net for fishing in surf.

Chochoca, maize flour.

Choclo, green corn on the cob; an ear of green corn.

Cholo, mixed-blood inhabitant of Peru.

Choza, a rustic house.

Chuno, a float made of a globular gourd, used on fish lines, and boat lines.

Chuño, sprouted maize kernels.

Cohete, rocket, firecracker.

Cojodito, small globular gourd for drinking *chicha.*

Colegio, high school; in Moche refers also to any school, primary grades included.

Compadrazgo, co-godparenthood.

Compromiso, commitment.

Copita, small liquor glass; by extension, a drink.

Cosecha, crop or harvest, also called *siembra.*

Cuadera, light rope forming part of the setline for fishing.

Cuarto, quarter; a quarter-bottle of pisco brandy.

Cuerda, cotton three-ply line with hooks forming part of the setline for fishing.

Culambra, colloquial, supernatural snake guardian of a garden.

Curandero (a), magical curer, but not a witch (*brujo*).

Destajo, task work, job of work to be done.

Encomienda, grant of land and Indians in trust to Spanish colonists.

Enguayanchar, to bewitch by love magic.

Espinel, setline with hooks for fishing in surf.

Estera, mat made of reeds tied together in parallel fashion.

Estiradura, inguinal hernia.

Fanegada, measure of land area, equal to about 3 hectares, or 7.77 acres.

Forastero, a stranger; in Moche, a Peruvian who is not native to Moche or who is not culturally identified with Moche.

Fulano, "so-and-so" (anonymous personal name).

Garúa, drizzle or mist, characteristic of winter season on Peruvian coast.

Granja, a poultry or stock-raising enterprise, small scale.

Hacha, single-bladed European-type ax.

Hacienda, plantation; influence of *haciendas* on culture and social life of Peruvian coast, on Moche.

Haciendita, "small hacienda," a land-holding in the District of Moche.

Hectarea, hectare, 2.59 acres.

Helada, colloquial, a cold night.

Hermandad, semireligious organization of laymen.

Horca, wooden pitchfork.

Huaca, Quechua, "holy place"; in Moche, the Mochica ruins.

Huanarpo (*Matropha macrantha*), an aphrodisiac.

Huangana, binding for reed raft.

Huerta, garden or orchard; in Moche, usually surrounds dwelling house and contains kitchen vegetables and fruit trees.

Intencionamiento, process of asking for a woman's hand in marriage.

Jora, mash made from sprouted grains of maize.

Lancha, motorboat used in fishing.

Llano, plain or flat place.

Machete, a one-handed knife or cutlass for cutting brush and weeds.

Madrina, godmother.

Malero, literally, "evildoer," usually applied to an evil witch or practitioner of evil witchcraft.

Mallero, wooden block used in making fish nets.

Mano, hand; grinding stone held in hand; "hand of bananas"; a procedure employed by the assistants in a curing seance of *brujería.*

Marinera, a social dance.

Mate, large, shallow, platelike gourd container.

Mayordomía, a group of laymen organized to celebrate a saint's day or other religious feast day.

Médico, scientific physician.

Médico boliviano, itinerant herb peddler.

Melgar, plot or subdivision of a field, usually for alfalfa.

Mesa, table.

Mesa de brujería, sort of altar laid out on the ground used in witchcraft cures; by extension, the seance itself.

Minga, a voluntary or semivoluntary work group democratically organized and involving recreational features as well as labor; a mechanism for exchanging labor.

Mocheros netos, real or true inhabitants of Moche, persons identified with the community of Moche.

Mondongo, animal intestines eaten as meat.

Muy-muy, sea shrimp.

Nasa, conical trap of cane for fishing in streams or irrigation ditches.

Novio, fiancé, lover, or suitor.

Ojéo, Moche colloquialism used in place of *mal ojo,* evil eye.

Padrinazgo, godparenthood.

Padrino, godfather.

Palana, shovel or spade; used in agriculture.

Patrón, protector, master; e. g., patron saint, master of a plantation, master of a sailing boat.

Peón, manual laborer or servant, usually an agricultural laborer.

Pescado, fish.

Pescador, fisherman.

Petate, a mat made of flat elements by checkerboard or twill weaving.

Picante, hot seasoning of various types.

Pico, pick-ax, used in agriculture and irrigation.

Pisco, a type of brandy originally made in Pisco, Peru.

Playa, the beach or seashore.

Playero, one who lives on the beach or is identified with that section of the community.

Porongo, long-necked, gourd *chicha* bottle.

Poto, a drinking cup or bowl of gourd.

Poza, puddle, a form of irrigation.

Pozo, water well.

Pueblo, town; the pueblo of Moche.

Quebradura, umbilical hernia in infants.

Quincha, a type of wattle-and-daub wall construction used for houses and fences.

Quirana, binding with which the reeds composing a roll or bundle is bound in the reed raft used for fishing in Huanchaco.

Rastro, garden rake.

Raya, target or mark at which to throw in quoits game.

Rebozo, shawl.

Red, net, for fishing.

Regante, one who irrigates or uses irrigation water.

Remada, outdoor vine arbor.

Revendadoro (a), an individual who makes a business of buying country products and reselling them in the city market.

Saca, sack; in Huanchaco, the crab net or trap.

Sala, sitting room of a house.

Salon, commercial refreshment parlor.

Sancochado (referring to a food preparation), cut up in small pieces and boiled.

Seviche, dish of raw fish prepared in various ways.

Shapingo, familiar spirit, or spiritual messenger and/or servant of an evil *brujo.*

Sorgo, sorghum.

Surco, furrow, types of planting furrows.

Susto, a form of illness believed to be associated with loss of the soul.

Tapia, wall and fence construction of earth laid up in wooden forms.

Tejos, quoits game.

Tienda, retail shop or store.

Tocayo, namesake.

Totora, a wild reed growing in swamps, used for making *estera* mats and fishing rafts (*caballitos del mar*).

Vergüenza, embarrassment or shame.

Vestido, costume, clothing.

Yapa, small good-will extra given by a merchant with a purchase.

Yunta, yoke; by extension, a yoke of oxen.

Yuyu, sea weed, water plant.

INDEX

Adobe making, 37–38.
Agriculture, 12–26; religious and magical aspects, 26–28; 154, 157.
Alforja, 80.
All Souls' Day, 150, 158.
Aphrodisiacs, 95–96.
Archeology, 4, 11–12, 154–156.
Art, 87–89, 156.

Bands, 86–87.
Baptism, 106–110.
Basketball, 85.
Beer, 48–49.
Betrothals, 111.
Births, statistics, 9; customs, 136–137; birth control, 95.
Boats, 31–36.
Borrowing, 75–76.
Brujería (witchcraft), 117; table of, 119–125; procedures of "good" witchcraft, 125–128; evil witchcraft, 128–129; Mochica elements, 156; Sierra influences, 157–158.
Brujos (witches), 116–117.
Budgets, family, 77–79.
Busses, 81–82.
Business dealings, 72–75.

Catholicism, Roman, 142–151, 158.
Census, 7–9.
Chicha, 46–49; recipe for, 53.
Childbirth, 136–138.
Children, numbers, 10; care, 98–99, 137; games, 86; dress, 63; in the family and household, 98–100.
Chimu, elements, 157.
Chucaque, 138.
Cinema, 86.
Class, 113.
Clocks, 91.
Colic, 136.
Communication, 80–82.
Compadrazgo, 104–112.
Confirmation, 110.
Constitutional type, 9–10.
Cost of living, 77–79.
Courtship, 96–97.
Creole culture, 151–154.
Crops, rotation, 15–16; techniques, 18–20; plants, 18–24; Mochica elements, 154.
Cultural position, 151–160.
Culture, Creole, 151–154; Mochica, 154–156; Tiahuanacoid and Chimu, 157; Sierra, 157–158; European, 158–160.
Curanderos (curers), 116–117; 129–130.
Curers (*curanderos*), 116–117; 129–130.
Curing, magical, 115–142; Mochica elements, 156; Sierra influences, 157–158.

Dancing, 86–87.
Death, 149–151, 158.
Devil, 148–149.
Disease, venereal, 136; others and cures, 115–136.
Distribution of economic goods, 75–77.
Dress, men, 61; women, 61–63; children, 63; Mochica elements, 155; Sierra elements, 157.
Drink, 46–49; preparation of, 49–51; consumption of, 54–60; as recreation, 82–84; Mochica, 154.
Drugs, 49.

Ear piercing, 110, 155.
Earrings, 155.
Eating, as recreation, 82–84.
Economics, 66–79.
Education, formal, 89.
Environment, 5–6.
Epigrams, 89–91.

Estiradura, 134.
Etiquette, 44–46, 48.
European, elements, 158–160.
Evil, eye, 135; spirits, 119–121, 128, 148.
Eye, evil, 135.

Family, budgets, 77–79; familial and pseudofamilial relationships, 93; and household, 98–100; larger family relationships, 101–102; names, 102–103.
Farming, 12–26.
Fiestas, 89; religious, 145–148.
Finance, 72–75; incomes and cost of living, 77–79.
Fishing, 28–30; in Huanchaco, 30–37; Mochica elements, 155.
Food, preparation of, 49–51; miscellaneous dishes, 52; "hot" and "cold," 53–54; consumed, statistical study of, 54–60; effect on illness, 53–54; Mochica, 154–155.
Football, 84–85.
Forasteros, 8, 112; comparison on food with Mocheros, 54–60; element in the community, 112–113.
Foreigners, 8, 112.
Funerals, 149–150.
Furnishings, of houses, 41–43.

Ghosts, after death, 150–151; Sierra elements, 158.
Gourds, 155.
Guinea pig, in witchcraft, 125–126.
Guitars, 87.

Haircutting, 110.
Heart, pain, 136.
Hernia, umbilical, 134; inguinal, 134.
Highways, 81.
Historical tradition, 91–92.
History, 10–12.
Households, 98–100.
Houses, 37–43, 154.
Huanchaco, fishing village, 30–37.

Illness, effects of foods, 53–54.
Implements, agricultural, 17–18; house building, 37–38; culinary, 44–53.
Inca culture, 157–158.
Incest, 96.
Incomes, and cost of living, 77–79.
Industries, 64–66.
Inguinal hernia, 134.
Instruments, musical, 87.
Investments, 73–74.
Irrigation, 12, 16–17.

Kinship, 101–112.

Labor, division of, 66–67; specialties, 67; distribution of male, 67–69.
Land, 10; ownership of, 69–72.
Language, 7, 89–90.
Learning, 89–92.
Lending, 75–76.
Literary treatment of Moche, 7.
Longevity, 9.
Lore, 89–92.
Love magic, 95.

Magic, love, 95; in marital situations, 100–101; curing, 115–142; beliefs, 142–143.
Maintenance, 12–37.
Market, public, 75–77.
Marriage, 97–98.
Mats, 155.
Measures, 91.
Meat, butchering, 51–52.
Medicine, native, 115–142.

Aerial photograph of Moche and surroundings, including Trujillo, Chanchan, Huanchaco, and Huamán. Area enclosed by dotted line is enlarged on plate 2.

Aerial photograph of the District of Moche, southern part, covering area enclosed by dotted line in plate 1.

FERROGARRIL

PANAMERICANA

CARRETERA

HDA. MONSERRATE

RIO MOCHE

THE MOCHE COUNTRYSIDE (CAMPIÑA)

Upper (left): Field of alfalfa and sorghum.   *Upper (right):* The *campiña.*   *Middle (right):* Bed of Moche River in dry season.   *Lower (left):* Field of alfalfa and sorghum.   *Lower (right):* A part of the *campiña,* looking south from the Huaquita.

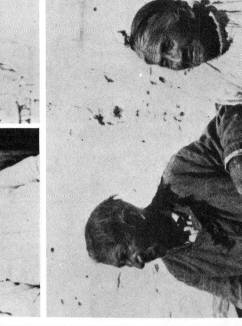

MOCHE PHYSICAL TYPES.

Upper (left): Mother and daughter, considered "true Mocheras." *Upper (center)*: Mochera *neta*, full face. *Upper (right)*: Same, profile. *Lower (left)*: True Mochero types. *Lower (right)*: Old man and old woman, "true Mochero" types; man claims to be 89 years old, woman 88 years.

MOCHE PHYSICAL TYPES AND AGRICULTURE.

Upper (left): Young woman; mother is "true Mochera"; father has Chinese, Negro, Spanish, and Indian blood. This young lady is justly considered one of the beauties of the community. *Upper (right):* Old man, claiming 89 years of age, considered "true Mochero." *Middle (left and center):* Front and profile view of woman, half Mochera, half "*sierra*" blood. *Middle (right):* A brown-cotton (*algodón pardo*) bush. *Lower (left):* Earth and wood dam for diversion of water in irrigation. *Lower (right)* (left to right): *Palana* (spade), *calabozo, palana, hacha* ax), *machete, pico* (pickax)

MOCHE AGRICULTURE.

Upper (left): Husking corn. *Upper (right):* Cultivation with spade. *Center (left to right):* Calabozo, hacha, horca (fork), machete, rastro (rake), barro de acero (iron bar), two spades on ground. *Lower (left):* Plowing. *Lower (right):* Scarecrows in field; cloths hung on limber poles moved by wind.

DOMESTICATED ANIMALS.

Upper (left): Animals at pasture. *Upper (right):* Feeding poultry. *Lower (left and right):* The faithful donkey (*picajeno*).

FISHING IMPLEMENTS AND CRAFT, MOCHE AND HUANCHACO.

Upper (left): Fishing boats raising sail, Huanchaco.   *Upper (right): Chinchorro* net hung up to dry; round object in center is gourd float (*chuno*), Moche.   *Middle (left):* Plaza of Las Delicias.   *Middle (right):* Fishing fleet putting to sea, Huanchaco.   *Lower (left):* Crab trap (*saca*) used with *caballitos del mar*, Huanchaco.   *Lower (right):* The dip net (*cahuán*); note *quincha* wall at left, Moche.

HUANCHACO FISHING.

Upper (left): Caballitos and boats on the beach. *Upper (right):* Left, Felipe Carranza, chief pilot of the fishing fleet; right, Lino Seguro, chief of the port and first sergeant of fishermen. *Middle (left) Caballito del mar* loaded with three crab traps; owner, with paddle of split bamboo, is ready to set forth; beach is at low tide. *Middle (right):* A fisherman's house. *Lower (left):* Preparing to launch a *caballito del mar. Lower (right):* Part of the fishing fleet, motorboats in foreground, sailboats in background.

THE TOWN OF MOCHE.

Upper (left): The *plazuela* near the railway tracks with windmill and water tank. *Upper (right):* Unplastered adobe house. *Lower (left):* The plaza as seen from the tower of the church, with the bus from Trujillo just coming in. *Lower (right):* Street scene.

HOUSE CONSTRUCTION IN MOCHE.

Upper (left): House with walls of tapia. *Upper (center):* The plaza, from the northwest corner. Directly behind the bandstand is the former Mercedarian *convento;*
to the left is the government building with the entrance to the girls' school and the Municipalidad on one side with the Gobernación on the other side. To the left
of the government building is the public market. *Upper (right):* House with three types of wall construction; lower part of side wall to left is *tapia,* upper part
is *quincha,* and front wall is mud-plastered adobe of "cut-out" construction. *Middle (left):* House with two types of wall construction; main room at right is of
tapia, kitchen to left is of *quincha.* *Middle (right):* Plastered adobe house. *Lower (left):* Dwelling with walls of *totora.* *Lower (right): Tapia* making in *minga;*
shoveling moistened earth into sack; woman stands by with gourd of *chicha* for workers.

HOUSE CONSTRUCTION IN MOCHE.

Upper (left): Adobe house with low, double-pitched roof and window in end wall. *Upper (right):* House entirely of *quincha*. *Middle (left):* Back-yard view in pueblo, showing sloping roofs, ventilators, and other features mentioned in text. *Middle (center):* Typical door. The house rented by the author for interview purposes, decorated by local acquaintances with hand-made Peruvian and American flags as a spontaneous token in honor of the 1944 presidential elections in the United States. *Middle (right):* House with one lime-plastered adobe wall. Note "saw-toothed" top of far end of plastered wall, suggestive of Mochica construction. *Lower (left):* "Sophisticated" type of *quincha* fence or wall, Note upright of sawed lumber. *Lower center):* Roof construction, inside view, showing rafters, canes and *petates*. *Lower (right):* Interior of roof structure with one set of canes over sawed rafters.

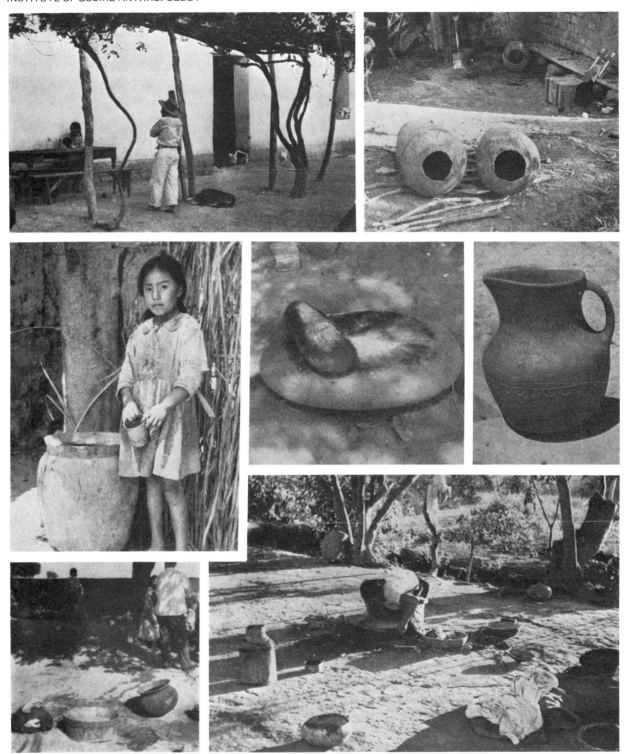

FOOD PREPARATION AND UTENSILS.

Upper (left): Typical outdoor arbor or *ramada*, used as dining room.   *Upper (right): Botijas* for *chicha*.   *Middle (left):* Water storage jar and tin can used as ladle.   *Middle (center):* Grinding stones.   *Middle (right):* Earthenware pitcher of the type frequently used in Moche houses, purchased in outside markets.   *Lower (left):* Wooden tub and cooking pot.   *Lower (right):* Woman heating wash water on outdoor fire.   To her left are two gourd *mates*, used as wash tubs; in front of her is a metal milk can.

EATING AND DRINKING.

Upper (left): Children eating their noonday meal from gourd plates and seated on a reed mat.   *Upper (right):* A *chichería's* sign of business, indicating that fresh *chicha* is available inside; a basket covered with red and white tissue paper; a green leaf is attached indicating that *causa* is also available.   *Middle (left):* Open-air kitchen with adobe stove and *quincha* wall.   *Lower (left):* Floor fireplace on loose stones.   *Lower (center):* A housewife.   *Lower (right):* A *copita* of *cañaso* (flavored cane alcohol).

MOCHE CLOTHING.

Upper (*left*): Toddler's costume, shirt only. *Upper* (*right*): Costume of 4-year-old child. *Lower* (*left*): Woman's "old costume." *Lower* (*center*): University student (Mochero) and small brother. *Lower* (*right*): Woman's "old costume" with *rebozo* (shawl).

MOCHE CLOTHING.

Upper (left): Women's costumes; woman farthest to left wears "cotton-dress costume"; next three wear "modified costume"; woman in dark clothing is in "old costume"; two women to extreme right are in "modified costume,". *Upper (right):* Woman's hairdress, ends of braids braided and wrapped together with brown cotton yarn. *Lower (left):* The influence of modern modes on the younger generation. A youth group of pure Mocheros, all working or going to school in Trujillo. *Lower (center):* Woman's "modified costume." *Lower (right):* Woman's "old costume" with *reboso* and hat.

MANUFACTURES: BASKET MAKING, WEAVING, AND ROCKET MAKING.

Upper (*left*): Basket making: splitting and scraping *carrizo* strips with knife. *Upper* (*right*) and *Middle* (*left*): Basket making. *Middle* (*right*): Grinding powder for rockets.
Lower (*left*): Young woman weaving in Monsefú, using type of loom said to have been employed in Moche until recently. *Lower* (*right*): A whirling rocket mechanism.

ROADS AND TRAILS; RECREATIONS.

Upper (left): The lane, passable for automobiles, entering the *campiña.* Note the *tapia* fences made with peaked tops so that they cannot be used as footpaths. *Upper (right):* Wood and earth bridge across an irrigation ditch. *Middle (left):* Foot and animal lane graded up with *tapia* wall. *Middle (right):* Trophies and diplomas won by the Moche Tejos Club. *Lower (left):* Flageolet and drum player with "American Indian" headdress, modern singlet, motorcycle goggles in procession of October 22. *Lower (center):* Trumpet player in the brass band. *Lower (right):* Foxtrotting in the public market.

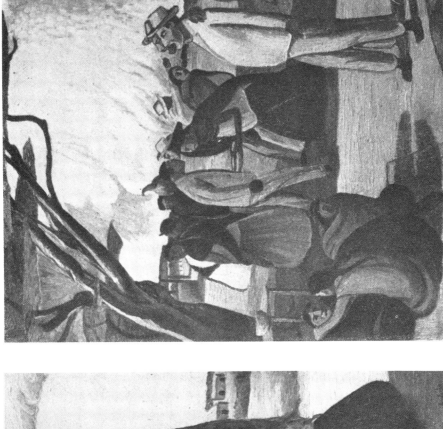

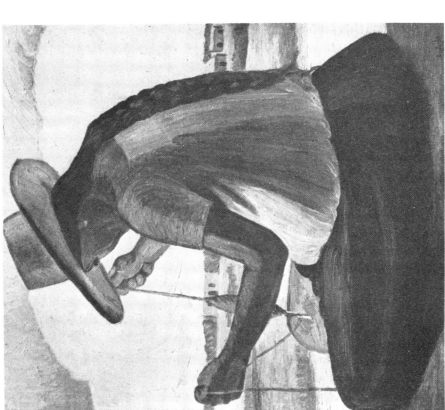

PAINTINGS OF MOCHE LIFE BY PEDRO AZABACHE.

Left: "La Hiladora" (The Spinner).   *Right:* "Fiesta in the Campiña."

PAINTINGS BY PEDRO AZABACHE.

Upper: "Salida a la Pesca" (Going Out to Fish). A painting of Huanchaco. (Property of Dr. Miguel Capurro.)   *Lower:* "También las Campesinas chismean" (Also the Country Women Gossip).   A painting of Moche life.   (Property of Carlos Salazar Southwell.)

Paintings by Pedro Azabache.

Upper (left): "Pescadores frente al Mar" (Fisherfolk at the Seaside). A painting of Huanchaco. (Property of St. Enrique Dammert Elguera.) *Upper (right):* "La Comadre Manonga." A painting of a Moche type. (Property of Sra. Mercedes Gallagher de Parks.) *Lower (left):* "La Minga (The Minga). A painting of Moche life. (Property of Sr. Luis Bentin Mujica.) *Lower (right):* "Callejuela de Moche" (Little Street of Moche.) A painting of Moche life. (Property of Sr. Carlos Blondet G.)

CURER'S TABLE (MESA DE BRUJERÍA) AND SUSTO CURE.

Upper (left): Operator starting to set up the table; just off the white cloth to the left is a piece of the medicinal cactus, San Pedro. *Upper (right):* View of the table when set up. See explanation of figure 8, pp. 124–125, for identification of articles. *Middle (right):* Close-up of a part of the table. *Lower (left):* Operator in position for work, shaking his rattle. *Lower (center):* Cure of adult *susto.* Patient strips leaves from herbs, in white bag at her left are her blankets and change of clothes. *Lower (right):* Patient watches while *curandera* mixes and kneads herb leaves.

CURE OF ADULT SUSTO.

Upper (left): Patient sews double *escapulario* while *curandera* continues to knead leaves.   *Upper (center):* Curandera stuffs *escapulario* with leaves.   *Upper (right):* Curandera prepares shelter of *esteras* for patient; herbs, moistened with "waters of *susto*" are heating in earthen pot on fire.   *Middle (left):* Patient has entered shelter and disrobed except for her shift and has put double *escapulario* around neck, front bag of which is seen here.   *Curandera* is beginning massage of head, squeezing juice into ear.   *Middle (center):* Curandera massages patients' body with herbs mixed with "waters of *susto*."   *Middle (right):* Curandera massages patient's legs and feet. *Lower (left):* Draped in blanket, patient stands over pan of hot coals to be smoked by incense of *San Mério*.   *Lower (center)* Patient, wrapped in blankets inside shelter to left, while *curandera* with garment in hand calls spirit.   Patient will be left to sweat over night.   *Lower (right):* Curandera buries herbs and incense used in cure.

CURE OF SUSTO IN CHILD.

Upper (left): Curandera and mother hang double *escapulario* about child's neck; mother has one of the sacks in her right hand. The sacks have previously been filled with herbs moistened with "waters of *susto*" as in adult cure. *Upper (center): Curandera* begins massage of child's head. Pot in foreground contains mixed herbs and waters of *susto* and frying pan contains hot coals. *Upper (right): Curandera* massages child's body. *Lower (left):* Massage of abdomen. *Lower (center):* Child is smoked in incense of San Mério. *Lower (right): Curandera* burns herbs and incense prior to burying them.

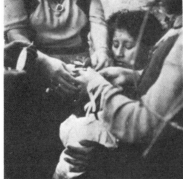

RELIGION AND CRISIS OBSERVANCES.

Upper (left): The church of Santa Lucía de Moche. *Upper (right):* Interior of the church with main altar. *Middle (center):* Haircutting ceremony for male child; *madrina* cutting first lock. *Middle (right): Amas* carrying children to church for baptism. *Lower (left):* A *mayordomo* rearranging the clothing and ornaments of an image during a pause in the parade through the streets. *Lower (right):* Tombs.

DEATH OBSERVANCES

Upper (left): Entrance to the cemetery of Moche, the Campo Santo. *Upper (right):* Procession through the streets. *Center:* Cemetery, a new adobe tomb, partly finished. *Lower (left):* In the cemetery. *Lower (right):* Coffin is lowered into the grave.